The Malfunctions Of A Bipolar Mind

Joss Smith Wesson

chipmunkapublishing
the mental health publisher

Published by
Chipmunkapublishing
PO Box 6872
Brentwood
Essex CM13 1ZT
United Kingdom

http://www.chipmunkapublishing.com

Edited by Aleks Lech / William Kettle

ISBN 978-1-84991-934-0

Chipmunkapublishing gratefully acknowledge the support of Arts Council England.

I find this book a beautiful piece of retrospective writing full of sensitive insight and tender descriptions. The introduction is quite breathtaking as an anticipation of the events that will come later and is also a glimpse of the author's thoughts and especially his character. The introduction is also important in the way that it starts the question about the arrogance of society in relation to the painful misfortune of a person enduring so called "mental illness". Society lifts its shield of indifference in order to build its precarious opulence out of the pain of the mentally ill person. I became familiar with the way that events are communicated so powerfully and particularly enjoyed witnessing the journey through the hardships and wonders of the author's adolescence in Africa. I was taken by the miracle of his description of the mysterious landscapes and places that inhabit his many memories. His work in various farms, weekends with friends, the awakening of love, his impressions of the Zulu workers and the motorbike...all early memories that have a mix of innocence and candid enthusiasm coloured by a tender sensuality. The episode with the girls in the bus leaves the impression of being at one with the author in being fully aware of the experience while being acutely conscious of his feelings and meanings.

In another chapter I found myself dramatically touched by his experiences as a schoolboy in England and the difficulties of learning and relearning the peculiarities of the culture and the feelings of vulnerability at trying to find his place in a foreign country. The author shows a lot of courage enduring this moment in his life. Another one of my favourite chapters was the unforgettable journey across Australia as a hitch hiker, a journey coloured by freedom and friendship.

Everything in the book is an anticipation of the author's meeting with Belinda. All women (including Beauty) are only affinities which lead to the real essence of love, all preparations for it. It is not difficult to understand the author's good fortune at being capable of holding in his mind and dreams the power of love and to be loved by a woman. This is the heart of the book.

The mix of styles and poetry is a powerful strength of the book. Many great authors have tried these combinations (Goethe, Emerson, Flaubert and even Shakespeare) with amazing aesthetic results. The poet knows the language of the spirit. Life and death, love and sadness, loneliness are all mystical reflections which are the nourishments of the poems. All elements of the author's reality are beautifully drawn in a rhythmic space.

This book travels beyond the intentions of comprehension of a medical condition. The mental pain experienced during the outbreak of depression is the material which gives birth to a reflective piece of art. Beauty comes from unexpected sources and this book is about the beauty of life.

Luisa Jamarillo

This first book by Joss Smith Wesson (for one so good must surely be followed by others) is essentially an autobiographical account of young Joss's adolescence and his progression towards what he perceives to be insanity. The author takes us on a journey which lurches from Cirencester Agricultural College through to the South African Veldt, portraying in so doing the inner anguish of a sensitive young male caught between two very different cultures.

The writing is a fascinating blend of wry, contemporary social narrative (a la Nick Hornby), yet conveying a message about the divisive South African culture reminiscent of J.M. Coetzee. Some of the brutally honest accounts of Joss's early sexual encounters would probably shock if taken out of context but he somehow manages to make them seem wholly acceptable as he struggles to come to terms with his manly desires in an Apartheid-governed world.

If the prose is easy and enjoyable to read, the poetry which adorns each chapter is sublime; indeed the substantial piece which closes the book so completely could well be published in its own right. It is almost as if Smith Wesson is using this opening work as a demonstration of his writing skills across a range of literary styles.

Although the author recounts a gradual descent into insanity there will be many readers (albeit mostly men) who will identify with some of the agonies described by Smith Wesson in his developmental years. Anyone capable of creating such a work must, by definition, be a sensitive type and the combination of a displaced adolescence and so many disappointments in his working life would have taken its toll. The author's rich sentimentality can only have been at odds with the cynical commercialism and petty villainy which dogged his entrepreneurial progress.

So familiar are we with Joss and his family by the time the transition from 'normality' to 'insanity' supposedly occurs, it is hard for us to work out what went wrong and how he became interned. This makes it all the more shocking when reading Smith Wesson's vivid account of the asylum's more colourful characters' antics, knowing that the man we thought we knew so well is now apparently powerless to escape from the institution. For many not too familiar with the British National Health Service, it will be shocking to contemplate how someone with an outwardly balanced existence can suddenly find themselves thrown in with mad people. It is a credit to Smith Wesson's narrative skills that he manages to convey this damning criticism of our woefully destitute mental health facilities without resorting to vitriol.

I read this book twice, so as to be sure that it was as good the second time around as it patently had been the first. Certainly, this book will stand as a work of literary prowess in its own right; it will inform those fascinated with mental health issues and entertain in the process those who simply want to read a good book rich in humour and frank social observations. It is as original as it is witty and I therefore commend it to you whole-heartedly.

Rupert Reid

ATHENA PRESS - Readers Report
Title "The Malfunctions of a Bipolar Mind" by Joss Smith Wesson
Date 19th May 2008

This novel is something of a tour de force. It is writing, not exactly of the "stream of consciousness", but certainly and inherently, of what one might call the stream of imagination, untrammelled, and this – even in today's "modern" technique is the first thing that strikes the reader.

"The Malfunctions of a Bipolar Mind" is certainly a novel – and although it may be a "faction", it is actually a novel, of a high order, and allows the imagination to roam freely around reality – it is a work of literary quality, which could attract comment. Not all of it by any means can be guaranteed to be favourable, simply because it never is. It could have a success d'estime. I liked it, but I have a taste for the oddball and the offbeat; hopefully I am not alone.

But it makes sense, however much it may be decorated with extravagantly creative phrases and uses of language. It is literary, and also, unusually, quite an "easy read"; it is almost rewarding at the end. It is metaphorical and imagist; the protagonist in particular, the autobiographical narrator, is a symbol of the universality, and all the other players, another symbol of the same universality, the other side – but, again, the reader will ask: the other side of what? The dilemmas are a symbol of the human dilemma. As in Kafka's "Metamorphosis", improbability becomes fact – or again, does it? The asylum passages at times could rival Genet.

This is not a book for everyone. But if the reader does enter this rather hermetic world that Joss has created, he or she will find themselves involved and unable to leave. What on earth will happen next, we ask ourselves, and in fact, has anything happened? What is reality? We see symbols, but of what are they symbolic, of life, of death, of disgust, of loss and finding again? What, anyway, is sanity?
It is highly contemplative, internal, and intellectually demanding, and on another level, seems to connect with nothing significant, resonant, perhaps almost pure decoration, it doesn't matter. The prose is both baroque and

fluid.
Joss uses language – and dialogue – with economy on the one hand, every word doing its work, and reckless generosity on the other; a torrent of ideas rolls out. It is unusual to find a considerable amount of plot advancement (in so far as there is a "plot" in the conventional sense) in a literary novel of this nature.

The idiosyncratic style takes the reader along with the flow of the narrative.
It is certainly not mainstream material, but should attract a readership. It expresses a contemporary wish for something more profound and meaningful than daily reality.

Penelope Plunket – Reader
Mark Sykes – Editor-In-Chief - Athena Press

I have this book, "The Malfunctions of a Bipolar Mind" with me all the time, in an e-book format, and am reading it now for the third time; it is as exciting as the first time I read it. A brilliant approach to describing the day-to-day torments of life in South Africa, a hint of Hemingway passion for what life has to offer, a wonderful debut for an author that I hope will continue publishing precious gems like this one. I recommend it to anyone that enjoys reading quality literature.

George Cozmenco

Heather Pennell
01 October 2009

An extremely invigorating and exiting read, that takes you through the thoughts and times of a man and his mental illness. Spanning two eras of time full of love and fight, the loves of his life and the fight for it too, both beautifully brought together in humour and triumph, sadness and reality. It takes a snap shot of the cultural awareness and awakening changes that have occurred in South Africa, and can put Apartheid into some perspective of understanding. A book that also so refreshingly talks about the mental health system, of what the reality of living with mental health is, how the slow descent happens over many years and through not just one cause but is in fact attributed to several factors, both physiologically and environmentally with social pressures, cultural inadequacies and love in its many forms. A book for all mental health supporters who want to find out what it is like to be right on the edge between long term management and return to the community and enhanced relapse and what it takes to be able to walk away from the system back to your life again.

Waterstones.com
http://waterstones.com/waterstonesweb/products/j2c+smith+weston/aargh21/5692507/

There are many books out there on the shelves of bookshops which all fall within the areas of fiction or factual. However, no book I have ever read before has being able to combine the best of both elements, that is, until I read this book.

The author Joss Smith Wesson in this book is able to display the factual events of his life, from his time in South Africa to the suffering of Bi-Polar disorder, like they were something out of a best-selling fiction novel. However, all the stuff mentioned actually happened to this guy. To read this book will lead you to feeling a great amount of inspiration for the author. In no way does he act superior in his writings as do so many other autobiographers. Instead, he portrays himself as he really is, a human like the rest of us, with weaknesses and strengths, and how he best handled the circumstances that happened as they took place in his life. When I say that this book ought to be on your book shelf, I mean it 100%. Reading it has shown me the upper and lower sides of being human! A Grade "A" book.
Alex Gadd amazon.co.uk
http://www.amazon.co.uk/product-reviews/1847470858/ref=dp_top_cm_cr_acr_txt?ie=UTF8&showViewpoints=1

"Sometimes disturbing, sometimes funny, sometimes heart-breaking, always poetic, never offering excuses – you are drawn in all the way through the book while being kept continually at arm's length. I found it intriguing."

Gemma Robaczynski

A selection of reviews from the first edition when the book was entitled "Aargh!"

Every year, almost one million people die from suicide; a "global" mortality rate of 16 per 100,000, or one death every 40 seconds.
In the last 45 years suicide rates have increased by 60% worldwide. Suicide is among the three leading causes of death among those aged 15-44 years in some countries, and the second leading cause of death in the 10-24 years age group; these figures do not include suicide attempts which are up to 20 times more frequent than completed suicide.
Suicide worldwide is estimated to represent 1.8% of the total global burden of disease in 1998, and 2.4% in countries with market and former socialist economies in 2020.
Although traditionally suicide rates have been highest among the male elderly, rates among young people have been increasing to such an extent that they are now the group at highest risk in a third of countries, in both developed and developing countries.

Mental disorders (particularly depression and alcohol use disorders) are a major risk factor for suicide in Europe and North America; however, in Asian countries impulsiveness plays an important role. Suicide is complex with psychological, social, biological, cultural and environmental factors involved.
World Health Organisation
http://www.who.int/mental_health/prevention/suicide/suicideprevent/en/

Contents

Intermittent Poems

Seven Ever-Changing Women

Lizzy My Love

Ode to a passing beauty

When you are old

Romeo and Juliet

not my own= *

For
all women in my life,
both real and imaginary
who are all portrayed here as
Belinda
Belinda, my love, forgive me
I am but a fool

INTRODUCTION

The titles *"The Secret Road To Sanity*", "*Little House Of Sanity*" and "*How To Live And Die Sane*" all seem to be taken. I was vaguely tempted by "*Out of Aarghfrica!*", "*Mad about Aargh-Stralia*", or "****hg Aargh uhm Insane!"* Even *"***hg Aargh uhm lost somewhere between Heaven and Hell*" crossed my mind.

OK, so "Aargh!" was not the best title for a book and have changed it to this one, reflecting the subject matter **[after consulting my editor]**.

The author **(that's me)** attempts to recount some of his bizarre experiences through a journey towards, partially through and hopefully out of insanity, depression and thoughts of suicide **(with some irreverent notes by the editor, which, to be honest, is also me)**. Despite its sombre subject, there are many moments of joy. It begins in adolescence and continues through to the present when I recently spent (**Ed. a lot of**) time in a mental asylum. One in five of the population suffer from one sort of mental illness or another, so I strongly believe that this work will be of interest to those in that category. Also, to those that believe that they have somehow escaped, it should be of interest to see what constitutes the condition, or rather something like it, as there are so many variations of any illness. Understanding Manic Depression, or Bipolar Affective Disorder as it is now referred to, is hard enough from the outside. This is an attempt to make sense of the condition from inside.

It starts out with a dream that I have repeatedly. Perhaps I am the character in it? Many of my dreams are also of continuously falling, of drowning or of suffocating. If only dreams were like a cinema in which one could choose the films...

I believe that my self-stability, my ability to maintain my own character, depends on my being able to recognise my mental state of health. There are times when my self-esteem fluctuates. In being able to measure my own self worth, I believe it is important not to do so against that of my contemporaries. In the majority of people, the measure of one's self-esteem is simply a measure of one's financial success. People may not be as successful as they wish to be, however if they believe that their contemporaries believe that they are successful, then they have high self-esteem. The measure of one's self-esteem is a reflection of one's perception in the approval of others. By nature of my being one of the same race that we all share, it is undoubtedly the case that these factors affect my self-evaluation. I may be less concerned with the views of others and am prepared to swim against the flow. I am able to set my own criteria for what is success. I was bound at the time by the constraints of running my own company, being a husband, a parent, a son, and a sibling. By being bound, I mean all these people closely analyzed any perception of my underachievement. These people could equally uplift me, as their reaction to success would have an immediate impact.

I have tried to intersperse various events of my decline from cheerful-chappy to sadly insane, with some of my attempts at poetry. The book is written retrospectively, and, although I honestly feel that no one has been libelled in any way, I have decided to change everyone's names, to protect the innocent etc. It was certainly not my intention when starting out to offend anyone. But if you do recognise yourself, Mr Head, I was hoping that either you would be happily tucked away for good by now, or that you would have the good humour to realise that it is just part of my long term plot to spring myself, so no insults intended – Richard. As a registered loon, I felt little point in changing someone's name from Bill to Bob, so if there are some really obscure names out there, just try vocalising them. My reason for inclusion of some apparently isolated events or chapters in my life, is to attempt to illustrate the extremes in mood variation. These swings become more violent later in the book, eventually culminating in my hospitalisation. I also try to portray a journey from reality into fantasy that becomes indistinguishable as the illness progresses.

Before taking the plunge in a bookshop, at about this point I would always love some third party to give me an unbiased, objective and yet critical opinion of the book I am considering buying. There is one juicy bit in which I had just excitedly 'spotted my 14th zebra.' I was reinforcing the actions of an outward-bound sane healthy person sitting in the back of a bouncing land rover in the wilds of Africa, against those of an introverted sick-o loon who later could hardly make head or tail of peeling and faded hospital wallpaper. **(Ed. Actually that event never happened. You were using it as an example to emphasise the change in your character from one extreme to the other.)** My humble estimation of my own work is, well...very funny...very true to life and also very depressing. If I were standing there, with the till beckoning, I would have a bit of a read, burst out chortling, thinking that I could understand the predicament. It begins in South Africa in 1981 when I was apparently without a care in the world. Plotting the course through the causes of deteriorating mental health across two decades, the symptoms becoming more and more manifest, although perhaps not necessarily easier to understand, was not easy. As I sit here now in Christmas 2011, taking my endless tablets, friendless, shunned and even hated by many, I write this in the belief that I can somehow contribute to a growing awareness of the condition. In an increasingly fractious society, the opportunities for otherwise mentally well people to become sick are enormous. As a society, we have the ability to vastly improve the lives of the unfortunate mentally ill people who have been left by the wayside. Perhaps I was never ill as such and, as with many crime authors who study murder scenes to get their authenticity, I have simply let my imagination go. Perhaps I have an over excited imagination, perhaps I enjoy seeing my beloved family suffer; perhaps my abilities do not extend beyond that of road sweeper. Honestly, this is not the case and I have really been there and really am in this desperate plight.

My objectives at the moment are: to fight myself back into mainstream society (so far after a year I think that perhaps, being slightly eccentric, I have got away with being perceived as almost normal); to hold my youngest daughter Sophie's hand all the way to school every morning and back in the afternoon (the reason why the poor darling has no friends is because all the mums know that Sophie's dad is likely to be in the news for some horrific crime committed on their beloved child – people can be so fickle and so unforgiving); to be available to take the older two, Tilly and Felicity up to school when they miss the bus, which hopefully is not too often. They frequently need lifts back, as the school bus does not bring them home if they are involved in any extra-curricula school activities. Felicity has made it into the school netball and running teams and Tillie has Business Studies on Wednesday afternoons. Actually I can manage to help Little Sophie with her homework, but as far as Tilly and Felicity are concerned, I don't remember having to work out how to get to Mars and back when I was fifteen. Long term, I am determined to complete this degree I have started...

A brief summary of some of my on-going daily mental health medications

Rispiradal
Risperidone is an antipsychotic used to treat schizophrenia schizoaffective disorder, the mixed and manic states associated with bipolar disorder, and irritability in people with autism. It is associated with significant weight gain and metabolic problems, as well as tardive dyskinesia and neuroleptic malignant syndrome.

Venlafaxine
Venlafaxine is an antidepressant licensed for the treatment of major depressive disorder, as a treatment for generalized anxiety disorder, and co-morbid indications in certain anxiety disorders with depression. It is used primarily for the treatment of depression, general anxiety disorder, social phobia, panic disorder, and vasomotor symptoms. The US Food and Drug Administration body requires all antidepressants, including venlafaxine, to carry a black box warning with a generic warning about a possible suicide risk. In addition, the most recent research indicated that patients taking venlafaxine are at increased risk of suicide.

Depacote
Valproate semisodium is used for the treatment of the manic episodes of bipolar disorder. It is also used as a treatment for major depressive disorder, and increasingly taken long-term for prevention of both manic and depressive phases of bipolar disorder, especially the rapid-cycling variant. It is also used in treatment of epilepsy, certain side effects of autism, chronic pain associated with neuropathy, and migraine headaches. The most severe side effect is a ten times higher-than-average incidence rate of serious, irreversible birth defects (teratogenic) such as births of brainless babies (anencephaly). Risk of birth defects such as spina bifida has been demonstrated among populations of female patients who took the medicine in childbearing age.

Zopiclone
Zopiclone is used in the treatment of insomnia. It is a tranquilliser drug and works by causing a depression or

tranquillisation of the Central Nervous System. As it is sedating it is marketed as a sleeping pill. After regular dampening down of the Central Nervous System the body becomes accustomed to functioning under the influence of zopiclone. When the dose is reduced or the drug is stopped these adaptions which have occurred when a person's body has become addicted to a drug are revealed. The side effect most commonly seen in clinical trials is taste alteration or dysgeusia (bitter, metallic taste, which is usually fleeting in most users but can persist until the drug's half-life has expired). Palpitations may occur in the daytime following withdrawal from the drug after prolonged periods of use. Zopiclone induces amnesia type memory impairments similar to triazolam and Rohypnol. Impairment of driving skills with a resultant increased risk of road traffic accidents is probably the most important side effect. This side effect is not unique to zopiclone but also occurs with other hypnotic drugs. Long term users of hypnotic drugs for sleep disorders only develop partial tolerance to adverse effects on driving with users of hypnotic drugs even after one year's use still showing an increased motor vehicle accident rate. Patients who drive motor vehicles should not take it unless they stop driving due to a significant increased risk of road traffic accidents in its users. It induces impairment of psychomotor function. Driving or operating machinery should be avoided after taking it as effects can carry over to the next day including impaired hand eye coordination. Patients with a history of substance abuse should not be prescribed it, as it has a very high potential for problematic drug misuse. Zopiclone is known to, in some case, induce a state of amnesia. This can extend to sleep-eating, sleep-talking, to dangerously 'sleep driving'. It is a drug with the potential for misuse. It is well known amongst drug addicts as a drug of abuse and they commonly seek it from their doctors. It is abused orally and sometimes intravenously and often combined with alcohol to achieve a combined sedative hypnotic-alcohol euphoria. Patients who do abuse the drug are also at risk of dependence. Withdrawal symptoms can be seen after long term use of normal doses even after a gradual reduction regime. The symptoms of addiction can include depression, dysphoria, hopelessness, slow thoughts, social isolation, worrying, sexual anhedonia and nervousness. Zopiclone and other sedative hypnotic drugs are detected frequently in cases of people suspected of driving under the influence of drugs. As with other hypnotic drugs it is sometimes abused to carry out criminal acts such as sexual assaults.

Aspirin

Aspirin, also known as acetylsalicylic. It is a salicylate drug, often used as an analgesic to relieve minor aches and pains, as an antipyretic to reduce fever, and as an anti-inflammatory medication. Salicylic acid, the main metabolite of aspirin, is an integral part of human and animal metabolism. While much of it is attributable to diet, a substantial part is synthesized endogenously.

Aspirin also has an antiplatelet effect by inhibiting the production of thromboxane, which under normal circumstances binds platelet molecules together to create a patch over damaged walls of blood vessels. Because the platelet patch can become too large and also block blood flow, locally and downstream, aspirin is also used long-term, at low doses, to help prevent heart attacks, strokes, and blood clot formation in people at high risk of developing blood clots.

(I went blind in one eye a few years ago and as a result have been prescribed Aspirin for the rest of my innings – no, I am not going to tell you about that episode...)

Ventolin Inhaler

Salbutamol or albuterol is a short-acting β2-adrenergic receptor agonist used for the relief of bronchospasm in conditions such as asthma and chronic obstructive pulmonary disease. It is marketed as Ventolin among other brand names. Salbutamol was the first selective β2-receptor agonist to be marketed — in 1968. It was first sold by Allen & Hanburys under the brand name Ventolin. The drug was an instant success, and has been used for the treatment of asthma ever since.

Fostair Inhaler

(beclometasone, formoterol)

Main use Asthma. Manufacturer Trinity-Chiesi. Fostair inhaler contains two active ingredients, beclometasone dipropionate and formoterol fumarate (previously known as eformoterol fumarate in the UK) Beclometasone is a type of medicine known as a corticosteroid. Corticosteroids are hormones that are produced naturally by the adrenal glands. They have many important functions, including control of inflammatory responses. Beclometasone is a synthetic corticosteroid and is used to decrease inflammation in the lungs. Corticosteroids are often simply called steroids, but it should be noted that they are very different from another group of steroids, called anabolic steroids, which have gained notoriety because of their abuse by some athletes and body builders.

My personal observations on these medications

Regarding the first three mental health medications, Yes, I do feel that they do have a beneficial impact on my life in that I have less violent mood swings. However I have only just learnt that I need to take my sleeping pills much earlier than when I would otherwise had before going to bed. Their effectiveness can vary enormously. Some nights I can sleep like a baby, and on others, not at all. Having left the hospital, I do feel somewhat abandoned by the NHS. My feeling with virtually all GPs is that these medications are not those that they are used to prescribing and rather than refer me on to someone more qualified, all they do is simply re-prescribe the same medication. Not that there is anything necessarily wrong with this, after all, on assessing the patient before them, I appear to be in control of my life. I have come to accept that I will probably be on these medications for the rest of my innings, but I would like to know that they are being reviewed by doctors that are properly trained in this field. Ideally I would like to reduce the amount of the medicines I take down to a bare minimum. Currently every time I take my medications I am reminded that I am suffering from a mental health problem.

Without my asthma medication I would be lost.

CHAPTER ONE

...one of my many adolescent, repeating, disturbed dreams...

"They're lifting the last few bales, are you ready lads?" Pitchforks and spades raised above shoulders. The question hardly needed answering as the few remaining parts of our previously safe home were toppled over. Exposed, and surrounding us, were our enemy and their dogs. They were huge, barbaric, merciless killers. For milliseconds we stared at each other before...

"Get 'em!" The barbarians shrieked. About twenty yards to make it to the long grass, and then another ten to the barley, Ben and I were running, breathlessly, desperately, together. He was young and powerfully built, and if anyone could make it, he would. The men-of-war were stamping and beating the ground with sticks and blades and screaming when they killed one of us. The dogs were yapping, howling and baying incessantly. Those bastard, evil terriers – tearing flesh, maiming and killing us.

Ben was slightly ahead of me, nearly there, almost safe, when a pitchfork seemed to hang in the air before plunging into his side. He immediately whirled round, screaming, and breaking his teeth on the cruel steel bar that had brutally pinned him to the ground. At the grass verge I stopped. A very ugly violent man stood over Ben grinning, then his steel heel crashed heavily down. Ben had been screaming in agony, the bar tearing through his kidneys, his liver and his gut. Now he lay still, his race over. Others lay dead and bleeding as the now insane dogs tore at our bodies. Madmen ran after those of us who were wounded; some with legs broken, and some even with broken backs were mercilessly killed.

I knew I was not yet safe. The sea of pasture only gave a little cover so long as I remained still. Caesar was an old bull terrier. I knew him well and had managed to stay one step ahead of him for the last four years. He had seen me get to the grass and had come to within five yards of me before I smelled him. I sprinted for my life for the taller, deeper barley field. Caesar did not yap as he came up behind me. He may have been old, but not slow. I hurled myself to one side as his hot, rancid, poisonous breath passed over the terrified hairs of my back. I made it to the high barley just before having to side step again to avoid him. Now Caesar slowed down as he crashed loudly into the field. Fifteen yards in, I stopped. The bad men who had been watching our race had lost interest. Their dogs did not usually catch us in there. Caesar was not breathing and he was down-wind now and in a different row. And suddenly he was there again, crashing down on me. Three. Two yards to go! I leapt frantically to the right and ran for my life once more!

Suddenly to my horror, I was out of the barley and on the concrete loading bay again. I knew that the old hole in the far wall was my only hope. Only too late as I sprinted towards it I realised it was boarded over. Breathless and terrified, I turned to face Caesar. His tongue flashed in and out of his horrible-pointed, evil head, his glazed eyes staring in triumph. He had time as he had me cornered. He had to be careful though; cornered and terrified, I could still give a nasty bite. He lunged and I sank my teeth deep into his lip as he crushed my back right leg in his jaws. He howled as he hurled me in the air. He was going to snap me in half!

A loud, near, explosion and my battered body was racked with an even worse agony. One of the killer enemy men had seen me come out of the field and dart for my hole which had been boarded up. As the fearful dog threw me in the air, the man lifted his rifle and fired. The bullet tore through my skin, throwing me into the fertiliser stack.

That autumn, when the men took down the last bags of the fertiliser stack, they were ready again with their sticks flailing and dogs yapping. Most of us rats were killed, although one with only three legs and some of my sons somehow made it through...

CHAPTER TWO

...before symptoms manifest themselves...

I arrived at Johannesburg Airport ready for action and passed through the Customs and Passport checks without any trouble, although was given plenty of agitation by supposedly 'helpful' black taxi drivers to whom I must have been the first potential customer for a week – they were like vultures around a carcass – to use relatively indigenous terminology. I spotted Ludwig van der Hum, with his cardboard airport sign, and he pulled me away from them. He was a Swedish Veterinary Student who worked for my cousin Steve and had been sent to fetch me. His long blond straight hair was almost down to his shoulders,

"You are going to have a ball!" he laughed as he crunched my hand. With his blue eyes and broad shoulders, he could have been a film star.

"Is there anything you need from the airport before you leave civilisation?" His accent was so strong I could only just work out what it was he was saying.

My first 'taxi' as such was as a passenger with Ludwig in a cattle truck full of cows and much cow dung, as far as a bike repair shop where his motorbike was being fixed. The cattle were on their way to market and lowed forlornly, drowning our attempt at introductory conversation.

"I am only here for a couple more weeks and then a pair of right chicks are coming out to replace me. You will be in there." He laughed loudly at the thought. "Eileen and Marina, they go to the same college as me and they are coming out to get some experience working with wild animals. Steve likes to have pretty girls around him, you know."

"I've got a girlfriend." I elbowed him playfully, hoping he would not recognise the lie.

"That is no excuse. This is Africa and you must sow your wild oats." He laughed even louder.

"Heh, heh, heh." I chuckled at the prospect.

We continued on two wheels, interesting because of the numerous enormous 'black' holes in the roads that Ludwig weaved expertly between. Arriving at the office he introduced me to Steven Baldwin, my cousin, and his charming American wife, Dorothy. Steve had transformed his traditional cattle ranch back in Kenya into a game farm and strongly believed that indigenous wild species were far more suitable for the commercial production of meat. They were better able to survive the extremes of nature, their impact on the soil was less detrimental, they have higher meat to fat ratio and importantly, it was an important avenue to protect one of Africa's most endangered attractions; without tourism, the economy in Africa would probably collapse. His experiment had largely been a success in Kenya and his objective was to make his second farm in South Africa economically viable to be able to prove to the government that it was worthwhile. Equally, to prove to his sceptical fellow ranchers to abandon the practices they believed to be right just because they worked in Europe. He grabbed my hand in a handshake like a vice-grip;

"You look just like your Uncle Joss," he announced, inspecting me closely. "He was one great guy and we all loved him dearly. He was a great loss. You never met him, did you?" - finally letting go of my hand.

"No, but I feel as if I have. He's certainly a huge influence in my life." My Uncle Joss had been great friends with the Baldwin family before he died, just before I was born.

"He would have been delighted that you are here," Steve continued. "We have a few loose ends to sort out before we go back to the farm, why don't you have a look around old Joeburg and we should be ready in an hour or so." He dismissed me rather like a tour guide. Steve was about six foot four with a thickset square moustache; he had piercing blue eyes although he spoke in a quiet almost teacher-like monotone. Dorothy's long straight blonde hair was beginning to grey. She looked tired and her skin had a slightly sickly, bluish hue. She clung to his elbow in a possessive manner and I thought at the time that perhaps she was ill. Days later she was to disappear off to the States for treatment and I was not to see her for a while.

I was amazed at the number of healthy young men who spent their whole day wandering about the streets apparently trying to cheat people. They tried by selling worthless trinkets or offering drugs and, if that didn't work, they would offer to change foreign currency into South

African Rands. While I was waiting outside Steve's office I began talking to one of these people. He seemed quite friendly. I asked where he got the drugs from and why he sold them and why didn't he get a proper job, etc. **(Ed. As you do in a Patronising-Colonial-White-Man kind of a way.)** After that, he then said the 'change' bit and I asked him how many South African Rands he would give me for a UK Sterling pound.

'Three', he announced, knowing I had taken the bait. It was certainly better than the rate I had been given at the bank. At this point I should pathetically say that I had not been warned about these crooks and that I didn't see any reason why or how he would cheat me. I mean, he looked honest enough, Guv. I never even suspected it. Yes, I must have been born that morning. Anyway, before I really thought again, my money was whipped into an envelope and hit onto the ground by a supposed passer-by who said something, in Zulu, to the effect of,

"What's going on here, you cheat?" The two of them sprinted off triumphantly together down the street. I picked up the envelope to find a piece of paper inside, surprised not to find,

"Ha, ha, fool" written on it.

We had lunch with the Man from the Ministry who was responsible for Steve's permit. This was the permit that would allow Steve governmental permission to shoot wild game on his farm; it had not come through yet.

"Jeez, I am going to die of old age by the time you lot eventually get yourselves around your ridiculous bureaucratic tomfoolery." Steve jogged the man's elbow jokingly. He had apparently been waiting for months to hear from them.

To get rid of us, Steve suggested that Ludwig and I collect his samples before we left for the farm. So I spent the afternoon speeding around Joeburg on the back of the bike with Ludwig, going to various laboratories where he had his veterinary samples. The Highway Code, and possibly even driving lessons of any nature, could not have been part of his driving experience; other road users and pedestrians alike were merely hazards as he sped from one pit-stop to another.

Much later that evening Steve and Dorothy and I arrived at their farm, *The Heart of Africa*, near the village, Orange River Tributaries. I spent the night in their spare 'room' which was a house on its own, about a hundred yards away from theirs. The whole of the front side of it was made of glass. I thought I would never sleep, due to the prospect of some nasty creatures being about to leap in and eat me. I slept very well though, probably out of exhaustion, although I probably dreamt of wrestling lions, tigers and giant woolly mammoths all night long.

"Yebo Baas." Godson Banana, the black farm supervisor seemed to know everything there was to know about cattle. He almost curtsied as he gently shook my hand. I rather liked the idea of a man probably thirty or forty years my senior calling me 'Boss.' He was branding and then dipping a large herd of cattle. Dipping. Later in my life that word came to have a rather more interesting interpretation, but then it simply involved forcing cattle into a chemical mixture that would kill all the ticks on their skin. **(Ed. OK, dipping came to mean a euphemism for casual sex!)** I was surprised at the generally healthy condition of the animals. I had expected them to be a lot thinner because the grass was so brown, almost non-existent on the farm. The cattle certainly needed to be dipped though, judging from the amount of revolting ticks clinging to them. The tame eland was persuaded to go through. The poor thing was covered in ticks, like huge black ripe shiny grapes, particularly around its arse and its armpits.

Godson took me to notch calves at Uncle Tom's kraal (a circular fence made of thorn bushes to form a corral to keep cattle in overnight). Godson's English vocabulary, although far advanced compared to all the other workers on the farm, was still relatively limited and our conversations reflected this. I would try to break the stony silences by asking the name of a particular buck we passed and he would answer,

"An animal." Perhaps he was resentful of the whites that Steve employed to do what he perceived as being his job. Steve had equipped me with an 'Upcountry Zulu Dictionary and Phrase Book' that proved invaluable for the other indigenous Zulu staff. He had succeeded in getting work permits for some Arab Bedouin workers from his farm in northern Kenya. He said they were more reliable and knowledgeable than the Blacks in South Africa when it came to wild animal husbandry. I wasn't very impressed with their methods used to catch the poor calves. It involved using a crook, the same kind that Mary-Mary-Quite-Contrary had. **(Ed. Wrong Mary, I think. Should be the one who had a little lamb – or her cousin Little Bo-Peep who lost her sheep!)** A calf's leg, or anybody's leg for that matter, was not supposed to stick out at right angles to their body. The sounds of extreme agony did not seem to detract the inflictors of the pain. Torturers, murderers, rapists and child molesters all seem to understand its meaning. Quite why such Bedouin expertise was necessary, I could not see. Still, I did not want to interfere with the local system, not when I had only just arrived anyway. The Bedouin herdsmen at Uncle Tom's kraal had the unpronounceable names of Arheddis Varkenjaab and Aywellbe Fayed. I understood immediately why I would need a notebook as their names vanished out of my memory almost as soon as Godson had introduced me.

Ludwig, the up-and-coming Scandinavian actor, showed me around the whole of the farm on the motorbike. The experience was something like being with a slightly out of control Barry Sheen – very fast and very scary. Barry of course had been the World Motorbike racing champion and had supposedly broken almost all the bones in his body at some time or other. Something I did not relish.

"Are dere any sick cattle 'ere?" he drawled in his heavy Swedish accent to the herdsmen. How they communicated was a mystery to me as they did not speak English and he made no attempt to speak their language. Although, to be fair, some of my attempts to communicate with him also failed.

"Can't this thing go any faster?!" I screamed in his ear as we hurtled along through the untamed African bush. It was really liberating to be out in the wilds of Africa and to feel that I was going to contribute towards the running of an important experimental farm. His work was particularly interesting to me, especially when he did post-mortems. A sheep could equally die from a piece of wire in its gut here as in Britain. I remember my father saying when we had sheep on our own farm in Natal when I was a child, ironically called 'Sheep Heaven', that he only needed to look at a sheep and it would die.

One morning I took Steve his milk up on the motorbike. We had chatted about what I was expected to do and what I could expect of him.

"Your responsibility is to keep on top of the cattle. You must check and double-check all the herdsmen's counts. There are nine different herds and the opportunity for cattle to go missing is enormous. They can easily wander through the gaps in the perimeter fence or be herded out by thieves. Your responsibilities also include checking that the kraals have enough salt and that they were not overflowing with muck. You need to get to know all the herdsmen by name and they need to know that you will be at their kraals by six in the morning to count the cattle out with them." He showed me a map of the whole farm with all the European homes on it, the roads and importantly all the kraals.

"To be perfectly honest, Karl was hopeless. I am hoping that you will sort out the records and really become part of the cattle management on this farm. Become Godson's best mate." He added cheerfully. Karl Gut was going back to university in Holland, thereby creating a job for me. Initially it was quite daunting as the farm was about the same size as an average English county. When I set about actually doing the job I immediately came upon some unexpected difficulties, like getting completely lost.

"How many are there?" I asked the herder, Arheddis, when I eventually found the right kraal.

"288, with five still on the hill coming." I understood after counting the scratches on his arm and his pointing towards the hill. The herders counted the cattle by scratching four marks on one of their forearms, and then crossing these out to indicate five. A supervisor could then come along and count the number of batches of five and any remainder to work out how many cattle were present. Once counting was complete and checked the scratches would be wiped off, like a slate.

Ludwig and his pretty English girlfriend Lorraine Jones invited me to go to the Joeburg National Game Park at the weekend. It was an absolutely gorgeous day, with the sun shining brightly, although early in the morning it was still bitter. We had probably overcompensated because by midday the car was strewn with discarded clothes. Lorraine stopped short at a sort of pink tank-top-type-thing, probably only because I was there. She had magnificent breasts; but then, in my limited experience of actually seeing any, almost any would be classified as magnificent. She also had an annoying forced erotic-manic laugh, which came out at the slightest provocation. There are only so many jokes that could be extracted from a group of monkeys. Perhaps, with surgery, she could have had the laugh removed. It was good fun, the first of my many excursions out of the farm, but on that occasion there were few more animals than there were on the farm. Although we were extremely lucky enough to see some curious giraffe from about eight yards away.

Back at the farmhouse Malcolm Edwards had arrived with Madeleine, his girlfriend. He was the farm's General Manager and mechanic and Madeleine was an excellent photographer. He decided that he wanted my mattress... He did not say how he had managed without it before Madeleine arrived; perhaps she was the Princess and had a Pea Problem.

Each night we went out to catch game to use in experiments to closely monitor exactly what they ate.

"This doesn't involve wandering about with a butterfly net and a magnifying glass, but in a land rover without lights in the pitch black of an African night, little suspension, and often jumping out without knowing exactly where the ground is, and before the vehicle has stopped." Steve chuckled as he gave the basic instructions of the whole operation.

"No chance. I'm not missing this caper, if that's what you reckon." I think that he thought he might frighten me into staying behind. Madeleine came as the official photographer and Malcolm drove the land rover. After chasing a couple of animals about for a while, which involved running about and frantically diving at terrified creatures and in the vast majority of times not coming close, we were about to give up when I caught a Springbok. To catch the animals involved someone perched on top of the land rover, shining a very bright light in the prospective victim's eyes. It would then theoretically run around in circles or try to run on its side or try running up in the air, totally disorientated. The ideal conditions were an inky night with an obscured horizon. The night sky was cloudless, and even just sitting in the relative safety of the land rover was very disorientating for me.

At the conference on African Animal Husbandry, Steve gave a speech on the benefits of farming indigenous African animals as opposed to stock brought in from Europe and Asia.

"Commercial farming and breeding of indigenous wild African game animals is one of the most effective ways of ensuring their survival. This is not simply the sentiment of an over-eager game warden, but of years of experimental work to prove that, by harvesting game, we can ensure their long-term survival." He was almost shouting as he punched one hand into the palm of the other at this crucial point. He was an incredibly rousing public speaker and it was the sort of speech that, if the right people were listening, would have guaranteed his permit to crop game in ten minutes. It just seemed inconceivable that the authorities would not listen to his brilliant idea. To provide meat for the conference we had woken very early that morning to kill a wildebeest. Malcolm took charge of the gun, Ludwig drove and I badly bruised my back on the roof of the land rover trying to aim the spotlight. No animal seemed to want to be shot. We chased around for a few hours before Malcolm eventually shot a wildebeest in the shoulder. We followed after it for a while until it stood exhausted, facing us from about twenty-five yards away in the darkness. It leapt in the air after the shot had been fired but then miraculously it just ran away even faster. We spent ages looking for it but couldn't find it. The poor creature; imagine the agony of two bullet wounds. All we found in our search were aardvark holes that made our drive as much up and down as along. The poor wildebeest presumably either died of its wounds, or somehow survived to tell its grandchildren the tale of woe. Steve was undoubtedly the best shot. His first shot went straight through a zebra's brain; a brilliant shot. No running around in agony for him, lucky creature. iNja, the Muslim gatekeeper, ceremoniously grinning, cut its throat; Ludwig collected a couple of test tubes of blood and a guy called Mudi Aazohl who worked for the National Parks Board took official pictures. We then took them back to the slaughterhouse where they were skinned and gutted. We finished at about one in the morning. Later some government inspectors came to inspect the meat. They didn't find anything wrong although they looked very thoroughly. While they were doing so, an unfortunate sheep had its throat ceremoniously cut by dear iNja. It was still kicking while it was being skinned, poor thing.

We occasionally went into neighbouring farms to shoot game. We did not shoot our farm during the day as it scared the game away but our neighbours did not mind them being scared off their property because they competed with their cattle for grass. Once, while doing so, we saw a large herd of eland led by a magnificent bull.

"Don't be afraid of dem, dey are probably more 'fraid of you," Ludwig sarcastically tried to persuade me as he abandoned me in the bush at a strategic spot in our attempt to chase the herd into the farm through one of the funnel shaped gaps. I was supposed to wave my arms frantically and steer them into the trap.

"Shoo, shoo, whoa, whoa!" I screamed as they sauntered past me, and also past the entrance to the funnel.

The milking process was the single most different aspect from what I was used to. In the pristine milking parlours of greenest England, milking was a science, done largely by machine, controlled largely by sexy, well-built, well-paid English girls, on beautiful, healthy, almost happy, manicured, well-fed cows. Here, in the African outdoors, exhausted low-paid filthy African calloused hands grappled reluctant, bedraggled, unfortunate filthy beasts. The Arabian milkmen's curious names were Arhevbin Fayed and Bybeiev Rhibodie. Milking made my whole body ache, particularly my back; I certainly would not make it as an African Milkman.

Karl, the Dutch chap whose job I was to be taking over, arrived back from holiday with his eighteen year old girlfriend, Sheemha Krak, who was doing the standard year-out experience thing. She was yet another gorgeous shaggable compulsory Dutch-Asian mistress. They had come to South Africa together to work on the farm and had been on holiday to the coast. Apparently they had to go through a bizarre act of signing into hotels separately thanks to the Immorality Act, which stated, "Thou shall not have sex with someone not the same colour as oneself but it is compulsory with one's cousins and preferably one's siblings." It was Karl's job to manage the cattle on the farm. He showed me the records;

"Der in ur hel offa mess. If you can sord dem oud while you are ere den you are ur ero. Whoever was doing id before me did not know his aas from is elbow and I ave to confess dat I ave not rilly tried as it is such ur difficult jub." His explanation of the records being out of date sounded like a confession. "Don worry if you can't manage. Nobody ever lugs at dem anyways," he added just to confirm my suspicions. Karl and Sheemha disappeared off to Europe soon after to continue 'normal' life, leaving me to supposedly control the domestic cattle on the farm. All the cattle had to be inoculated against the dreaded Foot and Mouth disease and seven vets were employed to do the job.

"Thank God for modern science." Steve proposed a toast after they had finished.

"Thank God for modern game farmers," one of them replied. They all understood and appreciated the nature of what it was that Steve was trying to achieve.

"Life on the range must be heaven?" one of them asked me.

"After this year, next year will be a difficult act for me to follow," I laughed. "Besides going skydiving, scuba diving, and playing rugby virtually every weekend in season and getting more than my fair share of stitches, going to endless college parties, I feel that this trip to Africa will be the cream on the pudding for me." We all had a good chat over a couple of cold beers.

I was awoken one morning at 5.45 by Gaucha Bitaguly (who was also known as yisiThutha by the non-Zulu staff), the night watchman, knocking at my window and I set off for the kraals to go and count. I went straight to Number Four kraal, where there appeared to be fifteen cows short. The herders and also the milkmen there had the extraordinary Arabian names of Steelaygot Maowenbach and Tuka Piziniztee. I sped back to ask Godson how many there should have been, in other words how many there were on the previous Tuesday, their dipping day. I returned and counted them again and then there were sixteen more than there should be, and also one extra calf. No explanation was offered as to where they came from. I took my scraps of paper to ask Goodmansson. He was Godson's eldest son, about seventeen years old, but was not technically employed on the farm. He was under his father's own tuition. I think that even if I had had a calculator, a computer or a special cattle-counting machine, I would never have kept on top.

"How many cows and calves?" I asked.

"194 cows and 181 calves," the scratches told me. Maybe the herders' idea of a joke to break in any new farm manager was by playing musical cows between the different kraals. I arrived early enough at Loriba's kraal and the cattle had not been let out. Loriba himself had long gone and Aynayda Pizaqvick and Malexa Kriest, the Bedouins, now manned it. I counted them out to reach 371, the right amount. At Number Seven kraal they had also been let out. They were also sixteen cows short. Lister ran Lister's kraal coincidently as one might imagine.

A task Godson seemed to relish was castrating steers. I was sure that it was unnecessary to have to do it quite so brutally. The soon-to-be-steers could be put in with the actual bulls in the Central kraal and sold from there. What difference would it make if they were soon to be made into steak anyway? A steer is of course a male cow that has had the ability to reproduce removed. The unfortunate beast would be caught, thrown to the ground, one of the boys would grab its balls and Godson, with his huge pliers, would crush the part of the animal in between. The pain must have been terrible. In Britain most cattle were not branded but have their numbers painted or tagged on. I thought that that could also be done there. The combined effect of branding, castration, the stress of being cooped up all night in very restricted space, and being dipped particularly when the dip was almost empty, not to mention the diet of parched African grass, must have considerably reduced their weight gain compared to their European cousins.

I was determined to make Godson appreciate the benefits of my system of maintaining the cattle records. Despite the uncertainty of acknowledgement of understanding, I would have hour-long talks with him about the bookkeeping in general and how I wanted to keep records of where all the cows were at any one time. To begin with, the dairy numbers didn't seem to be the same through the week. At the end of my speech (the word 'chat' would suggest a two way process) he would respond blandly,

"Yebo, Baas", which left me again feeling that he had not understood any of it.

I was really getting to know the herders well, but without my notebook to record their names I would have been lost; the herders at Sales Group One's were Awul Dasfilsshabeda and Nowaynada Zheet. Cows and Calves Two's herders and milkmen were Makollig Jezvahted and Levdaroum DeBahzted. Steve had assured me that they were actually very intelligent and that once I got to know them and could speak their language, we would get on like a house on fire. I started to make a wooden filing cabinet to keep my records in. Each kraal had to have its own drawer, a total of ten drawers including the hospital kraal. Woodwork was something, besides running, that I really excelled in at in school. The woodwork teacher used to let us Smith Wesson boys use the circular saw. One could just see the headline,

"They said they knew how to work the bloody thing," accompanied by a picture of one of us holding up a bloody hand without any fingers. Fortunately we never had an accident at school on the dreaded machine, although since then, Dad, Jonathan and I have all snipped off bits of our fingers on our own machine. My speciality was making elaborate bowls on the lathe, usually with dozens of different coloured woods. So, I set about making a deluxe cabinet to keep all the records in. I planed down the wood, getting my hands full of splinters and blisters.

Sybil arrived one afternoon with a sick ostrich that died before anything could be done to save it. She was an incredible person, with a truly magical, eccentric character; but then living in the middle of Wildest Africa on one's own, one was bound to be. She had wanted Ludwig to try to save its life. Her house was an ocean-going yacht, complete with masts and rigging. How or why it got to be in the middle of the farm, I never found out. She had short brown hair, was very tanned and freckled, about forty years old, did not wear a bra, about my height and still quite pretty. I accompanied her back to her extraordinary house to see other sick ostriches and meet Gerald FitzPatrick. He was a friend of Sybil's that was staying permanently with her. He was evidently a bit queer, but likeable all the same.

"What are you gays up to to...night?" He lisped in a typically gay manner. I suspect that Sybil took comfort in him in that he was not a threat to her, and he probably considered me as a bit of a challenge. Whatever the reason, the three of us got on very well. He plied me with beers, presumably in the hope of taking advantage of me. As a result the next morning I did not get up on time. I liked to think that I always had an appropriate excuse. Sometimes I had cramp in the night and my legs wouldn't feel up to it. Sometimes I assumed that we were going to catch animals early in the morning so I didn't set my alarm clock and sometimes the motorbike was locked in the workshop so even if I did get up I could not go anywhere. Horrendous excuses, but hey, I had turned into a Pom and getting up before eight was contrary to the Laws of Nature.

I had only been on the farm a while when I received very good news in the post; I had passed all my exams at Agricultural College, which meant that I did not need to go back on the 1st September to retake any. This was a bit of a surprise, considering the amount of studying I had done. It also meant, of course, that I had got into the second year with half the National Diploma in Farm Management behind me.

I put a load of logs and bamboo poles onto the Grump and set off for Steve's house (the Grump being the farm's very old temperamental and appropriately named land rover, which had no starter motor). On the way, I caught the bamboo poles in a bush on the side of the road, probably because of my unnecessary reckless driving, but, hey, in Africa everyone drives badly, it is part of the driving test. The whole load went everywhere. Luckily I was giving a black chap a lift and he helped me put it all back on again. Even more luckily, neither of us was decapitated. Only three bamboo poles were split. Luckily also, Steve never found out, although I never did get to find out what offences amounted to summary dismissal. Arriving at Steve's, I met Marina Belring and Eileen Dover, the two long-awaited Swedish Vet students that were going to replace Ludwig. I immediately realised that any possible liaison with either of them was definitely out of the question as they were decidedly ugly. Eileen was beyond any hope as she was fat beyond obese, however, Marina had the most beautiful buttocks and thighs and was wearing very tight jeans to prove it. We had hardly been introduced when she turned to stroke one of Steve's dogs. She had bent over away from me with her knees straight in a most provocative manner to show off her wonderful womanly crease.

From one delightful view to another...We watched some giraffe that could not have been further than a hundred yards away, behind one of many gloriously beautiful African sunsets that was best appreciated from Steve's beautiful step.

"I believe," Steve began, raising his wine glass and languishing in the arrival of his new 'beauties,' "that a man is his own worst enemy. If only he could be persuaded as to the futility of war and engage in constructive use of the world's resources. At the rate that we are going mankind will be extinct in the foreseeable future." He looked around to see who was going to take up the debate.

"I think you are wrong," Eileen ventured. "Man has the capacity to realise the danger he has put himself in and will be able to do something about it, even if it is only at the last moment. Look at how Germany has been able to be rebuilt despite the horrors of war. One could argue that war was necessary to stop the ideology of Hitler." She took a sip of her wine.

"No. Look at Mahatma Gandhi. He achieved more by passive resistance..."

"Oh, I disagree," she interpolated. "The strong will ultimately always conquer the weak. History proves that." She leaned further back into her settee comfortably.

"Perhaps that may have been the case in the past, but surely the more civilised mankind becomes and is able to communicate and understand himself better, the less likely war becomes. This is why it is so important to educate the whole world. If there is going to be a Third World War it will be started by Third World countries. I can't see democratic First World countries going to war with each other any more," Steve argued philosophically. He was beginning to get angry and flustered judging by the shade of red he was going. I think he was a pacifist.

"We could argue the point all night, but there are still fundamental reasons why there will be more and worse wars. To name but a few: differences in religious beliefs, in culture, in wealth distribution and in language all seem to be diametrically opposed. Personally, I think the best way is to reconcile oneself to the inevitability of war and to try to protect oneself accordingly." Eileen was certainly not getting too stressed by the argument and was as convinced as Steve was that she was right. I thought both of them were philosophically right, as well as being technically wrong. I had to agree with Eileen in that I could not see man ever stopping his favourite game and equally I agreed with Steve that if we did not find a solution to what often were ultimately ridiculous reasons for war, we would soon be close to annihilating ourselves. I listened intently as we watched the magnificent oranges, reds and gold interwoven into a tapestry in the sky in front of us. There is always something totally awe-inspiring about an African sunset. Steve seemed to have a never-ending stream of volunteers willing to get off aeroplanes to work for him for either nothing, or close to it. I have to confess that I was there as a self-financed fool, but it was certainly worth the experience. Maybe, if I had had any sense, I should have approached Steve after I had qualified at college and asked him for a permanent job. I certainly loved being on the farm and I loved Africa, it was my home, although there were moments that were less than wonderful. Once I had helped Malcolm with what seemed an impossible task. He had asked me to clean out the septic tank at the back of the farmhouse. I was standing shoulder deep in the pit shovelling out the contents. We were supposed to take it in turns as to who was the lucky winner of being in the pit. The 'loser' had the lesser job of taking the wheelbarrow loads of poo away. Being the junior and newest arrival I was the winner and spent most of the afternoon in the hole! It was a fairly dirty job. **(Ed. That has got to be an indication that you had inadvertently become a serious Pom. In any other language that would have read: It was a totally**

absolutely, completely, revolting, disgusting job – emphasis on the word 'job'!)

After supper Marina, Eileen and I washed up. We bumped (**Ed. caressed for milliseconds**) buttocks, elbows, backs and even fronts in what was not a particularly small kitchen. They laughed and joked,

"Many people would say that you are very lucky, being a prisoner here in the middle of Africa with two unattached beautiful Swedish girls." Perhaps Ludwig had told them the same story. Perhaps he had told them that I was good for a threesome. The three of us were starting to get rather cosy in that we chatted and joked a lot, but one of my preconceptions about girls that I had been born with was that my future wife or any bed-mate had to look like a magazine cover model and not some terrible science experiment that had gone horribly wrong. So my letter writing sessions were presumably to girls that in my distorted mind looked like Marilyn Monroe but to anyone else's looked like the back end of horses **(Ed. isn't that the other way around?)**. Anyway, Steve, being a normal kind of a guy, saw them as beautiful...

Soon after, Eileen was to leave for Cape Town for a few weeks to visit her ageing Uncle.

"How would you like to go to the Kruger National Game Park?" Steve asked me as he finished playing an incredible piano recital, almost running the question out with the last few notes.

"...Yes..." I could not have been more excited at the prospect.

"Get yourself to Johannesburg by nine tomorrow and you can go with my cousin Sandra," he added with a laughing glint in his eye. "She's going for a long weekend and says she is dying to meet you."

I arrived at Sandra Street's fabulous antique auction showroom at about ten o'clock and we introduced ourselves. She kissed me like an old friend or a favourite nephew and immediately started chatting away as to what fun the weekend was going to be. She said she had not been for ages and had organised a guide that would show us where all the best game was. Sandra's husband had died a few years earlier. She had thrown herself wholeheartedly into the family business and according to Steve was either going to have a breakdown or had to have a break.

The roads outside the northern Kruger National Park were incredibly dusty; however, the wind was on our side and there were few vehicles going in the opposite direction. It had rained quite heavily just before we arrived at the Flat Earth Camp, which had settled the dust. We arrived to discover 'Flatty', a tame mongoose. I was first aware of her in Sandra's arms.

"Ouch!" squealed Sandra as Flatty bit her. She promptly dropped the animal and jumped onto a table. Flatty made a continuous bird-like noise as she went sniff-sniffing her way inquisitively around. Sandra was very sceptical about Flatty – short for Flotsam and Jetsam – so I picked the little creature up and allowed her to 'bite' me a couple of times. Her little nips were really just expressions of affection and after that Sandra would not put her down.

Our guide took us to see bat-eared fox cubs, a hyena kill, buffalo, as well as many thousand wildebeest. We also saw many topi, zebra **(Ed. Were there fourteen?)**, giraffe, Springbok, impala, vervet monkeys, vultures, as well as many other types of birds. When the average tourist goes, they might just see a few bits of road kill and have fun trying to identify them. After breakfast I jumped off a fifteen-odd-foot-high cliff by the river into sand. I think it was a subliminal way of showing Sandra how courageous I was. I was a young buck in my prime and the sandy beach below looked more like a mattress... In the process I mildly sprained my thigh muscles **(Ed. You were then in agony?)**.

We walked to Peep-a-rock near to the camp where Sandra and I swam alone together. She had been my Uncle Joss's fiancée and I was briefly either a long lost son or potential lover. Either way, we seemed to get on like a house on fire as if we had known each other all our lives. She had a magical girlish squeal when I splashed her. For a woman of her age, she had a magnificent figure, not looking remotely out of place in a skimpy pink bikini. There was a little waterfall that we hid behind and a rock that we were able to jump into the pool from. She sighed heavily as I dried her back, and then disappeared behind a bush to change...

Exhausted but elated in each other's company we arrived back to meet Naase Bittim, the famous Afrikaner big game photographer and his two brothers, Fik and Sid (Fik spelled Frik, I think). Like us, they were taking a long weekend away from the big city. They were very interesting in their own way, although I got the distinct impression that all three of them did not have a picnic-basket of brain between them. Naase told me to tell Steve that he had seen to it that 'The Permit' had been organised and that it was in the post and should arrive by Monday or Tuesday the following week. On the drive back to Johannesburg it was raining heavily and we initially did not spot anything. Suddenly we stumbled across four buffalo kills in the space of fifteen yards and over the next brow were the seven responsible lions. Out came glorious sunshine, as suddenly the rain had stopped, and everything was wet, shiny and beautiful. We drove up to about five yards from the magnificent beasts and took photos of them until we were all metaphorically blue in the face. Sandra retired from driving at the Phalaborwa exit from The Kruger National Park and almost fell asleep next to me. I understood why it was so tiring to drive – the steering was very slight and therefore required a very tight grip on the steering wheel. It was very enjoyable, despite the natural obstacles, the indigenous drivers and the holes in the roads. When we arrived back to Sandra's house, it was too late for me to try to get back to Orange River Tributaries so she insisted I stayed the night at her house. I had a long hot bath, an excellent meal, listened to her wonderful music and her lovely conversation and then slept in a comfortable warm double bed. She was an exceptionally handsome woman and, had I been ten years older, or she ten years younger, I might have made a pass at her. She might well have made one at me but I was too naive to have noticed. Generally I was thoroughly spoilt by her and certainly enjoyed all her attention. If I had had half a brain, I would have organised to have gone and worked for her either in another college holiday, or after I had left – hi, ho, if pots and pans... She woke me fairly early to the rattle of tea in china cutlery in bed, and then breakfast in bed with her sitting on the edge of the bed, happily chatting away.

I managed to get hold of Dutch on the phone and he agreed to pick me up at twelve from Sandra's house. She dropped me at Steve's office to give him the good news about the permit. He was not in, so I told Aunt Isabella. Aunt Isabella and my grandmother were sisters. Dutch was waiting for me with his 125 cc motorbike on my return. After fondly saying goodbye to Sandra - she kissed me on both cheeks and then purposefully on my lips - Dutch and I set off on a short cut from her house to his – it was very rough and part of the way I had to walk. I met his parents Doc and Patty 'Benson' and had lunch with them. His claim to fame was that he had received a letter from England with "Dr. Benson, Africa" on the envelope. They offered me a job as manager in Grahamstown in their newly completed hotel. They dropped me in town and I went and asked Sandra her advice on the subject.

"I think that your Uncle Steve will be disappointed if you let him down." She looked me evenly in the eye and I knew she was right. I thought about it as I walked to Steve's office. He was very glad to see me and wanted to know the whole story about the letter with the Permit and Naase from beginning to end. He was also a bit sceptical and even phoned Sandra to confirm it. I was not surprised, after all the time he had waited. I was running back from the Doc's office after telling him that I would not be able to take up his offer of a job, when a black peasant ran along next to me trying to sell me a trinket. He waited for me to come out of the office. Eventually I bought it for a fraction of what he had offered it for just to get rid of him. Conmen rarely bothered me and never more than once, which was cheering. Steve and I sat for a while in the Wild Buffalo until it started raining and then we moved inside where we sat and chatted with a German family. Steve showed them an incredible piece in the previous day's newspaper – President Daniel Arap Moi of Kenya saying that drinking was bad for the country as he laid the first brick in a multi million shilling brewery.

Back to the 'routine' of life on the farm, I was woken up at about four o'clock by Bangbang's incessant barking; I climbed out of bed to see what it was. There was something by the skins on the garage roof. It could either be farm dogs, wild dogs, jackals, hyenas, burglars or even lions. I decided not to go and see exactly as it may have been dangerous. The thought of being torn to shreds by ravenous beasts had the coward in me take charge. That was one good reason I would like Malcolm to show me how to shoot. My brother Jonathan was a big cheese in our School Army Cadets; if only it was not so un-cool in my year. If one was caught being into it in my year, one was immediately labelled as a 'Cor-Plug'. I remember the test one had to do: breathe out, squeeze the trigger and keep your eye on the target. Either way, I was hopelessly inadequate or deliberately missed; I had missed an opportunity to train up as a homicidal psychopathic gun-toting killer. Anyway, as a result I did not get any more sleep that night. Jonathan would have stormed out there and massacred the lot.

We went out shooting and Malcolm shot a Springbok and two rabbits and knocked out a bird that flew into his chin and we ran over a jumping hare. It was shot so that Ludwig and Marina could do a post mortem together. That was the strange and absurd nature of the adventure; in any normal situation, two vets would go for a drink together to get to know each other better, but no, they chose to pick at the remains of a hare, you can see the turn-on there. Maybe I was just jealous that I had not been invited, or that I was not qualified to give an opinion, but it seemed to me that any blind fool could diagnose that it died because it had been run over and then shot. Godson reported that a calf had died that night and two others were very sick. I thought that it was something to do with their kraal being too small. There was not even enough space for them all to lie down at night. We had just finished our breakfast when Goodmansson came over to say that a cow had died at UmFuyana. Marina and I first went to UmFuyana to inject a sick cow with Ngombicmyocin then came back to fetch the dead cow. It had been half eaten by jackals and stank to high heaven. I towed it behind the Grump and dropped it in the graveyard and picked up a cow that had Maligned Catarrh and it was duly slaughtered. I went speeding to umFuyana where I counted Sale Group One and Two and injected cow number 1037 with fifteen cc of Ngombicmyocin and then sped over to Musimba's kraal and the Central kraal. When I arrived back Steve was very angry about the cow that was slaughtered because it was not reported sick early enough. He wanted me to tighten up the management system and draw up a guide that any manager could follow to prevent the same occurrence happening again. Of course, my well-oiled war-cabinet with all the records of the cattle up-to-date and correct was largely supposed to achieve this.

Marina had not yet been out to all the kraals. Initially she tentatively held onto my belt above my hips as we sped along on the motorbike. We stopped for tea with Gerald, Patrick and Sybil and then went past Number Seven kraal to count the cattle at InDuna's, and as it was then getting late we had to hurry. The result was that the bike broke down at the exact point at which I had had an accident in the Grump and also where I had twice broken down before. I pushed the heavy motorbike all the way to Steve's house after trying desperately to start it many times. We arrived at Steve's after dark and, frustratingly, he started it almost immediately. One would have thought that after Marina and I had been stranded in the wildest parts of Africa where only days before lions had trod, our souls would have embraced; well, I had either been so piously snobby and would have preferred one of the local semi-tame goats or perhaps I was gay or something. I mean, come off it, what other explanation could there be? There was no bag to put over her head? Although, to be honest, something was stirring, as we hurtled faster and faster through the African bush with her arms tightly around my waist, and her sharp breasts pressed against my back; perhaps that is why bikers' women are always so hideously ugly, but then again, bikers themselves are not exactly handsome. **(Ed. As far as sweeping generalisations go, this must be near the top of the list.)** Anyway, I certainly enjoyed those high-speed hugs.

The drought finally ended and although it was only raining slightly I still got mud in my eyes as well as getting the bike and myself totally filthy. I was to count cattle at the dip as well as trying to organise taking water around to the kraals but, as it was still raining at lunchtime, I cancelled the job. Steve had phoned on the two-way radio to say that Marina and I should go up to his house for supper. We set off on the motorbike. The roads were like ice. We bumped into Sybil in her Toyota and she said we were mad to even try. We were about a hundred yards up the road before realising that she was right. I drove to about a kilometre and a half from Steve's house on the grass verge but was eventually foiled by a fence. I turned to come down to the gate but the bike became stuck in the mud that was on the road.

Wild scenes... my experience of life (despite developing exponentially almost by the day) had not brought me to imagine a totally windswept, soaked, almost totally naked woman, clutching me as her hero in the middle of a darkest Black-African night. **(Ed. Perhaps cruelly you left out "beautiful" in that list of adjectives; the truth was that she was actually by any standards quite pretty. Perhaps if you had just reciprocated and given in to her, you would not have been able to simply leave the farm and Africa dispassionately. Perhaps you were petrified of falling in love with anyone...)** Marina's thin cotton dress had become completely transparent in the deluge. We walked the rest of the way to find that Aunt Isabella was there. She found dry clothes for us. She was amazed and delighted that we had come all that way just for supper in the terrible weather. We had a very enjoyable evening despite the weather. Of course she refused to let us consider going back to the farmhouse that night and the only place we could sleep was in the vast spare bed... Perhaps Marina was not on the pill, perhaps it was the wrong time of the month, perhaps, perhaps... whatever, the expression merely 'sleeping together' never had a truer meaning. Judging from the movement from her side of the large bed, she also did not sleep all night either.

We visited Sybil, Gerald and Patrick on the way back the next morning. Gerald tossed me a beer with his usual suggestive wink.

"What's a good looking English boy like you doing in the middle of an African game farm?" He tipped his wrist at me as he spoke.

"I suppose I just have friends in high places." I laughed. "And how did you get to be here?"

"Sybil invited Patrick and I down last year and we have been here ever since. I think she loves us." He put his other hand on his hip. I was never intimidated by either of them, because it was clear from their teapot gestures that what they said was tongue-in-cheek. The rumour amongst the European staff was that Sybil was Steve's ex-wife, which might have explained what she was doing there. Maybe Marina had led Patrick and Gerald to believe that I was gay, as I had not made any progress with her, given that we had actually slept in the same bed together and not done the deed. My impression then was that she wished that things had happened and given another opportunity, I was going to make certain that any ridiculous shyness, lack-of-experience-in-bed-department, or even potentially gay excuses were not going to be used.

One Sunday night Godson came to announce that the whole of the Far Valley herd was missing. I went out to look for them in the land rover. I drove around until one-thirty in the morning but could not find them. I woke at six to go and look for the missing cattle and still could not find them, so came back at seven o'clock to go and tell Steve but he had just arrived at the farmhouse. Steve went out with a carload of people to go and look for them. Annoyingly, he couldn't have been looking for more than ten minutes before he found them. The reason why they had got out of their kraal was because two bulls had had a fight and the one had probably chased the other over the kraal wall and the rest of the herd had followed.

iNja was fiercely muttering a lot of African mumbo-jumbo. When I eventually translated it, with the help of my Up County Zulu Book, he was in fact trying to tell me that fourteen cattle were missing. I took the Grump with two black berks to go and look for them. I could not persuade them to stand up to look for the cattle so I continually had to stop and stand on the back and peer around for them. When I also became too cold I climbed back in and drove again. I was absolutely delighted, however, when I found them just going out through one of the traps by the main road. If I had not caught them, they would have disappeared for good.

There were supposed to have been fourteen missing so I was over the moon to have found twenty-five.

Marina persuaded me to take her to Orange River Tributaries on the motorbike. When we started our mutual high speed fantasy, she wore her corduroys and denim shirt and she would clasp her hands firmly around my ribs. By that time though, we had become extremely familiar with each other and the whole experience. She wore her flowing pink cotton dress with no bra. I could distinctly feel her aroused nipples gouge provocatively into my back. Her hands casually slipped into my crotch to find the extra gear stick in my jeans. It was a wonderful sexual game we played. The faster we went, the more aroused we became. Despite my supposed normal resistance to ugly females (or being gay, or whatever), it was something that my alter ego allowed; after all, she was simply a passenger on the bike whose face I could not see anyway. Being thus distracted, on the way, I foolishly started to overtake a large truck on a blind rise, only to find another speeding lorry appear out of nowhere, bearing down towards us in a terminator kind of way. Fortunately my immediate instincts were to swerve off the road to the right, and off a foot-high precipice. Luckily, I was able to control the bike as it skidded in the gravel. A millisecond later, the two of us would have added to South Africa's already impressive road death toll. The things I did as a young and impetuous teenager, keen to impress the most ugly woman **(Ed. Isn't that a contradiction in terms)** in Africa. The incident more or less cured me of such driving practices though. Anyhow, we lived to tell the tale, although Marina, not surprisingly, accepted a lift back home with Ivan Itchyanis to his farm Luandoo, possibly because she was embarrassed as to the contents of her knickers. Although, it had to be said, that at the moment that we flew off the precipice, she could hardly have been clutching me tighter – it was gorgeous. I followed them on the bike to see where Ivan's farm was. Of all the people that I came into contact with in my travels, Ivan had the most ridiculous name. It was the cause of much merriment in a juvenile adolescent way. Steve always warned new employees about him and gave strict instructions not to laugh at him about his name. At his farm the blasted bike would not start again, although that time it was because I had not switched the damn kill-switch on. Arriving home I ran a hot bath for Marina to allow her to recover. Maybe I should just confess... Marina, naked, phew... I could not have resisted an invitation to hop in with her... **(Ed. Joss, stop that.)** From the neck down, she was extremely well built. There was no firewood so I chopped some up with some excessive sweaty, manly violence to take my mind off her totally glorious naked, wet-female, otherwise-unavailable, available body. Later the two of us went to visit Sybil together, needless to say, on the motorbike. She wanted Marina to treat an ostrich but we could not catch it and had to admit defeat.

When we arrived back at the farmhouse, Aunt Isabella was waiting in the dark. The 'dear old thing' wanted to give Marina a pot of marmalade for giving Steve some flowers. Steve turned up and he invited us up for a grand supper at his house. We had another very depressing discussion about the certainty of man destroying himself. We drove back down to the farmhouse listening to *Regatta de Blanc* by The Police and, in the haze of alcohol and darkness, Marina was becoming increasingly more and more attractive...

One of my secret thoughts of what would make an excellent book was all of Dave's letters. I would either have to wait until he was dead, or get his approval, which I doubt he would consent to. However, he was without doubt the funniest, chirpiest, happiest, most normal person I knew and his many letters always cheered me up. For years we had a postal game of chess going, the pieces held in place with blue-tack. It suited me well because he was always accusing me of taking too long with my moves. Dave Green was a devoted school friend. We had been in the same gang: him, me and another friend, Dennis Churchill.

Again, I aggressively broke up another heap of firewood and prepared a roaring fire in the dining room and was just getting down to writing when my conscience decided that I ought to go out and do some counting instead. I sped over to umFuyana kraal. The herd was not close to going in so I asked them to wait and then went to Number Seven kraal and counted the cows there. Then the bike, true to form, refused to start. After many fruitless efforts I had no choice but to push. With a bad attack of asthma looming, I had no option but to press on.

Bad. **(Ed. Back to English lingo, Joss, bad - 'bad'. Actually, honestly, that should translate as 'very nearly actually died!')** OK Bad, bad. I was in total misery, desperately dragging in each breath. It is difficult to describe, but imagine one has a wet sponge in one's mouth, which one has to breathe through. If one imagines that a whale can exhale ninety percent of the air in its lungs with each gulp and that a normal human can exhale around ten percent, well, it felt as if I was pushing out less than half a percent. The echo of my own pathetic breathing sounded like someone else's, away over my shoulder. Sometimes it sounded like a mouse's squeak, also in a bush over my shoulder. On other breaths, it sounded as bad as a stick in bicycle spokes. The net impact, of course, is that my pathetic body, and particularly my brain, were simply not able to operate, starved of oxygen, and began to shut down. I eventually arrived at Steve's house just as he did. I managed to pretend that all was well and infuriatingly, he fixed it almost immediately and I set off again in a black rage. Incredibly, I only got as far as where I had broken down four times before. Steve had given me a torch so that I could signal to him if I ran into trouble but I decided against it and pushed it the rest of the way home as I felt I could not bear the indignity of having to be rescued. Marina had made a delicious supper. **(Ed. Now the truth, you have edited out the bit where she kissed you passionately as you pushed open the back door and murmured, "Did you have a good day out on the ranch today, Darling?")** I did the washing up and went out and battered to death more firewood... I opened one of my bottles of Guinness and we both wrote letters together until eleven o'clock in front of a really blazing open fire. When I arrived back from my bike-pushing episode, I had hardly any asthma at all; also I was not completely exhausted, which meant that there was hope. It was the first time that my asthma has subsidised by itself.

I had just started to do some ironing when I was whipped away by Steve to make the storeroom suitable for fifty waterbuck. As any normal male will confirm, ironing at the best of times is women's preserve. So I was delighted to be made otherwise busy all day, although I avoided working in too much dust. Steve had managed to get permission to bring fifty of them into the farm, which would be a huge boost to the wild game collection. Waterbuck have big white rings around their back-end and the adults have ominously long curved horns. Later, Steve and I went to Ivan's farm to collect the Mazda truck. I drove it back to the farm and filled it up with diesel. Steve and I and a gang of the farm's workers put two traps on the back and secured them with rope. I also put in the tents and other camping equipment. I made supper and washed up as well as making a blazing fire. We put the last of the things that we needed into the traps on the Mazda and Marina and I set off for Luandoo on the way to Lake Bloemfontein. We filled up again with diesel on the way and arrived at eight-fifteen, a quarter of an hour later than we had agreed. Still Steve was about half an hour behind us, but Jan Grotéhuis was very late. Jan was the coloured expert on the drugs needed to knock out the waterbuck. We obviously could not start without him. We waited at Lake Bloemfontein Hotel for about an hour, drinking beer. When Steve and Jan arrived we had some sandwiches for lunch and then set off for Crescent Island. Steve had brought his two nieces who were left with Marina and me in the Mazda. They were two ripening young pretty girls of fourteen and fifteen, Bianca and Jordan, and they made the long journey more interesting with their continual banal teenage chatter. I think that I must have had a bad girl-boy experience when I was a child, as I seemed incapable of relating to girls or even getting past 'Advance-to-Go'. However, I certainly would have been mad to even consider them as fair game but it was nice to abstractly chat them up in a 'we're-almost-in-the-same-age-group' kind of way. We stopped once because the two ropes holding down the traps had sheared through so we tied them back down with wire. Had we gone on much further, they would have fallen off the back of the truck...

We eventually gained access to the island via a narrow causeway. On the one side of the causeway there was a thick layer of algae that looked as if one could walk on it and, on the other, the water was clear bright blue. The tiny island was terribly over grazed. There must have been three to four hundred waterbuck on it and it was only about a thousand square acres. There were also three wildebeest, two zebra **(Ed. Not fourteen?)**, dik-dik, rabbits, bat-eared foxes, bushbuck, and some black mongooses. We set up camp at the far end of the island and unloaded the crates off the lorry while Jan started to prepare the darts. Jan had also brought two Indians brothers called Yesh and Vilai Deesmai. They were to act as extra drivers and general helpers.

We set about darting the frightened waterbuck. The first dart missed and we spent about half an hour searching for it. The second hit its target and when the unfortunate waterbuck eventually collapsed, Steve bellowed to me through his cupped hands,

"Go grab it, Joss!" It was still flailing away when Marina and I arrived to deal with it. Marina and I took a blood sample, faeces sample, tagged its ear with a number, and gave it some Nilverin followed up with the antidote. After the antidote had been given, it only took about thirty seconds before the waterbuck woke up again so between Yesh, Vilai and myself it had to be secured in the crate very quickly. We only caught one on the first day because of all the time wasted. We gathered up a load of firewood and made a huge camp fire. Steve mocked me because I put on a huge log that was supposedly part of the camp site furniture and consequently the fire blazed until the same time the next day. After a delicious supper, cooked mostly by Marina with a little help from the schoolgirls Bianca and Jordan who also did most of the washing up, I went to sleep by the fire.

"Nothing can beat sleeping under the stars next to an open fire. That is were I will put my sleeping-bag" Steve boasted, and as it certainly did not look like raining, I said I would join him. Actually the main reason was because I was not going to sleep in the same tent as Marina, which was the only other option. In retrospect, I was not sure that excuse washed as, although she might not have been a contender for Miss Sweden, she was pretty enough and getting prettier every time I looked at her. Funny thing, love or infatuation, she probably thought I was an arrogant prig whom she barely tolerated. Or perhaps she was scheming night and day over ways to entrap me forever. Perhaps it was because I did not want anyone to know about our blossoming love affair... I slept very well with the bright stars as my ceiling, but Steve said he only slept between three and three-thirty.

After breakfast we set out to catch more waterbuck and were immediately beset with more problems. The darts, once fired, were being blown off target by the strong wind. Jan prepared and handed the darts to Steve who crouched in the land rover to shoot while I drove the Mazda with Marina, Yesh and Vilai. He would shoot one and we would get it back into the crates. When we stopped for lunch we had caught four.

During the lunch break I went out on the lake in a little boat with the flirty holiday-mood young girls.

"C'mon muscles, can't you row any harder?" Jordan tormented me. I was finding it difficult to row against the wind so I jumped out and pulled the boat along. "You're not very strong with all those muscles" she continued, so I tipped the boat over – that shut them up! Straight after lunch we shot another waterbuck but it refused to go down so after about half an hour Steve shot it again, after which it immediately collapsed. We gave it some antidote as soon as we arrived and I drove as fast as I could back to the camp but by the time we got there it started to flail about madly for about thirty seconds then stopped suddenly. A few moments later it was stone dead.

The next morning, Steve and I and the two girls set off for home in the Peugeot and three workers and Yesh drove the truck. I was crushed into the back seat between the schoolgirls. We went into Bloemfontein to phone Aunt Isabella's house to see if Malcolm was there. We caught up with the truck and followed it all the way back home. There were seven police checks along the way and at each one of them Steve talked his way through without having to produce any permit or without them checking inside the back. One section of road had three police checks on which no roads joined so no other traffic could have joined or left the road! We had the waterbuck unloaded and the crates back on the trucks by one-forty in the morning. I put water in the bathtub and grass in with the waterbuck. They were all very edgy and nervously concentrated on being closest to the far wall. One of the bucks got fairly mean and decided to charge me. He missed me by about two millimetres. Bruised, I decided not to have a friendly chat with them after all.

The film *Bloemfontein in my Blood* was going to be filmed on the property. Sheila, the producer, particularly wanted to use Steve's ancient rusty old car that had long since blended into the farmyard. She felt that it would add to the authenticity of the film. There were of course only to be two-dimensional buildings but to us non-film types the whole experience was enthralling. The book had been a best seller. It was all about the English–Afrikaner post-war confrontation in which both groups claimed to have equal inheritance to the country. It was set around a family which was English on the mother's side and Afrikaans on the father's side. Sheila was very pretty; it would appear to be part of the requirements of the 'Wild-White-Man-in-Africa-Thing' to have an appropriate dolly-woman in one's retinue, although to whom she belonged, I was not sure. Film making morons continually hounded me for bits and pieces, the worst of whom was the Gaffer called Ben Down. It was incredible how realistic the two dimensional 'buildings' were. Until then, I had not been privy as to how such films were made. They looked as if a strong wind would sweep them away. I could just imagine John Wayne and Clint Eastwood coming face to face in the street with their guns blazing. The film was far removed from gratuitous violence – it was all about a young English family and their determination to settle in Africa. It dealt largely with the question of identity. The one son quickly embraced Africa and learnt its customs, languages, laws and nature. Equally quickly he purposefully forgot any connection with Mother England. Conversely, the second brother saw their stay as an extended holiday in an English Colony. The film followed the paths of the two brothers who eventually became alienated.

I arrived back at the farmhouse to find that Yesh had brought more waterbuck. After we had unloaded them from the truck, I left because Aunt Isabella wanted me to stay the night up with her because she did not like to be alone. **(Ed. Marina would have been furious!)** The next morning after a good breakfast I set off down to the farmhouse. Godson must have started dipping very early because he was almost finished when I arrived. He was as keen as mustard and the truth was that the farm would not have operated as smoothly as it did if it had not been for his commitment. He must have been something of an authority on dipping, judging by the number of offspring he had. I then cut a large heap of fresh grass for the waterbuck and watered the area around their tank so that the grass would grow faster. I then instructed Goodmansson to saw a barrel in half so that we could use it for water for the buck. I filed the edge, cleaned it and then put it in and filled it with water. I edged within six inches of number twenty-one waterbuck before he tried to run me over again. Their new-found domesticity could sometimes be deceptive.

Marina and I went to Orange River Tributaries to buy groceries on the bike again; by this time the high-speed hugging had become a mutual fantasy. She would pull her dress up into her crotch, climb on behind me with her gorgeous white knees either side of me and when I lent back I could feel her soft cheek in my neck. Perhaps we didn't really go to buy anything, it was just an excuse to get really close to each other. The motorbike had become our cupboard under the stairs to secretly play with each other's fantasies out in the wide open expanse of wildest erotic Africa. The two of us had become something of a pair, we must have seemed inseparable; the next step would have been to be caught actually holding hands...

Godson and I decided, or rather I had suggested it ages ago and he had only just taken it up, to do the dipping in two days rather than three which meant that there would be another day free for weaning, notching and castrating. After counting cattle out of the dip the following morning, I took some Africans and some Asians to see the Tomlinson herd and the two sale groups. I could not find any of them. The men supposedly had a meeting in town so they had to hurry off but Steve just caught them as they were leaving and took them about a hundred yards further than where I had looked, and found the cattle. The man seemed to have instinctive radar to find his own cattle. Having expressed an interest, they were more or less committed to buying them; perhaps seeing them was just to verify that they existed.

That evening we went off to catch Springbok. In the dark, the land rover hit a monster hole in the road which shattered the back window. An aardvark was very much like a monster with its strange nose. I had luckily jumped off about five seconds earlier, avoiding any serious injury. We caught two babies – both by unnatural means. One smashed into a fence and knocked itself out and the other seemed to run out of energy and just sat down. In the Grump I spoke to Steve about the night watchmen and he had agreed to only have three on the whole farm. He gave poor iNja another bollocking. Quite why, I never worked out as my Zulu was not up to that speed by then; perhaps he was just saying,

"Howdy mate, how's life, how's it hanging?"

Steve's landmark statement of the day was,

"The world was made of ideas and people who tried to carry them out." Perhaps it was not the most mind-blowing of thoughts. Leaning out of the oncoming vehicle, Steve introduced me to Beth Tomlinson, his sister;

"You must come down and stay with us for a few days, I insist." She swooped in and kissed me unexpectedly through the back window.

Later, he dropped me at the station. My compartment was full of women and in normal circumstances that might have been heaven. Amongst others, there was an Asian woman who couldn't stop talking and a big fat African Mamma who stank and never opened her mouth. The window was open all night and as a result I caught a bad head cold.

The train arrived in Cape Town at eight o'clock and surprisingly taxi drivers did not harass me. I eventually decided that Pin-yah van der Westhuisen was not coming to collect me, and the only phone I could find did not work, so I was forced to resort to a taxi. It could not have been more than five kilometres, which cost an incredible R40.00, almost as much as the whole train journey from Johannesburg to Cape Town. Pin-yah said that his uncle had just died and no one was staying at his house. He suggested that I go and stay in the Sunset Boulevard Holiday Centre. His driver dropped me off at the bus station and I caught a bus bound for Fishhoek. It seemed a hell of a long way and I was the only white man on the bus.

When I eventually arrived, I had 'Diet A' supper with some people that were having a conference on bringing the different denominations of the Church together. They were kind and well spoken and did not seem to mind my nonconformist opinions.

"The differences in the Church only seem to be getting bigger and the different factions further and further apart," I pointed out. They probably had loads of negativists try and persuade them of the hopeless nature of their cause.

"God works in mysterious ways. Each offshoot is a new understanding of Christ's teaching," they tried to explain patiently.

"Some of the different denominations are so far apart they are effectively different religions," I continued.

"Yes, but on the Final Days, all the Churches will come together and the Glory of God will be revealed to all Man." The saving of Mankind just seemed too big a mission for me, although I did think that at some point in the future I might see the light and spring forward to enrol. I had 'Diet B' breakfast with them as we continued the discussion. Five aspirin pills and a malaria pill seemed to have defeated whatever I had the day before. I only had to wait about ten minutes for a matato, as they were known as elsewhere in Africa to arrive. **(Ed. Sadly it is just a polite translation for the term that you have tried to avoid using – Kaffir-taxi.)** It was a death trap, to put it mildly. There were people on the roof and people hanging out the doors. The brakes were almost non-existent, the steering was bad but, worst of all, there did not appear to be any suspension, but somehow it managed to get there. I found Fort Riebeeck. A nice black conman bobbed, weaved and floated around me as I made my way about. He tried to pretend to be a tour guide by saying things like,

"...and that was where the soldiers stood..." He sure worked up a sweat. A fat black guy was also being forcibly shown around. He must have come from Swaziland or somewhere, because he was really amazed by every little thing. My 'guide' kept calling me his 'Little White Brother', which was a little annoying as I felt that it was obvious from our different colours that I was not his brother and being considerably taller than he qualified me not to be called 'Little'. No whores bothered me. In some parts of the world they are part of the tourist attraction but I could not find them mentioned in my map but, then again, it was out of date. Old Cape Town, under gently flapping washing, past naked snotty brown babies, past part-naked, tit-full, fully-fat, ugly old native black women, around drunken, abusive, loud, unemployed, shabby, grumpy, prematurely old men, over open, revolting, medieval, turdfull diseased drains and through tourist-free squalor. My options were somewhat limited as I had blown all my money on shells and therefore could not afford to go romping around the country because the banks were closed.

I walked in the rain to the top of Jan Van Riebeeck Street and caught a government bus. On the crowded back seat were two of the most beautiful black African teenagers I had ever seen. They could certainly grace the front of any European Glossy magazine. They were about my age, with cheeky, smiling, healthy, bashful, dimpled white sexy grins that just caught my alert eyes. One wore a bright tulip-yellow, sexy, frilly, above-the-knee dress and the other had a red designer top and new blue studded, very tight jeans. The only space on the bus mysteriously appeared between them in the back row. There was such a crush that Tulip put her arm over my shoulder, and Lipstick Red had her arm lying between her thigh and mine. Tulip had her other arm between her thighs and every moment of the jolting vehicle caused it to gently move up and down.

"You drank enough last night to down an elephant!" Tulip's eager shining beautiful brown face was inches from mine. She had an immaculate English Public School accent. I had to be in some kind of unscheduled, unrehearsed dream.

"You didn't exactly hang back yourself!" Lipstick Red chirped back in her refined Pucka Peerage voice. She had turned her right shoulder towards me, clearly showing the space between her magnificent brown breasts as far down as her pierced belly button in a delightfully provocative manner. The aureole surrounding her tantalising nipples was millimetres from the edge of the red top and her nipples themselves also just visible through the near transparent material.

"Did you see that jerk dancing with Jade last night? He really made a real fool of himself!" Tulip laughed at the memory, her face even closer.

"Actually, I rather fancied him." Lipstick's hand had now bumped its way onto my thigh. "I bet he would have been good in bed!" She beamed into my face.

If only I had the nerve to jump into their game. Perhaps I should have introduced myself... The side of her beautiful face momentarily blocked my vision as Tulip leaned forward to her friend.

"Nah. Nonsense. You know what they say, hopeless dancers are hopeless lovers." Tulip's cool cold brown arm just slightly increased the tension on my shoulder. I could taste the toothpaste on her breath. She was just so wickedly pretty.

"You're just jealous because he did not look at you." The tips of Lipstick's fingers had now slipped or rather pushed their way between my thighs. The whole reality fantasy trip was rapidly getting out of control. My stop was getting ominously close and there I was, trapped beyond any adolescent young man's most erotic fantasy; what was I to do? Perhaps realising my predicament, Tulip dug her sharp fingernails into my shoulder;

"Why don't we just take this good-looking boy home? You would love to come and play with us two gorgeous African Princesses, wouldn't you?" she whispered into my ear, nibbled, and then licked and kissed it softly.

"Brilliant idea! C'mon Big Boy, you know you want to!" Lipstck whispered coarsely, licking inside my other ear. She turned my face gently with her hands and kissed me first on the cheek and then directly on my lips, her tongue darting momentarily into my mouth. Her hand had deftly undone my belt and gently began tugging up my stern member.

"Good God, here I am on a public bus virtually being raped!" My inadequately prepared teenage mind's only defence was to retreat. Another few seconds and the three of us would probably have been thrown off the bus anyway. Perhaps everyone on the bus was enjoying the show as much as we were. Perhaps my own sexually deficient education had me cringe at the prospect of what I ought to do with two raging nymphomaniacs and my embarrassment tolerance level had shot thought the acceptable ceiling. Struggling with my jeans, I leapt forward and spluttered pathetically,

"Oh no, this is my stop!" I knew I would never see them again and, as impulsively as I had pulled away at the moment of no return, I lurched awkwardly back and kissed them both.

"Girls, we must meet again and go the whole way together!" I tried to whisper but the bus had become totally silent. I almost fell off the bus, fumbling with my belt and the excited package that had appeared in my jeans. They giggled and held hands and waved to me through the back window. They mouthed something as an ocean of chemistry ebbed and flowed between us. The sensual touch of their fleeting hands and their clean brown, young seductive bodies pressed provocatively against mine was completely erotic. In reality, that was the moment when I lost my virginity. Why I did not stay on the bus with them I would never know. I regretted getting off the moment I did so. We waved goodbye to each other like old friends that would see each other again soon.

Their ghosts haunted me then as they do now, their golden-brown, naked lithe bodies playing with my mind and soul. I was besotted with their exquisite tantalising perfect smiles, polished white, camera teeth surrounded with blood-red-rose kissing lips, and they looked straight into my eyes and beyond as they kissed and consumed me. The thought of recounting the tale of how I was nearly seduced, nay, raped, by two gorgeous black woman in a bus, in darkest Africa when black women were perceived as little more than slaves, at a period in my life when to have one vaguely pretty white girl look twice at me was unusual – what would my grandchildren say? The thought of it made me chuckle to myself.

Arriving back in Johannesburg, I met Lorraine, Ludwig's ex-girlfriend, and talked to her over tea at the Red Bull cafe. If only she did not have that nauseating laugh she would be quite desirable. It was difficult talking to her without knowing whether to make her laugh or not. After all, the basis of mine, and I presumed any normal man's chat-up technique, was to appeal to the woman's sense of humour. In the end, I just became immune to it. Marina however, had magically stopped being ugly and I found myself pro-actively chatting her up. Where had that steep chin and clipped accent gone? Her bedroom was next to mine with a door between. Although hers was not a double bed, it was certainly big enough for two. I just had to encourage her to invite me in... Maybe it was the wrong time of the month again, or the right time, whatever, she was very friendly but did not take the final plunge.

On my last morning Godson Banana insisted on writing his name and address in my diary and a list of books that he wanted me to buy for him in England and to send to him. Marina and I did the fifteen miles round trip to tell some herders to bring their cattle to the farmhouse to be weighed. It was the best trip and journey ever. There was definitely a correlation between the speed of the motorbike and the tightness of her grip on my gear stick. We had had a truly unique relationship, erotic and sensual which had totally revolved around our journeys on the bike. On this last goodbye she undid the top buttons of her dress so that her bare nipples pressed cool-hard and then hot-sex against my bare back. She undid my belt and zip and tugged furiously at my willing tool gear-stick; her glorious white naked legs lifted onto the petrol tank around me, her pink cotton skirt billowing behind the bike. With one hand on the handle bar I stroked a magnificent white calf as far back as her stomach where she led my hand between her legs. Judging from the wetness of the saddle and my fingers, I guessed that she enjoyed the trip as much as I had. How we did not crash was a miracle. I stopped a few miles away from the farmhouse,

"We must meet up in the middle of Africa and do this more often!" She laughed aloud. We hugged very closely and kissed as a sort of closing gesture to our non-sexual yet very sexy intimate relationship.

"Riding a motorbike will never be the same without you!" Suddenly she was very, very beautiful.

"Perhaps we could meet up on Steve's farm again and get a bigger faster bike" I laughed.

"Or perhaps we should just share one room, next time." She tucked in her beautiful delicate white breasts, which I had only just seen for the first time, back into her dress and buttoned them away. When she climbed back on behind me she was able to sit on her dress in such a way that it looked much like trousers, covering her beautiful legs, and primly held me around the waist with just her hands. We skidded into the yard and believed that no one was any the wiser as we casually dismounted. Marina also wrote her address into my diary and although we wrote to each other a couple of times, it did not really last. Marina was very sweet, but ultimately not on my short list of potential wives **(Ed. Liar, liar!)**.

Vilai Deesmai dropped me at the airport. I had no trouble getting through, however the passport officer thought it was very strange that as a student I was without a pen. A really outstandingly beautiful sunrise was visible from my window the next morning. It epitomised the tremendous holiday I had had. I arrived home to continue life as an Agricultural student in the English drizzle. Although I had other adventures, this at the time certainly rated as a holiday of a lifetime. I was bronzed, muscled and my tales made me the envy of my fellow students.

Laugh last

Life is like a hat; living just goes on and on.
Tomorrows come, and tomorrows will blow,
The great churning Wheel of Time digs low.
Time for your inspection, time is perfection.
They have to stop time though it's all wrong.
Yesterday is past care, they did not see it go.
It's out for them, they've ended in the furrow.
Fill-up all time; call-up every second's song,
What is not wanted is wasted, all ticking by.
Mould every day as if it were your very last.
Keep to the narrow path and don't tell a lie.
When the clock stops, you are under grass,
Stop bleating; you know what it is like to die.
You can say to them now, 'Forget me, fast!'

Forgotten Friend

Faster, fearless, feckless friend
Flying, falling, following flop
She's a tease, a menace,
A bully, a threat, a bother
A girl, all female, all woman,
An enticing exquisite beauty,
She's mine as we wrestled
As we rolled and fornicated
She's not mine as we fought
And made passionate love/hate
She's exorcised and transient.

CHAPTER THREE

...continuing sublime, glorious normality...

A year later... ***(Ed. Marina was articulate, intelligent, foreign, and your pubescent-adolescent mind realised she was only fantasy)*** *...After achieving a National Diploma in Farm Management, I began life for real. I was offered a job on a pig farm which should more correctly be described as a meat factory and I was not able to handle the inhumanity of it and so turned it down. My father had just started an exciting business venture and it seemed a logical step to put the agricultural career on hold for a while and to assist building up the family business. It was very hard work. Initially I assisted in the building of the warehouse offices and then as a salesman, driving many hours trying to find buyers. We were just about to have a major launch when the rug was proverbially and literally pulled from under us. The company was declared insolvent. It was of course devastating for the whole family and I seized the opportunity to get out of England. I had bought the legendary escape ticket to visit Den in the Land-down-under, Australia.*

Sydney, Gateway to the North, or was that Watford...? Instead of going north, I went further south to Melbourne. The flight down had taken twenty-six hours and to pass the time I had watched a few soppy films as well as being waited on hand and foot by the legendary obliging air hostesses. In those early flying days of mine I still had not heard of the Mile-High Club and, even if I had, I doubt I would have managed the acrobatics required to do it in an aeroplane loo, never mind the extraordinary fast track chatting up required beforehand. I have never really looked, but there are bound to be 'Confessions of a long distant air hostess' type books about. The little I have ogled them, they always seemed far too busy and I imagined that sex would be the last thing on their minds. Perhaps the books would relate that between the first and second in-flight films, they could select a suitable single, good-looking bloke to take an unsolicited drink with a note, "Meet me in the back loo in two minutes and I will be naked and ready..." My favourite **HATE** TV AD is one in which a young couple agree to do it on board. Off he goes and strips off in anticipation while in the meantime she is offered a drink and prefers it to her boyfriend who is being raped by a gay male flight attendant.

Den had been out in Australia for two years working in various copper mines and he had just left one in Tasmania and was in the process of finding another job on mainland Australia. He was an old school friend and the two of us had remained close. He was the same height as me, but was always a few pounds heavier. He was one of those people who looked as if he was more closely related to a gorilla in that he was very hairy. I, on the other hand, had an embarrassing half dozen hairs sprouting pathetically on my girly chest. My theory-excuse was that the more civilised and cultured one was the less hair one had. Den's theory was that the less hair one had the more effeminate one was and of course more hair meant being more butch-masculine and grown-up.

"G'day Cobba!" he rumbled unconvincingly in his newly acquired primeval accent as he shook my hand at the airport.

We stayed the night in Melbourne with a friend of his. In the time that he had been there he had acquired an army of friends around the country. They were to come in extremely handy as we made our way around. We swam at Mentone Beach and threw a stick for the friend's wolf-like dog and after buying our host some chocolates and flowers we caught an overnight coach back to Sydney on the Monday evening. We had not seen each other for years and so we talked for hours until we finally arrived in Sydney eleven hours later at five o'clock. We caught a taxi that proudly managed seventy miles per hour along the main street, had pancakes for breakfast and caught the ferry across the harbour to go to Manley. We were just in time to see a most glorious sunrise over the Sydney Opera House and an ocean liner dwarfing tiny tugs that struggled to bring it into the harbour. My apologies for the lack of Bruce-and-Sheila jokes at this juncture – they usually revolve around the Opera house and Bruce saying to Sheila at the end,

"...Not only are you a darn good shag, but you are a good sport as well!" My impression was that everyone in the West had heard them, but in case of some conspiracy and anyone had been left out of the loop, just send a stamped addressed envelope and I will send the gory details. Anyway, it was exceptionally beautiful and despite both of us having quite good cameras, we could not do justice in capturing the moment. When the sun came out from behind darkened clouds, it appeared to be shooting rays of golden light down like eternal spotlights on the famous domes of the Opera House and the ocean liner.

Bernard and Katie Strange were also friends of Den's. We were lucky to catch them, as they were about to leave for work. We played squash that afternoon, and true to our schoolboy form, he won four games to three. Great game it was, although I played barefoot.

Den went to see his ex-employers. "They have got a job for me up in Townsville, I just have to get myself up there," he announced cheerfully when I found him and added that there might be one for me.

We were hitch-hiking for twenty-five minutes when we caught a lift in a small yellow truck. The pillock must have averaged twenty-five miles per hour and took us on some back road. It was already two o'clock by the time we eventually arrived in Newcastle. I had had a similar experience hitching from Oxford to college in Cirencester not many years before. I was sure that man who had given me the lift had no intention of letting me out. He said he would take me all the way to Cirencester; he just had to pop into his RAF base to pick up something. When we got to the main gate, I seized the opportunity to leap out of the car even though I was in the middle of nowhere. Fortunately I found a phone box and a friend drove all the way out to come and rescue me. Perhaps the bastard was going to murder me – or even worse... After four hours of hitching we walked five miles up the road to a caravan park where we were told about some unfortunate German hitch-hikers who had recently been brutally murdered there. They had apparently pitched their tent as any ordinary campers do, and they were found the next morning with their throats cut.

"...and they've still not caught the killers," the campsite owner added, rolling his eyes. The suggestion was that he subliminally approved and the area would be better off without hitch-hikers. Den was never really in favour of the whole hitch-hiking option and on hearing this news he was determined to get out of the dreadful place as soon as he could. Not that I was far behind him; the only thing that made me slightly reluctant to jump on a bus was the cost element. We woke up the next morning feeling worse than death as we had not put the tent up properly and it collapsed in the night so we almost froze. We spent at least half an hour in a hot shower and were hitch-hiking by seven o'clock to get out of the awful place. We had a cup of coffee and breakfast in a garage when the amazing character called Gavin entered our tale. He looked like a traditional hippy, complete with foot-long knotted-beard, bare filthy feet, half-length dirty torn jeans and a contagious effervescent laugh. He gave us a lift to about 130 kilometres short of Brisbane. His truck was on its last wheels and every time he filled up with petrol, he also filled up with oil. He was going simply to see the sun set from the most easterly point in Australia where he was going to abandon the truck.

We then thumbed a lift with a drunken beer deliveryman; at a guess, his name should have been Sterling Moss. His missed vocation in life was to have been a racing car driver. The next was with another truck, a furniture removal lorry, and I had the rucksacks uncomfortably heaped onto my lap. I listened to a long debate Den had with the driver on the social implications of genetic engineering. Den was something of a 'pro' at biology at school. He had to be, as he sat next to Kate Buckingham-Stratford – the most gorgeous girl in the sixth form. The driver felt it was inevitable that all our food would one day be genetically modified. He dropped us at Tweed Heads outside a bus stop just as a bus was about to pull off. Hurriedly we clambered on and went as far as Southport and found a camp site. We put the tent up securely that time and, as it did not collapse, we slept fairly well.

We started hitching again at seven o'clock and after an hour we were just about to get a bus into Brisbane when a car stopped. The driver was a recent immigrant from England, from darkest Birmingham. He and Den jabbered away about motorbikes and race meetings, starting with the Isle of Man TT, the Mecca for any motorbike enthusiast. Den knew a dangerous amount about bikes since he had also been to the Isle of Man a couple of times. Almost reluctantly, we were dropped outside the main station in Brisbane and we caught a train to the outskirts. In a small shop we bought a pie each and were given a shoebox lid on which we wrote 'Rock', hopefully an obvious abbreviation for Rockhampton. It was the sign to hold up to show to prospective 'lifters' our desired destination. We walked for about two miles to find a suitable spot from which to hitch. The next lift was with Sue and Helen, two mildly chubby giggling middle-aged girls, who were going all the way to Rock. We shared the back of their small truck with their three enormous and only just tame Alsatians. We had our first experience of being nearly wiped out when the wheels of their Ute locked while trying to avoid some other moronic driver. Our view out the back was somewhat hampered by their caravan, about two feet behind us. But hey, when one is hitch-hiking one can't be picky. At the caravan park in Rocky, Den phoned Cathy MacFlattery, another 'Old Friend'. Some skinny Aussie official enquired why I had not booked in at reception yet. I did my "No speaky dee Ingleesh," trick. Cathy arrived about three quarter of an hour later in her Ute. She took us to Wreck Point to have a look at Great Keppel Island; a great place to commit suicide from, a sheer drop down. Then she took us to their house. It was in a beautiful spot, overlooking the beach on to the island.

A major marathon squash session in which the last game I won the score was 13-11 and the score in games was five-four. If I had lost that last one the score would have been six-three, so not such a major defeat after all. Dennis the Menace's first entry in my diary was,

"[I won!]" – Always was a man of few words...

On the road home we hurried past a flattened, festering, revolting possum that had long gone to meet his maker a couple of weeks earlier and to say it smelt appropriately, disgustingly ripe would be a gross understatement. The other possum saga was on the island. The little shit insisted on eating a hole in our tent to get to our bread. It woke me a couple of times in the night to wage war, although I never quite got to fixed bayonets. I eventually gave up and let him have the bread. Annoyingly, Den just lay there snoring and groaning while the possum ferreted away behind us, or was it a ferret possuming away? Anyway, I feel it important to differentiate between the live and dead possum stories.

The roads in the Australian outback were mostly gravel with hundreds of holes and other deterrents such as creeks and dead stinking kangaroos. When we saw a dead kangaroo coming up in the distance, we would get as close as possible before taking a large gulp of air and then the driver would accelerate as fast and as far as possible before breathing out. The stench was beyond nearly visible, it WAS visible, a sort of blue haze of flies.

We would kill time between lifts by reading Trash Mags. Now slow down, 'trash mag' is not going to be one of those unexplained terms that leaves one with the distinct impression that one were reading the diary of a pervert i.e. porno magazines. Actually, it would probably have been better if they were, because in reality they were a reflection of our own non-academic minds. 'Trash Mags' were schoolboy war comics. I must quickly add before Den flies over seeking litigation for suggesting that he was a thick-o, that he later went to Camborne School of Mines in Cornwall and was one of their top graduates. Although I don't read them any more, it is not necessarily because I am above them intellectually, it is probably because I can't get hold of them! One only had to read those little bubbles, 'Donder und Blitzen' etc, whereas with a porn mag, after the pictures, one actually has to read them to get down to the nitty-gritty. **(Ed. Was that a lie?)**

We slouched in the back of the next Ute (small trucky thing – translates into South African as 'Bakkie' and of course was short for Utility; Australia was fast becoming another state of the USA, culturally anyway, but then again so was England...) with the countryside fast disappearing behind us and were dropped off at Yabboola about twenty kilometres north of Townsville. We walked the couple of miles to the Nickel Smelting Plant where Den had been promised a job. We filled in some application forms and I was called in first;

"...Sorry Cobba, but not without experience in this country," the man at the hatch pronounced without looking up. He had filed my application form into a ball and had missed the bin while I stood in front of him. Den was offered a job as promised, but because the bastards had turned me down, he turned them down. We walked to Mickey and Chalky's house (more friends from magician Den's inexhaustible list); they said we could stay.

Den collected the plans for 'his house' at Townsville Post Office. They looked tremendous. The plan was to build it near Camborne School of Mines while he studied there. I have to confess that, despite a lot happening over the last twenty-five years, I have still to get down to 'My House'. I know that it would have a back door with an orchard, a paddock with some horses, three or four dogs and some cats. I also want my own office with a soundproof lockable door. **(Ed. Don't stop buying those lottery tickets...)** We wandered past the cinema and then decided to see how much a trip to the Great Barrier Reef would be. We were shown a couple of slides and given a couple of application forms. After chicken and chips for lunch we decided that we had to go on it, so we paid the $20.00 non-refundable deposit. They gave us the address of a doctor we could get our medicals from. In those days I was blissfully unaware of the damage diving could potentially do to asthmatics. The reason why asthmatics are not normally allowed to scuba dive is because small bubbles caught in their lungs can explode on the ascent back up to the surface. If this were to happen, they would be likely to die. Yet again I was first up. After a few sweaty lies, jumping up and down, peeing in a bottle, I passed. Naturally so did Den but then he did not have any ailments to hide.

Saturday - slept and watched the box.

Believe it or not, I had coaching from 'the Best' as to recording a day's events in six words and making them into a best seller, Jeff Archer was the Man. Actually, I didn't, and certainly would not want his coaching, but he is undoubtedly a master. Don't you hate days like that though? I should have phoned up Lord Archer; how he manages to still be referred to as 'Lord' and be a Fully Qualified Villain I do not know. Of course the truth is that at the present moment my sad life revolves around virtually nothing happening from day to day, hence the need to record my passage through time. Saturday, for instance, I won the lottery and bought a fair slice of Northern Queensland. One might spot that one as a porky. How about, Saturday: was seduced by three gorgeous, insatiable, totally naked, blonde virgin beauties whose only wishes were to satisfy my every need and perhaps even some that my innocent mind didn't know about. **(Ed. Why stop at three, go for a whole Persian carpet full of them...!)** I think I was normal in that department in that I spent my every waking moment on thoughts of women and little else, actually that should also include while I slept as the evidence was usually there on waking up with a canoe in my pocket. Sorry, a bit of a digression...

At the famous Mingala Races – a total rip-off to get in to watch four races with the same four horses. When I get to have my go at being World Dictator, which should be coming up soon, the first thing I would do is to ban bloody horse racing; Rugby League can go too, come to think of it. I will also ban other people having a go at being World Dictator.

We were at last signed on the diving course and had a three-hour introductory lesson practising the skills needed for the next day. It was great fun, particularly because I had a tasty partner or, to use dive terminology, 'buddy'. The problem with female diving kit was that there was little left to see other than the eyes and teeth, and from those I could see she appeared to be tasty. Still, it was an illusionist thing, the possibility that she probably did not have any clothes on under all the rubber... the thought of that lucky rubber rubbing itself up against her fanny... I think she was called Michelle... Every third fifteen metres we dived down ten feet to swim along the bottom for five metres. **(Ed. There is much confusion in these garbled memories between Imperial and Metric measurement. You wrote it back in 1981 and also perhaps you are not the sharpest of wits?)** I had mastered the equalisation thing and we swotted up the diving manual.

The Meat Works was miles and miles away on the edge of town and my heel was in agony after the various games at the pool the day before. I was told to come back the next morning at six o'clock. So I woke up at five and peddled to there and waited until eight-fifteen to be told that there were still no jobs going. There must have been forty to fifty of us miserable no-hopers all hoping for a job.

Den had started work at a golf course. He took the bike so I walked into town for an interview with a farmer,

"Can you ride a bucking bronco?" Brawled in true native Oz.

"No..." I stammered.

"End of interview... Next!" Shouted over my head.

Increasingly desperate for a job, I arrived at the Meat Works five-thirty and left at seven forty-five still without one. Charlie, our host/unpaid-so-far landlord, went off on a serious grog session and came home around midnight with a paralytic friend. They sat in our room telling sordid jokes for about an hour. We lived in the room below the house – the house being on stilts so we had the pleasure of first encounter with any interesting fauna and flora, poisonous snakes, spiders and there was an interesting very prickly poisonous bush just outside our door.

I was quite chuffed at getting ninety percent in the dive exam, but Dennis the Menace was a secret swot and, like the Squash and table tennis etc., he just had to get more than me with ninety-four percent. I attempted to read *Sense and Sensibility,* and sort of lost interest. I continually had to, and still have to fight the 'I'm a retard syndrome', so the next best excuse I can come up with is that I thought that it was a girlie book... anyway I gave up on it.

Sorry.

I did some serious sleeping. Retrospectively, I think that the reason why I felt it important to record at the time that the sleep was 'serious' was probably because I did not wake up more tired than I went to sleep. In other words I did not have a tent pitched in my pants...

A job would have meant self-financing the next six weeks and no job would mean disappearing off to Cairns, owing Den a fortune and messing up our friendship in the process. I set off despondently at five-fifteen and at seven the bloke in charge at the Meat Works, bellowed,

"Ian Smith Wesson!"

"Now that's not me..." I thought for a few milliseconds as I leapt awake before springing into action. I tentatively approached the window.

"Are you Ian Smith Wesson?" he demanded.

"No, I'm Joss Smith Wesson..." I answered in a 'surely-that-will-do' kind of way.

"Oh. You'll do..."

"**YES!!**"

He just needed bodies and I was a close enough fit. Anyway, I was in. I was togged up with white trousers, white Tee shirt, white wellies, a white helmet, long white rubber apron, hair net and gloves, and so began my career in the Plant. I was led off into the pre-packing site where I steam-cleaned some machine all day. After work I pedalled to the local shop to buy a triumphant Mars Bar.

I started again the following day at six o'clock wearing blue overalls and pushing empty meat hooks back to the steaming room. The supervisor then asked me to do the following shift doing the same thing; that ended at ten that evening. By the end of it I was totally exhausted and totally starved, as I had not taken any sandwiches or any money to buy any. The next morning, still exhausted, I had to go to the employment office at the main gate but had my status changed from Casual to Daily-Regular, a major breakthrough psychologically. I was still pushing hooks. It was quite tiring and I did not take any smokes to try to keep up. After my shift, I did another two hours overtime.

On the way home, a Saint Bernard puppy mysteriously fell out of a Combi in front of me as I pedalled along.

"Oi!" I bellowed at the top of my lungs, skidding to avoid it.

I screamed again, "You've dropped your dog!" I just managed to catch the attention of the driver, as he was about to turn a corner. I had long since abandoned the bike and was standing over the dazed, hurt puppy furiously waving my arms. It certainly occurred to me that it was not an accident but other than return the poor creature to its owners what else could I do? I suppose had I not actually seen it fall, I could have taken it back home...

"I can't think how it happened," the driver grovelled, "I think that the back door was not closed properly." I could only hope that if it were his intention to dispose of the dog he would not go for the more direct route and drop it off a bridge and rather go for the more humane method of giving it to a pet rescue sanctuary.

Our host's bloody cat was practising to be in the local orchestra and I did not feel it was right to kill it. I think I was hoping that they would do the deed, the sound was so awful, or perhaps they did not need to get up so early. The general plan was that as Den and I both had jobs, we would stay in Townsville for another six weeks and then set off South again. Den, of course was as 'happy as Larry' as he was getting nicely suntanned working on his golf course. During his two years in Australia he had been like a 'mole in a hole' down various mines staying pommie-white. I, on the other hand, working on farms etc. and coming from South Africa was, on many occasions, accepted as an indigenous Australian with my convincing accent ("Arl rart mate") and tan.

I phoned Simone Thomas in Germany. Great news, she only had three weeks to go and she would be back in England, ha! I had convinced Den she was my actual girlfriend back home and had almost convinced myself. He had never met her and was not entirely convinced. We spoke for ages. We had met at Agricultural College and had been sort of boyfriend and girlfriend. She was extremely pretty and posh, horsey and chatty, and mine. Actually, I was not sure she ever actually was, in the proper sense of the word, however I was definitely very fond of her. She was going to be studying in Bournemouth when I arrived back and I could hardly wait.

"I am really looking forward to your coming home. I really loved going skydiving with you." Maybe she really did love me. The skydiving weekend was one of total fear for me; in fact to this day I am convinced that, despite our extensive training, I was simply thrown out of the plane by the instructor when it came to my turn to jump. Fortunately, I went after Simone so she never found out what a coward I really was.

"I promise I will phone you next time." Her voice was warm and tender as she ended the conversation. What was I doing at the opposite end of the world when I could have been with her? I remembered the bare concrete floor of the aeroplane hangar and squeezing into her large warm sleeping bag. After cuddling and kissing and whispering soft sweet nothings in each other's ears we succumbed to the laws of nature and, as quietly as was possible, made love. The surrounding snoring echoes of fellow jumpers were probably staged to make us believe that the coast was clear. The last time we had made love was when I had dropped her off at a hotel just outside Heathrow just before she was to go and work in Germany. We had giggled as we booked the room in the name of Mr and Mrs Smith. It was an almost surreal part of the relationship; if only we had been able to somehow remove sex from the equation, we may have lasted longer. As a male in a posh hotel room with a beautiful girl, who I would not see again for many months, I felt almost contractually obliged to do the deed. I often wonder if she felt the same. If I had just said,

"Listen Simone, I really, really like you. I think I even love you. I want to be friends with you more than anything. If you feel at all uncomfortable about making love we don't have to do it. I just don't want to lose you." It may have been that I was too sensitive to the possibility that she did not really want to make love, but also sort of felt obliged to, that I did not perform too well. She probably remembered me as a hopeless lover, which would be awful as I may well have been. I really was genuinely very fond of her though. I wondered what would have happened to our relationship if on that first morning when I woke up to find her as a stranger in my bed, instead of leaping out in horror, I had started to gently massage her and then made love to her in the comfort of my own big bed? I may well have never seen her again… Life is a game of speculation…

Great Britain had lost two damn ships in the war with the Argentine bastards. Those illiterate shits, how dare they. If they believed all the crap that was in their comic newspapers, then they deserve to be blasted to hell. Still, anyone that reads our 'Sun' newspaper has to be a few sandwiches short of a full picnic. I believe Sun readers have a vocabulary of around 500 words. English troops were still dug into the Islands but had yet to come into contact with the enemy. It was amazing the priority of the news broadcasts in Australia. It went something like this:

First

"A toad was nearly run over by a lost tourist on the road to Cairns. The police, army and air force are out looking for it etc. etc."

Half an hour later and last (PS almost)

"...and by the way, England had two battleships sunk today."

Pay day, and I started by pedalling at five-fifteen as usual and began mopping the ceiling in the factory at six as usual. At seven o'clock I was pushing the trolleys around and at nine stopped for a smoke still as usual. Then the boners **(Ed. Not like the 'canoe' or 'tent' terms, but something to do with the beloved artisans that hacked the meat off the Bovine Travellers that also find themselves on board this ship we call Earth?)** decided to have a meeting. The day before, Chain Three walked off for ten minutes because the temperature dropped below eight degrees centigrade. They still wanted to be paid while wasting Company time. It was a Principle Thing, one had to understand. After some heated 'discussion', up came the 'management' delegate. What a fool, what a tool, what an idiot. Instead of listening to their side of the argument and trying to reason rationally with them, he just told them that they were wrong and ordered them back to work. Naturally they did not take to that and so an hour later all the factory workers were outside for a meeting. After much talk, Sensible Man stood up to the mike;

"Listen Fellows, our officials do a good job, now if you want something changed, you've got to do it properly. Just because some of you would rather have the day off doesn't mean that we all have to go home. Maybe it was wrong and maybe not, but whatever, it should be sorted out properly and not like this. The whole thing has been blown out of proportion. Now I say we all go back to work and let the management guys sort it out. You know they do a good job." He desperately appealed to their reasonableness.

Next Union Man took the microphone and announced,

"Yes, they do a good job, but I say we go home!" He cheered himself as the workers clapped him.

Well, if I was the boss, I would have sacked the particular layer of management who didn't know his arse from his tits who in this instance was short and fat, and the bearded union shit-stirrer who had the strange ability to convince his colleagues that the one degree drop in temperature was the beginning of the end. The end, of course, would be all of them being carted out in cardboard boxes and being used to fire the furnaces of hell.

Incidentally, before I go on, I have translated that into England English. The thing about the folks in Australia was that mostly they do not speak *Neighbours*, particularly in that meat works. 'Fellows' would sound something like 'Fielhlarhs,' and even that is remotely discernible.

"I move that we go home and keep going home every time the temperature falls below eight degrees centigrade. Also we clean out what has been cut," Union Man the gorilla shouted into the microphone. They had a vote on the motion and I happened to be sitting on the side that wanted to go home, as I was too afraid to get up and walk to the other side. For an hour I pushed carcasses into the freezer and then taped up the doors.

After clambering on board *The Reef Seeker*, a large, magnificent, ocean-going catamaran, so began our weekend of bliss. We were shown our bunks and the boat left the harbour at one-thirty in the morning. We woke up fifty-five miles out on Grubbs Reef to a sumptuous breakfast, a large choice of cereals, fruit salad, melon, toast, scrambled egg and bacon followed by filtered coffee.

In our first dive we started by snorkelling around a 'bomb' – a large pillar of coral with many different types of fish, including sharks. At midday we had our first real scuba dive with navigation lessons. We descended to sixty feet and practised buddy breathing. One classic line Den came out with was,

"Do we have to do an emergency ascent on the way up?" The reason of course why it was so funny was because one could hardly imagine doing an emergency ascent on the way down. Anyway, everyone thought it was hysterical. We all seized the opportunity to tease him mercilessly. After supper some of the advanced divers went for a night dive. We could see their lights far below from inside the glass-bottomed boat. All of us aspired to reach the level of being able to dive at night.

On the Sunday we were kicked out of bed at some ungodly hour and after the same five-star breakfast we were scuba diving again. We started by going through an underwater canyon. Den and I sat on a ledge while the instructor indicated to take a photo of us with our masks off and without our breathing regulators in our mouths. We put our masks back on, expecting to find him in front of us with his thumb up, except we found him gone. The instructors must enjoy making fools of the novices. Den and I also went snorkelling and saw some of the most beautiful fish and coral only three or four feet or so from the surface. Sadly, all too soon it was time to set sail for home. Den was certainly beginning to enjoy the holiday. The idea of endless beer, working in the sun, and continually beating me at virtually any game or sport was bound to make him grin. Back in England, he had had girlfriend problems and two years later was still suffering.

Scratching his head, Den ordered me to log that,

"I get bullied by you Joss all the time!" I don't know which one of us was showing henpecked/henpecking symptoms in our hitch-hiking relationship.

"I should get my major sports colours for always winning at squash, table tennis, snooker, darts, space invaders, hitch-hiking and the highest score in the dive exam," he boasted cheerfully. He definitely also had the edge in Black Jack and a few other card games. Major sports colours were when one got presented with the full coloured scarf at school, which sent girls into a mating frenzy. Still, someone had to come second. Here is another Dennis Churchill (aka The Menace!) intrusion in my personal, private, intimate, soul-exposing diary. In a vague attempt to look like my writing,

"Mustn't think about sex. Try harder Joss." I think that he meant that he shouldn't think about the opposite sex and that I must think about them 'harder', possibly because of the lack of any tangible evidence that I actually possessed a thing called a 'girlfriend'. Perhaps we could add to that list, 'chick-pulling.'

In getting to work on the bike, I had perfected the technique of riding along without my hands on the handlebars. It could have something to do with when I worked in Northumberland a few years earlier, when I had come back to the place I was staying at with blood coming from my forehead, the side of my face, palms, and knees. I had tried pathetically to sit strategically with my injured side close up against the wall hoping that my landlady would not notice the mess. When she did suddenly notice she demanded, roughly inspecting the damage,

"Were you riding that bike without your hands again?"

"Yes, I was..." I muttered sheepishly. I could hardly expect any sympathy if I had told her that I was in fact also riding it without my hands, with my feet on the handlebar and with my eyes closed.

Sometimes I worked in the Bull Ring, which involved lifting heavy boxes of frozen meat all day. It was a huge improvement from pushing hooks and an excellent way of building up my biceps. On some days I worked inside the freezer. It must have been at least minus twenty degrees centigrade and I had been issued with tons of clothes. It was so cold that my moustache froze and I could flick bits of it off. Another day I swept floors until eight because the boners were having yet another meeting. At nine o'clock work stopped altogether. The day before, a man had been sacked for walking off the job before time although he had finished his tally of carcasses. The meeting went on until eleven-thirty and again a motion was held as to whether to go on strike or not. This time I voted to go back to work, but the motion was lost.

"Wakey–wakey, rise and shine!" laughed Den as he jabbed me annoyingly in the ribs just before leaving for the golf course.

"Go away and work on that suntan," I murmured pleadingly from out of my sleeping bag.

"Heh, heh, heh!" he chuckled, as that was exactly what he was going to do. At eleven forty-five at the Meat Works I was collecting my pay. In total I was paid $895 for three weeks' work and had only spent $395 in Townsville. I then joyfully pedalled into the centre of town, which was about six kilometres away, then pedalled up Castle Hill, the huge mountain just to the north of Townsville, without stopping. I was of course extremely fit and determined not to give up. It was a magnificent view, although I think that one would expect me to say that after all the energy expended in getting up there. Talking of views, I persuaded "Mr and Mrs Complete Stranger" to take a picture of me with Townsville somewhere in the background. It is surprising looking at the photo now as to what a lean, mean, brown, healthy stick of meat I was. The ride going down was beautiful and yes, I was tightly clenching the handle bar, mainly to have control of the overheating, smoking brakes.

We started hitching by the Meat Works by nine to set off South again. Den and I had just worked out the best technique of hitch-hiking in Australia; one had to be wearing shorts. The first three were all single businessmen giving substance to our theory that the best policy was to appeal to lonely gays. A crazy bloke that drove along those dangerous roads at ninety miles per hour and most worryingly did not seem to look where he was going took us as far as Mackay arriving late in the evening. We retired into a pub. Australians all seem to share a similar sense of humour, many of their revolting jokes revolved around the sound that the Queensland Cane Toad made when it was run over, the sound becoming louder and more obscene with each passing beverage. More Trash Mags. Sorry. **(Ed. Proof that this is not made up?)** The irony, although probably lost on us at the time, was that we were assaulted by an attractive nineteen-year-old saleswoman selling encyclopaedias. We were like flies around a flame listening to her endless sales patter.

Then to the town Sabrina, thirty-seven kilometres down the road, with an ancient octogenarian with three-inch thick glasses and his eighty-eight year old wife/hag. We were eventually sitting in the back of their Ute, going South after spending ages helping our 'hosts' to attach a boat to the back of their trailer. They let us off in the middle of nowhere and we were getting that definite 'we're going to be murdered tonight' feeling when Howie stopped. He was moving house, literally, so consequently only went at about thirty miles per hour. He was in convoy with his wife Kathy in the Ute in front. We eventually arrived at the Rocky junction at seven and then, to balance the day, caught a lift from Rocky with a psycho that managed to do the thirty-four-kilometre journey to Yeppoon in about five minutes. Den's friend Cathy picked us up outside the Strand.

I woke with a terrible cold and, after snivelling pathetically, I had a double whisky and a XXXX beer and a dose of pills. Den and I played Space Invaders and he won again (grrr…). This bit in the diary is interesting, honestly; it simply reads,

"Had a drink with Kerri." God, I remember her now, she was gorgeous, no wonder I never got my colours for pulling. She was minute, about five foot two, and very slender. She had wavy, shoulder length brown hair and brown almond-shaped eyes. Maybe the snivelling and constant wiping my nose on my sleeve turned her off me.

Den and I played squash and, this is going to be a surprise; Den won five games to four, although I did come back from four-two down. Eight bikinied, virtually-naked bronzed teenage women approached us that afternoon. That bit must be made up; I certainly can't believe it so why should I expect anyone else to, except that it is here in my diary. Maybe they were lost; maybe we looked like tour operators; Maybe we looked gay and therefore safe to approach. God forbid the obvious option, we were dead gorgeous and looked as if we were up for it. So instead of chatting them up like normal blokes, we played pool. Yes, Den won six games to one.

For my forfeit in a game of Piggy, I had to kiss the player on my right, which happened to be Kerri. I presumed a quick peck would do the trick but she grabbed the back of my head and went the whole ten seconds. I almost died of embarrassment as I thought she was just doing it to engage in the game. The girls came to watch Den and I play squash, now in reality this line should be in font size 48, because I actually won! Yes me, Jauss, Smeeeth Weessin, Josstick, Gin West-In etc. The reason retrospectively is obvious; it was simply because Kerri was watching. The score was nine games to three. It was nine nil but he managed to pull back three. But the next day, with his morale in tatters, Den proceeded to thrash me nine games to one, the shit.

The highlight of the whole holiday was when Den, Kerri and I went into Rockhampton for a Chinese meal. She was wearing a white, knee-length, nearly-see-through skirt with pretty flower patterns on it and matching shoes, making her look like a life size Barbie-doll. The cute, brown-eyed little minx slipped her hand into mine under the table and gave me a,

"Let's-slip-off-somewhere-quiet-together-and-cement-our-budding-relationship," kind of a squeeze. She certainly looked stunning, however if there was more to the Piggy kiss, I was not to find out. We had settled into our seats and were chatting away, the crab claws were served and then I had possibly the worst asthma attack so far in my whole career/ journey/ trip/ existence/ life. In my previous worst experience, I could at least rasp out some words but in this incidence any form of speech would have been a luxury. A total shut down of my breathing apparatus. Fortunately for me, 'Den the Doc' was on full alert, possibly at the thought of phoning up his ex-friend's parents and saying that they were down one. Anyway, he got me around to the local hospital, I think in a taxi, but he may well have sprinted the forty-eight blocks with me on his shoulder bouncing like a corpse. Now that has blown the illusion of the place Rocky, it was probably only one block from end to end, but it was all part of the intricate fabric of the unfolding drama. **(Ed. Also shatters the illusion of Den whom it was felt could easily sprint with a corpse around his neck to the nearest A & E or morgue.)** The point is that I was in no condition to remember any sort of detail. The irony was that Kerri might even have made an actual pass at me, and it was subsequently erased from my memory. Den barged his way to the front of the queue, I imagine – bear with me – the other patients had probably just got pick-axes in their heads with blood spurting everywhere, and demanded that I was seen to immediately. They give me a mask to breathe in, presumably oxygen and liquid Ventalin, the stuff that was in my inhalers. Maybe the whole episode made me more intriguing, vulnerable, human and desirable, but in my blind way I never noticed any advances she may or may not have made.

Partially recovered, Kerri took Den and I to a game park a couple of miles north of Yeppoon. Of course, any fool can see, it was obviously the adorable (wrong word for a male to male description – but this was from a female perspective) Den the fanny-magnet that she was after – no wonder; he had shaved off all the chin mange. The usual wombats, Tasmanian Devils and miniature kangaroos were there which were all very cuddly and photogenic. After saying goodbye to that woman, I think that the ever-hungry Churchill probably swooped in for a kiss/ snog/grope, but that may be total imagination/fabrication, mainly because she had totally disappeared from my memory and I now find her five times in my diary. Maybe I suffer from 'willed Amnesia' because, realising that it would be totally impossible to proceed to stage two, I deliberately erased her. If you are still out there Kerri, "Hi" and "What colour knickers were/are you wearing that/ this night?" Pathetic, but as a chat-up line it seemed to work for 'Scuttle' Worthington at College. Another chat-up line (which I never quite understood) that he used to good effect was,

"Sit on my face for five pounds!"

Kerri dropped us on the main road very early the next morning. She stayed until we caught our first lift in a Ute. She gave me a long kiss, saying goodbye. She had caught me in an extended version of our 'Piggy Kiss', perhaps in the vain hope that I would return and swoop her off her feet... The driver had worked on the same golf course as Den so again they had loads to chat about. In Brisbane we stayed in the 'People Palace'. It sounds grand, but it was more like the YMCA. We caught a coach to the Gold Coast and got off at Surfer's Paradise to find a new electronic game called Gobblers. I won, amazingly, although

Den got the highest score. We stayed in a good motel. What an incredible difference having a few dollars in one's pocket; it made one's whole outlook on life different. On the way up, we slept under bridges and ate road-kill. On the way down, we enjoyed all the worldly pleasures money could buy. Well, neither was entirely true, but one should get the gist.

We ended the adventure, catching a coach to Mawaloomubar and then a seventeen hours to Sydney.

"Thanks for a really fantastic holiday. I have really enjoyed the last couple of months. We must get together as soon as I get back to England." Den vigorously shook my hand before hugging me sincerely. There were tears in his eyes.

"It has certainly been fun!" I agreed as we stood just outside the International Departure Gate. "See you back in England!" I called as I disappeared inside.

I was armed with all my Aussie presents, mostly for Simone, in a vain attempt to persuade her to be mine in both body and in spirit. I don't think, like many things in life, that I ever worked out what went wrong with the relationship. She was definitely approved of by my college friends, as she was earthy, horsey, apparently rich and definitely very pretty. With hindsight, perhaps I saw that the forthcoming episode in South Africa would just be another adventure and I would be able to go back to her. How wrong I was to be. Simone may well have liked me, even momentarily loved me, but she certainly was not interested in an adventurer who was going to flit his life away in far flung parts of the world. Despite her sweet and sensual letters, she rapidly moved into the category of ex-girlfriend.

CHAPTER FOUR

...normality begins to be replaced ...

Perhaps I should have married Kerri and lived sane ever after, but then I would not have met my beloved Belinda and, let's face it, Kerri would have dumped me faster than she could say 'loony bin'.

Well...

I found myself back in South Africa, the land I was born in and spent the first thirteen years of my life in. A series of almost lucky accidents brought about my acquiring a British passport. My great-grandfather was definitely British. He had owned a Cider factory in Taunton and eventually sold out to Appledorph Ltd due to bad management. My grandfather disappeared down to South Africa just after the Boer War (1899-1902 I think) presumably for some colonial-style adventure. He met my grandmother and together they started farming. My father was born there while South Africa was still a British colony. He met my mum when they were both at Rhodes University and when I was nearly thirteen they decided to head for England. My parents had seized the first opportunity to escape life in Johannesburg and moved the family to England mainly because they were unhappy with the politics of Apartheid but also because a business opportunity had opened itself to my father.

Before we left, my father took us to the parts of Soweto (South West Township) that Europeans in a car could not normally reach, and certainly were not permitted to enter by law. He wanted us to see for ourselves how the majority of South Africa's population lived simply because of the colour of their skin. The stench of sewage, despite the luxury car windows being wound up, was awful. Few buildings had proper roofs as such, just bits of tin held down by stones. There was no electricity, no drains, no nothing. My parents and us, their family, ultimately left South Africa because they disagreed with and could not tolerate the policy of Apartheid, along with many others.

I would have had to live in England until I was twenty-eight before I could say that I had lived at least half my life there. During those sad long years I always wanted to leave to get back home to South Africa. Five years in an awful English Public School, of learning a new language, as English effectively was. Learning English etiquette, forgetting Afrikaans as a culture and a heritage, learning French, forgetting Zulu, meeting people, forgetting people, learning English culture, manners and mannerisms and forgetting my past. Thirty years later writing this record, I have still to master the intricacies of accent and regional verbal differences. Native English people immediately still, and probably always will, identify me as an alien.

After a week at my new school, and having not said boo or baa to a soul, our class were all called in to see the House Master. It was late October and the Smith Wesson family had moved from the relative warmth of South Africa to the beginnings of cold winter in England. We were all sitting in a semi-circle in front of him. He asked us in turn if we all were happy. The other boys all came out with,

"Sir. Couldn't be happier, Sir, What-what!" (I came to learn that the upper class always use expressions like 'What-what' and 'top-hole', although I never learnt the appropriate moments to use such expressions. For instance, what the hell is the difference between 'Tea' and 'Supper', for God's sake!!) Anyway, I was last and, upon being asked, I answered in perfectly good English,

"I am very cold at night and need another blanket." The Master and the other boys stared at me and after I had repeated myself four times, one of the other boys eventually ventured tentatively,

"I think he says he wants another blanket..." Much later, when I heard on a tape recorder how I actually spoke, realised that I had indeed, as far as my merciless bastard classmates were concerned, arrived from another planet.

I had left the Preparatory School in Johannesburg with exemplary exam results in Afrikaans, Religious Studies and Maths and so I was put in the top set for everything. I think I managed to hold my own in Maths but as there was not much demand for Afrikaans in England, they put me in the top French set anyway. My well meaning parents had sent me to French lessons just before we left as well as continuing with the Afrikaans and Latin, and I spoke a splattering of Zulu and other native languages to our staff at home. In the first week we had to do a translation. The kindly teacher said that if we did not know a word, to have a go, as we would not get any points for a blank sheet. A few of the bright boys achieved around fifty-five out of sixty, ranging down to the sadly uneducated with nought. Then as if it were his clever magical party trick, he thought it would be fun to read out the translation of the boy that had got minus sixty-out-of-sixty. To say that the class was in hysterics was an understatement. I made a solemn vow to myself that I hated him – and French – and would make every effort never to learn it. I told my dad, who immediately rang the Headmaster. So I had the last laugh, as he was fired soon after.

I had not been at the School from Hell for more than a month or so when I decided to run away. I had climbed a fence in a far corner of the grounds and set off in the direction of where I thought my parents were staying. Unfortunately I went into the wrong town where the local yobs thought it was great to find a lost Public School boy running along the pavement in their rough neighbourhood (in South Africa we would have referred to it as a Township). Their contribution towards my settling into England was to firstly hurl obscenities at me and when that had no apparent impact, probably because I did not understand them, they rubbed stinging nettles onto my bare calves. I had no alternative in my misery but to run back to the dreaded school to escape them.

Yet somehow I managed to survive. I achieved very little academically, and was not a great sportsman, in fact not a sportsman at all, spending an inordinate amount of time in the San (the school hospital). I learnt a lot in woodwork, pottery, metalwork and in art though. Religion – definitely learnt a lot, or rather I thought I did. Girls – absolutely nothing (when I left school, I still thought they were a different species). I enjoyed biology and geography field trips, although, regrettably, they did nothing to further my education about the strange anatomy of the opposite sex...

Then, after eventually leaving the awful school (this place of internment, where my parents were determined I should become an English Gentleman), I spent a year on different farms around the country in the freezing cold, forking steaming silage and making my own tracks in the thick virgin snow, along with those of badgers and foxes and other wild carnivores. Driving tractors; pheasants, wheat and bright-yellow oil-seed rape; dark English tan, hardened hands and patches on patches on my jeans. Making summer-hay was great; grabbing the bales with that grab-thing and then driving them odd miles back to the farm. Cows, calves, sheep, ewes and rams etc., I learnt a little about them all.

Two years at the Royal Agricultural College in Cirencester in which I found great friends, many beers, fast rugby, faster cars and much sex. Oh hell, if one were not permanently on heat then there was something wrong, but truthfully I was not a success at any of them. The friends did not last. I threw up after only a few beers and my car was too slow. I only just managed the second team, and the women? God... What a disaster! I was too emotionally involved with the wrong ones. Which may have been my biggest problem – not involved enough with the right one.

Sally, oh Sally. She had been the nearest thing I had had to a 'normal' girlfriend at college.

"Knock, knock," on a door a million miles away. A very pretty woman answers and jabbers away incomprehensively in Norwegian.

"Hello... it's me Joss, Joss Smith Wesson. Um ... I.... I want to talk to you, Sally."

"Yes, yes, come in, come in. Ha, ha, I never recognised you. What are you doing here?" She twists her long fingers through her apron and flicks back her gorgeous dark hair. She had of course remained exactly as I had left her, Goddess-perfection. Oh no, how would it go? I wanted so badly to say,

"Sally, I don't seem to be able to exist properly without you. I want you. I love you. I want to marry you."

Hell.

Instead I cleared my throat and mumbled into my coat,

"Well, I was just passing and I thought I'd see how you were keeping. How is Peter? He must be getting on a bit now?" Would I have kissed her? Would we?

I could never have gone in there. I did not even know where in Norway she lived. I had spooky dreams about her and still do. I had gone to Norway to look for her and found strange things. I eventually found her living in a sort of a water tower – a round building on a very long ladder enclosed in a tube. I climbed up to find a whole lot of old hags knitting and sewing and a young boy of two or three, but no Sally. When I opened the trap door the boy, who was obviously being held prisoner, fell down to his presumed death. In another, I found her in a flat in a huge dilapidated apartment block. I brought a couple of bouquets of flowers and dressed up as a delivery boy to take them up. I was about to knock when two women arrived, one huge, one tiny. The tiny one said,

"It's Joss," and to me, "What do you want?" It shook me awake realising that it was Sally and Peter.

We had held hands and laughed. Those few precious months in Cirencester were truly Heaven. If only you were not pregnant, Sally. We were in love, not because our minds met and had decided to spend the rest of eternity together, but simply because we had made physical love and our bodies had made a temporary pact of adolescent allegiance to each other. We were two young people who had not experienced serious love before. We satisfied each other's need to have and to hold somebody. Oh Sally, you beauty, if only I had had the strength of character to say damn what everyone would say and stayed with you. Why didn't I, instead of coming back to South Africa, slink back to Norway or run away to Australia with you? Without proper entrance papers, we could have said that we were simply going there on holiday. Anyway, there must have been somewhere we could have lived happily together. And Peter, Oh God forgive me. What if that boy was mine? I deserve all this punishment and more. Even if he wasn't I should still have claimed him. I love that boy's mother.

"Ha! I heard that!" Lucifer pounced. "You said 'I love her', got you!" There was triumph in his terrible evil voice.

"You may well be right, Devil, you bastard. I'll give you something; you sure as hell win sometimes. Today, what a bad day and you had the whole of it."

And then suddenly Simone, she was a stranger's body in my bed. I had ceremoniously dumped Sally on my fellow housemates' advice, or rather their instruction, the day the second rugby team came back from beating our biggest rivals, Harper Adams, and we were all invited to a party. I *had* to dump her. Being a coward and afraid of their disapproval I did what I did. She was pregnant and I was not the father of her expected child. I thought I loved her. I thought I loved her and, to this day, do not really know. I must have been seriously drunk that night. I woke, rolled over and felt Simone's bare, strange rounded bottom next to mine and was suddenly amazed and disgusted with myself to find it wasn't Sally's. For long seconds in the drunken blur, I could not remember how she got there. I leapt out of bed and went downstairs and made myself a cup of strong coffee. I realised that I had to move on from Sally, so I washed and filled the bath for Simone. The other lads arrived back from the party just as she was leaving and of course would not believe that we had not 'slept' together. It would have ruined my credibility if I had said that we only shared a bed so I let them believe what they wanted to. Still, it was the beginning of yet another strange relationship. Simone and I did eventually become technically lovers; however, I think that it was presumed on both sides that it was just part of the contract. Perhaps she had also just come out of a damaging relationship and did not want to become emotionally involved. We were really just good friends that enjoyed doing the same thing. Actually, the truth was probably that in our peer group one was a bit odd without a partner and we just found each other holding hands at the right moments.

Then a year on the loose…

The year after college and before ending up back in South Africa a second time. It was to become the beginning of my search for this sanity thing. Six weeks before the end of the last term at Cirencester I drove my brother Jonathan's little car 'T T' (Tank Two) into London. Jonathan had more or less written off the little blue mini pick-up van on a Kamikaze hill on a Kamikaze night. He was very lucky that the tree stopped him; otherwise it would have been a non-stop drop. He had left to hitch-hike to South Africa with our great pal, Dutch Benson, and abandoned the wreck to me. I tied a chain to the dented front frame and the other end to a stout tree. By reversing at full speed against the chain, I sort of straightened it out. All around the windscreen leaked badly and at 70 mph the steering wheel vibrated so badly that after only half an hour's driving my hands would be quite numb. The wheels needed re-aligning and there was no spare. But it worked, and off to London I went. I parked around the corner from Jackie's flat and disappeared into the heart of London. I walked into Australia House to get an application for a visa, wandered along the Embankment for a while and then went back to Jackie's place. Jackie and Dave had been going steady ever since being at school together. Actually Dave had stolen Jackie from Den, which was of course a great bone of contention between the former friends. School friends, Dave, Jackie, Sam and I ended up in the Winchester Arms where I announced that I was off to Australia. Sam had just finished a year working in Paris and seemed set on a career in the City. He had done very well at school. We had sat next to each other in Biology class for our A levels and we always had a bit of a titter behind the teacher's back. Australia, Australia, I love you, ahem; great days of security and insecurity, of blissful college days with those outside, open days, leering, beckoning. Those days of coping on one's own, of making up one's own mind, deciding days. Deciding what that was all about. Sanity or insanity, security or insecurity, responsibly or irresponsibility, South Africa or not... We sat around the bar, drinking round after round of lukewarm beautiful English bitter, with the occasional burst on the Space Invader machine so that we could curse it afterwards for being such a waste of money: down the motorway, in a beery haze with the radio doing its best over the crackle and the rain and the leaks. Since I was young and strong, I easily drove the ninety-odd miles back after the eight or nine beers.

With brothers Daryl, Jonathan and I in the red Alfa and the radio seriously blasting down the M40 laughing about school, college, women, sex, about the big wide world, about working. With the three of us together, we discussed at length everything and anything. World problems – was Ronald Reagan the idiot he looked? El Salvador, Vietnam, the Middle East, Northern Ireland, always skirting around South Africa. Then it was South Africa with a vengeance. The other subjects we could discuss rationally without tempers flaring, but South Africa made for a hell of a debate. Daryl was always right on moral and ethical grounds. I stuck my arguments to practicality and what was possible given the circumstances that existed in the country. We arrived at Dave Green's pad on a fairly even keel, having decided which women would be present and how they should be divided. Dave's twenty-first – big occasion. We bundled out our smart clothes and presents, the radio was still blasting; we were in party mood. The barbecue was already in full swing. Sam and his new pretty girlfriend were there already as were Dave's many aunties and grannies. We settled into a circle on the lawn with some fine looking nosh and beer. J S W, that's me, had grown my umpteenth beard so nobody noticed. The gentle English evening wafted into the growing dusk with the smoke.

6.00 pm. Blast Off! From Broxbourne, just above London, and I was trying the impossible, to get to two parties in one night, the other being in Leicester at least two hours up the M1. Fantastic, Dad's car, and 120 mph all the way, my blood pumping, racing, my hands wet on the wheel. I had promised Matthew that I would be there, and come hell or high water I was going to do it. It was just one of those unfortunate things that both important parties happened to be on the same date.

8.00 pm. I slid the car onto the grass verge outside Steve and Lulu's house. Steve was Matthew's brother. Matthew was there with Sandra, his girlfriend from college.

She looked radiant, almost pregnant. She had the most beautiful golden waist-length hair and an equally beautiful healthy tan. They almost immediately jokingly made love on the bonnet of my bright red car as I pulled up. They were both very pleased to see me. I was the only college boy that had made the effort. We talked for a long time. It was to be the last time for ages. Maybe we both knew it. He crunched my hand goodbye and I kissed Sandra and Lulu and then got back on the motorway.

10.00 pm. My hands trembled, my eyes lids twitched, the signs flew by, it was a beautiful, black, dangerous winter night and the car loved it. Together we carved dangerously, recklessly through the dangerous darkness.

12.00 pm. Everyone drunk as lords, back at Dave's, all reclined untidily in the sitting room still seriously drinking. I was the obvious driver – only an hour and a half to home. Easy!

Daryl and I had a few great days at The Old Cock Inn. One evening an old guitarist played the songs we all knew and loved. It was a totally olde-worlde pub, which sadly no longer exists. The landlord had a permanently red nose from excessive alcohol; actually it was more like a huge hooter on his face! There was no counter as such and when one wanted more beer one either just gave him the money if he was about or simply left it on one of the rickety stairs on one's way up from the basement after helping oneself from the barrel. It is now probably called the "Slug and the Lettuce Leaf" and a half metric pint would cost around £10.00! If I ever were to be mad enough **(Ed. Hold it...!)** to want to have my own pub, I would have a place that anyone over let's say five foot five banged their heads on the rafters, the settees would be made of leather and would be at least a hundred years old and when one sat in them one would disappear. The whole place would be covered in nicotine-yellow stains and famous long dead people's graffiti, or failing that, nearly famous people's doodles. If the nicotine was off-putting, we could negotiate down to say, Tee shirts from around the world, or Tee towels? Stone drunk, usually after a 'Lock-in', we would stagger home, crawl up the stairs and collapse into bed.

We careered into Reading along one of Daryl's famous short cuts. Daryl was a born psychopathic manic driver. Anyone in front of him was an opponent, an enemy, someone to be destroyed and totally eliminated, not to mention overtaken, which of course was the very least that had to be done. One device that he considered patenting was an enormous foot that would come out of the roof of his car and would crash on the car in front, allowing him to simply step through the wreckage! We would spill out of his van at the warehouse in Reading where another day of building, banging and bodging would begin.

It was during another one of these hazy days of hammering, drilling, screwing, and shouting at Eldred Hettersley, the man manning the Home Exchange Telephone Company next door, that Dad confronted me with the 'Big Proposal'. He wanted me to work for him for a while. We were sitting outside The Farmer's Adopted Son **(Ed. Fine name for a pub – really!)** in Chiseldeane when he asked me. It was one of those idyllic beautiful English summer evenings when one can really enjoy sitting outdoors. Scratching the back of his neck, stretching and searching for words as he clutched his pint in the other hand,

"Remember 'Sheep Heaven'?" he began awkwardly.

"I remember that fool of a careers' advisor at school who said that I would end up as a sheep farmer in New Zealand, he was a bit of a soothsayer!" Everyone in the family had got used to the fact that my thoughts did not always flow directly.

"The problem with that farm was that it was too small to be financially viable. I would love to own a farm here in the UK so long as you were going to run it with me." He had stopped scratching, and the setting sun from behind me caught his glasses for a second. "If this business makes money we will have enough money to buy one. I always fancied living in the Cotswolds. How about you?" He knew I had loved my time at Cirencester so it was a bit of a loaded question. I eagerly took the bait and we chatted late into the dying summers' evening as to how it would work. The idea was that we would make lots of money together on the family farm.

"I reckon we should have some crops like wheat and barley as well as sheep." It was already becoming a reality as we excitedly planned.

"It depends on the size of the place which will depend on how much money we have". Dad was always the clever schemer, but sometimes let his imagination get the better of him.

"What about the name of the place?" I could really see myself out there in the windswept moor with my Wellington boots, Barbour jacket and a crooked stick.

"What about 'Sheep Heaven'?" Dad laughed!

Although the original Sheep Heaven in Natal was an unmitigated disaster, we agreed to call it that in its memory. We talked for hours about what we would grow and where exactly we would look for the farm.

So the visa was lost for a while and I stuck to making that second floor in the warehouse with Daryl. We were an orchestra and Daryl was the conductor. Doing similar work much later, making doors and door frames in the Zulu staff compound, I realised how important his organisation was. Very rarely were we without the right tools, materials, or equipment. Good old Daryl, we would work like hell all morning with Eldred giving us his never-ending unhelpful-cockney commentary from his overlooking balcony. At lunch we would buy an extra large portion of fish and chips each. Never was the dispute settled as to which was the best fish and chip shop in England. Eldred and I preferred going a few extra miles to the Bear where the chip portions were enormous and fantastic, but Daryl liked the ones in the nearby shopping centre. He was a great pal with the chap behind the counter whose big joke was that there was arsenic or something in the chips at the Bear. We would go up to Eldred's little hovel with his porn mags and continuous telephone and gobble our chips. Every single chip was always eaten.

Dave Green and I had a bicycling holiday in Italy, one of the cheapest and one of the best holidays I had ever had. We set off on the day of Prince Charles and Princess Diana's wedding. The night before, we were in Hyde Park with children on our shoulders watching the fireworks. It was fantastic. Pedalling through London with Dave in the front of the tandem was agony on my crotch as my seat had not been properly attached. We arrived at Victoria station and loaded the tandem onto the train. Dave had bought two *Tom Sharpe* books that had come highly recommended. **(Ed. Yes, yes give them a go, but after this though!)** Down to the coast and onto the ferry, we concentrated on beer and chuckling, just enough not to throw up on board. On the train to Dover we had top two bunks and we spent the evening chatting away. Two pretty French girls underneath us somewhat objected to our endless banter, probably because we were not making any attempt to chat them up. We also had the Rubik's Cube that kept Dave fascinated for hours, as well as the Famous Chess set. The whole holiday was one long competition. By the time we arrived in Rome, Dave had a convincing lead.

The twenty-seven hour journey went very quickly. We climbed off the train only to find that the tandem was not on the same train. So we wandered into a nice, quaint little Italian restaurant to find nice huge, Mafia-type thugs, probably gay, glaring at us. So we quickly left and found another, less intimidating restaurant. We spent the first afternoon looking at Saint Peter's and other things that were in ruins and that everyone photographs. **(Ed. Further proof that this was not made up as years later I was to write vast essays on the Coliseum which is mentioned here only as 'ruins.')** In the early evening we decided to look for a youth hostel or something of that nature; somewhere to spend the night. After wandering for a while without success we decided that a beer and some supper was the next best thing. Having found a bar, we eventually left at 1.30 am when the cleaners were cleaning around our stools and showing us the door. We found a park bench and had a cup of coffee. Dave brought out the thermos and chess set. In an appropriate break in the traffic, we jumped over the hedge behind us and set up camp and passed out almost immediately. The next morning we were woken up by a rather surprised Italian gentleman watering his flowers, furiously shouting,

"Mama Mia, Mama Mia!"

"Is it a garden?" Dave protested.

"It's a lovely little garden," I tried to pacify the man.

Dave then got the hysterics, which only made the dear chap even more irate. We left quickly with him muttering something about the English. We wandered into a large square with a large needle-type monument in the middle. We had a wash and shave and a few more games of chess.

At the station the next train did not have the tandem. We took the bus somewhere and saw something and spent the afternoon drinking. To save money we decided to share a single room. Dave went in and I sneaked up the fire escape. The room would happen to have a stone floor, which I duly slept on. The next morning I was spotted leaving and so we took off in opposite directions. We happened to bump into each other a few hours later and spent the day lying low. That night we slept in a park. Dave took the first watch. All our stuff was at the bottom of his sleeping bag. We had spent hours wandering about trying to find a suitable spot, as he was convinced that someone was following us. I was supposed to take the second watch but slept like a log. Next morning I set off for the station and lo and behold there it was – the tandem! On the way back to Dave and the camp site, I lost my wallet, passport and travellers cheques. I went back along the way I had come, but could not find them. I told Dave which cheered him up still further, after my sleeping-on-duty offence! I went to the police at the railway station and reported it to them and to the main police station. They made me fill out a large questionnaire; one of the questions was,

"Where were you staying?" I could hardly write,

"Wherever we happen to be," so I wrote down the first camp site that was in our tourist information book. So when we arrived at that self-same campsite we found a note on the gate saying,

"Joss Smith Wesson to go to the Police Station." After trekking back into Rome to the police station where I had filled out the form, they knew nothing about it. I went to the main police station. They knew nothing about it. In fact the Head-Chap-Sergeanty-Type person was rather indignant when I suggested they had it, whereas he knew they had not. I went back to the police station at the railway station and after a long struggle with the non-English-speaking Italian-speaking devils I eventually managed to find another very small, almost hidden police station on a distant platform. I was eventually ushered into a little room with a huge bald man with no neck and who was sweating profusely. He also spoke absolutely no English and had obviously played the Bad-Wicked, Very-Evil Prison Warder in the film about the American bloke smuggling drugs in Turkey – *Midnight Express*. I thought at first that he wanted more details of what I had lost. He eventually produced all the goodies from a drawer in his desk, which I was very relieved to see, but he was in no mood to let me have them. He extracted every little piece of paper and read out my name from each,

"J-A-U-S-S-E-E,"
"S-T-E-P-H-E-A-V-E-N,"
"S-M-E-E-V,"
"V-E-S-H-A-U-O-N,"
long pause,
"S-M-I-T-H,"
longer pause,
"W-E-E-E-S-O-N!"

After an hour and a half of heavy interrogation I was eventually handed my stuff. I had dreadful images of deBahzted attempting to give me the same treatment the hero in the film was about to be given at the same point. I was grateful, but my gratitude was somewhat diluted by having to suffer for it.

I arrived back at the camp site and had a serious drinking session with some chaps from Newcastle where Dave was at University. As punishment, or because I was slightly more sober, I was left to put up the tent and the only place I could find was on a forty-five degree slope. I woke the next morning some distance from the tent wrapped around a tree that had saved me from going all the way to the bottom. Dave had either slept in the Bar or had had the foresight to strap himself into the tent.

So we set off on our great pedalling marathon. Past many pastures, up many ups. It was actually quite competitive as the person in the front would set the pace and the one at the back would be the unthinking 'engine' and would simply record how many kilometres were covered each hour. Dave and I had roughly the same build and much the same strength. **(Ed. Yet another lie, the truth was that he was a lot butcher than you ever were, which was why you had to change Dave's name. It was really Freddy. I think the only redeeming snippet of truth was that you could and did occasionally beat him at squash.)** Anyway, we would pedal for hours at great speed, completely draining our bodies' resources. On one occasion we had just surmounted a particularly huge hill without stopping when we both almost simultaneously blacked out at the crest of the hill. We pedalled for thirteen days in all, during which time we covered an average of eighty-three kilometres a day and the most we managed in a single day was one hundred and forty-three. We arrived in Milan looking like models out of Playgirl, bronzed, muscled, hair swept back and available. Although, yet again young Dave was completely accounted for in that department with Jackie, although whether he would have said 'no' to an Italian beauty I would never know. Dave was usually on the front, sweating like hell, while I tried to keep up. We were both as fit as sprinters, naked, except for our shorts, thighs pumping as we churned through Italian mountains. Flying down hills, feet up and hair blowing. One day we had stopped and pushed the bike up a little mountain path and found a tiny patch of flat ground to put the tent up. We scurried about for a bit and then went to the local cafe for a beer, or was it tea? Probably tea, Dave was really a bit of a Secret English Gentleman. That particular evening, I thrashed him three games to nil at chess. The locals pulled up chairs around our table and were intrigued by the game. By the time we had reached Milan, however, Dave had resoundingly won twenty-one games to nine.

Home to Greenest England.

Switched from manual to auto, from human to robot, from jeans to suits, from holidaying to sales repping. Driving from dawn to dusk and beyond, looking smart, good impression, trying to sell. Oh hell, it was hell. The only time it was worth it was when Simone came back from Germany. I went up to visit her at her home in the north of deepest, deep-dark Wales, where English and England were foreign. Her brother Altern was crazy and her mother even crazier. He was stone crazy because he insisted on shaving his hair off on a whim and the mother pinched all the gifts I had brought for Simone. I think that the only reason they accepted me was because I was not really English, although I did not understand a word when they jabbered to themselves in Welsh. We went down to Cirencester one weekend and ended up on the floor of her old digs. It was freezing cold. We hugged each other all night inside her sleeping bag and never got to take our clothes off. The next night we went to the Gables, the cottage I had lived in. Rod Peterson, its current tenant who was away for the weekend, let me have my old room for the night for old time's sake. Simone was so exquisitely beautiful. We had had so much fun together. Holding hands with her in Hyde Park, carrying her and kissing her was heaven but somehow I knew it was going to end.

No Virgin

Those legs tucked under your bottom
Visible brown thighs below your nightie
Twinkling, inviting eyes force me in.
My brother's room and his girlfriend
What are you doing here, princess?
What are you doing here, intruder?
You unwind those legs of heaven
Drawing, tempting, hypnotising me
I stall, fascinated. Who are you?
And where do you come from?
Before I realise what was said
I have invited her down to me.
Down to my cottage, my place.
She comes, two weeks pregnant.
I immediately fall in love with her
And have truly been ever since.
Despite not having ever seen her
Or heard from her whatsoever
These twenty-five years now

CHAPTER FIVE

...abnormality descends...

So... a million years later, in January 1983... I found myself in a small room with room enough to swing a proverbial cat, or in that case slap at an elusive fly that had landed on an envelope under which there was a painful drawing pin... found myself muttering to myself, that I knew something was amiss.

Sanity, or the lack of it, had always been an issue with me. As a young man, working on that farm near Pietermaritzburg, in Natal, Africa without any other people of the same language, without a clear commitment as to where my allegiances and loyalties lay, without my family's immediate support, without the succour of a partner, I easily started doubting my every action and motive. What's the story? Well, take me from the farm that I grew up on, and get stuck in darkest Johannesburg for five years after getting flung about the country for a bit. Something like seven schools in four years and then I was dropped in the heart of England. England, where the accent, climate and culture were totally different. I might as well have been on another planet. Nine years later, twenty-three years old with a British passport, English accent and not thinking anything in particular, I came back to South Africa. Came home! With my alien accent, an inability to really fit in with my supposed English contemporaries, a determined adolescent fixation with 'wide open spaces,' and a desire to explore the land of my forefathers, I came home. Anyone that comes to an unjust society like that, has an option, and says they were coming home, had to be insane. Poor blacks, downtrodden, abused, stepped on and crushed as the bottom rung in society's ladder. The whole South African system depended on keeping the majority of its population submissive. Its methods of doing so were brutal and callous. Its system of government was bound to end in bloodshed. Not just the blood of a few, but also probably the annihilation of most of the white population. Move to Australia, with its huge open spaces, no blacks, no problems. I could have gone to Australia and not have done anything to help the situation in South Africa anyway. Fantastic, if I were safely in the tightly woven First World country. Looking down at that end of Africa, the Press fed 'Unjust-Bound-For-Extinction-get-out' option. Tightly woven? Europe is so 'First-Worldly' that it cannot imagine parts of the world being anything else. Black people are civilised individuals that one kisses and dances with at parties. They chatter gaily and laugh in the same language. The poor are poor, but not desperately starving and destitute. Generally they live lives and begging is not totally commonplace. The rich are rich, and getting richer in their fat-cat cars. But in South Africa... The man in the street in Europe or the USA does not comprehend the word 'savage'. A savage – someone with a hatchet and a glint in his eye, with no education and clothed in skins? Such people exist, and exist in South Africa. Possibly they were the vast majority of the population. South Africa was very much a Third World country with a splattering of First World. A few hundred years ago the indigenous African people were cultured. They had their own culture. The Europeans came along and introduced their White Northern cultures, material possessions and their morals and beliefs. Would these peoples have been better off without them?

Apartheid – the word springs thoughts of bitter oppression in the minds of most people outside South Africa and the majority of those within. No doubt they were oppressed, but whoever thought of the blacks in the rest of Africa and the state they were in? Whoever thought of this busy little community with its impressive motorways that cut through beautiful hedged countryside that link together huge sprawling urbanisations? Urban growth comparable to anywhere else in the world. Did the press ever tell of the progress being made? Did they write about the black man in a suit with matching crocodile skin briefcase and shoes sitting next to me on the plane? Or the pretty black girls, in their short, colourful, knee-length skirts, shiny calves and laughing white teeth, winking? What about the broad shouldered, tree-trunk legged, handsome black man playing against me in rugby? Did they? Did they tell me of the complexities of the problems here? These morally and culturally uneducated people were about to leap up and kill every white man. Huh?

I had an identity. I would have done if we had stayed, or would I? Identity could have been the crisis. Who was I and who am I? No doubt the answer is blazingly simple as most people know who they are, and therefore I should know who I am. Maybe who I was was not quite the issue, but where my loyalties lay. On the side of Table Mountain is a small graveyard. My forefathers were the Von Weilleghs. My mother's father must have been furious to see his two daughters marry English Imperial colonialists. Where would the dynasty end? What would happen to the family name? What of the family traditions, the Afrikaner way? I looked at those graves as a foreigner, as an Englishman! Through them, my roots had been in the country longer than most. My mother's father's family were the Great Von Weilleghs from Bloemfontein, in the heart of the Orange Free State. Then the Wilkinsons; my father's mother's father was a Colonel in the British Army that fought against Von Weillegh. My gran grew up in Pietermaritzburg. Smuts used to call her 'my little Jenny' when he stayed in their house. He and her father had been great friends.

Fat, naked, beautiful brown babies waddling in the dirty mud. Doubtless if one were to kidnap one of them and put them through an average First World education they would end up civilised. The parents and grandparents and children all have to be brought forward eighty years in eight. So I thought that that was the issue; to stay and to try to help find the answer and to face the music when it starts, to stay and build a home and find my own identity here? I was born there but have a UK passport. Do I forsake the British passport for a South African one and South African Citizenship? All male South Africans of my age have done National Service. I knew my lungs were useless. They never seem to work when I want them to. The business of doing Military Service could be a problem. I could confess to being an asthmatic, but even the South African Army would reject me. Still, a few porky-pies, as on the diving trip, and I'd have been accepted. Having done my Service I would be able to answer the big question of my life. I would be able to go anywhere in the world and anyone could ask me,

"Where were you from?" and without having to think about it, I could say proudly, "South Africa!" That would certainly solve the dilemma of loyalty, nationality and identity and then that whole business of insanity would disappear. If only…

A savage, in my mind, is an individual who kills another without remorse, without considering the consequences. A savage is one whose morals and values are those that belong in the past. One who is without education, without principles or ethics, one whose identity is confused, whose sense of loyalty is lost. Ephraim could be described as such. He was the farm's supervisor. Initially he was indispensable as he was my translator. He had a wizened little goatee beard and enjoyed rubbing his hands together importantly. After repeating the same line in an argument numerous times from his book, he attacked Tollie, one of the farm workers of distant European descent, with it. Maybe this is a racist point of view, but he had the intellect of a bean! So he was a savage, so what? He probably used his own culture's criteria to decide that I was a savage. Brixton, Toxteth, Bristol were examples of racial disharmony, incidences of racial hatred which showed that black and white people did not get on together. If they did not wish to live together, why not make it mandatory that they should live apart?

The tomato farm I was working on belonged to my cousins the Kennedys. My uncle Arthur had offered me the job, after my numerous attempts to get gainfully employed in England in farming had failed. It was because I had no farm management experience, although I did have a Diploma in Farm Management. The experience of being a farm labourer for a year of course counted for nothing.

"You cad!" I exclaimed to myself. It was then that I realised that things were seriously going wrong. Talking to oneself was a sure sign of madness. A monster on my Mini Pacman game had just eaten my 'man'. He was not being a particularly bad sport either. He was forced to catch me because of my abstract stupidity. Given the option and knowing the dilemma I faced, he probably would not have!

Yes, me, really, whether to go potty or not…

"To sleep and then to dream, aye – there's the rub." Of course all things could be thought over and then carefully re-analysed and then thought over again, whether it was worth thinking about in the first place. But in this instance – whether to go insane.

"Whether it is better to suffer the slings and arrows of outrageous fortune." Whether or not? Well, points for. Crumbs, points for... Made me dribble at the mouth just thinking about the sanctity of happy premeditated oblivion. Ha! No more logical, troublesome rational thought, no more earthly problems. Presumably when one did achieve a state of madness one did not bother with things so menial as food, money, life insurance, mortgage, sex, transport, etc. No, of course not. There was bound to be some friendly state institute that would have a full time chap who would sit pulling faces at me all day long, making me laugh. Of course there would. What more did a thinking predetermining man want? To be able to release that hormone that made one laugh for no rational reason. Just to sit there, gurgling all day! I would get quite fit as the very few times I had done it I had got a stitch quite quickly. Now, for me, the options of chortling from dawn to dusk as a formula for getting the most out of life seem to be fairly limited. The line between sanity and insanity was fairly marginal even in people who thought it wasn't. At that moment, I thought I was one of those who weren't exactly sure where the line was drawn at all. To begin with, let me illustrate. Take a puppy, eight inches long, four inches high, a white woolly bundle that bounces around with endless energy and joy. Happy to curl around on its back, biting a finger, then to sprint off to a tree five feet away, and then hurtle back to the fray with its jolly yip-yipping noises! When picked up its eyes sparkle and its nose is wet with happiness. The same creature in five years would receive ninety-nine percent less attention, its life spent unnoticed by anyone. Back on the farm, when I was a pup, when I was sane, because there was no option, I may well have been content. Those willow trees with the weaverbirds and their upside-down nests over the dam; the chug-a-lug irrigation pump, the rocks in the river, dogs, potatoes, cows and fertiliser. I may well have been swimming naked after first breaking the ice, getting hurt in older boys' games, fights and getting lost. Getting lost was awful, as any little boy will tell you. But not awful-awful, not suicidal awful.

"Anyway, Lord, what shall I do?" My eyes squeezed shut, I prayed.

"What should you do forever, or just today?" It was definitely God's voice.

"What should I do in general?" I stammered, making conversation.

"Put off the decision." It was unquestionably Him.

"That is what you said yesterday." My hands were pushed hard over my eyes.

"You're still not ready for the answer." He sounded kindly and gently. Maybe, in truth, it was God.

"Come on God, Old Chap, you could at least give me part of the answer." I was talking to the Almighty Creator of the Universe inside my head.

"You know the arguments. Think it out for yourself." He seemed infinitely patient with the likes of non-responsive me.

"Well, for a start, I'm healthier. I use my inhaler a lot less. Aunt Sarah reckons I'm taller. I am probably larger and heavier than I was six months ago. I have servants waiting on me hand and foot. I am learning a lot about farming. I have made some good friends. In all, it has been good little adventure so far," I reasoned.

"Was that for, or against?" he mused. Did He use those tactics against Moses?

"You've got a good point there, you really have. All in all I am just exploiting the situation. Am I trying to defend being here justly? No, it is exploitation. What would have happened if I had gone to Australia, worked on a cattle ranch, and put on a stone in weight?" Desperately, I just wanted someone to tell me the answer.

"You know the answer to that. I am still not clear as to whether you were trying to justify being here or not?" His voice was loud and clear inside my head.

"Oh God, Oh God, Oh God!! I wonder if staying here any longer will provide the answer?" I implored.

"Yes it will, one way or another. I say stay," He commanded with some finality. My hands came down and at first my eyes would not open as I had been squeezing them so hard. Maybe sometimes decisions are not made but happen simply by inertia.

The farm 'Make-Me-Rich' belonged to my aunt and uncle, the Kennedys, Aunt Sarah being my mother's sister, Uncle Arthur being my Godfather. They lived in Durban, on the coast, and the farm was many miles inland, relatively near Pietermaritzburg. Arthur had taken the neighbouring farmer as a partner but needed an on site manager, which was me. The partner was an enormous archetypical South African 'Boer' farmer that spends 90% of his life in the sun, shouting at Africans. He went by the appropriate name of 'String'.

Chris Smith lived on a farm on the opposite side of the dam. I met him when he had come to Make-me-Rich to deliver sawdust. He challenged me to a game of squash and we became firm friends. He had done his two years in the army here, but still held a British Passport. This shocked me. How long before they would call me up? Was I frightened? I certainly wouldn't want to make a career out of it. I wonder, what would the folks back home think? I wondered what the Kennedys would think, and specifically, what would Martin think? He was their oldest son who had become a pacifist and a conscientious objector and had refused to serve in the South African army. He had gone to prison because of his religious beliefs. He had refused to wear army uniform in prison and went naked until they issued him with prison clothes. His argument was that if he was still wearing army uniform, then he was still technically in the army. I know what my beloved gran would think and even do. She would immediately phone saying,

"Good for you Joss, go kill a few Commies!" She was famous for repeating the expression, "Better dead than Red!"

But I really didn't know what to think or do.

Eleena, the enormous rotund housemaid and Ephraim's wife, trotted, or rather lumbered, down the garden path, stopped at the garden gate and howled, initially it appeared to no one in particular, to tell me that I was wanted on the phone. Kneeling on bits of wood over wet concrete that I was trying to level, I got the message. Earlier I had discarded my shirt as it dangled in the way. My numbed, filthy knees were hardly working and my trousers covered in dirt. A sort of agonised hobbling gait was all I could manage as I attempted to hurry. I think the staff thought I was doing a gorilla impersonation. 'Horse', as he came to be known, however, didn't notice. 'Horse' being a little three-year-old infant boy with a remotely horse-shaped piece of wire tied between his legs, and another piece of wire for the horse's head in one hand and his riding stick in the other. I was slobbering along with my knees in agony when I noticed Horse click-clicking, pounding the ground and whipping himself, running next to me. I arrived at the farmhouse still chuckling at the sight we must have looked together.

The farm's workers had all been talking about the coming Friday for the previous few weeks. I had had windows put into my white bakkie. With its two doors and four windows it was naturally nicknamed 'The Hotel' by the cousins. It was Pay-Day weekend and I was taking most of them back to where they came from, Fawn-Liza, their distant village in far-remote Zululand. With the front of the vehicle pointing skyward, the Hotel struggled upwards. There were ten of them with as much weight in luggage jammed in. The Hotel had to climb the long hill up to the Polo Club in first. I eventually stopped at the shop in Fawn-Liza after an hour's drive, where they bought what seemed as much weight again. Fawn-Liza was the first stop out of civilised, tame White-land and into wild, barbaric untamed Black-land in which there were no tarred roads, drains, and pavements, in fact not much of anything. I left Mighty-Magnificent-Manly Maruanda and told him that if he were drunk on my return he would have to walk home. I dropped off Tollie and his wife and all their clobber. Then Rita and her four children, and then Bogkile, which entailed driving along a road that had long since ceased to be a road and was then barely even a drain. Finally large teenage Jablisse, with her strangely large protruding buttocks and wholly magnificent, totally erotic, partially-naked brown breasts, at another Darkest-Africa spot, and then back towards home. The Hotel must have been immensely pleased to no longer have the incredible weight on board.

Moronic-Mad-Maniac Maruanda managed to look me in the eye fleetingly for a millionth of a second, denying being drunk or even having been drinking. Once he had climbed in the front seat, it was absurdly and abundantly clearly not to be the case. The closer to home, the worse he became, demanding beer in a slur of Zulu that was untranslatable even to a fellow Zulu.

At home I had a shower, set off for town and James' party to meet the promised Monica. What could be said – great party, great fun, great music? The question was did I ask her for her phone number? She seemed fairly nice but how would she have measured up in the cold light of day? Still, I did wonder if she would have phoned me. On the way home, I fell asleep driving for the first time. Fortunately I woke as I drove over the bumps on the side of the road. The only casualty was one of my bottles of stout, which by the next morning was causing a hell of a stink, worse than Maruanda-the-moron-the-shit in full swing.

Monica never rang and I never heard from her again.

I was completely exhausted as the previous three nights had been spent keeping the tomatoes warm. We had had forty-four gallon drums sawn in half, filled with sawdust which we tried to keep burning all night to keep the frost at bay. It was exceedingly good fun though. Smoke in my eyes, my clothes reeked of smoke but as a registered pyromaniac it was a hoot. That whole great country caused smoke in my eyes.

Tales of owls in the house, of snakes in the garden, of sparrows and mice, of chocolate-coloured howling native babies, of coffee-coloured toddlers, of buildings and builders, of chemicals and poisons, of tomatoes and sawdust. Tales of squash and beer, of hockey and beer, of rugby and beer, discos and beer, women and beer, of black men and beer, of beer and beer, ears singing tales of adventure, emotion and tears.

Chris's bakkie was brand new, ran on petrol and of course he, being a psychopath, would not accept coming second to my non-racing vehicle. On one occasion I actually managed to leave the squash club just before him and thought that I would be able to keep him behind me with a subtle combination of the huge column of dust and by swerving from side to side on the road. It seemed to work for a while until I noticed his bakkie in the field to my right, bouncing along alarmingly, almost out of control and at great speed. He managed to swerve into the road seconds before me and arrived home in triumph. There was of course no need for him to apply the same tactics to me because as soon as he was in front he applied his foot and zoomed off.

The chemicals required to try to control the various diseases that plagued the tomatoes were deadly not only to the diseases but also to anything or anyone else. Twice a week the sprayer would be attached onto the back of the tractor and a mix of the lethal stuff would be poured into the tank. It was quite a science and part of my job to attempt to get it right. In those youthful days it was not the done thing to read the very small print that came with such chemicals, if indeed there were any. Anyway, on one occasion, I accidentally spilled some onto my hands. I immediately rinsed them in water and thought nothing more of it. A few days later alarming holes began to appear in my hands, some of which are still there today.

Depression, depression, deeper and deeper, blacker and blacker...

My thoughts spiralled into a vortex of sombreness...

How to get out?

How to get out!

Treacle-black giddy thoughts churned around and around. How the hell had I got into that? Was it all to do with my lack of woman? Since the disappearance of that bitch Sally things had gone rapidly downhill. As an adult I had never cried until then. Now it seems a regular occurrence. Damn her... Had I really loved her? Hell, did she really love me? What the hell was love, that thing that most pop songs are made of, what the diamond business depends on, what sturdy families are made of?

Tomatoes, tomatoes, tomatoes, were they really the answer to the world's problems, to South Africa's problems, to my problems? What was I doing there? Was I achieving anything? If only I was doing something real, something for which the results were visible. Those black people did not know me, solely because they were black and that was South Africa. What a pit, what a palace! God, you brought me here, let's get that one clear.

Saturday afternoon and the Hilton versus Saint Andrews rugby match was compulsory. I could have gone to either of the two schools but, as a ten-year-exiled hated English boy, I felt distinctly out of place. It was bloody cold. The beer and that stuck-up Pommie girl... On Sunday the incompetent imbecile Ephraim had succeeded in destroying my bakkie, the pillock. Wayne my-son-went-to-Eton-on-a-grant-but-I-could-pay-for-the-whole-school's-fees Kerr could only wind down the window an inch for the statutory,

"Goodbye-come-up-and-see-us-sometime." The bastard saw me at the rugby match and when I greeted him he chose to ignore me.

I put the tractor battery into my bakkie and it started perfectly. Then I fixed the lights and went up to String's farm to fill up with diesel. I was all set to meet Martin at Pietermaritzburg Cathedral. It was the centenary of the death of the Bishop of Colenso. He was a great lover of all black people. I had reached as far as the beginning of the tarmac into town when the headlights failed and had to abort the mission in the gathering darkness; I could hardly drive on the main roads into town without lights in the dark. I had to cautiously feel my way back along the dirt roads in the darkness. What a disaster. No doubt Martin had written me off as a non-starter Christian and not worth bothering with. I could have phoned him to tell him how long it took to try to jump-start the bakkie, to put the tractor battery in, to fix the lights, to get diesel. Then to tell him I had left early enough, but that the lights had failed again... I disappointed you Martin, and you God, old Sport. Still, with not too much effort you could have kept those lights on for another few hundred yards to the tar, and I would probably have made it from there...

Another day, another notch in the depression machine inside my head. I sat on the arm of a dappled-green-leaf armchair with one foot on the windowsill and one on the other knee, holding my head feeling my shave, quite close, some great patches. Real baby-bottom bits and places where the stubble had beaten the razor. I sat there looking at my reflection in the glass. My green eyes, my moustache, and my hand moved slowly over my face. Was it really the same person I used to be? Sally would be disgusted by me.

The music was hushed in the next room.

"Hide in your shell, there is no room for anyone else. Loneliness is such a drag." So quiet I could not hear it from another room, yet so loud every word went straight into my brain. Sitting there, looking at those green eyes looking at me, thinking. Thinking, what was I going to do?

That night I really had completely slipped up. What a disaster! One of those silly letters I had written. One of those I would never be able to send. Vicky was Sally's lifelong friend. They had shared a room together in Oxford for two years.

"To: Vicky Saunders
3 Parish Cottages
Mapledurham
Oxon
RG6 PJ7
England

Dear Vicky,
I am going to visit Sally. What is her address?"
Love
Joss

Not a lot to ask. To anyone other than the green-eyed bastard that sat opposite me it would have been a reasonable request. Why not go and see her? After all we were great pals once, deeply in love. Why not? Oh hell, why not...

He slowly ran his fingertips along the bottom of his moustache and then licked the top lip with his tongue. My tongue, dammit. My lips, and briskly I sat up. The answer was simple. I had to get out of that vortex of my own thoughts, otherwise... otherwise the green-eyed moustached bastard in the window was going to drag me down. I had to get back into contact with people, lots of people, white people. Oh shit, so those people were black, brown whatever, but they were Zulus. They were a different culture. We could laugh and joke together, but I was not strong enough to step over the apartheid line. Or was it that? I was honestly not attracted to any of their women folk, nor was I inclined to sit down and drink beer with their men. No, I had to hop into bed and get mortally drunk with white folks only. Or was that really the case, I wasn't sure. As I sat there and mused, I realised that I was twenty-four and after that year it would be too late for any further education for me, and I really did need further education. Two years at the Royal Agricultural College had taught me nothing and left me without direction. I had to have something to aim at. Hydroponics and intensive vegetable production under protection could have been an answer. I needed to go to an institution where I could be taught South African farming, Zulu, rugby, squash, football and holidays, and could come out with a First. I would have time to visit Gran, the Van Tonders in Bloemfontein and all those family in Johannesburg. The Prinsloos in the Karoo, Dad's old pals the Andersons and the Newtons in Howick. I could go to Sun City, see the Kimberley Hole. Then I would have been really employable. I honestly thought I was older and more mature than I had been at Cirencester. I thought that I had a better attitude towards studying.

I saw the black clouds swirling around the brink. I saw that the balls of my feet were on the edge, tottering. In front of me was that sea of black, ominous, infinite, transparent clouds, so easy to fall into. That solid block I was on, that foundation that has taken so long to build, just waiting... I stood there and swayed for days. My centre of balance had gone over, and then suddenly... claw back... claw back!!! Stay, survive, and fight those tears, fight to be alive. I stopped those thoughts and somehow I stayed on top.

But that letter.

That last letter. Some girl electrocuted, found dead on our lawn. My parents had organised a large party in the garden, complete with a large marquee, band and champagne. There must have been some dreadful accident with the electrics, or maybe she had taken an overdose. The letter simply said she was found dead on our lawn. No more to feel the delights and pleasures of life. No more to laugh or cry. Oh, to cry, that outpouring of the problems of the living. To be living. Life, I could laugh. Poor girl. Death, so sudden and so horrible; what had she been thinking? Was she happy? Was she married? Imagine dying without finishing one's life. So she died, and on our lawn. At first my mind rejected what I read. It went completely numb. My poor, poor parents... Those bastards from the gutter press with their sordid headlines, trampling their dirt all over the place and gloating over every detail. No doubt it would have been on the front pages of their shitty smutty papers. Poor Dad, so human, so sensitive, so vulnerable, and what could I do out there? Hand in my notice now...

"Sorry String, but I will never make it in this country. I am going to look for my fortune elsewhere. I will be gone at the end of the month." The moment to burst out with it was kept at bay with his perpetual exuberant enthusiasm; it was on the tip of my tongue...

Music was blasting into the back of my neck, down to Durban, killing any conversation. Red carnation in my lapel, a clean shave, clean suit, a Stuttaford's neatly wrapped appropriate present, old Granny Jean Kennedy loved it. Aunt Sarah chatting away gaily had not heard the news. As Mum's sister she seemed to have taken on maternal responsibility for me. She was going to find out sometime, so I told her. Suddenly it was worse, the damn tomatoes, the women, my family, everything. How could I join the South African Army? I would never survive. If I left, I would spend the rest of my life wondering whether I would have survived. Stumbling over that little mountain to find whether things would be better or worse...

I stumbled on... and fell backwards from the edge. Things did get worse, but I was stronger, and I crawled away from the brink. Back at the farm from the party, all the tomato plants were dead, almost a joke really. On a day like that, such a minor blow, if anything was going to do it. Every one of them stone bloody dead, passed into the great beyond.

I was standing again. The edge I had been standing on was clearly visible. I could see my footprints walking away from it. It had been close. I was going to continue walking away. Surely now my future was with that arsehole of a country. I have got to somehow make things better. Old Hole-in-the-Head Tollie's children, Ephraim's children, all those black illiterate people's children, and the next generation that were going to rise and change things. We had to beat them to it. There had to be hope for the country. Black people have their own culture, customs and identity; they just had to be educated. They were not going to be subjugated forever. So there I stood, quite steady. I would have to learn to farm properly, perhaps buy a farm, and make an example of how it could be done.

That would be the answer.

Blazing, fiery-red, the sun wallowed slowly, hippo-like behind silhouetted black, fearsome mountains. Changing to bright translucent orange-yellow, further up, to clear turquoise, baby blue. Perfect wisps of cloud looked like the Eternal Artist had painted the mountain-beast up into the sky, joining the two by a momentary snapshot umbilical cord. Shades of colour ranged from bright blue in the sky directly above and behind, to approaching ominous darkness in the near foreground. Into this intimate warm foreground a naked brown beautiful child sidled innocently into my workshop. The fluorescent light caught her there shining in the doorway with the riot of colours wrestling behind her. She chuckled and gurgled musically as she twisted her toes in the sand

and played with her little fingers in her mouth. Now the sun was living blood and the wisps of fire were more pronounced, almost like huge locks of hair coming out of the monster-mountain. The child is as much part of the painting as were the hippo and the monster. The evening mist gently shaded in the foreground and the middle distance began to blacken. For many precious moments these three creatures vie for centre stage, the innocent child uses magic in her voice before two small boys trot into my fast fading paradise.

They announced importantly that a pipe was leaking somewhere. I told Tembisen, the elder of the two, to put all the tools away and to lock up. I climbed into my bakkie and drove into the priceless picture only to find a tap had been left on. A gathering of small children had followed me around to the tomatoes and demanded a lift back as payment for spotting the supposed leak. Into the back of the Hotel they climbed. Tembiseni demanded to go in the front, presumably because he needed most payment. I may well have let him, except for the fact that he was demanding. He collapsed pathetically on the ground, writhing in agony and making odd groaning, crying dying noises. It was then almost totally dark. The black mountains were hardly discernible from the black, totally deep space black sky and I laughed uncontrollably at the weeping child. I was laughing because the day had been yet another one of those brain-dead depression days.

Tollie, the chuckling hole-in-the-forehead man was sort of second in charge. The hole was so large another irate Zulu with a pick must have made it. How he was still alive was a mystery to me. He came up with some strange gurgling choking noises whenever I kicked Maruanda, which I could only translate as a chuckle of approval. He and Maruanda were always at each other's throats. Tollie would come to tell me that Maruanda was drinking and Maruanda would sidle up to me and whisper in triumph that if I went to a certain spot on the farm I would catch Tollie loafing.

Tollie was married to Mangati. She must have been quite beautiful in her day; tall and slim with tribal slash marks in her old cheeks. Perhaps Tollie had won her in a man-to-man combat. Mangati pottered around, sweeping the compound, did a bit of cooking and was one of the old hands on the farm. She appeared to hold some authority over her peers, but it may simply have been because of her age.

Niki and his wife Mbonambi had four children. Niki did his best to keep body and soul together. Six mouths to feed was a lot for any one. He managed, and still laughed heartily at the end of it. He was a responsible, very likeable chap, as strong as an ox and, unlike Maruanda, he never drank. He managed to drive the tractor without major incident. It was his job to spray the tomatoes with fungicide and insecticide twice a week. The tomatoes were perpetually covered in a whitish, greenish powder. As much as it was designed to kill fungus and insects, I thought it would probably do the same for a human if the poison was not removed first.

Mbonambi always had a baby strapped to her back. She was a very slight, pretty woman, almost boy-shaped. She could not have been much older than I. Her eldest child must have been six or so. She worked twice as hard as the others to make up for the children. The baby was getting older, exploring the packing shed, splashing in the dirty water. Gurgling with its two little front teeth and laughing eyes and then howling like crazy when it wanted its bottle or its nappy changed. The six of them lived in the middle building of the compound in one tiny room. They shared the room with a small girl called Tembi. On stifling January and February days she used to work with her pretty little bee-sting breasts peeping out at me provocatively, although she was so young that they could only just be described as such. She could not have been much older than fourteen or so. Where did she go when Niki and Mbonambi made love? I didn't know, maybe she was his second wife. She definitely was not another daughter as Mbonambi was not old enough. When it was very hot, many of the younger women would work with their equipment out. Whether this was a deliberate ploy to entice the newly arrived man from 'Overseas' over the Apartheid fence, I was not sure.

iButho was the farm's groom. It was his job to daily groom and exercise Uncle Arthur's two thoroughbred Polo ponies. He had got the job because he had the savvy to answer when asked,

"Do you have experience with horses?"

"Yebo Baas," he had lied, after all how difficult could it be? He was also the junior supervisor on the farm in the absence of Ephraim. His reputation with the ladies preceded him. There was not a single one of the black women on the farm that was safe from his advances.

Rita lived in a tiny room with five children. Bongiwe, her youngest, was a fairly large contented baby, and could waddle about most of the farm. She had just reached the point of being able to communicate. She jabbered away, usually the same thing over and over. She was still breast-fed and Rita would pop out a rounded, plump, brown, beautiful breast whenever Bongiwe was hungry. Incredibly, she would carry on sorting tomatoes while the child fed from her. Thembisini, her eldest, was a very small boy. He was sixteen but, presumably because he was so undernourished, he looked as if he were only nine. Still, he tried hard and was always trying to impress me. Sipho, Rita's second son, must have been about ten. Once he went into Pietermaritzburg with iButho. Imagine one's horizon being so limited that the edge of one's world was just over the hill, all of thirty kilometres away. Maxchu, Rita's third son's nickname was 'Horse'. About seven or eight, he spent most of his day either bent double pushing an old wheelbarrow wheel around making motorcar noises, or pushing his wire car or horse about. He was sometimes very sick and would stand crying with the tears cutting deep channels through the dirt on his face. A couple of tablets were usually able to do the trick. Rita's fourth son Samuel was about three. He was not old enough to run without fear of falling over. He was happy to play in a heap of plaster sand all day and say importantly when I walked past,

"Ja," or "Ja, Nkosane," at which point I would pick him up and swing him about while he made happy, chuckling baby noises.

Beauty caught me having an early morning manly upright, testosterone-convex pee in the garden. When I had recovered from the embarrassment, it was to become the gateway to our unique relationship. Her eyes would look momentarily deep into my soul, see the real me, smile shyly out of the corner of her face, knowing that I was not the façade I pretended to be. She seems to be a different race from the others, tall, shoulders back, proud, efficient, well spoken and very beautiful. Her figure, especially her magnificent buttocks and breasts, were a cross between an expensive slave's and a high-class fashion model. She was probably a year or so older than I was and a little shorter. On her pursed lips she wore cherry flavoured lip-ice, which made them all the more impossible to ignore. She had an alluring smell, distinctly African, yet totally provocative. She worked in the kitchen and was an excellent cook. Unlike all the other black women that worked on the farm, she did not have a boyfriend or any male acquaintance. In the way that a light bulb attracts flies, beautiful women attract men. As a man on one side of the Apartheid fence, I was wary and yet undeniably fascinated by her.

Jaina must have been about sixty. She looked like a friendly giant panda. When she wore her silly woolly hat with a matching scarf over it and a blanket over her shoulders, she looked exactly like Paddington Bear. To see her lumbering and shuffling along in a hurry with her outfit on was hysterical. She must have been on her last legs because she was not that intimated by the various threats and cajoling used to make the blacks work.

Old Esheena was shacked up with even older Dolphus. She had found him down-and-out in a drain under a road. They seemed to get on well together, sleeping in one tiny bed. They were both huge. Dolphus was Tollie's chief crony or sidekick and was good for a laugh. The two of them were responsible for the compound buildings being in the mess they were in. Dolphus was not aware of the subtle difference between a chisel and a screwdriver.

Gun and Sipho Ndlovu were both new arrivals. Both were eager to show their willingness. Both were fairly hot on sorting days. Sipho manned the stapling machine and produced tomato boxes all day long. Gun weighed the field grade tomatoes and gave the girls more tomatoes to sort.

The two of them smoked and were continually taking 'smokos', their mandatory five-minute smoke breaks. They had obviously worked in Australia so I thought I'd better not try to stop them otherwise they would get their union on to me.

Jacob Ndlovu, known just as Ndlovu, was quite wise – about eighteen. His voice had not yet broken. He was Ephraim's apprentice, great for watering and counting. He had to walk about five miles across the river every day to get there. He came with Eunice, probably his aunt, who was always ill and asking for pills. She was often late and was forever going to the toilet, if it could be so called. How anyone could sit on one of those things was a mystery to me. The cloud of flies buzzing around one's arse and the horrible fear that the whole thing was about to collapse would certainly keep me away. The thought of falling into a pit of human excreta made my skin prickle, and then having tons of mud and concrete fall down... one would probably be killed. What a way to go! I would rather do it in the long grass. On the other hand, they looked sturdy and the flies would disappear once the bacteria had started to work...

Tollie – sweet, kind, moronic, total idiot, hole-in-the-head Tollie – hurried to come to tell me that Jablisse was about to have her baby. Jablisse herself could not have been much older than fifteen or sixteen, although a lovely well-built girl. iButho, I believe, was the father but he may well have been the father of many other young Zulu girls' children. I phoned String and spoke to his Constable-Els type wife (Constable Els being a superb character in one of Tom Sharpe's brilliantly, hysterically cutting books. Els is both totally racist and stupid);

"Take her into town and drop her at the bus stop," she commanded.

"Fine." I wondered how my trial would go? Would I be able to plead that I was only carrying out orders? I think that I had already decided to take her all the way to hospital. By the way that she waddled awkwardly towards the bakkie I realised that the baby's head must be already appearing. Jablisse somehow managed to clamber into the back. She was no longer the alluring sensual, sexual female I had first seen six months previously with her magnificent naked, enlarged darkened areola and cheeky flashing sideways glances when she had immediately recognised that I found her attractive. She moaned in agony, a pitiful creature about to give birth. I waited for a few moments for Eleena, who was going to come with us, when the baby cried. I felt totally helpless; being white and male and having no medical experience, there was absolutely nothing I could do to help. Poor bastard. Poor bastard indeed... I would cry if I was born into the world in the back of a dirty bakkie, assisted by three big fat black Mammas, all dirty as hell. Calling for hot water and getting it in dirty, fire-burnt containers and unclean, used beer bottles. Calling for a razor and getting a horrible revolting looking knife, another ANC terrorist was born. What did I do to stop her from becoming one? NOTHING!!

"Baas Baas, my daughter's leg is very bad. Please baas, I need petrol to take her to hospital." Ephraim rushed to tell me. About ten days previously his daughter Spongille had badly burnt herself stepping on burning plastic near their compound. Old McDonald's wife had put some methylated spirits on it, and a bandage. It proved disastrous because when the bandage was eventually taken off, the scab had stuck to it, ripping the wound wide open again.

"Here is R10.00 for petrol which is all I have, but you know you have to pay R5.00 to buy petrol on Sundays." Shame, now he was not so keen. He ambled off to ask McDonald if he was going into town for any reason. He was all set to go and ask a few other surrounding farmers. I knew damn well it was his diversionary tactic. Lyle appeared;

"You can siphon some petrol out of my car." Deep down he had a heart of gold. We tried for about five minutes but could not get any out. The answer was staring me in the face: I could see that I had to go.

"Don't worry Ephraim, I will take Spongille to the hospital." I rubbed my face in resignation. He immediately had something more important to do and organised for his wife Eleena to go in his stead. After being promptly dealt with at the registration desk in the black hospital, I left Eleena and the child at the back of the very long queue. However, I had been sitting in the bakkie for only twenty minutes when chubby Eleena lumbered out to come and call me,

"The doctor wants to speak to you," she announced excitedly. He was an incredible chap; working on a Sunday amongst those diseased and battered bodies, probably getting paid a pittance, the sort of person that makes the backbone of our society. Behind us in the queue was a person that had been run over; blood poured out of several head wounds. His one hand was in shreds, his legs hardly working. He must have been in agony. One must have been stabbed in the forehead, a huge horrible wound which I would have thought, in normal circumstances, would have killed a person. Another had had his throat cut – blood everywhere. Somehow he was also not dead; a doctor was about to give him a plasma transfusion as we passed.

"You have to wash her wound properly twice a day every day with antiseptic. Bring her back to me next week for a skin graft. You must do all the washing to make sure it is done properly," the tired but dedicated doctor instructed me.

We were then ushered into another room where a pretty businesslike nurse with a saintly expression dressed the wound and gave Spongille two injections on her bottom. All in all, we were not there for more than an hour. We went back past the mutilated bodies, the amputees in their wheelchairs and sewn-up pyjamas. Eleena and I stopped in town to buy some bread and things, the first and only time we shopped together. She bought essentials for her family and I bought sweeties to feed my car-cleaning gang. Tearing towards each other on that dusty road on Baboon Hill, creating an enormous cloud of dust, my white box of a vehicle, the Hotel, veered to the right and then to the left, playing 'Chicken' with Lyle who was hurtling towards us. We slowed and then came alongside and said something short and polite before another car dusting the road forced us to carry on our separate ways. Another weekend over.

I shaved off the moustache and changed from looking something like that fellow Magnum back to the McEnroe image, the day Vicky Saunders got married. I remember taking a sweet out of her mouth with my tongue at a party, in front of her totally enraged, livid boyfriend! Vicky was a great upholder of one or the other image, bearded or clean-shaven. She loved me with a beard and said I was handsome clean-shaven, but with a moustache... I loved her barrage of continual comments about my caterpillar. Vicky, my last and only tie with Sally. No doubt your first offspring would have been born a year or so later. Peter must be coming up for twenty-three years old. Peter, you should have been mine...

I should have forgotten Sally, Vicky, and Simone a long time before...

There I was on Make-Me-Rich farm, on Midmar Dam, Howick near Pietermaritzburg, managing a tomato farm. That year we had produced 135,000 kilograms of tomatoes. The next year I had to produce 450,000 kilograms. I thought I could overcome most problems, having overcome some so far. Maybe it would be possible. That year, 1982, was the year of the drought, the worst for centuries. The rest of Africa was in a real mess. Appeals for food; forget the politics, they were hungry. South Africa was taking a blow but was not as badly affected as its neighbours. Some puddles some way down in the valley sadly represented what was left of Midmar Dam. Brown sad stone, dry dead grass not having water for months. The whole country was parched, famished. Drought prevailed; every single person in Natal was affected. Restrictions applied – four hundred litres a day per household in Durban and Pietermaritzburg, and they were thinking of reducing it further. I had come to South Africa to see what things were really like and I found myself totally unaffected by the drought. If that was why I came... Surely there could not be a stronger indication that I was in the wrong place. That brown barren wasteland all around me and I wasted hundreds of litres of precious water a day. There was no stopcock on the reservoir so the only way to tell when it was full was when it overflowed. Often hundreds of gallons went to waste before anyone noticed. The only effect the drought had on the farm was that I had to move the water pump further and further into the dribble that was once the river. I should have been working in darkest Zululand where they really were in trouble, where I might actually have been of some use. Make-Me-Rich Farm was an allotment of a farm. The first farm I had worked on, the 'Heart of Africa', was over twenty thousand acres. This was only six acres. If you blinked while walking past, you would miss it. It had only two hectares under shade cloth intensively producing tomatoes. I had to get the hygiene right. It was of paramount importance. We had to have a formalin dip and we had to get the irrigation and the spray programmes right. It all had to be done that coming season. Make-Me-Rich Farm was an isolation camp. My mind was in turmoil; it was almost as if in the Grand Almighty Plan it has been prearranged for me to have that period on my own to work things out. I reckon Jesus was fairly fast to come to his in a mere forty days. So far I had taken two hundred days and I was certainly not convinced that I was willing to be crucified for a cause. Or maybe I was. Maybe I decided ages ago and did not have the courage to take the necessary action. Maybe Jesus made up his mind on the first day and spent the other thirty-nine wondering if or whether he should go through with it. Maybe he did not decide at all. Maybe Jesus was not an aspiring tomato farmer in Africa. Maybe he came out having resisted the Devil's temptations but things just worked out the way they did. Was that what I was hoping for? Just waiting for something to happen. Maybe String would sack me? Maybe I would be called up? Maybe when I got to Amsterdam airport I would go north to Sally and... I had to stop allowing myself the luxury of such thoughts.

Make-Me-Rich Farm was a little haven of beautiful weather, warm sunny days and bright clear starlit nights. It was away from the continuous drizzle of England. It was a place of perpetual luxury: servants making my bed, cooking my food. No rent, not having to buy food, a vehicle, and a fantastic, though somewhat small, dam to play on.

"Maruanda, you drunken idiot!" I screamed at him, hitting the back of his head.

"Baas, baas. I not been drinking," he promised, momentarily convincingly; like the price of an antique, the value changing by the second, depending on the buyers, the weather, the enthusiasm of the auctioneer and possibly the activity of any ringers. Previously he had duped me with a fleeting case of rigor mortis and a sharp intake of breath. I looked him in the eye and suddenly had to gasp away for fresh air.

"Look at that hole in the roof of my room." Lifting his arm he moved his centre of balance, making him stagger and fall over. He always babbled when he had been drinking. No one could keep him quiet. I honestly felt like killing him. I kicked him a bit, strangled him playfully and threw his hat away. He sort of chuckled in Zulu as if it was his reward for getting drunk.

"Please Baas, my baby she want job." His eyes had that glazed dead-dog look, there was the characteristic stagger, but the dead give away was the smell. Hell, he didn't half pong when he'd had a few. Now he wanted me to employ his 'baby'...

"No chance! She's an even worse raving alcoholic than you are!" She was totally blind drunk once, slobbering around totally inexcusably. In her paralytic state she had made something of a pass at me, which had virtually made me sick. She could go to hell, which was quite ironic because, being black and in South Africa, was more or less where she was.

"Tomatoes and tomatoes and tomatoes, creep by at this petty pace from day to day to the last syllable of recorded time. All our tomatoes have lighted fools the way to dusty death. Life is but a brief tomato that ripens and rots its hour in the field. It is a vegetable full of goodness and vitamins, signifying nothing." **(Ed. So much for your education at Agricultural College, a tomato is not a vegetable but a fruit.)** At that moment, my life did seem to revolve around tomatoes. The following year I was going to make the farm tick. At all costs we had to avoid soil coming into contact with the tomatoes. The platforms were being made higher so that when the tractor went down the aisles it would not splash mud onto the plants. We were going to build a bar onto the tractor that pushed the tomatoes out of the way so that they did not come into contact with the dirty wheels. We were going to make sides on the rotivator so that it did not spray dirt everywhere. We had the fertiliser application sorted out and the irrigation sorted out. Labour relations were no longer a problem now that we had five star accommodation. I could almost have written a book on it:

"How to grow tomatoes under shade cloth in sawdust in Natal."

This Christianity Thing...

As someone that had been presented with all the facts about the life of Jesus, his crucifixion, resurrection and his ascension into heaven, I was more or less forced to agree that there was a God and that Jesus lives, that he died for our sins and that there is hope for the world. Having been presented with these arguments many times at school I considered myself a Christian. Martin, on the other hand, had taken the argument a lot further. When Gran took me to the Moral Rearmament (MRA) Headquarters in London, I knew that I would have to give up any other career. I would have had to dedicate my life to God and the salvation of others. Not a bad course but, sitting cross-legged on my bed with my notebook and pen in hand, on those mornings no great 'inspired thoughts' came to me to say that it was the right path to take. Martin, however, had taken the path. He was off to save the world. The same attitude could be taken when presented with the facts of the future of South Africa. According to my adolescent calculations (remember that in 1981 Aids had not begun to cull the black population to the horrific degree that it since has), there were going to be around eighty million blacks and only five million whites by the year 2000. Sounds frightening; something had to be done. Some of the problem was that a lot of the 'do-gooders' did not have a clue as to the real problems that the country faced. Those black people, their different cultures, their different languages, their dislike for work, their proclivity for alcohol, their lack of education, their lack of worldly status, their hatred of each other; sweeping stereotypes, and that was before I had started on the Afrikaners. Those bastards were so bigoted that to get a new idea into their heads one would have to drill a hole in their thick skulls and push it through. They were really naïve about the changes occurring. They honestly thought that five million whites would be able to suppress all those blacks. Had they a reason? The Zulus and every other tribe knocked hell out of them in the last century. The English drove their wives and children into wire cages and starved them to death, thereby inventing 'concentration camps'. Maybe they had a right to be so bitter. Then surely so do the Zulus and the Xhosas and every peoples that have suffered at the hands of another. The imminent big bang would be quite fearsome. But would it be a bang or would it be a gradual deterioration of law and order until things got totally out of hand? Or would the Afrikaner-led bigots open their hearts to the right path? It was not just the Afrikaners. I had heard many English-speaking people express a 'put-them-all-in-ships-and-sink-them' attitude. What was the answer? God, what was the answer? Did you really send me there to find one?

However, whatever way it was put, my own underlying question remained the same, whether to go insane or not? All the questions were still there staring at me, glaring at me, demanding answers. The answers were coming but they were all so contradictory that I was having trouble understanding them. If I decided on one course, would I spend the rest of my life regretting it? Tomatoes were the only apparent answer. I had to get the tomatoes right and then at least I would have a weapon at my disposal. I would be able to speak Zulu, manage a farm, and hopefully make some money. I could then be useful to some lost cause.

The rain was coming down, making for a sad, grey day. Coming off the thatch was a curtain of drips just in front of the window. Wet shoulders, hair and thighs, I had almost forgotten what it was like; that gorgeous aroma of newly wet Africa is something I would never forget. That beautiful all-soaking drenching, but would there ever be enough? The dam was so empty that one could walk right across the middle. The country was crying out for rain and there I was, quietly cursing it. No work could be done and we were miles behind in the work that had to be done before next season. Pots to be removed, platforms to be remade, drippers to be flushed, everything sterilised in formalin and, oh, so much other work. The staff had had the morning off because it was impossible to work in the rain. The rest of the country probably had the morning off to fall to their knees to praise God in thanks for it. Was it the end of the drought, for South Africa, for me?

For me, the beginning of the new era had already started. A heavy blanket was lifted off me. Life had a new purpose, a new meaning. I grinned and chuckled to myself. I did not have that mad glint in my eyes any more. Instead of bumbling and fumbling my way into the next day, I looked forward to it. I would wake up in a state of exhaustion, shake myself awake and attack the day, knowing that in the evening things would be different. To be able to look into those clear blue eyes and laugh with her made my spirits soar; I felt I was a new person. Fumbling with my hands in my pockets and looking at my feet, I knew what I was supposed to do when the evening came to an end. I knew because of bitter training at the Agricultural College. One grabbed the girl and gave her a slobbering kiss and, if that did not work, it was because one was a poof. There I was stuck in the wilds of Africa with almost no friends. Suddenly Belinda Swart appeared and was exactly that, a friend. The fear of losing her was such that I was afraid even to touch her. Yet, on the other hand, if I did not behave like a normal male, she would think exactly that – that I was not normal. So I fidgeted at her front door and she smiled sweetly at me. The first time I had seen her on a horse she was pretty, but certainly not on 'my type of girl' list, simply because she was a horsey girl. Simone had been horsey and I had sworn 'No more horsey types!' But then, no jodhpurs, riding hat and crop, no horsey hairs and importantly, no horsey smell; she was transformed into a swan! She had large eyes, or perhaps it was just her pupils that were so attractive. They mesmerised, hypnotised and transfixed me. Shoulder length gorgeous brown hair any model would envy. She casually swivelled on her heel, blowing her beautiful patterned blue dress into a flower in a breeze. I realised it was now or never. I leaned gently towards her, my hands still in my pockets, and kissed her. My lips brushed those soft lips, just for a half a second, and my mind went crazy.

"Goodnight," I chuckled and fell into the Mercedes, my sensations burning around me, my heart pumping ten times more blood than was necessary, and drove off as carefully as possible. Wow, what a girl. What a woman. Those blue, blue eyes and large sexy pupils. Did she find me attractive? Did she want to stay just friends? What were her thoughts on sex? I wondered how long I would stay on cloud nine musing about it? I thought that as a normal well-adjusted (**Ed. That's a laugh**!) adult human being, I would have been happy to leave things the way they were. But that kiss... so soft, so gentle, so long, so suggestive and all of half a second...

I had just ten days before I left for England to find out.

England and Angie.

Whew, regular as clockwork, her sweet love letters made me sweat. She had organised my seduction. Tickets to go and see Peter Gabriel in London performing "Free Nelson Mandela". Little Angie, little hard working, beautiful Angie was my neighbour back home. We had only met a few days before I was due to leave for South Africa. The memory of her was delicious, particularly when I also received a letter from Simone. She may have been petite but was very strong and she excelled in every sport. Yet she would never survive in South Africa or I in England. Still it would have been fantastic to make love with her, so long as I was not emotionally tied down. Mate – isn't that what otherwise unattached adolescent animals in season do? We were certainly friends, if only pen pals. If I had had a normal job in England at the time and had not hurried away to hide in South Africa, we might have become an item.

Days before I left I did not technically owe Belinda anything. I wondered what she would think if she knew I had a girlfriend in England, if I did? Although I had been writing to Angie regularly, I felt that she could not be categorised as a girlfriend. I had no idea as to how long I was going to be in SA and perhaps I misled her into believing that we would be together on my return. Did Belinda have a boyfriend in Durban? I did not think so and, yes, I would have been upset if she had. We were so right for each other. I could not say that I was madly in love, but it did make me wonder if I ever was before. Maybe I was, I had never felt like that before. So I was in love with a girl I had only known for a week and had not even slept with her. Maybe that was my mistake before. Maybe the only reason I told Sally I loved her was so that I could keep on making love with her. Was that the reason she said it back?

Belinda, what was she doing? Was she thinking of me? Just thinking of her elevated my whole being. I could consider anything and solve some of the world's problems.

No honestly, listen…

Now don't cloud your mind with how it could not happen – rather think of the positive consequences. Our fragile breaking world is ever increasing in hatred, separating cultures, disparate races, beliefs, values, and income so widely different where single individuals are worth more than the GDP of many countries.

Imagine if every single human being were to hold hands at once.

A thought so huge you probably can't take it in, but why should it be so ludicrous? There are about seven billion of us scurrying about. We could all stop what we were doing for a moment and join in this infinite human chain. Where continents begin and end there could be people of significance such as heads of state. In each chain would be both poor and rich, all differing religions, cultures, colours, ages, professions, varying height, weight, ability – yes, everybody. If our planet earth/life raft is hypothetically to survive this trip eventually all our descendants will inevitably be a conglomeration of all of these attributes. In other words, they would be a beautiful light brown colour, neither too rich nor too poor, with an interfaith belief (hopefully not too fat, or too tall and with similar abilities etc.). If we consider what mad governments spend on arms and wars, sending idiots into space, on grandiose unnecessary buildings; on what most western cultures spend on vain and cosmetic ephemeral beauty.

Let us show ourselves, and whoever else is out there, that we do have the ability to live together in peace and not go up in a blaze of suicidal glory that seems preordained for us.

The phenomenal subliminal message of simply acknowledging each other's existence and therefore right to exist; after being part of such a chain people of violence would see the error and futility of their ways. They would realise that we were all one people, all trying to survive on this tiny and ever-shrinking boat in a vast expanse of desolate infinite sea.

Everyone participating in the scenes of mass crowd joy would become intoxicated with goodwill and would go into a frenzy of camaraderie and bonhomie. If we, fellow occupants–tenants–travellers–passengers, achieve nothing else, then let this be it. Let's do it!

One can see it happening.

Life was pushing me up for the next big slide. Realising that I did not go over last time, I would have to be further away and higher up and approach the cliff much faster to stand a chance of going over. I was going over to England chuckling the whole way, probably crying for happiness. Oh God, I had not seen the family for ages. Then up to Cumbria to Matthew and Sandra's wedding to see my old college pals for many beers, many stories, much backslapping and shaking of hands. I would come away feeling fifteen feet tall. Then to brother and sister, Jonathan and Melissa's party for more friends, more slapping and kissing, great times ahead. Then Angie, what would happen there? She had certainly decided that I was her returning boyfriend. Was I her hero, or was she just to take advantage of? Still, all to be looked forward to. Then I was going back to South Africa, back to Belinda. Oh Belinda, I was totally depending on you to be there, if I was not going to suffer a quick and complete defeat. I needed to come back to you and, more importantly, I needed to go from you. I could see the 'Graph-of-Life' thinking that one out. Let Joss climb on to the Plane-of-Euphoria and let him stay there. Then no more friends, no more family, make the issue of his identity stronger; force him to make a move. That mad see-saw life he led. Dave wrote me another of his funny letters which were all from the same sane person. Was it because of Jackie's stabilising influence? Must have been. I would have been stable if I'd had her. Still, if I could catch Belinda, I could stop my life see-sawing between the deepest extremes of emotions. It would stay on the highs forever. I wondered if she was on the same boat? Would I provide something solid for her to lean on? I would have liked to think so.

She, like champagne, bubbled through me, lifting my mind, flying me higher. First nervously leaning on her stove and chatting, laughing carefully. Then in the slouched position next to the heater, cross-legged on the couch next to her, playing cards. Her thigh just touching mine, my immediate bodily reaction was to go erect. Her hand on my knee and just as quickly it was gone. Playing cards with the pack just above my crotch on the duvet and laughing and teasing, with coffee and cocoa. Suddenly it was midnight and I was caught. Do I kiss her there and then? Would she get the wrong idea? What was the wrong idea – two young people sitting with no space between them? Maybe she already had the wrong idea that I was a raving queer. Was I staying faithful to some bitch in England? Did I realise that sex was not solely for the reproduction of the species? Was I a tease? I remembered that label. So she wanted to be just friends. Was it possible between male and female? Was it possible for me, after nine months of total drought and three years of short rations? What would happen when we reached the stage of 'past girlfriends and boyfriends'? Would we ever reach that stage? With all my friends, Dave, Sam, Matthew, 'Scuttle', Chris and my brothers Daryl and Jonathan, because we were the same sex, there were no restrictions on conversation, no inhibitions as to what we could talk about. But with a female you had to guard every thought before you thought it, never mind said it. Guard every expression, every movement of one's body. At all costs, that friendship had to live. How long could I go on without sleeping with a woman, without that particular woman? I desired her and needed her so badly.

Oh Almighty, and most Incredible God! Oh Magnificent Creator of all things beautiful and lovely. Oh Lord God Almighty, you had that strange ability to raise my spirits to the very pinnacle of human experience, taking me to such heights of happiness I thought not possible. Oh Lord God, what a sunrise! Bounding down the uneven, stony hill with the dull red glow of sunrise warming itself along the horizon below me. Flying on air, my senses out of my body, captured by the time and place. Glorious brighter red slowly reflected off the dam as a cockerel told me the time. It was such a clear, crisp sound on a cold, still morning such as that. Time to get up indeed. Cockerel, cockerel, old time lord, you were completely and utterly late that morning. That morning was yet another miracle of colours and splendour, as the different shades of red, pink, orange, and magenta fought into the blackness of retreating, defeated night. Another miracle for me, I thought I could fly. Could it be worship? Hell, sure it was. Sorry, Heaven, sure it was. Oh strange and invisible God, you heard that, I said, "I love her!" I did not say "I think I love her." I loved her then and always would. Her soft, warm, smooth, Goddess, alabaster body, her sparkling eyes, her beautiful laugh, her smile, her teeth, sheer perfection, oh just to touch, just to kiss her, Belinda Swart, I was hers. How could such a perfect angel be left in such an obscure place? I thought I would never find such an ideal life friend in such a strange place. My senses had been transformed although we were not yet lovers. However, we had slept together and agreed that we loved each other. Belinda was going to go on the pill and we could begin our physical relationship when I returned.

Arriving home in England, I remember telling poor Angie about Belinda. Even though we were not physically committed to each other, we might just as well have been as she was devastated. She had so wanted me. She cried inconsolably. I tried to console her; it was as effective as a butcher telling a cow that being slaughtered was good for it.

Three weeks of holiday, beer drinking, burping, talking and laughing with friends and my beloved family. But for Belinda, it was three weeks of desperate loneliness. I wrote to her on the plane, on the train, from Cumbria. I sent her silly love cards. I bought her little presents. I would phone her every day. I would go crazy waiting to get back to her, back to kissing her and possessing her.

However, on my return, back on the farm after my holiday, I told iButho, my black buddy, I thought I still could not take it. I said I was going home to England again, to my family and friends for good. I said I did not like it there, that my uncle and aunt were not my parents, that I was not a racist and that I could not help being what I appeared to be. I told him that I considered him as a friend and that when things were different we could share a beer together. I told him that I could not run the farm without him. I told him that I desperately hoped that Belinda would come with me back to the land of Equal Opportunity. I was standing on the top step looking down into the reservoir and he was at the bottom. Why I felt it necessary to explain my desertion of the farm to him, I will never understand. Possibly he was more of a friend than I care to admit now.

"You cannot leave. I have been here since February and I have been watching you, we have all been watching you. We can see that you are good, that you are not like the others. You cannot leave. I like you too much!" His tears and his tone showed that he really meant it. He stood for a moment pointing his arm at me with his palm outstretched. Our heart-to-heart conversation was interrupted by the sudden arrival of String. I told him that the contents of the new reservoir had leaked out. He went on to tell me what he would like to do to Gabbergass – the incompetent Indian builder who had built the reservoir. iButho quietly walked away. iButho, a black man in South Africa, born into poverty with no hope other than that he made for himself. Was I the hope he was banking on? Christopher 'String' Rodgers on the other hand was the sporting hero that was born white in South Africa. He went to the best school, the best university and was able to be irresponsible because someone else had always paid. String went into partnership with Arthur Kennedy, my uncle, who was loaded. He couldn't lose. Where was the comparison? What was the difference in IQ of these two men? Had the one a natural born athletic ability? Was one automatically entitled to a better standard of living?

Was it courage or cowardice? If I had any real courage I would leave. It was so easy to bumble along not achieving anything there, watching the farm going to pieces. That was cowardice...staying. And it was only the next day. Loving Belinda only made the decision agonisingly more difficult. The day after I had decided to stay and now the whirlpool had come around another 180 degrees. Did I lack courage? Could I deny to myself that I was incompetent? Who else could ask the question? I suspected that String thought I was, but the poor bastard was also caught in a trap. He could hardly sack his partner's nephew, unless of course I forced him to. Put the question the other way around, was I competent? Well, at some things at most, I suppose. It was just that awful dead weight on my mind. I used to be so fit; now my all muscles in my entire body ached like hell. My back, my spine, my pelvis were in perpetual exhaustion. My eyesight sometimes blacked out; my teeth grating together, making that sickening dentist smell and sound. Sure I was competent, it was just that... that black fog clouding rational thought, logical deduction and happiness, replacing them with sadness, with doubt and despair, with remorse and hopelessness. It filled me with confusion and a terrible desire to do something drastic to change things.

Beauty, you brown beauty, you picture of elegance and grace, you princess of your race. You popped into my life with your obsession with cleanliness, your immaculate white teeth smiles. Your clean white apron and chequered blue and white uniform with a pretty white cotton cap always ironed immaculately. Your happy, sweet, obliging innocent smile and occasional whistle as you busy yourself about the house. With a towel wrapped around my waist and still clean and wet after a shower, we bumped unexpectedly into each other in the corridor. Alone in the house we gazed at each other momentarily for long seconds. To me she was perfection that I had not fully noticed before. With her very pale perfect brown completion, almost childlike little button nose and gorgeous freckles under her eyes, she could easily pass as my sister. Perhaps she might have been at least slightly interested in my young, wet, athletic, totally forbidden male body only inches away from hers. Still only a little distance apart, involuntarily I moved my hands towards her. She dropped the folded linen she was carrying and entwined her fingers in mine to keep me away from her. It was the first time we had ever touched. Her fingers were strong. Still looking into each other's eyes, I let out my breath, pulled in my stomach, allowing the towel to fall and in the same moment gently pulled her towards my naked body.

"No, no Joss- uhua, you cannot do this." She gasped; her mouth was only inches from mine.

"My name is just Joss." I gently twisted her arms behind her back, hugging her, her apron wet against my chest.

"In my mind you are Joshua because you are a Servant of the Lord." Her body did not resist me. Her lips were made for kissing, slightly large, pursed and pouted. Her eyes closed, her head stretching up to meet mine, and she trembled in my grasp. With her African sweet corn scent, she was truly delicious. Two young creatures, momentarily innocent of our differences, caught in a tiny box of some vast experiment, one of us male and the other female. Born to mate, make love, breed, procreate, fornicate, we arrived together, mutually, temporarily agreeing terms. My eager erect member pushed hard and wet against her stomach, somehow as a third person to our mouths which sought each other's souls. We kissed softly with our eyes closed for what seemed like an eternity. Still holding her strong fingers, I lifted her skirt and was immediately driven beyond control when my fingers came into contact with her magnificent, soft, bare, perfect brown buttocks; she had no knickers on. Perhaps initially I had just wanted to touch her, let her touch me, and then to kiss her. But at that point I had to make love to her, to penetrate and conquer her. I did not think that what I was doing amounted to rape. Up until that point, she had been willing and even seemed to enjoyed the kiss, being close to my totally naked, muscular, white, illegal body and my first touching her bare bottom.

"In my mind you are Sleeping Beauty, because you do not belong here. You belong in a magical far-off palace in a looking glass. You are a true Princess." I caressed her glorious buttocks with my knuckles.

"No, Joss, No. Leave me. We will get into trouble," she begged as the fear of realisation of what was happening seized her.

"Please Beauty, we must do it," I implored her, hurting her.

"No, no, no..." she pleaded, her fingers twisting and fighting against mine as she panicked.

"Yes, yes, you know you want to..." I gently but firmly forced my knee between hers, my crotch coming into contact with her calves. Big tears splashed down from her brown eyes.

"Please don't do this Baas, I beg you." Her reddened, wet, unhappy, spoilt face was no longer pretty as she squirmed desperately against me. Holding both her hands in one of mine, I used the other to lift her one leg slightly. I pushed my weapon upward, coming into contact with her intimate wetness and muscled into her.

"Aargh!" She screamed black ugly rage into my face. "Now you are an evil, wicked man. Go away and leave me alone!" she commanded, pushing me forcefully away and at the same time stooped to pick up the folded sheets she had dropped. I roughly pushed her flat down on the carpet, pulled up her skirt again and forced my nakedness down onto her again.

"Aaaargh!!!" Her piercing scream was louder, longer and more desperate and immediately I leapt off her. "YOU! ...You are going to die, you bastard!!" She looked at me with deadly hatred as she stood up. "I will tell iButho and he will kill you the next time he sees you!" I knew instantly that it was true. She brushed her clothing straight as she turned to walk briskly away.

I fell to my knees and touched her foot. "Oh Beauty, Beauty, please, please forgive me... You must forgive me! It will never happen again, I swear!" I was totally petrified. She had won. She looked at me in utter contempt,

"I will think about it," she murmured just as we both heard Eleena's laboured heavy breathing arrive at the back door. I darted into my room and dressed quickly. God, what had I done? What had I done...?

I had to get away. There was no option for me but to commit suicide. With no particular plan I ran to my bakkie. I was just scrambling for the keys when iButho appeared at the side window. He had one hand on his hip and the other slowly came up and held the rear view mirror.

"Now Beauty she says..." he paused. This was it; I could see his knife strapped under his armpit. He was going to stab me! "She says that the hot water in the Medeme's room is not working. She says you must go upstairs and fix it." He looked into my face for an instant. I must have been ashen. "And where are you going, Nkosi?" he added. (Nkosi meaning prince in Zulu, which iButho often called me.)

"...to... to check on the pump at the river." I stammered.

"I come with you." And he climbed into the door directly behind me and opened the window into the cab so his face was just next to mine. For the couple of miles down to the river he did not say a word. I could not hope to outrun him. I certainly could not fight him. In the mirror I saw him touch the knife handle. I parked the bakkie near the pump and fell uncontrollably out onto the grass. I slowly picked myself up.

"There is nothing the matter with it, Nkosi. Let's go back, the boys need me to play football!" he laughed.

"Thank God for that!" I heaved a sigh of relief and sped back. "I'm just going to fix the water," I muttered hurriedly and rushed inside.

I was putting up the ladder to climb into the loft when she appeared. I tried to ignore her. She touched my elbow,

"Let's forget the whole thing," she whispered quietly. She had fully recovered and was even more beautifully radiant.

"Oh Beauty, Thank you, thank you. I don't know whatever came over me. Please can we still be friends?" I stammered pathetically. Although how anyone would want to be friends with a rapist was beyond me.

"You will always be my friend. In another country and another time we could have been lovers." That radiant beautiful smile appeared on her wonderful face. She was an angel. She gently squeezed my elbow again and I climbed into the attic. I could hear her and Eleena chatting happily away in Zulu in the kitchen below.

Where in the depths of my sick mind did the thought of wanting to make love to her come from? Not that it was particularly sick that she was brown. It was sick, almost perverse, that I had a woman who loved me, whom I adored, who was beautiful beyond compare and I suddenly wanted to share myself with Beauty. Just as she was the Immaculate Virgin Beauty, I was the Revolting Evil Beast. Was I just another dominant male of my species that was genetically driven to mate with as many females as possible in order to ensure the success of my genes? She was truly beautiful both in body and being. I could not deny it. God I did not, I did not. You, oh Lord God, how could you do it? How could you let such thoughts invade my being? If I could take a white-hot, sterile scalpel and cut out that black-bad, decayed part of my brain...oh God...

...oh God...why such a mess on the farm...

Was it entirely my fault the damn pipe exploded in my face that day?

"Ndlovu, you sure that that tap is open?" I called, standing at the main control panel.

"Yes Baas," he shouted, nodding.

I switched on the pump and the pipe immediately shattered, spurting water and pieces of plastic pipe all over me. Despair, despondency and depression seemed to pounce onto me, determined to crush and defeat me; it was almost an effort to stay on my feet. My soul seemed to float away in the water that gushed around my feet in the shed. Involuntarily I crunched my teeth, forced open my eyes and slowly tried to think how I could get around the problem. I switched off the pump. Slowly the fog in my brain lifted. The new reservoir that we had just built held 140,000 litres. It leaked so much that it had completely emptied overnight. We had committed ourselves to using it as we had taken all the pipes away from the old reservoir and dismantled it. The only old pipe that remained was the agitation pipe which was used to pump the water back around and out through the same pipe. There had to be a non-return valve there that now made that impossible. I phoned String. I had to. He would know what to do.

To add to my frustrations, someone chose to steal the tractor battery that day. Sod it, why our tractor battery? I phoned the police – what else could I do? A chap that obviously modelled for Mr Plod or Humpty-Dumpty pitched up and asked such idiotic questions that I had difficulty in suppressing my laughter. Would you believe it, his real name was Constable Arma Duisdoo? **(Ed. Is that as in 'I'm also a Duis?' – Presumably a recent immigrant from Holland who was related to Amadeus.)** So some bastard nicked the tractor battery. No great blow, we could always buy a new one. It would only cost R80.00 odd; about six months of someone like Dolphus's wages. The new pump was over capacity. It was supposed to draw fifteen amps but drew over thirty. It blew the main fuse box after only five minutes or so. Eternally cheerful fellow String-a-ling found an answer to that one too; just as well, the options were horrifying – just take out all the pipes and replace them with larger ones...

...The fog could be so thick and black...

The whole farm was a sludgy, muddy mess. The poor, bedraggled, filthy women slipped and skidded about the place trying to cart pots filled with sawdust. It was an awful, horrid job, trying to earn a crust. Big cakes of slimy red-black mud stuck to their bare feet like revolting snowshoes and the mud all over their clothes was like unwanted body armour. The clay-like, disgusting mud effectively became super glue. You would not get me doing the job for R2.00 a day, not even for R200.00! Amazingly they managed to keep cheerful and joked with each other.

Recounting those times now, so many years later, it is difficult to explain some of my actions back then in 1983. I now attend our church and am a Sunday Club teacher; I have been a vegetarian and have not eaten chocolate for the last nine years; generally I love animals and my daughters have always had pets so I am ultimately at a loss as to why I killed that sparrow. Perhaps it was a symptom of the gathering maelstrom in my mind. Momentarily I actually found myself getting some enjoyment in insanely ripping its head off. God, what had I come to? Could I ever get out of that predicament? The vermin had been the bane of my life ever since I arrived and I had successfully evicted them from the house and intended to keep them out. One was forever checking the furniture to make sure that one was not going to sit in bird-shit. This particular one had broken in and had just shat directly in my breakfast cereal as I was busy eating it, presumably just as I was having one of my worst turns. Without thinking, I knew I had to exterminate it.

Chris arrived and announced that Louise's bakkie was stuck in the mud on the side of the road on the hill. I set off with him with our heavy cable. We went to collect Elijah and Silissor from String's place to help. They were two of his most reliable workers. It was getting dark as Louise and her stepfather, Murray, arrived on the one-eyed tractor. Old Murray Johnson was obviously seething and matters were not helped when we lifted it out without the use of his tractor. I offered to drive it back for him. He refused and set off on it. Chris disappeared with Louise leaving me with his bakkie to take back the boys. We got our wires crossed as I thought we were going to meet back at the girls' cottage. I took Chris's bakkie and passed Murray on the way. Louise and Chris wanted to keep their love affair secret from him. He would have suspected something if I had brought Chris's bakkie to Make-me-Rich so I abandoned it at Summertime Stud, Murray's farm, and made straight down the hill and immediately phoned Belinda.

"I love you so much. I love you. I love you. I miss you. I miss you. I never want to be without you." The fog instantly cleared. We talked and talked. My whole being seemed to slip behind my eyes and down the phone line. I imagined I was there with her, looking into those beautiful blue-blue eyes, touching that gorgeous body, kissing those delicious lips. Then…

"…bye-bye, bye-bye, bye-bye..."

Goddess

The dip in her back before the gentle rise of the hills of her buttocks,
My fingertips float down the warm slopes into the suntanned dunes.
Her shoulders and ivory neck, her chin and that smile, so precious.
Those magnificent banks and seaside that are her wonderful thighs;
To feel those curves, that softness, that body; to drink her, is heaven.
To be with her, to feel her pulse, to touch her all over is to love her totally.
To run and hide and play; my palms slide down between her knees
Massaging softly, gently around and around; naked, glorious and mine.
To know you is to love you, to be close to you is to worship your body,

To touch you is true ecstasy, to love you is divine.
You're all beautiful,
Making love with you is magic, is joy past compare. We fly together,
Forever entwined, our souls knotted together in an eternal embrace.
Apollo, Aphrodite, Zeus, Eros; we meet and leave them as we journey
Through time and space; imagination and beyond; infinite in my mind.

The receiver and the fog came down together, for minutes the fog won. It was so black inside I could not see out. I wanted her so badly. I staggered to the tape recorder and put on some noise. It helped. My ears were not listening to the awful silence. Maybe that was it. Buy a boogie pack and 'bop' all day.

The next day's issue was, not surprisingly yet again, courage or cowardice. Let's face it, another one of those days I took in the teeth. So, if I were to have resigned it would be cowardice. But it did not stand to reason. Just because I had a bad day does not mean that the state the farm was in was my fault. Not all of it anyway. How much did I know about farming? Uncle Arthur argued with me that rotavating was better than mowing for getting rid of the weeds and I could not argue with any conviction. If I had any courage, I would go. So I was a coward, for that day anyway.

"Louise has missed her period by four days!" Chris almost boasted as we commando-crawled down the hill in the early morning light. The fog wrapped around me and tried to choke me... Sally, Sally!! She was pregnant by two weeks when we had met. His mind must have been whirling... abortion, marriage or dump her? Strangely though, he did not ask for my advice. If anything he seemed quite happy with the situation.

"I'd love to have your baby," Louise had teased in the heat of their passion. Yet now it was reality, had she changed her mind? Was it possible to have an abortion in that country? Was it legal? Did he love her? Beyond making love, did he even know her? She was certainly loaded so they would make a good pair. Abandon her. Why not? God in heaven, be my witness, that was what I did. I abandoned Sally without knowing one way or the other. Did Chris love Louise? Did he have an option? I could just imagine old Murray-the-Wally forcing them into a shotgun wedding.

"Listen ur-hum... String... I want to have a word with you. I have thought this out very carefully and it is not a decision that I have come to lightly. I have put myself in your shoes, my uncle's shoes and the farm manager's, those I should be wearing. Each time I come to the same conclusion. I must leave so that the farm can go forward. From my own point of view, the present manager, I must go because I am not fully competent for various reasons possibly psychological – whatever. From my uncle's point of view, I see R300,000.00 invested here, and to have a less than fully qualified person in charge does not make good business sense. From your point of view, String, I see that you are employing your partner's nephew who you see as being incompetent. But I feel that, because of circumstances, I am possibly not entirely to blame. I am also not earning enough. I am not prepared to wait another year for the tomatoes to come right. I am not happy here. I have become disillusioned not only with Make-Me-Rich, but the whole South African situation. I went down with my father's business and I am not prepared to go down with another. I am very sorry that I have had to take this action but as you always say, 'Things always turn out for the best'. You have every right to be angry with me for abandoning you like this. Of course I give you a month's notice so that you can find a replacement. I will show the new manager all I know, although that should only take about ten minutes." String was milling around the new reservoir, ordering people about with his hands in his pockets, totally in command as usual. I was millimetres away from saying it. I had left earlier with the intention of meeting him face to face and telling him. That was not the same. So it went by for another day.

Later, after five, Chris arrived feeling good at the prospect of squash, supper, and more sex. I was forced to throw off my gown of gloom and grin at his endless cracks.

"Of course if she is pregnant, it means uninterrupted sex for nine months!" He laughed at his own sad joke. We went to the Armstrong's, hoping to get a game there, but they still had furniture stored in the squash court. Armstrong showed us into his shade house. He was growing tomatoes in pots and was wondering why they were not doing as well as ours.

"There were no holes in your plastic containers," I explained to him. He promptly poked holes in them with his finger.

"You ought to know a thing or two about tomatoes!" He grinned at my apparent expertise; although I think I could have given him that advice had my education finished at grade seven. Much later at the cottage I finished off a large glass of wine. Belinda brought out a bottle of ginger liqueur and some beer. I lay in bed with her for a while. She sobbed quietly to herself.

"What's the matter?" I asked.

"Nothing." She snivelled even louder.

"Hum." Nothing invariably meant something.

Long pause.

"Well... I'm listening." I sat down next to her and put my arm around her shoulder.

"You will only get upset if I tell you." Tears streaming down her reddened face.

"I'm getting upset because you are not telling me!"

Longer pause. Her shoulder quivered.

"This evening you hardly said a word to me. It was all to Louise, Louise, Louise...!" She pulled away from me in an accusing, judgemental way.

"Belinda... if you can dig up reasons like that to be upset, then I really must go. You know I love you. You know I do. I love you more than anything in the world. I have told you what I think of Louise and now that she has Chris there was even less reason for me to try to chat her up." I had said that although Louise was quite pretty, she was a certified snob and I would certainly not go anywhere near her.

She snivelled and cried some more. Whether it meant that she realised that she was wrong in that I have no desire for Louise, or she was snivelling because she had justified it to herself and instead of my admitting my guilt had made it worse. I knew she was down at that moment. Things could hardly have been worse. Although Louise was fairly pretty, in the cold light of day she was not a patch on my Belinda who, had she wanted, could and should have won the Miss South Africa Beauty competition. But then if she had, she would hardly have looked twice at a misfit like me. Then I threw up on her in the middle of the night and started to leave in disgrace. Thank heaven she had the sense to do what she did.

"Where are you going?" she screamed hysterically.

"Down..." I spluttered. She may have been wrong about my intentions for Louise, but my guilt over Beauty suddenly exploded. I certainly could not tell her and expect her to forgive me, not because Beauty was a maid but because it had happened while I was hers. I could no longer impose my life on her and the only answer was to get away.

"Get back into bed!" she commanded vehemently. Maybe she foresaw the end of our relationship had I gone. Belinda, I loved her so. I loved her for making me stay then in that crisis: for her strength and her ability to see my weaknesses and not hating me for them. Also she was my sanity then as she is now. I loved her for her golden-white seashore, beautiful, unspoilt and untamed body – her rounds and downs, her hills, dunes and dales. Her sparkling-laughing, intelligent-blue eyes, when she yawned early in the morning, when she slept, when she frowned – she was so beautiful then. To see her perched on her beloved horses with her rounded, perfect peach buttocks and hand-carved calves; her flat muscular stomach and straight upright back was a sight of rare beauty. Her shining dark brown wavy hair rolling around her riding hat in rhythm with the gait of the horse was enchanting in itself. She was able to speak directly to the horse and the sound of her instructions to the animal in her charge was as much of a command to my base instincts. I loved her for all that she was. I submitted to her and lay with her all night.

The next morning Chris and I set off down the hill from the cottage at 5.30 am. He was feeling particularly chirpy and went on to tell me in great detail his and Louise's gymnastic accomplishments during the night. The fact that I must have looked like a walking wreck probably made him feel better. He burbled on about squash and time for dinner and other things. My mind was completely numb. My only consolation was that if I was to choose between being either him or myself at that precise moment, I would still choose me. Louise still had not had her period and all that cheerfulness sounded suspiciously like a cover-up. If it were me, I would be saying things like:

"Should I marry her?" or "Where can one get an abortion done?" or "Should I just abandon her?" I was probably having more mental stress about his problem than he was! The options open to him seemed terrible. I tried to work out whether he really loved her. All they seemed to do was hop into bed and make love – rather frequently and furiously by the sound of their desperate, exhausted bedsprings.

Make-Me-Rich and I saw each other in the mirror – glazed staring eyes. Two days' stubble, stinking like a pig, I was disgusted with myself. Chris collapsed on the settee and instructed me to wake him at 6.30 am. I went crashing, stumbling, falling outside.

"You remember how I showed you how the standby irrigation system works?" My instructions to iButho seemed vague but he had to learn and I was exhausted. I came back in again at 6.50 am and woke Chris from his dead sleep. He leapt into action with some vigour that I found surprising. He had to take Louise's younger sisters, Babs and Sandra, to school and was supposed to pick them up at 7.00 am. He was still rushing about the house shouting for shaving gear, shaving lotion and underarm deodorant, when I fell asleep.

I woke at about 9.00 am and tottered out to the packing shed to be confronted by String. We had a little chat and then he questioned,

"And what were you going to do today?"

"Sleep." And with some finality I muttered, "I have just become more and more run down over the past two or three weeks and if I don't take a day off I am going to have a nervous breakdown or collapse or something."

"Why don't you see a doctor? Dr Hamilton is very good." He was being surprisingly sympathetic.

"OK," and I wandered off. The phone was not working and I called up my reserve strength to go and tell String.

"Go to the hospital. Hold on, which battery is driving the tractor? Yours? Well, you had better wait for me because I am going in later anyway. Go and lie down." He sounded like a schoolmaster. I made it to my bed and crashed out without any thoughts of being caught sleeping on the job. About half an hour later String woke me to say that if I took his bakkie and dropped the pump off at Monopump they would skim the impellers for us. So I hopped into his trusted vehicle and sped away. It was a cinch to find it in Longmarket Street. A rather well spoken girl, Vee P. Elle, an eighteen-year-old debutante Asian receptionist, took charge of the pump. She was definitely out to pull, as it were, but I only had time for a cursory glance at her bewitching bottom as she twirled it proudly in front of me. Then off to the hospital I went. Hospitals were always so full of penicillin, old witchy matrons and fogies in wheelchairs. Hospitals, with their endless forms to be filled in, smelly never-ending waiting rooms to be endured and grey-eyed pinafored white nurses. Grey's Hospital was at the top end of Prince Alfred Street. Just another hospital of strange smells and death, except that this one I had to go into. The enquiry desk, the forms, the waiting room, and then I went through to the doctor.

"Good morning, and how are you today?" he started cheerfully.

I always thought that as rather a sarcastic way for a doctor to begin an interview. I suppose it was to catch the unsuspecting idiot that answered,

"Fine, thank you."

"Fine, thank you," were the words furthermost from my mind but on the other hand I did not want to start off too deep with something like, "I feel I am about to die." So I eased in with,

"I feel totally exhausted and have continued to become more and more so over the last few weeks. Today the headaches are worse and I feel jittery."

"Urm." Nurse Virginia de Kok crossed her prettyish knees and stared even more intently at a fly on the wall while I examined her interesting name tag on her left well-proportioned breast. Temperature, blood pressure, urine sample, pulse, heart and lungs, all in perfect working order.

"Psychological." He stubbed out another cigarette and pulled his hands through his thick white hair. He went on to ask me about the pressures of work. More cigarettes later he leaned back with his hands entwined in his hair,

"Tell your boss the pressures you are under. Tell him what in particular you cannot cope with. Tell him you find it difficult to deal with some of the staff endlessly drinking. Ask him to define precisely the boundaries of your responsibilities. You mustn't get worried about things no matter how bad they look. No matter how impossible, just think quietly about it for a while and you will find a way through," he reasoned sensibly. If he could not flog me any medicine, then he would have to settle for some well-meaning advice. So I told him about the tomatoes all dying of Bacterial Canker. I also told him about Belinda's stepfather dying of Rabies. (The first time I visited their strange farm on the side of a hill he had already been bitten by a stray dog. He was living in an agonising wait as to whether he would become infected. He eventually died a slow agonising death.)

"If things get worse, come back and see me. I will lay you off work for a few days. These pills will make you sleep better, soothe you down as they are also an elixir." He spoke to his prescription pad as he scribbled away. I inspected Nurse de Kok's delicately carved ankles and calves; perhaps she was a fellow runner?

I drove away already feeling better. The whole saga could be compared to the battery being stolen incident. The fact that I had called in the police meant that something was being done. Well, I had given in. I no longer had to maintain the facade that everything was all right. I had a large swig of the medicine, collected the pump from Miss Elle and drove home. Belinda was so beautiful. We lay in each other's arms, kissing for endless hours. We had long passed the three million kisses mark.

...I remembered sitting in my brand new red Alfa Romeo in a car park somewhere in the middle of cold and wet Oxford, just a few miles from my parents' home in England, with my jacket off and waistcoat buttons undone. I was probably wearing my old Public School tie. It had been snowing and the slush on the ground had frozen. I was about fifteen minutes early. I sat there with a pad on my lap and a pen in my hand. In the left-hand column was 'Reasons for leaving' and on the right was 'Reasons for staying'. I sat there for much longer than a quarter of an hour. Maybe I didn't decide right there and then but it was certainly apparent to me that I wasn't cut out to be a sales representative and must take the first available opportunity to get out. At the time my thought seemed to focus on running away – literally – to Australia. I already had everything planned. I can't remember the precise moment when the pendulum clicked in my head because suddenly I had sent my passport in for a visa and was frantically phoning bucket shop travel agents. I just had to get out. Now I was in an almost identical situation waiting for papers back from the authorities to give me the go ahead. I think I had thought through the reasons for going or staying and had decided to go. I hadn't looked beyond that though. I certainly couldn't 'run' back to England. Previously I had gone to Australia. Now I was in a quandary. What would be my chances of getting a Chris Smith type job in town? I was as qualified as he was, i.e. I was white and had finished school. I would have to make options – damn it! I could have gone into an employment agency in town and seen what they had to offer. I bought the Farmers' Weekly. Whatever happened, Belinda was definitely going to come with me. How it would work, I did not know, nor had not even started to plan. I don't even think that Belinda understood my dilemma. Perhaps it was all in my imagination anyway. Either way, at that stage, we had, either as rhetoric or in reality, a relationship translating as,

"I only want to make love to you one more time," or seriously deep down in our psyche we knew we would be together forever.

I kissed her so softly on her doorstep in my gumboots.

"Did you sleep well?" she whispered softly into my tormented mind.

"Think so. Same horrific nightmares." I turned; "One more day." I suppose I looked quite smooth, black jeans tucked inside my gumboots with a cowboy type open-at-the-neck tracksuit. My thoughts must have been much the same as one would expect of someone that was about to resign, because that day was going to be the day. All had been said; it just had to be done. All that was left for me to say was,

"String, I am leaving."

I arrived back at the house at 5.40 am at the same time as the bulldozer driver – the keen bastard. I told him to get on with it – whatever 'it' was.

I went inside and started changing my shirt when I heard iButho's quiet 'Nkosi' at the window. I did up the buttons again and opened the back door.

"Morning iButho. We're picking tomatoes today. Tell Maruanda to put the trailer onto the tractor. Tell him to take some cardboard boxes to the packing shed. All the crates must be dipped in formalin. I'm coming now," I ordered as I usually did.

"Ja, Nkosi, now Mikeon he wants to go to Crammond. People is kill his sister. Is cut off his head and put him down." He looked past me, his hands twisted together miserably.

"OK, Mikeon," I nodded. Your sister murdered – big deal. My thoughts whirled in response to his announcement. You're all savages and you murder each other all the time anyway. I was in charge and would have to make the excuse to String as to why we were one key worker short on an important day. If my sister had been murdered, I don't think I would have stopped to ask... Perhaps a typical example of the total lack of understanding I had been brought up to have.

"He can have the day off." Mikeon already had his coat on when iButho told him. I touched Mikeon's shoulder,

"I'm sorry," was all I could come up with.

The day was cloudy, hazy with patches of sunshine. String arrived at about 8.00 am and I braced myself. It had to be then. I had to do it. It should be easy enough as I had rehearsed it enough times. He had brought the new sorting machine and was bustling about. I wandered after him hoping to catch him alone. Suddenly I did.

"String," I began, "I want a word with you."

Well that was it, the end of an era and over the edge.

"About the spraying," He folded his arms and looked over my shoulder towards the packing shed, "You will have to make do with what you've got." He rambled on about the problems of spraying, and somehow it never got said again.

I went down into section four to watch the girls getting the pots ready for planting. I sat down and started tying wire around plastic joints in the pipeline. The pliers slipped and I dug a slice out of my palm. Pain is a funny thing; a dirty black bruise immediately started to emerge on my hand. iButho appeared at my shoulder.

"iButho, do you know why Mikeon's sister was murdered?" No, he did not.

"But Africans like that, they like to kill each other. In 1981 my brother was killed. Six people came and cut off his head." He was sitting on his haunches with one hand touching the ground. From his bland expression he could just as well have told me that we had just run out of boxes or something.

"Why?" I was horrified.

"My brother was steal-em that other man's girlfriend and he come and call five friends and kill my brother. I kill him. I kill that man. I take a knife and cut him here." He casually pointed at his heart. "The police they take me. They put me in prison. The magistrate says that I was not the law and it was not right for me to do that. I go to Pietermaritzburg prison for two and a half years hard work."

I looked at him in a new light, not quite deciding whether it was fear or respect. He really had killed people as I had suspected.

"And Ndlovu too," he continued. "Last year people is kill his father..." I looked at him again. I did not tell him about Belinda's stepfather. What was the point? Death was all around. Death was seeping into the foundation of my sanity. I shook my head in sympathy,

"You poor bastard; all of you," I thought.

I was sitting hunched in the mud, African rain bucketing down and I was sucking my hurt palm, which was throbbing badly. My shoulders, knees, feet and hair were totally soaked. The only part of me not yet soaked to the skin was my belly, hidden against the elements. The rain trickled down over my eyelashes and splashed down my face into my mouth. Maybe it was tears, certainly it should have been.

"iButho, do you think I am happy here? You know in England I have many, many friends. Here I have only one friend. Do you count me as one of your friends?" I turned to look him in the face with my question.

"Maybe you should go home to England, Nkosi," he almost whispered slowly.

"Maybe, iButho, maybe..." We sat in silence for a bit longer. I was struggling with wire too thick for the job and he was putting in the rest of the joints in the pipe. After a while he quipped, his mood had totally changed,

"Hey you know what, my football shoes? I have no power with my foot because I have big holes in my shoes. I have a big hole right here and when I hit the ball my foot come out. No money, what can I do? The people is laughing at me now because of my shoes!"

"You will have to buy some more," I laughed, "or play barefoot or in your gumboots."

"How – my Nkosi. How can I do that?"

"What time do you start to play football?"

"Past five," he answered.

And so I found myself playing football with the indigenous boys. They varied in age from about thirty-five to ten, I'd say, and equally so in ball skill. Some were truly excellent. After an hour, I came away soaked in sweat but feeling fantastic.

"I can do it!" I almost screamed. I had found a way to really communicate with them. My plans were to go to bed and sleep but I was feeling so pleased with myself that I rung Belinda and she naturally invited me up. I found her busily cooking supper. She looked totally gorgeous. She was wearing a 'Get Physical' see-through Tee shirt with no bra with matching sexy see-through shorts. I hugged her and kissed her and laughed. And laughed and laughed! Her almost sharp nipples dug into my chest. I slipped my hands into her shorts behind her and squeezed her delightfully perfect, willing buttocks. She had been so worried and was dying to see me. We told each other about our days and ended up in her bed, the only island in that sea of insecurity and self-doubt. Her bed, where I had horrific nightmares, waking up sweating, and where I could sleep like a baby for hours. Her bed, its happy springs creaked and groaned musically celebrating with us. Her bed, my strange haven away from Africa, away from reality, wrapped in the security of her infinite love. Her alarm clock erupted at 5.15 am. She rolled over, kissed me and wrapped her arms and legs around me.

"I must go," I kissed her softly. Oh the pain of it. I really and truly did not want to go. But I had to and I tore myself away. I had a grim determination that that day was the day. I had asked God about it. God had forgiven me and agreed that the best thing for me was to leave. I knew with a certainty that I had never felt before that that was what He wanted. As soon as I had asked Him about it and heard His answer I had felt better.

However, it turned out to be another bad day.

But I did it.

I told String.

Man to man.

I told him.

He wanted to know what particular aspect of the job I felt I was not coping with. He felt I should delay my decision for a while – think about it and then we should discuss it again. I said that I would be happy to discuss it later, however my decision was made. Strangely surreally, I went down to the river to put the pump further into the water as it appeared to be sucking air because it was drawing too many amps. I succeeded only after a long struggle with a monkey wrench. I got back to the shed only to find that the pump had broken down altogether. No water was coming out at all. No water to drink, spray with, wash and sort the tomatoes with, or to irrigate with. What bigger blow could we suffer? After much discussion about it, String sped off into town in my bakkie to get another pump. I phoned Monopump to tell them that he was coming. In the meantime I tried to irrigate the tomatoes with the little water we had left in the reservoir. I started up the nutrients pump and filled up the agitation tank, part of the main tank. I stood there watching, mainly because when it was full I was going to put in a batch of nutrients. Suddenly there was an almighty thunderous crack; the sound of a head-on car collision, the sound of several gunshots together, and the partitioning wall in the reservoir was hurled across the reservoir like a leaf. It was a very frightening sight, seeing 20,000 litres throw a brick wall to within inches of where I was standing. With my heart crashing in my chest I fled to the switch to stop the pump.

I slumped down.

"About par for the course," I reflected as I tried to straighten out my thoughts. I opened the Johnson coupling-joint just outside the reservoir to drain out any stones that may have gone into the pipeline. I then irrigated with some of the water. String arrived back with the new pump. I told him what had happened. He stormed and fumed about, trying to think up a new plan of action. He went down to the river to connect up the new pump. He left Maruanda to look after the tractor, which was working the pump. All seemed to be going well. Then I noticed that no water was coming up. String shot back down to the river. He came back absolutely breathless; we had almost burnt out the new pump.

Some time after 5.30 pm the Indian driver took away the day's tomatoes and Chris arrived wanting to play squash. I left String to what were then his problems and went with Chris; I'd had enough of that day. The first rally was incredible – something like thirty shots, and then I went into rapid decline; total exhaustion. I could only drink milk afterwards. A poisonous spider had bitten Chris's mother, Caroline. She had terrible swellings on her leg and looked very ill. I gave my sympathies and left their garage-cum-new house. On the way home Chris was intent on blowing out the rest of my brains with his brand new, very loud, stereo. It went straight through me and grated my poor head, really hurting. At Make-Me-Rich, with exhaustion swirling around me, I staggered down the corridor. Aunt Sarah and Uncle Arthur's bedroom light was still on. I went into their room and chatted for a while before telling them. I expected them to get angry or to say that they always thought that I would, or to try and talk me out of it. We talked for ages.

The next day, the day after the bombshell, was a really quiet day. Pay day again. I accidentally took the staff pay with me to see Dr. Jay Stevens with Aunt Sarah. How potentially embarrassing – going to see a doctor when there was definitely nothing wrong with me. Still, I told him all he needed to know. Should I have asked him if Hodgkin's disease was hereditary, that my father's brother had died of it? I came away with a prescription for more pills and things. Back to the farm by 12.00 pm and I remembered to pay the staff. Poor Dolfas, R28.00 for twenty-three days work. In Australia I was paid the equivalent of R1,200.00 odd for twenty-three days work, R53.00 a day compared to R1.20 for doing the same unqualified manual labour. String gave him some sad story about supposedly being absent and not telling me that he was not going to work some days in December. I had lunch, organised the irrigation, had a nap, and then went down to the river to tell Maruanda-the-Muppet to stop the pump. He looked really funny curled up like a dog on the ground asleep. I felt like quietly unhitching the pump and driving it away. Next to him was Thembisini curled up like his puppy. Jessie, the Labrador, licked their faces and woke them.

The staff seemed to sense a change in the way that their lives were to be managed as that night they celebrated in style. They must have drunk something lethal. Months before, I had given 'Old Tool' Maruanda a couple of bottles of wine that he polished off in a night with no apparent ill effect the next morning. That Saturday he was a wreck. He knew that he was tempting fate if he did not pitch up for work that morning as I had told him on four separate occasions not to come to work drunk. I even fined him in advance saying that if he did get drunk he would lose R10.00. I honestly did not understand the reason why any human beings would want to drink themselves into such a state.

Then again, perhaps I did.

6.00 am. He managed quite a good performance to start with. He and his 'on-duty' crony Tollie managed to get the pump down to the river and connect it up. I went down to rehearse our signals. Waving the right arm up and down meant put up the tractor revs. Waving the left arm up and down meant bring them down, and holding both one's arms straight above one's head meant that it was just right. They were three incredibly simple arm signals, which we rehearsed at length. The packing shed was about a mile away from the river so it was impossible to shout instructions but arms could clearly be seen. I drove the mile up to the shed to find that there was not enough pressure and that more revs were needed. I waved slowly and deliberately with my right arm. The pressure fell still further. He had put down the revs.

"He's got the signals muddled up," I thought, losing patience, and so waved my left arm. Within seconds he had uncoupled the tractor and was burning for home. I leapt into my bakkie seething, and for the first time I was really exploding, red with rage, my temper completely lost. I bellowed at him and told him to get lost and that I would do it. He sobbed and said that he would take it back. I could have killed the bastard and thrown his body into the river and nobody would have been any the wiser. He helped me to reconnect the pump. I carefully re-rehearsed the signals and sped back to the shed. Too much pressure; left hand wave... pressure down, too much. Right hand. Up a little. Right again. No response. I just could not bring myself to go down there again. I went under the shade-cloth. The girls were putting strings on the tomatoes in section three. Mbonambi was fantastic, working busily away with the baby strapped to her back. What on earth inspired her to stay in that pit, I did not know. Back in the shed I found that the irrigation pressure was much too low. Right hand – frantic waving... No response. I sped down to the river. The tractor vibrations had slowly moved the accelerator arm down. I stepped over the sleeping 'Mud' and propped the accelerator up with a stick. I tried the same signals back to the shed with Ndlovu with no response. Thinking that it would be better to risk leaving it on too high than too low, I hoofed Maruanda in the stomach as I left. He moaned but did not wake up, as it was probably just part of his own distorted sad dream. A mile later at the shed and the pressure was too high... Only two girls left working on the string. I had told them all of three times on the three previous days that they would be on duty that weekend. Only Rita and Mbonambi had turned up. The rest were all pissed as parrots. I marked them all absent – minus two days pay. R4.00 lost, phew...

Now iButho had his own story. He had been stabbed directly over the heart with a broken beer bottle. Luckily for him it was a bottle and not a knife. He was slobbering, staggering, slurring and soaked in fresh crimson live blood as he told me the story. The team that his football team had beaten two weeks earlier had decided to wreak their revenge. As the one that had scored the two goals, he was their chief target. He was a mess and urgently needed to go to hospital.

My sister Melissa Smith Wesson was arriving at Durban Airport at 11.00 am.

9.00 am I was panicking. Aunt Sarah would not let me go without breakfast. I gobbled down some porridge as she wrote me a list:

1) Collect Belinda
2) Drop iButho
3) Get prescription
4) Fill up with diesel
5) Collect Melissa

I steamed off to Summertime Stud with iButho ranting incoherently away next to me. He was heartbroken at the idea of me leaving. He was going to leave too, he'd be my horse boy, and he would follow me to the ends of the earth.

"Oh don't go! Make-Me-Rich needs you!" His physical and personal agony seared together. Arriving at Belinda's cottage, I was trembling badly. On auto, I kissed her and strapped her in. iButho's raving subsided somewhat in her presence and I made small talk until we reached Pietermaritzburg.

"When is your horse running? What are the odds?" The blood soaked iButho left us to go to the Black hospital at the other end of town. On the motorway things improved: Neil Diamond's *Jazz Singer*, UB40's *Present Arms* and we arrived at Louis Botha airport ten minutes early. We settled in for toasted cheese sandwiches and coffee.

Melissa's 507 taxied in. Examining each passenger as they walked down those stairs, we realised that we must have missed her as the cleaners were just going in. Another ten minutes and suddenly she appeared. Tears burst from my eyes, my chest went heavy, trying pathetically to blink them away, and we kissed and hugged. We bundled into the Mercedes and were soon back on the motorway.

"How's home? How's the cold? How are things?" We chatted gaily for miles, and then it came out, mile after mile of endless excuses. It was pathetic, justifying losing. It sounded understandable somehow, when the opposite argument was not there to be heard, it always did. All the way to Make-Me-Rich I babbled on. My little sister, she of all people had to know why I did it. All the facts, all the innuendoes, all the pressures, all the untruths, all the lies, all the people, all the advice, she had to know why I did it. Melissa was highly intelligent, sensitive and, although being the youngest in the family, was always someone who held authority. She listened intently,

"Shame, poor Joss, you poor, poor old thing," she sympathised at all the right places. In reality, as her older brother, I should have been interrogating her. Before that episode it had always been my responsibility to check that she had the right boyfriends etc.

We arrived back in time for lunch. Cousins James and Lyle and their gran Jean were there. Everyone with his or her drinks had settled down on the patio. The subject disappeared, as if it were a cancer. It never existed. James's trip to Europe, Lyle's exam results and brother Martin's wedding were all discussed at length. The same at lunch, gaily chattering.

3.30 pm. I took Belinda back as she had to work. I got back and crashed out.

6.30 pm. I was told to collect Uncle Arthur from the Polo Club bar and then Belinda. Uncle Arthur was just settling down to his third or fourth scotch and was understandably in no mood to be moved. I skirted politely around curt remarks by String and Mabel and eventually disappeared to collect Belinda. She was in bed, but dressed and furious because I was late. Belinda must have been at the point of deciding whether to dump me. I certainly had given her the run-around and it would have been the logical thing for her to do. She and any other woman would certainly have told me to 'get lost' if they knew about the despicable thing I had done to poor Beauty. The business with her stepfather suddenly dying, her mother being evicted from their farm, perhaps I was a last desperate hope. Angelically radiantly beautiful as she always was, we headed for the Polo Club with new confidence. With Belinda as my bait, Uncle Arthur did not stand a chance and came quietly and he chuckled away at the prospect of him and Belinda being alone in the back seat and being chauffer-driven.

Sunday. Ian England, the farm's other side neighbour, agreed to take over from me. Aunt Sarah pressed me to go down to Durban with them and I agreed. After all, there was going to be someone in charge on the farm. Yawning almost continuously I managed to drive the Mercedes down in one piece. Melissa and I were treated like VIPs, a week of lie-ins, lying on the beach, Jacuzzis, fantastic restaurant meals, expensive shopping bouts, pills and more sleeping. Although my recovery really started from my decision to quit, or rather the moment I actually quit, that week did me wonders. Being pumped with good food, sleep and medicine made a new man of me almost overnight. My conscience bothered me though. I wanted to phone and ask String how things were going. Did he need me? How was old Ian England was coping? On the Thursday we went back to Make-Me-Rich. I bumped into Ian and he blurted out almost hysterically,

"I don't see how you coped at all!" He was delighted to have me around to help with the day-to-day running of the farm. I finished a number of minor jobs around the farm. The first was the paddock fence that had been left half finished for about six months. In incredible heat, it was done by 4.00 pm. Soaked with sweat and exhausted, I came inside just as the problems with the tomatoes were starting. The sorter did not work and there was no water. I reluctantly sent Maruanda down to the river, with a due sense of dread and anticipation...

Quickly I packed my squash gear into a bag and hurried up the hill. Chris thrashed me eight games to nil. At least four of the games the score was nine love. Lyle was wind surfing, which was a pity as the two of them would be quite a good match. Lyle had played squash for his school. Aunt Sarah was ill in bed so us 'young' spent an evening playing backgammon and talking. Belinda and I left at around 11.00 pm. We fell into bed together and I slept like a log but Belinda, who had her mind full of the future, didn't; she was becoming as messed up as I was about the situation. She was determined to stay with me.

2.00 pm. I was saying goodbye to Melissa at the airport. For her the whole experience was the beginning of her own journey of her return to the country of her birth. She was to abandon a successful executive career in London and later to marry a South African. I must be allergic to goodbyes. I managed the whole thing without a hitch until I turned to leave. Two taps inside my head turned on full. If I tried to stop I would only blub some other time, so I was sitting there, in my bakkie, with big tears splashing down onto my green canvas trousers. To add to my anxiety, I then got lost trying to find the racecourse, which was where I had agreed to meet Belinda. I hated horse racing because of betting, because of the vast fortunes lost on gambling.

2.45 pm. I had found the place most likely to be the place in her instructions.

3.00 pm. Came and went. Needed to panic.

3.05 pm.

3.07 pm.

3.10 pm. I could get a message broadcast over the loudspeakers. I could shout like a lost small boy. I could... and then she was there, Belinda.

Her horse 'What a Joy' had not won and she was terribly upset about it. We got into the bakkie and got lost again trying to find her mother who was staying with her in a house at the top of some incredibly steep steps. After some mandatory beers and 'cousin-bonding', I dragged her away.

Christmas Eve, 12 Woolacomb Drive, the Kennedys' town house was beautiful. So if it was like that to go over the top, well, I could highly recommend it. I woke up at 6.30 am after having slept like a baby. I crept into the spare room and into bed with Belinda. We kissed and cuddled and told each other how madly in love we were with each other. At ten o'clock we went into Durban. Hugging each other in front of the auto bank, under an umbrella in the pouring rain. Peering in shop windows, dashing across wet busy streets. We decided not to go to the famous party on the South Coast and had a take-away pizza instead. We parked at the Blue Lagoon and watched the sea crash in, the efforts of the fisherman, the ships stacked out at sea, the mist lowering itself slowly down. We wandered in and out of the arcades, drank milkshakes and coffee and we squeezed into a photo booth. We laughed and kissed and kissed and laughed with the flashes. We spent more money and laughed. I loved to tuck my fingers just inside the top of her jeans. She was mine and I was hers. We took many photos of the beautiful panorama in front of us. It had been the most beautiful day. On the way home she found her way inside my trousers, leaving me desperately wanting to stop and make love; the reaction she obviously wanted. We arrived at the empty cottage and immediately ripped each other's clothes off in a wanton desire to experience each other's bodies again... It was glorious!

Christmas Day 1983

– No snow, no carols, no cheer, no real Christmas, just a ritual handing out of presents. Money spent like there was no tomorrow. I seemed to spend more than most and certainly more than I could afford in a mad frenzy to get the 'right thing'. I so desperately wanted to blend in, to be accepted and to be wanted. So the day was Christ's birthday. What a miracle. All those years ago, Our Lord and Saviour, Jesus Christ arrived on Earth. Born to die a terrible death on a cross so that we might all be saved. Died with his hands nailed to wood with a crown of thorns, which dug deep gouges into his head and a sword thrust into his stomach. He was born an ordinary man, in a very ordinary way, although his conception was not. When he died the sky turned black, there was thunder and lightning, and the curtain in the Inner Temple was split from top to bottom signifying that Christ's death had opened access for sinful man to Holy God. So Christ was born on Christmas day. Was it such a great day? Should we celebrate less on Ascension Day? Maybe we should all forget the 'Jesus thing' and blow all that money with a clear conscience? After all, does any of it go to charity? And all those people that diligently go to church, Christ's birthday, are they true Christians? What was the subtle difference in morals and ethical codes between them and good people of other religions? Good grief, there I was, twenty-four, relatively well educated, and I could not answer that. Maybe it required a crash course on the Bible. What did Jesus preach that was so different from what the Jews already had? So I did not know, I was a lost soul anyway, lost and insane in a maelstrom world. A mad, fighting, seemingly suicidal world in which I was just one more piece of driftwood. I was that piece of wreckage that had just broken away from the main body of security to be tossed into that churning sea of confusion.

Christmas morning and my darling Belinda was fussing about in a sexy red and blue almost totally see-through nightie. The white frill came to millimetres below where her knickers should have been. The female form is so deliciously tantalisingly beautiful, especially when well wrapped. I caught her in her room around the waist and lifted my hands up to her breasts and laughed into her mouth. I gently rolled both nipples between my thumbs and forefingers. Her hand darted into my jeans and we kissed as we held each other prisoner. We fell onto her bed as she unzipped me and, for the first of countless number of times that day, we joined our bodies together in another act of passionate love.

Babs and Andrew, Louise's younger sister and baby brother, appeared and concentrated on pestering me. Louise was working with the horses in between making tea, hovering and generally tidying around the cottage. I sat on the couch and crossed my legs. I put one ankle on the other knee, then the other ankle on the other knee. Then I chased Andrew under the table. Then I put in a light bulb; then, suddenly, she was ready. Stunning, gorgeous, amazing. Quite, quite totally sexually edible! Light blue cling-on, one-piece slacks and top; absolutely totally spectacular; I wanted to rip it all off and start again. What was totally amazing was that she looked like that for me.

We rattled and bumped at top diesel speed down the dusty roads and then on to the motorway to Durban. Down those long, long downs. Slowly up those famous ups. That was The Comrades Marathon Kingdom where men were men and boys gave up. Every time I went to Durban, my mind plotted the race, every hill, every bend, low gear parts, and the easy bits. I had run the whole race in my mind. Almost ninety kilometres and eleven hours to finish it in, maybe some day I would run it for real. Anyone that had finished the Great Race was a hero in his or her local community.

The Bluff, a suburb of Durban and more turkey, more beer, more snooker, more sunshine, and still more beer, more jokes and back on the road again. Then, the terrible pang of wanting to make love to her all the way home.

We arrived to find pretty Beauty, beautiful Beauty still fussing about in her sweet flirty way in the kitchen. Always things to be cleaned, ironed, folded, lovingly put away. Polish the furniture, especially the phone, and scrub out the loo. It was way past the time she normally would finish work. Perhaps she was hoping that I was going to come home alone...

"Belinda, missus, you are so lucky to have such a wonderful man," she purred.

"I'm not. I can be a real bastard sometimes..." Our eyes met for half a second.

"Yes, he is wonderful and I love him to bits. You are so lucky because when he's not out on the farm he is cooped up with you all day. Sometimes I am quite jealous of you! What do you two get up to?" Belinda laughed.

"No Medem – He is white and I am black!" Beauty's laughter was a shy tinkling sound.

"Ah, but with his gorgeous tan and your beautiful light coloured skin, you two could almost be cousins!" Belinda continued the joke, the two girls laughed together. I was going to add that we played Doctors and Nurses but after the sordid operation I had performed on Beauty, the joke would probably not have been understood by either of them.

Belinda and I started a game of backgammon, a kissing, touching, thinking, pretend game of backgammon.

"What are you playing?" Beauty asked as she appeared behind us, as we sat on the settee, with her apron off and ready to leave. She ran her fingers down the back of my neck and gently rubbed under my ear for half a second. It made the hairs on my whole body stand on end.

"Nothing," Belinda giggled, "We are just waiting for you to go so we can go to bed to make love!"

"You don't have to wait for me!" Beauty laughed sheepishly.

"Goodnight Beauty," Belinda commanded and, "We're off to bed now."

Beauty, with her out-of-bounds, exquisite, perfectly rounded, regal bottom, and radiant yet knowing smile, winked goodnight at me and made her way back towards the African compound. Glancing after her disappearing bottom, I first noticed the compound lights and a deep blue, full African moon through her now invisible skirt enclosing her tantalising rounded, otherwise naked calves.

Then I noticed the ironing shed door banging loudly in the wind.

"The shed door is banging. We will never get any sleep with that noise. I am just going to pop out to close it – won't be a second," I called to Belinda who was already naked in the bedroom. Beauty was waiting in the loo just off the front step. She grabbed me and pulled me in, quietly closing the door and kissed me passionately with both her arms around my neck. Quickly she undid the two buttons on her shoulders allowing her dress to fall to the ground revealing her glorious brown African nakedness. She was truly beautiful, a combination of all my fantasies rolled into one. I was an unsuspecting fly caught in her fateful trap. Without saying a word she put her hands under my shirt and lifted it over my head and then deftly she undid my belt and buttons and pushed down my trousers and pants.

"For just five minutes," she breathed softly, "this room is your England in a thousand years' time." I could no more have resisted her at that moment than fly to the moon even if I had wanted to.

"What about Belinda?" I whispered pathetically. She was also naked but between satin sheets indoors waiting for me to come in and make passionate love to her. Not just a quickie in a loo, but part of our eternal relationship.

"Stop, Beauty my princess, not here... not now." I could hardly make love to her and then casually go back in and make love again to my beloved Belinda; it was not possible even for the most hardened of lovers. Perhaps this was to be her revenge, to get Belinda to dump me when she inevitably found out. However, the point of stopping had long since gone as she firmly tugged at my eager member. She had put the tips of her fingers inside her own body and wiped her erotic wetness onto my tool. It was true that our arms and legs were virtually the same colour, but the beautiful brownness of her perfect, rounded breasts clashed harshly against my pasty-white muscular chest. Standing on her toes she rubbed her hardened brown aroused nipples against mine and then arching her back she gently led my forefinger between her legs to find her clitoris. With her other hand she pushed my face onto her right breast. I began sucking gently on that golden brown sand dune, her nipple hard as a button with pleasure, at the same time gently moving my wet finger around and around and back and forth. She began to moan softly.

"Yes, yes, more, more..." she wiggled with pleasure under my touch.

"***hg,Aargh..." She sighed heavily in ecstasy as I continued.

"*hg,Aaaargh!!!"** She almost screamed through my fingers that were then cupped over her mouth as her glistening shining radiant body quivered with her orgasm and then slowly relaxed. Still holding my tool, she pulled me roughly closer to her, the same way as I had cruelly done to her in the corridor.

"Now…" she began.

"No, Sleeping Beauty, my Princess please let's stop, what about Belinda?" Her one hand was running up and down my engorged tool and around my balls and the other scratching my back.

"We could make love properly in a bed another time, but please not here and not now…" I vainly pleaded.

She did not hear me. It was going to be there and then, just as she had planned.

"Please Beauty, anything…anything, please…" She lifted her one foot onto the loo seat and with her flat, pale, beautiful brown stomach touching mine, slipped herself slowly onto me. She revolved her hips slightly and moved up and down. Any pathetic attempt to resist dissolved, as it was exquisite. She kissed my face, her tongue darting in and out of my mouth. With her peach-shaped hips and perfectly rounded lovely breasts fixed against me, her kissing lips on my mouth, she was truly shiny-magically beautiful. She smelled of sweet sawn pine, of distant cornfields, of friendly barbecues, a husky distinctly perfect African scent. The primeval animal in me wanted the act to last forever but to add to her revenge, I ejaculated in seconds. For a few precious moments we stood joined together, holding each other's naked bodies. I had raped her and now she had raped me in return. Her revenge was complete, as I could not see my relationship with Belinda continuing and, although I felt the victim, I felt again that my life was worthless. Presumably that was how she had felt when I had desecrated her.

"Now Joshua, we are equal. I now know that I can take you whenever I want, but this is to be the last time. I know that you are human and that you have failings, but I am sending you out of this room to do God's work," she whispered coarsely as she pulled herself out of my arms. Her smile was angelic. In one movement she lifted her pretty dress back onto her pretty body, did up the buttons, touched me on the forehead and, without looking back, left the room. If only I knew what it was that God wanted me to do for Him so I could get started; although quite why he would pick a reject jerk such as me, I did not know.

Apartheid: the irony of it. I was supposed to be the White Master of the farm, being paid a fortune for my inadequate services. She was the Black Lowest-of-the-low, being paid a pittance. Theoretically she was at my beck and call, but in reality I had become her slave. She could demand sex from me where and whenever she wanted. She had said that there would not be a next time, but what if she were sitting naked straddled on me as I lay on my back and I was almost swallowing one of her luscious breasts in passion? Or what if the next time she was under me in my bed with her legs wrapped around my waist as we committed the crime and Belinda walked in when she screamed that scream of ecstasy? Belinda could tell the police, my Aunt and Uncle, and would undoubtedly leave me. Beauty only needed to tell iButho that I had twice raped her and he would immediately murder me, irrespective of the consequences.

What if she became pregnant? God – perhaps that was her deliberate intention. Belinda and I were careful to ensure that that was not the result of our lovemaking. Yet with Beauty there was no rubbery contraceptive and, with her fleshy tight erotic grip, I stood little chance – she was probably fertilised already. As the loser, I had to go, anywhere, I just had to disappear off the planet. As quickly as I could, I put my own clothes back on and stumbled into the ominous black weather.

I had completely forgotten the ironing shed door. Automatically I sprinted to close it and almost immediately a very drunk iButho and Mikeon came rushing towards me brandishing clubs and knives. Behind them our distressed women staff were clutching their naked wailing babies. I slowed to a walk, wondering what was going on. iButho spluttered that I had to come quickly and babbled that I must bring a gun. I was almost in the compound. He was incoherently babbling something about knives, killing and guns and then he lost courage and disappeared as we went past the stables. I thought I spotted the boy called Gun and bellowed after him,

"Gun, Woza-la!!" (Come here.) The figure disappeared and I rounded the corner into the compound to be confronted by at least ten demented, unknown and very drunk blacks. They were sweating profusely, all with knives twitching in their angry hands. Two could speak quite good English and demanded that I open all the rooms so that they could find and kill the person that had 'poked' one of their brothers. I tried to reason with them, my back against a wall, knives to my throat.

"These people have poked our brothers and they were hiding here. We must be revenged!" they screamed, their hatred and rage clearly visible in their sweaty, pulsing, fearful faces.

"When you find these people, are you going to kill them? You know that is illegal. You will be taking the law into your own hands." I desperately tried to remain calm.

"The law will not mind as it was the way of our people, they will say that it was fair revenge," a very large man who held a rusty panga reasoned.

"Murder is murder and is no more justified whenever you do it. If you kill these people it will be murder and you will be treated as murderers. You are acting just like savages. I come from England, and the only people that behave as you are now are mentally unstable **(Ed. You've got a nerve!)** and are put inside prison to protect themselves as well as everybody else. You are only justifying to me that you are a race of uncivilised barbarians who have no right to vote. Now if these people have murdered or raped your brothers then come with me now and we will call the police. If not, I will call the police anyway, and they can sort this whole thing out. If you are not all off the property in two minutes you will be arrested!" My fear increased rapidly and I had to get away. My stomach had twisted so I was in real pain. I tried to move through them as they closed ranks and pushed my shoulders with knives in their fists to press home their intent. I forced through with them walking just behind and around me jabbering about breaking down doors and killing. One of them was only about fourteen. Quite hysterical, he was flicking an axe about in an alarmingly dangerous, uncontrolled way. I hurried to a very frightened Belinda inside. She had been wondering why I was taking so long and was standing on the stoep waiting for me in her nightie. I explained quickly what was happening. The phone was not working so I sprinted the few hundred yards up the hill to the cottage and phoned the police. Chris and Louise were there and I left Chris trying to phone the Howick police to confirm that the Pietermaritzburg police had radioed them. I sprinted back down to find that the police had appeared almost immediately. They had been dealing with another complaint by Mr Peppard at the Polo club. However, the black people causing the disturbance had mysteriously disappeared. I said I thought that they had all gone back up to the Polo club. I was leaving with the police to go there when Chris turned up with Louise. Louise was to stay with Belinda while we went up to the club. When we arrived Peppard came lumbering towards us.

"I have a riot gun that can kill nine at once!" he threatened.

A police van driven by a sergeant pulled up, with the presumably innocent people that the rampaging blacks had wanted to kill or at least wreak their revenge upon locked in the back. Police Constable Van Duisdoo stomped up. He was also the other adjoining farmer whose property abutted onto the Polo club ground. He wanted to wait for the station commander.

"Take that you bloody kaffir!" Duisdoo randomly promptly punched one of the terrified huddled figures in the face in the back of the police van without any reason.

"Why don't we look around the compound to see if we can find the real criminals?" I suggested, almost trying to protect the people from further indiscriminate violence. It had started to drizzle.

"Well, they are not here," Duisdoo drawled with finality.

"What would you know? We have not looked in all the rooms," Peppard argued. I had already said that to the Constable – that we should look in the rooms while we waited for the station commander. Station commander Van As arrived. He was a dishevelled disgrace, with shabby dirty denim shorts, a dirty Tee shirt and a revolver sticking out of his back pocket. He could not speak Zulu or English, an embarrassment to the forces of law and order. However, he did, in the midst of the tête-à-tête, take time to mutter sweet nothings to his beloved and betrothed on his two-way-radio.

From what I could gather from the conversation, they were going to break from tradition by not assuming the man's name after marriage and hyphenate their names – hers being Jurgenina Hoelle. Mr and Mrs Koojie Van As-Hoelle, truly a force to be reckoned with – people would leap aside.

Inside one of the rooms, lo and behold, there sat the barbarians. Except they were somewhat subdued, very unlike the raving lunatics they had been only minutes before. The only people that Station Commander Van As's ordered to be taken away were those with no permission to be there which was adjudged at his apparently random discretion.

Boxing Day and Chris was in Louise's trampoline/bed and I was in Belinda's. We awoke bright and early. Chris announced that we should start drinking straight away. By 8.30 am we had had three cans of beer each. By 10.00 am we were onto our eighth and then went into town to pick up some things, ninth and tenth on the way. We locked ourselves out of his bakkie outside the chemist. After drunkenly trying to break in, we gave up and used the chemist's phone where we had just bought a film to ask Chris's father Alistair to bring the spare key. He was at home just forty minutes drive away if he drove at ninety all the way. In the meantime we succeed in breaking in. Hoping to miraculously catch Alistair on the road coming in the opposite direction, we set off for the cottage. We missed Alistair and were immediately in more trouble because we had forgotten the ice. The journey back into town was fast, very fast. In my diesel bakkie I could manage a huge column of dust behind, mainly because of the upward downward contact the vehicle had with the road. But in Chris's bakkie we careered along with very little control at around 120 miles per hour! We went straight to the bottle store and straight back. It was past lunch and we must have been past fourteen and well past counting anyway. Louise asked me to slice up a watermelon and in doing so I sliced off a fair part of my index finger. With blood spurting everywhere, Chris was covered, as I showed off my gory new party trick. My hands were soon bright red. I staggered down the hill close to collapse. No sooner had I got there than Chris appeared, having driven round, with the next round of beers. He mercilessly drove me back to the girls at the cottage in my torn jeans covered in blood and now totally inebriated. With a terrible sinking feeling that I had hurt Belinda, I shrank back down the hill again. I lay on my bed for a while, my head spinning furiously. Then kneeling over the loo I was violently sick. Great, at least three pints came up. I shaved, brushed my teeth, put on clean clothes, bandaged my finger, and set off up the hill again. I found Chris and we retired to his bakkie and discussed the injustice of it all.

Inside Belinda was crying fit to bust. She thought I had left for good. I comforted her and then set about making the BBQ. It went well to start with. We chatted for ages during which time it almost burnt out. I heaped on more charcoal and then foolishly splashed on some petrol. It exploded into flame, which leapt up my arm. I ran back into the house using my other hand to try and put it out spraying blood everywhere again. I had badly burnt my hair and shoulder before I was able to put it out. Belinda and I decided to abandon the party and she drove us down to Make-Me-Rich. We fell asleep almost instantaneously in the spare bed.

Sleep...

The dark depths of one's subconscious where one's mind goes its own way, inventing strange and gory adventures in vivid colours that make them more than real. The worst dreams are when one is awake. Out of my unconsciousness, I was suddenly awake, alert and sitting. There was a muffled noise outside my door. I leapt up and ripped it open. A large familiar black man stood in the corridor holding a rusty panga. Unthinking, my leg muscles instinctively exploded and my heel struck him heavily on the chin. A sickening cracking noise as his neck broke and he slumped to the floor. I picked up his panga and ran to my Aunt and Uncle's room. Too late – blood everywhere – they had been brutally murdered. In the murky blackness of the house, the whole situation was clear to me. The war had begun. I grabbed jeans and a jacket from my room and slipped into them. The front and back porch lights were still on. I found a pen torch and some boot polish and switched off the mains. I dived out the front door and rolled as far as the first bush. The night was inky and starless. I could hear whispering Zulu. I slapped polish onto my face and hands. The voices wanted to know if they were all dead. I whispered coarsely in Zulu,

"They're all dead!"

"OK, let's do the Armstrongs." A torch came on and they trotted past me towards the shade cloth. Six of them, up the hill. I had done it a thousand times before, but that time, barefoot and in total darkness, I had to get there before them. I stumbled into the cottage moments before the black figures and locked the door behind me and grabbed the phone but it was cut. I woke Belinda, Chris and Louise. Louise started to scream and Chris clamped his hand over her mouth. There was a loud crunching noise outside as glass shattered. The bakkie was being smashed! There were terrible noises from the stables. The horses whinnied and screamed and thrashed against the stable doors. The bastards were killing them too. Chris took command – he had been in the army.

"Louise and I are going to try to get to the main house. We must warn them. We stand no chance together. Joss – We'll meet you at the Imperial Hotel in town tomorrow. Goodbye and good luck!" There was no time to argue, as there was a crashing at the back door. Windows were being smashed in, shrieking and shouting outside. Chris grabbed Louise's wrist and dashed into the kitchen. The large lounge bay window was being smashed in and a black body started stumbling through. I smashed my panga into his head and it lodged there as he collapsed dead in the window frame. Belinda was already in Louise's room, screaming for me to hurry. I sprinted for the door and she locked it behind me. I picked up the bedside table and hurled it through the window. I threw a blanket over the edge and we bundled after it. Almost immediately we were running, crawling, scrabbling, and falling down the hill with screaming, screeching and hooting blacks chasing behind us. Ahead Make-Me-Rich was burning; a huge red bonfire as the thatch roared high in the black night. A red ripple of flame was flowing, jumping, skipping across the shade cloth. Some of the poles ignited and burst into flame as lone torches. With the flames in front of us our enemy could see us so I pulled Belinda to the left towards the McDonalds' place. We crashed into a barbed wire fence and tumbled over it, falling onto stones and thorns, our hand, knees and faces bleeding. We stopped and I pulled Belinda to the ground, my hand over her mouth, my breathing laboured, hers worse. In the darkness I heard them crashing towards us, high on the hill almost level with us. Pitiful screams came from the McDonald house over the deafening roar of Make-Me-Rich burning higher and higher, gunshots from the Englands' place, the whole world was on fire. Hell was around us! Above the noise my ears struggled with the immediate silence around us. Then I heard it: stealthy creeping. We got up and start moving slowly, walking as quietly as possible down the hill. Our determined black hunters heard us, screamed with glee and started eagerly towards us. More sudden screams and then thuds behind us as we continued down the hill in a mad blind plunge. It suddenly occurred to me what had happened. We had run around the side of the gully and they ran over the top edge. In their haste to catch us in the pitch dark, they had fallen down the sheer drop, almost certainly to their deaths. No longer being pursued we stopped. I put black polish on Belinda's cut face. I could only imagine her terrified eyes through the blood and tears against my fingertips. From the light of the Armstrongs' burning house I could make out the Englands' pump house. We felt our way along for the wet bed of the Umgeni River. Pushing into the reeds we crawled along its bank, hounded like vermin. The whole country was under siege. Twenty-five million blacks all out to get even, all armed with hatred and revenge. Lie low until daylight, I thought. We had to make our way down the river until we hit something, a town or main road. Survival. My mind swam with alternatives. Our two wet bleeding bodies clung together in the reeds. At least it was warm. Survival. At least we were alive. We have survived the last hour more by chance. Now think. We had to get to Pietermaritzburg, had to get...

My mind erupted. I was lying awake, sweat was pouring from my body, saturating the bed. The siege of South Africa had started. The bastards arrested on Christmas day were only charged with Trespass! A body had turned up the next morning for identification. The rampaging horde had killed him, how totally barbaric! Where did civilisation begin with these people? What right have I to tell Mabel that it was right and moral for them to be able to vote? That black savage horde that went hooting and screaming down here on Christmas day was real. They were the same people in my dream.

COMRADES 1986

10,000 odd, black, white, men and women,
Huddle together, all comrades in arms now
Tracksuits, jumpers, plastic bags we wear
On this historic gallant day. Shuffle forward,
Finely tuned, enthusiastic determined athletes
On the street to the City Hall. The Start 500 metres
Now is our time, for seconds the cold is sealed out.
Cock-a-doodle-do and our heroic leaders race off!
Theirs is a different battle, fight for the country's pride.
Past spotlights – "Hello Mum" – the crowd cheering.
Onto the cold, dark, forbidding, endless, lonely road.
Abandoned, discarded old clothes tripping the unwary
Friends disappear, everyone starting at different paces
Exhaled breath becoming a haze-cloud above our army.

Slowly the African sun rises, the dew retreats,
The fun part is over, the real fight has started.
All the many months of training, the right food,
The correct psychological mental preparation
All for this single day – each of us combatants
Intent on defeating this mighty tarmac creature.
Some with genetic superiority and better training,
They attack the beast with purposeful vengeance.
Destroy or be destroyed, they run for their lives
Shoulder to shoulder, kilometre after kilometre
Taking and giving nothing to the grim enemy.
Hounded, followed, every grimace, every pain
All remorselessly reported on every TV station
To the millions watching fascinated at home.

Us mortals struggle behind, ours more earthly goals.
As mere footmen we trudge in their inhuman super wake
Glad of all passing signs, trees and many shouting fans.
As the sun rises to its full unrelenting, tormenting fury
We begin to suffer and wane. Blisters, knees and hips
The up hills are torture, they are far worse than imagined
Systems of replenishment, restoring re-energising bodies
Becoming less efficient with each passing water station.
Some of us gulp down too much, a fatal mistake later on
Others bravely dash by, not to disturb the momentum
Of the ever crucial flowing measured determined stride.
The fear and anguish of dishonour of defeat only when
The total agony of despair forces crumpled defeated
Runners to the unforgiving verge to stop collapsed.

For we who are left, there are no friends, no allies
We cling to that single hope, spark, that thought
Measure each stride, each gulp of healing water
Each gasp of racing breath. At absolutely all costs
The fearful, dreadful dragon must be conquered.
Stare doggedly at the tarmac of the beast's back
Concentrate grimly on stepping in the exact print
Of the noble yet expendable runner one pace ahead.
Come the inevitable mountain and he begins to flag.
Now! Force those desperate limbs! Ignore the pain!
It is the up hills that make the Silver-Time difference.
Glance at the top then fix on a spot three feet ahead
And hate it, beat it, devour and consume it, step on it!
Gods with their heavenly wings and potions can do it,
Then so must, can, nay – have to mortal, determined I!

The Grim Monster, the road; it sweats, it yawns
It is a mirage of illusion. It changes cloud into sun,
Hills into mountains, fellow runners into super athletes
It is a being capable of flicking the most strident runner
From its black, reptilian, loathsome, endless, living back.
It wakes slowly for each of us, grinning road signs
Its hateful teeth, eyes staring from over its shoulders
In every bank, in every glance over its terrible rump.
Yet we are like St. George with his noble holy lance
We stride on with brave heart and stumbling courage
It is partially afraid. Fear of fear is its weapon as it waits
It pounces! A runner is set upon, only to run through
The Demon-from-Hell, after being revived with a sponge.

Dripping sweat turned to crusted scaled harmful salt
On my eyebrows, in my eyes, and all over my face
Under my armpits, it rubs, sears and burns my skin
The skin on the end of my nipples has worn away
The acid salt burns into the flesh of the war wounds.
Between my legs is worse – it was never to be like this.
At each station I pathetically try to relieve the pain
The water is evaporated seconds after it is applied
The unforgiving merciless sun is at its peak, relentless…
Lesser mortals collapse desperately at the aid stations
Drink too much in an attempt to defeat the enemy
The liquid sloshes around in their defeated bellies
Incapable of resuscitating, dehydrated damaged
Exhausted all too frail limbs that can go no further.

Every cell, fibre, nerve, muscle, thought in my being
Focuses on the creature. It is alive, it moves, it thinks.
It plots. It has its own strategy. It sees inside my mind.
My being, my team, together strive to carry the whole
Towards the end. On my side every single human being
screams Mercilessly to me personally to finish the task,
To kill the beast, the monster from hell! Their energy flows
into my Exhausted soul, my spirit, and into my ailing legs.
For them, for me, my family, I whip my forgiving being on
I crash drunkenly through the line, eyes and fists clenched
To total euphoria, to total victory, to the ultimate glorious
prize
All pain, all agony, all hell – all gone, swept behind me.
Now in paradise I stand stationary; weeping, weeping
Gripping, clutching, wearing my badge of honour forever.

CHAPTER SIX

...Transient triumph...

The Comrades is a marathon of 89 kilometres run alternately between Pietermaritzburg and Durban every year. The vast majority of the valiant entrants take over ten hours to finish. There are some incredible, bionic super-fit, part-Gods that finish in five and half hours and there is one amazing Super-Hero, Bruce Fordyce, who has won it an astounding ten times. In the Fifties it was not unusual, however, for the winning time to be around seven and a half hours. I cannot say that I was ever possessed of a burning desire to run it as a child. In fact, I do not remember it at all. When Belinda and I first started dating, one of the first events we went to together was to see the start of the event outside the Pietermaritzburg City Hall. I was amazed at how many other apparent idiots were prepared to get up at five thirty to bear witness. I was even more amazed by how many participants there were. Although in all honesty, I do not think that I was inspired at that stage to have a go. At school, back in England, I had been singularly hopeless at virtually every sport. I would like to think that it was largely down to the dreaded lurgie, the bane of my life – asthma, although in truth I probably had zero ability... **(Ed – Rubbish, rubbish, rubbish, stop this negativity NOW and FOREVER!!!)** I wonder if Pinocchio could stick his conscience (Jiminy Cricket) in a matchbox at awkward moments...Jeez Ed, perhaps wallowing in self-pity is a form of mental masturbation...and I am not sure that explaining that desire is my intention. However, I do know that when I do have control of my mind I can focus on the positive... so on arriving at the farm and going for a jog with cousin James, I was mildly surprised to beat him home. The Kennedy boys were the exact opposite and had excelled in virtually all sports their school had to offer. James suggested that I give the "16 kilometres Magic Trophy" a bash that Sunday. Never before having run 16 kilometres, I set off to String's farm on the Friday to see if I could manage it.

"If you can manage the 'Magic' in under an hour, you are really flying," announced James with some scepticism. Of course I almost killed myself proving the point to myself that I could run to String's farm and back in an hour. So that Sunday, three days later I signed up for my first race. I was amazed by how skinny and apparently unhealthy the other runners all looked. After a seemingly endless period of milling about, the gun was fired and we were off! I don't remember the asthma thing being much of an issue; all I wanted to do was crack the hour. Consequently I was delighted to do it in 59.58 minutes!

James was determined that I continue my newly found running career and with a slightly more scientific approach to my training, the next big step was a 32 km race. I can't remember where I came but was astonished to come in under two hours. All runners at virtually all South African events live and breathe nothing else but the Comrades. I think that perhaps the very moment that I decided to have a go at "The Thing/ the Beast/ the Marathon" was at Mike Dixon's wedding up in Cumbria, when I met his friend the rugby legend Billy Beaumont, captain of the England rugby team, and his opening line to me was,

"Have you run the Comrades? ...and if not why not...?"

"No..., Billy...," (but I've had a go since!)

The furthest I ran in the first year was 42 kms, a standard marathon, which I did in about three hours twenty minutes. As any idiot novice, I ridiculously calculated that I would be able to therefore do the comrades in seven and a half hours, a Silver Medal. 42 kms is not even half way in the Comrades! Still, in my ignorance, I thought I could do it. Well, things did not go well from the start. It took me over ten minutes to cross the start line as there were over 10,000 runners. Strangely, because of the continuous impact on the knees and hips, running down hill can be as damaging as running up. When I finally did reach half way, I knew I was not going to make it; it was just a question of finding an appropriate spot to collapse in. I tottered along with a nice space approaching. I was about to pull in and die when a loud authoritative female voice boomed,

"You can't give up here! We are waiting for our son and we don't want you giving him any ideas!"

I staggered pathetically on. Then a bakkie passed with a load of fallen fellow Comrades. The sad forlorn looks on their faces could equally have been those on soldiers being carted away to be executed. I realised that, as dire as I thought I felt, I was not ready for that. So I decided on a tactic of staggering and falling down hills, walking and stumbling along the flats, and, if necessary, crawling up the hills. Although I did manage something akin to a gait as I stumbled past the Kennedys' car as the whole family cheered fiercely.

Not surprisingly then I was not physically able to get out of bed for three days. Belinda even had to get me a bedpan. Now at this stage, any normal citizen would have realised that the venture was only for the bionic. Not I, oh no – I just had to say I was going to have another go...

It is virtually impossible to convey that feeling of being totally fit and at ease with one's own body and to release one's mind as one runs along. I remember one ultra-distance marathon that, with hindsight, was too close to the following year's Comrades. It was the Escourt 51 kilometres. To get there I vaguely knew it was past Mooiriver, somewhere on the way up to Johannesburg in northern Natal. I was to pick up my black friend Simon Mkize and his mates up in the middle of Pietermaritzburg to take them to the race. They did not show up so I reluctantly set off on my own.

Some of the rules that were regularly imparted upon us white folk in South Africa were:-

1. Never give anyone lifts
2. Never pick up black passengers
3. Never, ever black hitch-hikers

and absolutely

4. Never, ever black hitch-hikers in the middle of nowhere

and on pain of death

5. Never, **never**, ever, **ever** black hitch-hikers in the middle of nowhere and in the middle of the night otherwise one will be chopped to bits and used for black voodoo-magic mootee and eaten!

So I was absolutely delighted when I stopped to find that the lone hitch-hiker on the side of the highway was Simon. Although it was not the middle of the night – closer to 5.00 am, but it was still pitch dark. He had missed his bus into Pietermaritzburg and was hoping for a long shot to the race. Simon had been running for decades and once came in the top ten of the Comrades before 1975 when blacks were not allowed to run. He was just ushered past the finish line without a medal. He is undoubtedly one of my greatest heroes. He has, however, run it officially seventeen or eighteen times since then. Simon met his friends there. One had come in the top five the year before and was determined to win it that year. At the gun they set off accordingly, with that in mind. The race was mostly on dirt road and there were only about three hundred runners. Simon and his friends were way ahead of me and initially I could just vaguely see them in the dust. It was one of those marathons in which one could run for kilometres and kilometres without seeing another competitor. The watering stations were just blokes with jugs in the back of their cars. My breathing was perfect and my training had just peaked. I popped the old Smith Wesson running machine engine into overdrive and started to eat up the kilometres, slowly overtaking more and more runners. The last four kilometres were down a long hill into Escourt town centre. I was able to more or less do a long sprint to the finish, overtaking another half dozen or so. Our hero from the previous year had slumped to twelfth and miraculously I was nineteenth. I was immediately not just the taxi driver, but also suddenly one of the chosen few.

That year I managed a standard marathon in less than three hours. I was doing 200 kilometres training a week since January. There were few races in Natal I did not enter. Certainly my whole life then revolved around the Comrades. All my friends ran, everything I ate was carefully considered as to its impact on my running. Every time Belinda and I went down to Durban to see her family, we drove slowly along the Old Road so that I could memorise every bend and hill on the route. I had drawn up a map of the route with the exact times that I wanted to be at certain locations. The original plan was to start ten minutes ahead of schedule, in other words, if I were to run at a constant pace throughout the race, I would finish in seven hours twenty minutes. For poor Belinda and her Beloved Dad, the race must have been equally draining on an emotional level. They had to know all the back roads to avoid all the traffic in order to meet me at strategic points so she could pass me my much needed secret supplies. The secret "thing" was a triangular plastic container which one would rip open with one's teeth. They contained high-energy syrup. Of course I took on as much fluids as necessary at the many watering points. The one watering hole was superb; at the bottom of the torturous notorious Fields Hill there was a rain tunnel. I came out completely soaked and revitalised. There was still more than 15 kilometres to go and I was down to the bottom edge of my time allowed to get the legendary Silver. I desperately needed a pee. I knew that if I stopped I would have blown any hope of getting the medal and as I was sopping wet anyway, I thought no one would notice it dribble down my legs. Now even in training and other ultra distance marathons I still had not run further than 65 kilometres. So with 15 kilometres to go, I was effectively running on empty. It is extraordinary as to how fragile one gets in such circumstances. I think that if anyone were to have stepped in front of me, I would not have been able to avoid crashing into him or her.

I knew I had to maintain the length of my stride, the ever-growing crowd screaming that a silver medal was still possible for me. I was running for them, with them, drawing strength and determination from them. Entering the stadium was extraordinary, even though I was 1200 or so places behind the legendary man-machine Bruce Fordyce, I still felt the same incredible exhilaration from the baying crowd. Every single one of them wanted me to make it. They screamed and screamed and my totally exhausted body responded. Shame, one of the most frustrating difficulties in those last few hundred metres was having to dodge the poor bastards that had given up. If only they could implore their exhausted bodies to make one final surge, they too could have achieved the desired medal.

The man with the gun, the man with the huge towel, the many, many men with their huge media cameras, the huge timing machine, my every fibre of my body pumping, driving, pleading, begging my legs to finish.

Across the line, the medal placed around my neck, I was unable to control the floods of tears in my own pride. Beyond my family's wildest expectations and belief, Joss the asthmatic, bow-legged baby, who had never achieved anything at school now had Silver in the Comrades. I had conquered "Inchanga", a hill (or rather a mountain appropriately translating from Zulu as "The Edge of the Spear"), Botha's Hill, Field's Hill, Cowies Hill, and Polly Shorts amongst many others.

Simon finished about an hour later. His proud strong arm on my shoulder again brought more tears of joy. In the car back home to Pietermaritzburg, he could not stop telling Belinda how incredible her "man" was. Uncle Arthur was the same. He made me feel ten metres tall with his continual boasting to his friends that his favourite nephew had a Silver in the Comrades. They were both right, they and the others I showed the medal too. Just completing the Comrades put me into a rather special category of heroic human achievement. Since the dawn of mankind the amount of people who have run 89km still only numbers in the thousands. More people have got PhDs at universities. More people have been CEOs of multinational corporations. More people have been multi-millionaires. More people have been members of royal families. Running the Comrades has made me special. Nobody can ever take it away from me…

I defeated the Comrades, I defeated my chronic asthma, I defeated the fact that I only have one kidney. I defeated all those people who said I could not do it.

My time was seven hours, twenty-nine minutes, fifty-nine seconds;

I achieved a silver medal by one second.

CHAPTER SEVEN

...On Licence...

... to succeed, gain wealth, popularity and fame ...

Years later and Belinda and I found ourselves in darkest England running our own little village shop. After I had left Make-Me-Rich I worked in a supermarket for a few years in Pietermaritzburg. Belinda and I were married for four years before we then decided to move because on the day of the referendum as to whether or not to include the Coloureds and Indians in the government, there was a corpse on the front step of the shop I worked in. The Liberal 'Let's-All-Have-One-Vote' party were defeated by the Raving-Loony 'Let's-Go-Back-To-Total-Segregation' party.

It was our dream that had come true and nothing was going to stop us. Ours was going to be the best little store in the village, and also the best little shop in the country. We were going to make it special by stocking unusual South African wines and spirits as well as sticking to all the favourites the locals needed and loved. As a result our shop was well known and well liked in the community. In the end we stocked over seventy exclusive South African Estate wines as well as a huge selection of other booze. We often had wine tastings, usually in the village hall, that were always well attended. We had an excellent selection of always fresh fruit and vegetables, a good display of frozen foods, our milk we sold at cut price to get regular customers in. We did extremely well with video hire, sold tobacco, chilled provisions and a wide selection of groceries.

We opened at 8.00 am and closed at 10.00 pm seven days a week. We worked extremely hard to try and make it work so it was just so depressing to find out that a staff member who had been working for us for some years had been stealing from us. In my mind I had thought over the trap I was going to set to catch her and had rehearsed what I was going to say to her when the police took her away. Even when they did, she had the last laugh, thanks to the wonderful society we lived in. I was struggling, and losing, to make a living out of the shop. My family lived in a tiny flat with no garden. I worked on average a hundred hours per week and only managed one holiday in six years. I bought all my clothes second hand so that I could afford to buy my children new and fashionable clothes. The thief on the other hand, boasted about how much she spent on clothes. She would not go to prison; she would not even be punished and would certainly not repay me for anything she had stolen. Betrayal? In my humble estimation, she should be shot.

Imagine one were in a queue at the head of which there was a heap of dead people that had just been shot by one of the many men armed with semi-automatic guns. The dilemma is simple. Just spit on the picture of Jesus ... or be shot. One arrives at the front of the queue telling oneself one is a Christian and that one is prepared to die for one's belief. Now reality. My wife, my children, and my life's work, what would happen to them... my mouth is dry... but then again it is only a story and there is no queue. Imagine she and I were alone on a deserted island. She is an attractive woman and I'm a man. She is happily married and so am I. I love my wife Belinda with all my heart and soul and all my might. I love her beyond reason, beyond beauty, beyond time. She is my being, my identity, my sanity, and my alter ego. She is my reason for living. Still... Belinda and this other woman's husband are somehow not there. It is a beautiful island and there is nothing to worry about. In the same way that I would like them to tell them to shoot me, I could only love her as a sister, but then where does fidelity really end? She is not my sister and presumably we would share the same hut. Secretly my corrupted mind had always desired her, but perhaps only just to talk to and to brush against as we were occasionally socially squeezed together. Presumably after a period on the island we would become familiar with each other in a purely platonic bodily way. Presumably in the same way we would probably have glimpses of each other's nakedness. Perhaps we became so blasé about each other's bodies that we began to take them for granted. I would wash her back in the bath... perhaps if I were to help her achieve an orgasm without actually having sex... If I were to keep all my clothes on, like a doctor performing an operation, do these thoughts in themselves constitute betrayal? Is it possible to have sex without full penetration? And if so, is it classified as sex or just heavy petting or foreplay? If we had convinced each other that somehow our mutual partners were not coming back, would that be grounds for allowing the relationship to slip into the physical? Perhaps we might have fooled each other into believing that if they were to one day reappear, we would simply go back to them and that would be that. Is my mind already irretrievably over the edge? I had never had an adult relationship with other women in which sex was not one of the ingredients. So was it only natural to confuse friendship with sexuality?

In the same way, I had never been able to sort out the issue of racism in my mind. I was strongly of the belief that racism had nothing to do with colour. People of different ethnic origins that find themselves in a new culture should, in my view, attempt to adopt the culture of the country they had chosen to live in. That of course might sound like nonsense to many people. I would not have liked my daughter to marry a man that never washed, had rings and tattoos in every part of his body, smoked, drank, was an atheist etc. but was white. Perhaps the truth that I would not admit to myself was that I hated black people but that I loved her... it was hardly surprising then that I found myself going insane. Perhaps I should have stuck to the original plot and written a book on 'The Shop-keeping Business' rather than 'How to go to Insane'. The surviving conscious part of me still believed neither to be the case... In reality I know little about shop-keeping, or not enough anyway, and who ever heard of a manual on how to go mad, for God's sake?

Selling our House

Years of snipping and dipping to get the hedge box-shape
perfect.
Lawn and edges – white paved front path, trees and garden
– perfect.
Shrubs, and flowers, wild birds; the frogs, sandpit, the
paddling pool
Garden furniture and bird boxes all perfect, inside everything
perfect.
The children's playroom with its giant smiling friendly
penguin, perfect
The kitchen complete with cutting-boards and cupboards,
just perfect.
Our dining room with its spotlights, striking carpet and
pictures, perfect
The mirror in the hall and the cupboard I diligently made – all
perfect.
The living room, so cuddly, so snug, so comfortable, so ours
– perfect
Our bedroom, our bed, our passion pit, our shrine to our love
– perfect
The office, my favourite room, my books, my history charts –
perfect
The children's bedroom and toys, all so familiar, so friendly –
perfect
So why then did we have to sell?

The English Weather

Clear blue autumnal days, leaves gently swirling,
Beautiful blues, yeasty yellows, opaque oranges,
Glorious greys, magical mauves, raspberry reds,
Tingling temperatures – summer's slowly sighing.
Winter gets ready, joy, colour, happiness – going.
Old and forgotten coats repaired – ice sharpened.
Deadly – dreary drizzle, snow secretly suspected,
Fat fog to follow; mild-mannered mist make man
Forget fellow forest fighters to fend off the freeze.
Fox frantically find faster furry frightened food.
Badgers burst boxes burrowing for bad bread.
Dear diving doves die, hibernating hedgehogs
Fearsome furious floods, Wild West wet winds
Life squeezed from the wet weary woodlands.

CHAPTER EIGHT

... insane sanity ....

One of the many mini adventures I had adding fuel to my James Herriot of shopkeepers' image. Let's start with the high point; it should not have happened to any shopkeeper. Imagine tearing down North Thames Bank Lane at seventy miles per hour in the back of a police car in hot pursuit of some villains.

The day started as usual at six-thirty. It was supposed to have been one of my rare days for a lie-in but Frantic Fran had forgotten that it was his turn to do the honours. Presumably his thirteen alarm clocks had let him down again. It was his morning to do battle with the early morning deliveries. So wearily I climbed out of bed and went down into the fray, only to find that the Little Tyke was in fact there, only just behind schedule. Actually, he was normally very reliable and was certainly one of the otherwise permanent part-time crew. One had to be well-hard to be able to deal with the enormous fruit and vegetable order, the milk and the bread orders. So after a bit of a cheerful reprimand, back to bed I went.

Now Thursdays always had the same routine, so there was no munching through the juicy bits of suppliers, customers and staff, although Jenny wouldn't forgive me if I forgot to mention that she was propositioned by a man who must have been at least a hundred! She was one of the old reliable stalwarts who had worked for us for ages. Customers often chatted her up but that was a record.

I was making tremendous progress with my 'Descendants of Gert Von Weillegh's' book. The hurry was to try and get it finished for brother Daryl's wedding. I was telling one of our suppliers, the infamous Ron, as in, 'Da, Doo, Da Da, Yeah, as she walked you home,' etc., that I was now up to three-finger typing. He said that in his youth he could type a hundred words a minute without looking at the keyboard. I said that I was up to three to four minutes per word. Ron was the cream, yoghurts, bacon and cheese supplier. He always arrived at the same time on the same day and his coffee was always waiting.

So that brought me to seven-thirty pm and I was typing away furiously. Yes, I really ought to have done that course. I was supposed to be at the Youth Club Annual General Meeting for seven-thirty. I quickly saved everything and closed down the computer. The last thing I wanted was for my own youths to fiddle with my work and set off only to find Sharon, Tracy and Father Tim. Sharon was a gorgeous hunk of a woman – I had yet to decide on an appropriate nickname for her other than 'Darling, honey-bunch, petal, lover, light-of-my life etc.!' Belinda did not mind because at least our affair was out in the open! Actually, it was really just an elaborate game of customer care, to ensure their continued patronage. Tracy ran the Youth Club and was desperately always looking for stupid adults to volunteer for a fate worse than death by helping supervise the hoodlums/apprentice jailbirds. Everyone else turned up a statutory half an hour late, which I must remember for next time if there was to ever be one. All started politely enough with coffee and 'Uncle' Tim did a sterling job of handing round the Gateway mince pies. I was still enough of an animal to scoff down a few of my enemy, the competitor's products. Everyone agreed they were bad. The two girlies, Janette and Sue did a wonderful performance of giggling throughout. Things started to get interesting when Father Tim said that everything that happened outside the Youth Club building was not his responsibility. The village had become one big youth testing area. It never got seriously out of hand, but there was no shortage of petty graffiti, and other minor damage to property. I had already resigned from the Youth Club for that very reason. The club was just a poor cover for irresponsible parents to dump their delinquent children in the village on Wednesday evenings, Youth Club night, to create havoc. Alcohol was notoriously easy to get in the village, although I prided myself that my shop wasn't the source of the underage drinking. However I was delighted to find some allies who shared the same view I did. It ended quite amicably in that we did not come to blows. One evening when I was in charge, one apprentice villain thought it would be fun to use the table-tennis table as a trampoline so I gave him a friendly smack around the chops as a reward. His mafia-type father threatened to kill me until I showed him the damage his son had caused, at which point he threatened to kill his son instead when he got him home.

I returned home, switched on my computer, scoffed supper, some revolting Chinese muck – I had to remember to tell Belinda to cross it off my preferred list – and dived in. I was just at the delicious scrumptious part of the day where the rest of the world disappeared and it was just me versus my computer, man-to-man, head-to-head, when scurrying down the corridor came my beloved Belinda – what an amazing creation she was. To say I loved her would be a serious understatement. She was my being, my sanity, my alter ego, she was mine and I was hers, no apologies for repeating that at every opportunity.

"Joss, someone is kicking down a door in the high street!" she fretted. Down I hurried to find Janet, James and Julian and a few mates drunkenly staggering past. They were tame-teenage, local, upper-class types and otherwise customers of mine anyway.

"Kids, have you heard any banging?" I asked.

"No, but there is a disco in the Badger, it's probably coming from there," they slurred and staggered on so I retired inside and was sitting sensitively by the side of my pool as it were, deciding whether to dive in again, when again she came sprinting,

"There was definitely something going on downstairs!" On opening the door, I heard the noise for the first time and ran down to the street. Two youths were standing outside the closed off-license with their backs to the window pretending to look innocuous. Ugly Thug A was happily kicking at the window with the back of his heel.

"What the hell are you doing?" I screamed.

"And what are you going to do about it?" Even More Ugly Thug B retorted aggressively.

"Get the police," I shouted and sprinted into the Badger. The music was louder than Led Zeppelin on a loud day. I dialled 999 and bellowed down the phone at the top of my lungs. Nobody in the pub seemed to notice my conversation. The police response was fantastic and they appeared about two minutes later. His hands on the steering wheel and foot still on the accelerator, the local Police Constable, PC Metcalf peered up at me from the car,

"What's happened?" he demanded.

I pointed to the broken window and explained that it would be better if I identified the likely candidates so I got in the back of their car. I said that they were likely to be at the railway station so we zoomed up to it. No. Not there. We zoomed down Maidenbottom Road, past the Five-till-Late shop and back into North Thames Bank Lane and quietly past the recreation ground. My side window was blurred by rain so I could hardly see a youth sitting in a parked car. Another, which I thought might have been one of the thugs, was walking towards us. We drove back into the High Street and dropped one officer outside the newsagent and drove around to the car park. Nothing. It was beginning to look like a wild goose chase and the best the day would get, as far as the diary was concerned, would have been 'Had a ride in a Panda Car'. However, in the Otter and Weasel I saw, as we drove past, the person I thought I had seen by the recreation ground. I immediately said I wanted another look at the people in the car by the recreation ground. As we turned back into North Thames Bank Lane, the officer driving, Diamond Geezer of the First Order, William Metcalf and Fiona, his partner, give them both medals, immediately recognised the car as the one which the suspect had been sitting in. It had just started driving off without its lights on. Will started to flash his lights as the suspects' car sped up. Then he put the Beee-barp siren on – as you do when you are about to embark on a high speed car chase!

The bends at the end of North Thames Bank Lane where it started to go down the hill, any racecourse in the world would have been proud to have as their chicanes. The thugs realised that the only option was to escape and flew past the parked cars in a desperate bid for freedom.

'We've been rumbled! Step on it geezer or we'll be done for!' The thugs must have relished the prospect of a good old-fashioned car chase. Thug A's adrenalin pumping, he forced the accelerator down as far as it would go. Thug B's high pitched excited commentary;

"They're gaining on us, Rizzo, faster, faster you stupid idiot!"

At that stage 'Diamond' was babbling into his gismo,

"Send in reinforcements, we have them cornered in Southern Oxfordshire/ England somewhere!" and at the same time he was imagining himself talking to the villain driver ahead, "Don't brake into the corner – you will get yourself killed…!"

Anyhow, there I was sitting in the middle in the back leaning through between them. It was a damned sight more exciting than watching *The Bill* on TV! Cameras rolling, metaphorically speaking, and my heart in my mouth, or perhaps more accurately it was on the dashboard. Sadly the excitement ended as quickly as it started. Fortunately or unfortunately, Thug A's driving skills were not up to that sort of caper and he ploughed into the end of the fence on the sharp right hand bend at the bottom.

"Book-em, Danno!" I shouted. William and Fiona (heroes, diamonds, give them both OBEs) leapt out and unceremoniously ripped the villains out of the car and promptly cuffed them. Totally unsympathetic over the fact that Thug A's nose was spurting blood, the reject, he should have been shot there and then, although that would make things even more bloody, I sat in the car for a bit while they babbled into their gadgets that they had apprehended the low lives.

"All is under control, have apprehended suspects, no need for further assistance." The excitement had gone from his voice, almost routine. Out came the notebook and they began to interrogate the scum. The thrill over, I walked home. Belinda sleepily announced that in all the excitement she had nearly forgotten to tell me that Paul had phoned while I was out. He was on duty in the shop that night and as usual one of his responsibilities was to bring the signs in after we had closed. He had succeeded in smashing the front window while bringing in the big revolving heavy sign.

Minutes later, and still deciding whether to dive in again, Belinda shouted that police had arrived. The whole incident from beginning to end could not have taken more than twenty minutes, however the statement took over an hour and a half. Among many questions and details PC Metcalf asked me for my date of birth.

"25th October" I informed him.

"The anniversary of the Charge of the Light Brigade," he enthused. He collected medals from Light Brigade soldiers and was an expert in great British military disasters and as such was also interested in Isandlawana and Ulundi. A few cups of coffee later, I had shown him my family tree, which although did not include any members that had fought in those particular battles, had certainly been involved in many others in South Africa.

Weeks later, He phoned to report that those particular thugs were not in fact trying to break into the Off-Licence, but hey, anyone that is ugly and resists arrest deserves to have their noses broken and be put in handcuffs. He said it made filling in the paperwork difficult, but it was well worth it for the adventure. William, and to a lesser extent Fiona, often popped in to keep a watchful eye on the shop. Fortunately we did not need their services too often and we had an excellent rapport with them regarding the sale of alcohol and cigarettes to minors. I often wondered what did make those particular thugs speed off in such a guilty manner and, of course, whatever happened to the real criminals who smashed in the off-licence window?

CHAPTER NINE

... sane insanity ...

My Birthday party, another sublimely ridiculous tale that James H would have been proud of. Instead of a birthday cake, the story revolved around an enormous live Halloween pumpkin.

6.30 am and I was out of bed, odd socks, to do battle with the milk delivery. No, this is not another one of those 'get-out-of-bed-at-10.30-in-time-to-feed-my-Persian-with-a-little-smackeral-that-two-thirds-of–the-world's-population-would-envy-for-Christmas-dinner' type of story. Not flat soled shoes because it was impossible to push a loaded milk trolley up the ramp without rubber treads. That morning I had to swap one of the trolleys with one from the basement because one wheel had died. It involved a lot of grunting and groaning and doing my Samson/Hercules impersonation. Yes, they were very heavy! People said I looked like John McEnroe and look what grunting did for him! People also said I was weird and eccentric – call me anything, but don't call me 'stupid'! It made me as mad as calling Pamela Anderson 'Babe!' I filled up the milk, putting half the delivery in the downstairs fridge and brought in the bread and the huge fruit and vegetables delivery, and sneaked upstairs in time to pretend to be asleep. Just in time, as six-year-old Feline-Felicity and eight-year-old Terrible-Tillie came bursting into Belinda and my room armed with my birthday presents and then they proceeded to rip them open. To their surprise, they were what there were when they wrapped them up! Flick had her own version of the Birthday song,

"...don't waste it, don't taste it, stick your head down the loo!" To my surprise, my presents were things I really wanted; a book on the Boer War, one on Feudal England and one on medieval biographies.

8.00 am. "Oi, Joss!" bellows John, the Frozens' deliveryman. He was standing just below our bedroom window in front of the shop. There was no delivery scheduled for that day but he still wanted his tea. I once asked him what was the meaning of life and after some thought he said “Snowking”, his employer, which I thought was incredibly profound. His life on a Friday revolved around the cuppa he was served from us first thing in the morning and not having a delivery for us was not going to put him off. So while I quickly dressed, Belinda, my darling and totally indestructible wife, made him his cuppa. Taking it down, I found that Ron the cheese man was also strangely ahead of schedule. While John told another verse of his Bruce and Sheila joke, I made Da-do-da-da Ron his coffee, pouring away last Friday’s milk before it had a chance to bite me.

8.30 am. There’s English Summer Time and Greenwich Mean Time, well there was also Works-for-Joss Time which was a standard statutory at least ten minutes late. In stormed the troops. Jim-bob ‘kill-em-with-my-bare-hands’ and Jeffrey ‘always wears a tie’ and the sound of semi-automatic price guns echoed across the store zone. Leaving Ron to John’s vulgarities, I disappeared downstairs to the relative safety of my office before the punch line, “…Bruce screams… ‘I’ll get the firewood!’” John was also a bouncer at a nightclub in Maidenbottom and was suitably tattooed from his shaven head to his toes.

10.30 am. On the dot, in floats the Legendary Linda and the front line troops were still doing battle with the cheeses. In a few minutes she showed the boys how it was done and the remains of the delivery slipped into its rightful places on the shelves. I popped over to the library to return my books on their last day. I also posted a letter to Daryl who had returned to live in South Africa now that Nelson Mandela was in charge and posted some floppy discs to a fellow genealogist who had shown me how he was also descended from William the Conqueror. Genealogy had gone beyond hobby into something of an obsession to me, much to Belinda’s dismay. On a few occasions I had forgotten the time and only returned to bed in the wee hours.

11.00 am. Rod and Chas came in to attempt to make an appointment to play squash with me. When I mentioned that I was officially over the hill, they let me off. I would need a lot more practice and training before taking them on again. The previous time we played I could hardly hobble for weeks. They delighted in calling me ‘The Village Pirate’ due to my liberal pricing policy, but hey, they had no idea what my rent, wages, bank charges, interest, shrinkage, rates, solicitors' and accountants' charges were. But they had to concede that one couldn't get much cheaper than free which was how much some of my videos were.

1.00 pm. Staff all abandoned ship, or in Linda's case go to lunch. It was one of the highlights of the week, the 'how-much-am-I-worth-this-week' moment - haggling in its truest form. On the plus side were enthusiasm, sweat and tears and on the minus side were the times caught loafing, unscheduled coffee breaks putting frozen stuff in the fridge and visa-versa, pricing stuff at half the cost price... Sometimes they should have paid me!

1.05 pm McVitie Biscuit deliveryman arrived with a hundred-odd cases which was always good for a laugh when one was on one's own.

1.59 pm McVitie man, sweaty and cross, drove off.

2.00 pm Linda arrived back.

2.05 pm Simon, Linda's husband, arrived with Penny, their baby.

2.30 pm Linda and Ollie and Fran and I started putting out the biscuits.

5.30 pm Changing of the guard, Linda home and was replaced by the Mighty Ben, nicknamed 'Adonis' because he was into slaughtering and maiming helpless cuddly creatures which was where he was off to the next day with his gun. He was hot on not letting under age squirts buy their booze from us, which was essential on a Friday night. It was a sort of revenge thing as he had just turned eighteen.. .

8.00 pm We were just shutting the door, when in came two sad-looking boys. "The bevvies are this way," announced Sad Boy A.

"You're not eighteen so you can get out," I instructed and to Sad Boy B,

"And how old are you?" I asked accusingly.

"Eighteen..." He answered almost reluctantly.

"Can you prove it?" I demanded.

"No, but I've been served in loads of places," he proclaimed as if that were proof.

"Not in my shop," I declared, and as I was not in any mood to dilly-dally as eight-fifteen was calling. I repeated to Sad Boy A,

"I told you to get out of my shop," and grabbed him by the sleeve. He did his best 'Look-Down-At-My-Hand' menacing look, which only made me angrier and I proceeded to march him to the door. Dom, another village Diamond joined in the fun by helping to throw them out the door, literally.

8.20 pm I arrived breathless at The King William III's Head armed with Jeffrey's champion mega pumpkin creation under my arm. He had carved it for Halloween to sit in the front window of the shop. It was frightening even to adults and that was without candles inside. Mike the Landlord initially did not take too kindly to the work-of-art glaring at him on his bar, but after William and Jessica arrived he mellowed and allowed it on our table. It looked really eerie with a couple of rapidly melting candles inside its evil eyes and shining through its menacing mouth with its serrated teeth. Quasimodo – the North Maidenbottom Bell Ringer (sorry Steve, only joking!) growled,

"I'll 'ave ut when u funus wi' ut," and proceeded to blunder drunkenly out into the pitch darkness with a fully loaded pumpkin head under his arm. Two pints of Guinness and our second bottle of Australian Chardonnay and I was recanting my now famous story of 'The Three Smith Wesson Boys at the Dinner Table'. I was vaguely aware of a descending silence, and as I arrived at the punch line, which involved the sound effects of the three of us in a full speed-eating sprint-gobble to get to the leftovers first, there was a terrible roar of laughter from the entire pub!

CHAPTER TEN

... brief inspired inane sanity ...

Mr Davies ambled in out of the English weather. It had been raining cats and dogs and we had just reopened after a power cut had forced us to close for three hours. He announced that that morning he had been in Athens where there was bright sunshine. He mentioned that he would rather be back there. I replied that he should look on the bright side. The English weather kept the English so English; it gave them strength of character, a sense of humour and, importantly, it keeps the non-English out. Let's face it, if it were not for the weather, the place would be crowded with other people. If anyone could tolerate the English weather, they simply become indigenous. I found it very reassuring that some characters in the village spoke of nothing else except the weather. Anywhere else in the world the conversation would be of the latest bombs, water shortages, food shortages, AIDS etc. Weather hardly amounted to something to seriously moan about. It was just conversation fodder. Seriously bad weather was, of course, something else. So fellow English, if it is raining on you, you're lucky – you're in England. In the days when I ran, I remember the total joy of running in the pouring rain... Maybe it was one of those necessary experiences to enable one to understand.

Hamish came to collect Linda, his daughter, at 5.30 pm at the end of her shift and did not like to hang around. One of the reasons I liked Ham was that he thought I was funny or at least gave a good impression that he did. James H could have had someone like Linda working for him. She could have been the charming receptionist or trainee vet.

"It must be 5.40 because the 5.30 staff have just come in..." I quipped to him as he leaned heavily on the counter.

"Heh, heh, heh, heh!" he chuckled.

"Linda is going to inflict terrible pain on you lot." The evening staff ambled past, nonplussed.

"Heh, heh, heh, heh!" The creases around his eyes and mouth folded in mirth.

"I'll know that the end of the world is getting close when the part-timers come to work on time," I said, continuing the line of thought.

"Heh, heh, heh, heh!" He held his stomach and spluttered.

"Maybe I should schedule them to start at 5.20 so that their late would be on time for the rest of us!" It was even getting funny to me.

"Heh, heh, heh, heh!" he roared.

"Ham, couldn't I issue you with one of those electric cattle prods so that when they arrive late you could give them a little nudge…"

"Heh, heh, heh, heh, heh!" Being a farmer, he liked that one.

"Late being any time after 5.20 of course!" was my final punchline.

"Heh, heh, heh, heh!" Fortunately, the evening boys had started work and Linda was leaving. Otherwise he might have done himself an injury, or rather I would have.

CHAPTER ELEVEN

... sanity façade deteriorating ...

An out of the ordinary encounter with a very strange tramp-like girl, who James H would have found in a haystack on a moor while out fixing a broken bull. The cracks in the dyke of my sanity were beginning to appear. Perhaps I recognised in her the same wounds of despair, loneliness, despondency and depression...

Jim-Bob-MacSlob-On-Heat held the record for closing the shop, cashing-up and mopping the floor in the evening in about five minutes. His all-animal girlfriend Gemma had a lot to answer for. I had never been able to come that close because, in a perverse kind of a way, I prided myself in doing the job properly. There was always something to forget. Was the fruit and vegetables light turned off, or the scales light? The floor had to be mopped properly, taking care not to step on the done parts, and very importantly, the mop washed out properly. On that particular day, however, I closed the shop at ten to eight; even so, I only arrived at the church after twenty past, after the two minute walk.

The mostly-Norman building was magnificent in the full light of day and even more so when lit up by spotlight at night. That particular evening a recital was being held for the music that Clive Wheelwright had written and it was being recorded to commemorate his eighty-fifth birthday. Clive was, amongst other things, the local weatherman. All the electric lights were off inside, the inside light all came from candles, a beautiful experience. At half time, coffee, wine and mince pies appeared. Having given up the wicked booze a while ago, I thought that they might have thought that I was being funny if I said that I did not drink coffee either. So I reluctantly accepted a cup. The mince pies were good even though they were from Waitrose – one of my dreaded enemies.

After chatting to various people, Clive Wheelwright said he would pop into the shop and sign my copy of his music; I made my way to the kitchen. It was quite obvious that someone would have to be washing up until midnight so, when the second half got under way, I quietly carried on. I could still hear the music through the huge ancient wooden doors. When the music was finished there were a few mince pies left over so I took them back into the church to see if I could find any volunteers to finish them off. By the door I bumped into a rather strange dishevelled looking young woman whom I had never seen before.

"These are delicious mince pies. Are there any more?" she enquired hungrily. I brought out another plate full from an unopened box that might otherwise have gone to waste and she scoffed the lot. The only other thing I remembered at the time about her was that she said she was from Bristol.

I next saw her on that Wednesday evening in the shop and she was quite obviously in a very distressed psychological state as well as looking physically very ill. I invited her to have a coffee in the back office. Now the reason why I did not drink the stuff, correct me on my thinking when one spots a mistake, was that we are all on the one little raft, our planet, and the majority of commercial coffee producers grow coffee without any concern for the environment. They are busy hacking down the rain forests in order to grow the crop just to satisfy our need. Well, here is one consumer that can do without it. Look at Fair Trade Coffee; at least the producers get a fairer deal.

"Have you got any more of those mince pies?" she almost pleaded. Nicola Blackwell had come to Hurley because she had been infatuated with a boy who had gone to the same university as her.

"I love James and I just know he loves me. If I could just talk to him he will see that I am the girl for him." She was adamant and determined not to leave without him. As a Christian, I was quite quickly drawn into a decision to try and do something to help her. After phoning the ex-would-be-parents-in-law, her own parents, the police, and the youth hostel, my options were getting smaller and smaller – she was determined to stay.

"James says he wants nothing more to do with her." The ex-boyfriend's parents answered my call curtly.

"It's not our responsibility," was the police response. "Try social services," they suggested.

"We cannot put her up if she cannot pay," the youth hostel explained.

I was rapidly running out of options.

"We certainly cannot have her staying with us!" Belinda exclaimed. "We will never get rid of her." I knew of course that she was absolutely right.

Nicola's resistance must have started to sink as her bodily functions started to fail her. What had previously been coherent speech came out as babble. Little of what she said made any sense. I cannot remember what I specifically said to eventually persuade her to let me take her to Reading and to put her on a train home to Bristol. She staggered as she rose to stand up and started to fall. I immediately caught her and carried her to the car. She was shivering, almost convulsing, continuously because of her damp cold clothes. The night before the temperature had been minus five and she had camped outside the boyfriend's house and was going to do it again that night! She was, however, very intelligent, her interpretation of the meaning of life was that in order to go forward one had to walk away from something else. In the circumstances, I found that profound. She had been deeply hurt by the whole affair and needed professional care and concern. I was glad when I later phoned her mother to find that she had arrived home safely in Bristol and that she had not got off at the next station and come back to Hurley.

CHAPTER TWELVE

... glorious, enviable normality ...

Intrepid explorers, bold adventurers, Jonathan and Susan, dream-makers extraordinaire – to infinity and beyond. My brother and sister-in-law had just returned from their holiday of a lifetime filled with great adventures and excitement – a two-year trip around the world...

Many of us idly dream of selling up and backpacking around the world, but few of us actually set off. Jonathan and Susan, Super Deluxe Pizza Makers Extraordinaire, had made the epic voyage. They had been beyond England, beyond Europe, out of Africa, left Australia and Fiji. Bronzed, muscular, fit as tigers, fit for battle, fit to kick start life again in England. They could start another company, work for a large organisation, write a book about their numerous exciting adventures, work for me, go into partnership with Belinda and me, or emigrate back to South Africa. That beautiful strife-torn country that was ours, or to somewhere else in Africa, or Australia, New Zealand or Canada or somewhere else that they fancied in their travels. That was of course looking at the options entirely from my perspective, they might decide on India, Chile, or even somewhere strange like Mexico.

Daryl and Fiona announcing that their first child was due that September rather put the pressure on Jonathan and Susan to start creating. Perhaps they already had, perhaps they had already decided that Hawaii was for them. I had travelled a bit, certainly not as extensively, but even without having seen the rest, I can quite categorically say that right here was Heaven. I do hope for the opportunity to take them up to our place called Heaven. The weather is tremendous; I love the cold, the snow, the drizzle, the fog, the ice and the worst of the winter. One could only fully appreciate the spectacular miracle of spring and summer after living through winter. Who said that one could only experience true happiness after experiencing true suffering? Spring, summer and autumn in England are quite glorious. We are extremely fortunate that we live in this green, pleasant and prosperous land.

With Jonathan's great woodworking expertise, he could help with my Great Railway Building Project. In a fit of 'what's-best-for-my-sons' moment – actually it was William's fault as he had the same successful project alive in his house – it was a Hornby railway line going all the way around the house just above the height of the doors. Mine worked tremendously well until Joshua dropped the control unit and the trains never ran again – much to Belinda's relief! Jonathan's recollection of Billy – William - was on one occasion he and Susan had come to visit us, they found Belinda and I as drunk as skunks out the back with William and Jessica! I think it was on the news of their engagement. Of course, his business expertise was what I could really have done with. Belinda and I, in our own little way, had done an enormous amount in reducing overheads, increasing our profit margin and increasing our profile within our market by effective advertising, within our budget. Yet there was always room for improvement and his new refreshed eyes would immediately see other avenues forward. Our sales had not improved almost certainly because I had taken the decision at the end of the previous autumn to close at eight o'clock. Sadly, the local people did not alter their shopping habits accordingly. We were in the distress purchase market and therefore, by definition, people couldn't and wouldn't alter when they would need to buy something from us. We were also in the convenience, rescue, impulse and emergency purchase sector of the market. All of these factors made it impossible for us to determine when our customers should do their shopping. Ideally we should have been open twenty-four hours a day! So the following year we were definitely going to go through the winter closing at nine. From May to September we had always closed at ten. With our gross margin and costs under control, I was really looking forward to the next spring and summer.

One could imagine James H having a similar story about a rival veterinary practice that was cheaper, or perhaps not as compassionate about the animals in their care. James H was of course a legendary vet that must have encouraged a whole generation of young graduates to follow his adventurous footsteps. I hasten to say to anyone that has got thus far, please, please do not go into shop-keeping!

I remember from some ghastly statistic that virtually the whole population steals at one time or another in their lives. Suppliers, banks, and service companies will all also rip one off at the first opportunity.

Of course, the current Big Issue, which was something I tried to deal with separately, was the off-licence opposite. They seemed intent on suicide, with their determination to press on with the practice of serving alcohol to minors. Ideally, I would simply have liked them to just stop doing it. However, it appeared, for whatever reason, they were not going do so. So, in my view, it was inevitable that their licence would ultimately be revoked. The consequences of this on my business would have been enormous, a huge increase in sales with an opportunity to increase my margins dramatically. What with the police catching them red-handed a few days previously, it could only be a matter of time before something happened. But, with my own experience of the English Judicial System, it would probably take years before a trial or hearing and no doubt they would be allowed to continue trading without even being forced to replace the manager. Even then, they would probably just get a warning or a caution. Just think of what input Jonathan and Susan could have given in that scenario. Jonathan, we could have turned the business into a serious money-making machine. Belinda and Susan could have done the paper work. Susan could be editor-in-chief of my attempted reminiscences and of your own far more exciting tales. I remember the story of you and your friend 'Dutch' going down the Nile on a boat with no loo and staying at the very front to try and stay up wind of the pong!

So, they came back, dragging their knuckles along the ground saying,

"Urumph arh..." as gorillas do, and "Cor Blimey Mate, chuck me a tinny, Cobba!" with matted waist-length hair and a Navaho arrow shaft sticking out of Jonathan's head indicating that he had a degree in Life and a determination to lead it to the full.

CHAPTER THIRTEEN

... deep fissures ...

We returned to South Africa on holiday to visit our parents in Durban and Cape Town respectively. After a week I was forced to return and attend to our ailing business.

Airports are great places for crying for joy on seeing long lost friends and family, and tears of sorrow on having to be parted from them. Saying goodbye to my three beloved women was awful, even though it was only going to be a week until we would be together again. We had hugged and hugged and kissed and kissed and cried and cried. I started crying as I walked around the corner away from them. I loved them so.

"Busy yourself, Joss," I told myself. "Get your mind away, book and weigh in, and meander through the departure hall shops." I found some tremendous books and bought them. The cashier had said that I could reclaim the VAT downstairs and so, armed with all my other receipts, I headed for the queue and then spotted little Jeremy Reeves. How did I tell a little boy who was sitting alone crying in the departure lounge that I knew how he felt? I immediately went over to him and tried to cheer him up. I managed to persuade the airline staff to change our seats so that we would be sitting together. Armed with my redeemed VAT money we went into the curio shop and bought a little chess set and some chewing sweets.

My parents had just moved back to live in South Africa on the assumption that Nelson Mandela would miraculously be able to resolve all the country's problems. My sister Melissa, who had already moved there, was expecting her first baby. Brother Daryl and his future wife Fiona had also moved back and my youngest brother Jonathan and his wife Susan were making their way down to South Africa overland on holiday. All Belinda's family were there and so were all my cousins. I have always had a strong South African accent and was always quick to say where I was from. The issue of identity as to where I belonged was never sharper, sitting next to that crying

English boy trying to console him. He was going home to all his family where he so obviously belonged. I was going away from my family, to a country that I was not sure that I even liked, to a business that seemed doomed to extinction, to a court case which at best looked like it would go on for another three or four years. He continued to cry and I did my best to reassure him. I came to realise that he was a highly intelligent young man. He surprised me when I realised that he was aware of how alone and afraid I was and I think that he realised that we were of mutual support to each other, possibly he was more so to me.

He was under strict instructions to go straight to sleep after his supper, which he duly did. I was left to my own foreboding, miserable thoughts. Prozac – the miracle cure for depression. There I was, more miserable than ever and I had been taking the happy-tablets for more than a month. What if...? What if...? Almost every thought that entered my head seemed to lead to a negative conclusion. Hate, despair, ruin, hate, despair, ruin...

After two years of suffering the stealing, the over charging by our suppliers, the bank's excessive charges, the very long hours and with no prospective escape in sight, I had eventually succumbed to Belinda's advice to go and see our local GP about my depression.

"Don't worry about it," he promised reassuringly. "You would be amazed by how many people in the village are on Prozac." I started the treatment but with no real belief that it would work because, of course, the main causes of my depression were all still very much there, as far as I could see.

When little Jeremy awoke he was a new person, although he cheerfully said that he had just been pretending to be asleep. Sprightly and eager to defeat me at chess, he duly did so. I cannot remember the name of the book that we read to each other, Brer Rabbit and the Gang, but he read it perfectly. I felt a little embarrassed at to how Felicity might have compared. Life was a game of snakes and ladders. She may have been behind little Jeremy Reeves at reading but in the unlikely event that she found herself alone on an aeroplane she would probably have made a nuisance of herself to the crew and pilot. On the way down to South Africa, she went alone into the cockpit and asked the captain if he was sure that he knew the way. It was little Jeremy's suggestion that we exchange addresses. A little reluctantly, I agreed; perhaps Felicity and Tilly would enjoy a pen-pal relationship with him.

When we arrived at Heathrow, I was brusquely informed that he was not my responsibility. I said that I had not assumed that he was but that I wanted to go with him to meet his parents. Six other minors appeared and the delegated short-straw stewardess chaperoned her little flock along travelators, escalators, and various lifts. Just before Passport Control one of the slightly older children announced tearfully that she had left her passport and all her travel documents on the plane. Miss Fluster, the Stewardess jabbered away into her two-way walkie-talkie with no response. I offered to go back and get the documents. My hand luggage was about five tons of books that I had acquired in various second hand bookshops around South Africa. In sprinting down one of the many corridors, the shoulder strap of my rucksack tore off. I had no alternative but to carry the contents awkwardly in my arms. The plane already had a few cleaners on board and at first the documents could not be found. I was just beginning to lose hope when one of the cleaners found them in the seat behind where the child had been sitting.

By the time I came through with my luggage, little Jeremy Reeves and his family had gone.

CHAPTER FOURTEEN

... momentary interlude ...

On another occasion I flew down alone to Johannesburg for just a weekend. I was my brother Daryl's best man at his wedding. Our wedding present cost £450.00 in excess baggage fee...

"We make a Living out of what we get, we make a Life out of what we give," read a Billboard for some church on the way to the airport. Fiona drove, grating the gears, third to first, Daryl in the back seat and me in the front. Vague memories came back, Peter Stuyvesant flashed as brightly as the rest of Johannesburg. So-and-so used to work there, and we used to call that the 'Hig-Tog' Tower when we were little. Actually I think it was just Melissa, the little mite was probably only two or three. There used to be a revolving restaurant on the top of it. It was no longer a restaurant and it did not revolve any more. They took me to Jan Smuts Airport and we drove along Jan Smuts Freeway from Melissa's house. Our gran used to sit on Smuts's knee as a little girl listening to his stories. Fiona's granny helped run Smut's campaign in 1947 when he tragically lost. Checked in, said goodbye, no tears. It was a short weekend of many miles, many smiles and many tears, but none then.

> A weekend in Johannesburg. I had left Heathrow on Thursday evening and arrived on Friday at 2.00 pm. I flew with the Portuguese Airways – TAP. We always used to joke that it stood for 'Take Another Plane!' Daryl and Fiona's wedding was to be on Saturday morning. I was rudely awoken at seven to an intense day that only ended when the final guest had left at eleven that night. The next day, Sunday: present opening, dog walking, card opening in their lovely new home and then back on board.

What a weekend, where do I start? My fumbling excuses for a speech, opening my legendary Honeymoon Hamper, the floods of tears, the very moving ceremony? - All of which were chapters in themselves. One of my supposed laughs in my speech was that I only started preparing my speech in the morning before at Heathrow whereas Daryl had had the last fifteen years to fine-tune his! I included a few adventures from our past that turned our parents' hair grey. We used to be called the Wild Boys of Sheep Heaven. I think it may have been the importance of the occasion to my beloved brother but I was unable to control my nervousness. There seemed terrible moments where I simply could not get the words out, possibly because I did not know the audience, possibly also because Daryl had also asked me to say Grace and I made a serious mess of it. I used the time before my speech to come up with an excuse. I fumbled that I should have said,

"Rub a dub dub, Thanks for the grub!"

Most of the people invited were Fiona's family and friends. Aunt Sarah and Uncle Arthur, out of politeness, I think, said it was a tremendous speech. Of course I could have a whole chapter on Tim's flawless performance as Master of Ceremonies. His jokes were impeccably timed and, oddly for a wedding, genuinely very funny. He was Fiona's elder brother. The meal started with a disaster caused largely by me. The string quartet had gone home. At the time I did not even know who Tim was and when they approached me to settle the bill, I sent them to Stephen West, my brother-in-law, who knew even less than I, promptly paid them and so naturally they left. Poor Tim handled his opening crisis admirably. Minutes later, a gentleman appeared with a piano and he proceeded to played superbly. If only I had been introduced to the charming and very likeable Tim beforehand, we could possibly have coordinated our act better. In view of my total lack of experience in that sort of thing, my nervousness, jet lag, and culture shock, he managed to stage manage it all very well.

When I thought of the many hours in my distant subterranean office in another corner of the globe, trying to think of the right etiquette I would need to follow, the right people to thank and the proper order to do so, I cursed myself then for not including Fiona's parents Mavis and Frederick's neighbour who so competently videoed the whole affair from beginning to end. I caught him at the party afterwards and he modestly accepted my apology. And Tim, if only my Toast to you did not appear to be such an afterthought. Such is the journey of life. No doubt the relationship between Daryl and Fiona and Tim and Carole, his lovely wife who was Matron of Honour, and Fiona's sister, would be strengthened by my faux pas when they have had the opportunity to laugh about it together sometime in the future.

Sitting next to me on the plane going back was Norman Stone, an engineer who had worked for the London Underground. He had just become engaged to a South African girl called Stacy and was going back again in a few months to marry her. I was astonished when he said that, due to Affirmative Action, it was quite difficult for him to get a job in South Africa and even more surprising to hear that, in his field, the level of salaries was less than in the UK. He was reading *Far from the Madding Crowd* by Thomas Hardy. Norman suggested the title 'On Licence' when I told him that I saw myself as the James Herriot of Middle England shopkeepers. As usual, I'd had absolutely no sleep because on that occasion I had lost Daryl's famous expanding earplugs so I munched on a page of the in-flight magazine and shoved them in my ears. It was extremely uncomfortable and ineffective so I gave up on them. However, chatting, scribbling and eating, the ten-hour flight to Lisbon went quite quickly.

Moments after we had touched down, applause broke out from our hosts' people, the Portuguese. I could understand in the 1920s, one might be eternally grateful to the pilot and his crew for one's safe arrival back on terra firma; however, a few years from the following century, I rather took it for granted. Perhaps I should not have.

It would be difficult to list completely the contents of the Honeymoon Hamper mainly because so much was crammed in and also because this book is only classified as an eighteen! It was a beautiful old black corrugated metal trunk with bright brass clasps and working lock and bolt. "11th January 1997 Daryl and Fiona Today Tonight

Tomorrow and Forever" I had carefully painted onto the lid and underneath the writing, just above the lock, I had sprayed a silhouette of a man and a woman dancing inside a heart shaped surround. However, when I had bought it, it was unrecognisable as anything. It was in a very dilapidated condition. I knocked out some of the worst dents, and completely repainted it both inside and out. I removed the clasps and locking mechanism and polished them and I had a key made to fit the lock. It took me hours to make the three shelves that fitted neatly inside. The four layers were in descending order of naughtiness with the Hardcore-Honeymoon-Conception stuff being in the secret layer at the bottom. When I said in my speech that it was everything that a couple might conceivably need on their honeymoon, the emphasis was on the word 'conceive'. So, with that in mind, I will not go into the specific contents of that layer! In the top layer was a Smith Wesson's Convenience Store Banking Box with some South African money, lots of chocolate money and a piece of paper on which I had written, "IOU my sanity, my character, my identity, much more than a trunk of trinkets can ever express." During the very black time, Daryl had helped with our accounts, taken the children for endless walks, but most of all, encouraged, coaxed, implored and begged me not to lose my grip. There was a time, despite my love from my darling, beloved wife Belinda and my two adorable daughters, when I felt that I could not go on. The pressure from the bank – we owed them over £100,000.00 – the stress caused by my parents moving away to live in South Africa, an ugly unnecessary dispute with our neighbours, a conflict within myself as to where my loyalties lay as to whether I was South African, British, both or neither, whether my eccentric behaviour was a symptom of impinging insanity or whether it was my real character trying to escape after being suppressed for so long. There were times, late in the evenings after coming back from Maidenbottom doing the banking through the hole-in-the-wall that I felt I would be unable to control myself and swerve into the path of an oncoming speeding truck; going to the bank became a phobia.

Both Belinda and I had to have our lives insured for incredible sums as part of the bank agreement. If I were to supposedly die in a 'freak' accident, it would wipe out all our financial debts at a stroke. The many options would revolve around and around in my mind. Simply diving into the river in flood wouldn't work. One, I could swim and more obviously, it would look like suicide. The speeding truck, the supposed momentary lack of concentration and it would all be over. What would the family do without me? Then my thoughts would go the full circle and they would become free, 'How liberated they would be.' They would be financially secure and no longer attached to a liability.

The top layer also contained two books that I had written; the ancestors of Daryl Smith Wesson, which proudly took Daryl's ancestors back to William the Conqueror and beyond, and the descendants of Gert Von Weiligh, the original settler on our mother's side who had arrived in the Cape in 1658. That was the core of my research at that moment and I would happily admit that my interest went way beyond harmless hobby into dangerous obsession. I considered myself a world authority on the wider Von Weiligh family. Actually, dear Reader, this is the real reason for writing my book. I feel that the only way I am ever going to be able to finance publishing my personal family history is to gain some credibility as an author outside that field. I strongly believe that the interest, pastime, hobby, call it what you will, is rapidly becoming an alternative to the paying public. The Genealogical Society of London – a registered charity of which I am a member – had recently received a large sum of money from the lottery. This was very exciting as it will enable them to employ people to enter data into a computer, making it available to a far greater audience. It always amazed me that these floppy glossy fashion magazines were able to demand incredibly high prices, whereas historic books appear to have no value. Perhaps the tide of ephemera was turning and mankind was looking back or forward for something a little more positive to do in his spare time. Perhaps studying one's genealogy gives purpose to one's identity. The greatest influences on any individual are his parents, and their parents on them, ad infinitum. I searched not just for dates of birth, death and marriage and occupation but also how they might have voted, their beliefs, their aspirations and their fears. Finding the character of my ancestors was the key to understanding myself.

Also in the top layer was a birthday diary, a crucial piece of equipment in family management; planning would be the wrong word here! As an expert on the matter, I had entered all of dates of the new family. I had cut out the pages prior to 11th January and entered, "Today is the first day of our lives together".

The most important thing in the top layer, and indeed the whole box, was a Bible. It belonged to our father's beloved brother Joss, who had died a painful death in 1959 of Hodgkin's disease. He was a devout Christian and a staunch supporter of Moral Rearmament (MRA). Many friends all over the world were inspired by the courageous and forgiving way that he had faced his death. He struggled against the disease for two long, excruciating years. Although I had never met him, I was honoured to have his name; I felt I knew him and that in an obscure way I would have loved to continue his work. The Bible was undoubtedly a treasured possession of his. It was certainly one of my most treasured possessions, but as a Christian I believe that one has to give with the heart, give not to receive, give what is really most precious, no matter if the recipient discards the gift in time. Even though the book now belongs to Daryl and Fiona, it is still mine. The words rather than the paper made it precious, Christ's words. At the ceremony, Fiona's brother Tim read from Saint Paul's letter to the Corinthians Chapter thirteen verses 1-13. It speaks of Faith, Hope and Love and the greatest of these was Love and that without Love we are nothing. I strongly believe that with Daryl's marriage to Fiona, a Christian, my insignificant influence, that of Mum and Dad, Aunt Sarah and Uncle Arthur and perhaps Alistair and Charlotte, although a bit distant, would change him from Saul to Paul. Daryl was certainly a man of great convictions and when he is called to move…

Lisbon and five hours to kill. Filled with notes on my adventures over the weekend and an expedition onto Portuguese soil. The bit on this side of Passport Control was still 'International', if such a State exists. I bought Belinda a cute porcelain doll to add to her collection. Wow, I could not wait to get back and to start making some serious money, to fixing up the flat and our miniscule little garden, to start living my life in attack rather than in retreat as I had done in the previous five years. It was difficult to say what I looked forward to most. Perhaps it was not. I will intimate to you dear Reader, as by the time one reads this hopefully the deed will be done. Belinda and I had decided to have another child! It was going to be fun and as you can understand I could not wait to get started! Although I had yet to have my operation reversed, it would be fun practising. I had the vasectomy reversed a few weeks after my return to England.

"It is very unusual for this operation to be done on a man with the same partner. Usually it is because he has remarried," the doctor explained. That would be a book in itself and I was certainly not going to reveal my thoughts and views on the subject, except to say to male readers, if through your technique you are unable to get your partner to achieve an orgasm regularly, then I suggest you seek help. Not in pornography, but in serious adult literature of which there is no shortage available. The basis of Belinda and my relationship was a metaphysical understanding between us – basically love. Initially, as with any couple, it was often a physical attraction. We loved each other's company, and our differences, and our rare separations, only brought us closer together. There will no doubt come a time when we will no longer be capable of physical love, but we will not love each other any less. By then, the rock of our relationship will be so steadfast that if Belinda were to die I feel sure that I would have no reason to carry on without her and would join her in Heaven. I am getting soppy and it was nearly time to board and I had only related half the weekend! Air Portugal appeared to have some clever plot to de-veggie their customers, as three of the four flights I had been on had no record that I was a sad vegetarian. On the second last flight home, the hostess, certainly not a contender for Miss World – I think that the old bag must have been doing the job for the last eighty years – suggested that I ought to eat flesh as everyone else did. I politely said that if they could not find me a veggie meal, then I would be happy without. Now the last leg home and I was first in the queue to book in. Wow, make an asterisk entry in the diary Joss! - Only to be spoiled because I was held up for many minutes while Biffo the Boffin surfed the Internet with his one finger to find me a vegetarian meal. I almost started screaming, "Yes, yes, anything, anything, I'll eat meat - dinosaur, hippo, tarantula, road-kill, human; just let me on the plane!"

The other layers of the hamper, the rest of my speech and the floods of tears, not to mention the slightly offbeat happenings over the weekend, were all to come. I sat next to an extremely interesting chap on the way down called Mat. Between us we resolved the world's problems and possibly some of our own. Certainly as soon as I got home I was going to make enquiries into the Alexander Technique. I was delighted that Fiona had heard of it and had nothing but praise for it. Mat was obviously a deeply profound man because his answer to my question, 'What is the meaning of life?' was,

"The meaning of life is the search for meaning..." I certainly enjoyed his company, even to the extent that I was highly embarrassed and felt his disapproval. At some point in our conversation, I had tried to explain my own difficulty with the concept of racism as I defined it, and culturalism. After I had given my best shot to the argument he quickly retorted that there was no such thing as culturalism and that a rejection of a person or people due to cultural differences still amounts to racism. I respect his viewpoint and sadly I feel that the vast majority of people will also agree with him. I put the point to Daryl and he immediately sided with me. He said that he would not object if his children were to marry someone that ate at a table, used a toilet, and had respect for law and order, irrespective of their colour. Conversely, if they were to bring home a man with rings and tattoos in every part of his body, with matted greasy unwashed hair that was full of lice, that felt that the police had no right to interfere with his life, used unnecessarily abusive and foul language and was white he would object. That was my rough interpretation of culturalism.

One of the long-term highlights of the weekend, other than Melissa and Stephen's magnificent shower, was definitely the discovery of the most amazing second-hand bookshop in the known universe only a few hundred yards away from their home. It was like arriving in Heaven. I could happily have spent a few days in it, but as it was, I was restricted to Friday afternoon. Needless to say, I came home with a veritable treasure trove of books that I could not wait to start researching. I could not imagine anyone visiting Johannesburg without going to that shop.

On the Friday evening I presented the hamper to Daryl and Fiona. They only discovered about twenty percent of its contents on their first rummage. They had another formal rummage through it on Sunday afternoon and still only found about eighty-five percent, the remainder hidden under the secret hard-core bottom.

It was tremendous to get all the dates of birth etc. from Fiona's side of the family. I later wrote to her uncle Henry De Villiers to get more information. There was a strong possibility that there was a connection between the Von Weiligh and De Villiers families, which would be both tremendously interesting and exciting. On the Sunday morning, other than the usual washing up from the party the night before, I unscrewed their front garden gate and planed it down as it would not open and close properly. I had encouraged all the guests to sign a copy of the order of service to add to the trunk as another memento of the day. Later, we had a very long walk around the lake in their local park with my darling Goddaughter, Melissa's daughter Nancy, strapped to my back. It was one incredible weekend, never to be forgotten and never to be repeated.

This was something of my speech; **(Ed. Just remind us exactly which bits we need to laugh at.)**

"I will introduce myself as Hurley's, the village in England where I live, only white Zulu and proud of it! I feel it important to state that I represent both of us Brothers Grim, myself and Jonathan, and if Daryl had not been such a traditionalist, he would have asked Melissa to be his best person. Brother Jonathan gives his sincere apologies for not being here for the day. He and his wife Susan are stuck somewhere between Outer Mongolia and the Bahamas. Thanks to the incredible flower organisers. If I go to another thousand weddings, I am sure that I would not see any better. To Frederick and Mavis for their organisation and for inviting us all and to all of us for coming. Particularly to Daryl and Fiona who caused that celebration to be necessary and for being foolish enough to choose me to be their best man. However, after this speech the term will have to be redefined as the 'Worst Man!"

"I was surprised that Frederick in his speech did not tell the story of Fiona, the parrot, the plumber and the time she got her big toe stuck in the bath tap! I however, will concentrate on embarrassing as much as I can, with personal anecdotes, the beloved groom. All I can say about Fiona is that she appears absolutely perfect and that the two of them are going to be blissfully happy together.

"In breaking with true best man tradition I feel that I will not allow the groom's speech to be an anticlimax, no, mine is not deliberately awful, it just comes naturally! Daryl made a tremendous best man speech at Belinda and my wedding about a hundred years ago. He's had the previous fifteen years to fine-tune his, whereas I started mine yesterday morning at Heathrow!" **(Ed. Boom, boom and faint titter of laughter?)**

"Part of the speech included a bit where I had Daryl and Fiona believing that the massive trunk I had brought out contained the set of 200 World Books that Melissa and Stephen had tactfully refused as a gift for their wedding.

"As you all know, Daryl's nickname for the last thirty-five-odd years has been Monkey. The origin of that was, when he was born, his eighteen month older brother, namely me, could not pronounce his Sotho name, uMunkuthi. Now Monkey suggests stupid and certainly not the academic giant we have come to know, respect and love. The time has come to add to his already sizeable portfolio a new, additional, updated and more appropriate nickname. I, the official arbitrator in these matters, present you with Buzz Lightyear, to Infinity and Beyond! As Buzz passes from boy to Manhood, I feel it important to give this particular story one more final rendition before it passes its sell by date. In our youth we were respectfully known and feared as 'The-Wild-Boys-of-Sheep-Heaven!' People visiting our farm would park their cars at the far end of the drive for fear of having useful things like potatoes or hosepipes put up their exhausts. One day Buzz, Chip and I aged 'The Old Boy' fifty years at a stroke when we invited him to come down and inspect our new waterfall. We had cleverly slit the sides of all the bags of fertiliser and the whole stack was coming cascading down like the Victoria Falls! Dad was pleased! - Not to say that he was not an authoritarian. I remember a time when Daryl had accidentally chopped a sizeable hole in his foot with an axe. Despite the excessive blood, he was so petrified of being thoroughly beaten that he could not be persuaded to come down from the tree in which he had taken refuge!

"Now, imagine transporting these three 'Wild Boys' into the backcountry of Little Tame England twenty or so years later. Sitting in the Kings Head we found ourselves labelled 'The Wah Boys'. Buzz and Chip had been reading a James Clavell classic in which reference was made to one's karma or peace of mind as one's Wah. That was the final and total insult, to go from 'Wild Boy' to 'Wah Boy!' To cut a long story short, the three Wild Boys stood back to back and fought two thousand screaming hatcheted Chelsea supporters whose side had just lost again. They even had tattoos on their eyelids! Needless to say, they never called us the Wah Boys again. Uncle Arthur was there, actually he wasn't, but his version is terrific, ask him for the truth!

"One could hardly be the Best Man at one's best friend's wedding without giving the couple some worldly advice. I have a number of part time staff working for me and although one sometimes has a misconception that they are of a lower order, intellectually, I was bowled over by the profoundness one gave to the question, "Who would you most like to be stuck on a desert island with?" It was in the middle of a boy/boy conversation after a particularly gorgeous woman had just left the store. The answer he gave was the Real Meaning of Love, or rather the meaning of Real Love. Anyway, he announced,

"My mum, because she cooks my dinner!" The moral of the story is, don't be stranded with someone just because they have nice childbearing hips to bear the fruits of your loins, but because they are your best friend. It must have been good advice as our mother's father, our Oupa, told our dad a similar story at their wedding. My two daughters, Felicity and Tilly have turned out to be Little Angels. This of course gives Buzz and Fiona licence to produce another generation of Wild Boys. You will have to check that there is a new management team at 'Stuttafords', or whatever is the poshest shop in town, when you attempt to civilise them. When the original Wild Boys were dragged in with a rather proper and civilised Auntie Sarah, she had to quickly abandon ship, screaming! Amongst other atrocities, we had just succeeded in killing the shop's parrot!

"With that in mind, I feel that I am sufficiently over the hill to give away some Boy-Having-Tips, or rather how to avoid them if you would rather not have grey hair, but I won't, except to say that Daryl is an expert in the key ingredient –Stress Management.

"Which brings me round to Daryl's greatest hits. He has two degrees, has been a director of his own company, at the same time as doing my company accounts, and now he is a Barrister. All these, however, pale into insignificance when rated by the Namer of the Monkey, namely me. To me, Daryl is far more than a brother; he is without doubt my best friend and what he has taught me, particularly in the last eighteen months, has been enough to kick-start my life again. If you have Daryl Smith Wesson on your short list of friends, then consider yourself fortunate because you have hit the big time!

"I will end on a slightly more serious note. Have you ever considered the meaning of life or the purpose of life? Is it that life is a dual universe and that every time one makes a positive decision one's life is enhanced and a negative decision results in one's life being degraded? Well, I am not going to disclose the answer except to say that Daryl has led me to it."

CHAPTER FIFTEEN

... escaping non-concealable symptoms ...

Reflections in the mind of a disturbed disorientated village shopkeeper rapidly heading for the cuckoo farm. Fifty referenda and forty years old that year, I had officially became an old codger.

It explained a lot; I was turning into an old fart. Pains in my back, pains in my hips, I could not lift as much as I used to, I was not as fast as I was. I was not the young buck that I was; younger, keener, fitter, meaner and hungrier boys had arrived to take my place.

"To be in our Regatta Rowing Team this year," Jim-Bob-MacSlob explained, "you have to lift the big heavy round sign up at least fifteen times". He continued in a manner that suggested that he felt that it was impossible for any other mortal soul to come anywhere close. His reasoning presumably being that he was the reigning village 'Mercy' Champion. Mercy being a finger bending sport that involves the opponent begging for mercy on defeat. So, to keep the conversation moving, I started the proceedings. The big round rotating sign was seriously heavy and the weaker members of staff had devised a clever way of using its base as a wheel and rolling it back into the shop at the end of the evening rather than having to lift it. I picked it up and started enthusiastically. Ten, twenty times - equal to Jim-Bob's record, thirty and still sailing, forty times and it was beginning to seriously hurt, but I was determined to go on, forty-five times and that was extremely painful but I had to go until the end. Forty-nine times but couldn't possibly stop here, fifty and my arms were in total agony.

"My arms!!" screamed the rest of my bodily parts, my hips, my back, my shoulders, to mention just a few. As far as it was vaguely possible, I nonchalantly walked back inside and continued serving. Ricky then had a go and could not even lift it even once above his shoulders! He was an average built seventeen year-old. Jim-Bob had another go. There was a lot at stake. After all, he was less than half my age.

"Thirty," he came in and announced, in a sort of 'it's-in-the-same league' kind of a way.

"Actually I thought it was only twenty," Ricky, following him in, muttered meekly.

The boys looked at me in a totally new light. They had just witnessed me do the impossible. If only I could have captured that moment with a medal or a photo or something. My immediate decision, after my old brain had finally switched back on, was that I was going to have another go at doing the Comrades Marathon again. Not to do it in a better time, simply to accompany Lawrence, Belinda's brother in about ten and a half hours. In 1987 I had done it in seven and a half hours much to the amazement of my family. The London Marathon could possibly be one of my qualifying races. The point of the sign-lifting/rowing story was not that I have made the decision to run again. It was a slow realisation that life was passing me by and that if I didn't get off my arse it would slip me by without my having noticed.

Running

Sprained my ankle last week, playing squash.

Pain had left me shivering, clutching my foot.

Waves of giddiness and nausea engulfed me.
Swollen and black, still, I thought I would run.
Under fit – damaged ankle, and torrential rain.
What a hero, give me another very big medal
Just for entering. Everybody looks at my
Glorious legs pumping, the road moves under.
Clapping, cheering, screaming millions of fans.
Then it happens – Total embarrassment at my
Ridiculous personal adoration; my ant complex
Next to me is a man, his courage is of sixty men.
He is Hercules and Apollo; he towers above me
In his adapted wheelchair he has no arms or legs.

Belinda, my beloved and cherished wife, partner, companion and friend, believed that I had a certain skill at this writing malarkey and that I should apply myself to it. Now, most of what I have written before I felt sure was of an adolescent, possibly immature and churlish nature. The lifting of the sign was significant to me because at that point a sudden rush of confidence spurred me to write my understanding of certain circumstances. We all have views and thoughts on issues when we watch the news; the majority of them never see the light of day I supposed, arrogantly believing that that was going to get further than my own computer. After a major finger nail biting session (God I wished I could stop that revolting habit) it was possibly because of the enormity of what I was taking on. Perhaps I should stick to my pre-adolescent ramblings – it would be just as interesting – bit more of a gnaw?

The main item on the news around Easter was the prospect of peace in Northern Ireland. They had all actually agreed. It was a miracle. One could be cynical and think that those Thick-o Irish Morons in a few days would soon be back to the activity that they seemed to enjoy most, and were best at – killing each other. And of course anyone else who looks at them oddly which I suppose would now include me – somehow that did not worry me as much as my readers thinking that I was writing gobble-de-gook. What a surprise. In the next week the Orange Order, pronounced in that retarded way, announced that they rejected the deal and that they would be canvassing people to vote in the referendum against it. Was it just me, but was it because they were all so in-bred that they were so thick. One of the parties was annoyed because the people of Southern Ireland were not going to have a referendum. Well, that was a fair point. What about this for a point... struggled not to have a mouthful of remaining fingernails. Nobody has suggested that there ought to be a referendum on the subject in mainland Britain. Nobody had ever asked me... nobody ever asked the whole country, did they, if they did, surely, the answer would for peace, Peace, PEACE!! We all live on that little life raft of a planet that has some serious leaks in it. Should the issues be, who holds the paddle as the boat goes down? Let's pretend, until at least we have reached the other side, that we were all prepared to put our fingers in the holes, throw out the broken bottles and any other instruments that could damage that fragile little raft, and decide which direction we were going to row in – I suppose we could have a little argument over that – however does it matter, so long as we were all rowing together? It was not a major point, you might think. Peace, such an original idea; a piece of cake? How much more does the raft have to be damaged before we stop squabbling over what in retrospect are infinitely miniscule issues? We are no longer subjects, because we can reject the principle of monarchy, we are no longer residents, because we can reject the principle of having to have any loyalty to the country one lives in – or even the one to which one has printed in one's passport – many, many people choose to live where they do for whatever reason, convenience, comfort, finance. And by the same measure, we are no longer citizens.

"What?" I hear them shout. "That is the nub of what we are fighting about." Old Dick Whittington was a citizen of London. Of course, he was also a citizen of England, and of Great Britain, omitting the Irish Thing. And today we would agree, although some of the 'Head-In-The-Sand' party may try to convince us that black was in fact a shade of pink and that he was definitely not a citizen of Europe. In ten years time I would be able to slip in the word 'State' after Europe. A lot of people would hurry to disagree; however it is, in my view, totally inevitable. The 'H-I-T-S' Party would have us all believe that they were all Krauts and that we won the war and that it was not fair that they win by insidious means. The English should go it alone. The Cornish are virtually as in-bred as the Irish and so are the Welsh, so declare them Independent states with their own constitutions, languages and border controls. Scotland loves itself to bits so let it, great... Oh, wake me up PLEASE! The nightmare was reeling on towards reality. Can the short-sighted politicians who supposedly act on our, the voters, behalf not see? We are all subjects, residents, and citizens, of the same place. Call it home, call it the raft, call it the planet, call it anything, but let's start believing and behaving as if it was the only one. I bet that millions of voters up and down the country felt that same disappointment when the Orange chappies, who no doubt had what they believed to be reasons, rejected peace.

"Fellow residents... and if you don't like that thought go and reside somewhere else with your infested terminal ideas..."

"You 'ave no idea wad ids lark to live wiv dose animaals, dose basdards, dose criminarls, we are going tu kill dem arl becaz Gaud haz tauld us doo and id is da riht ting tu doo..." Imagine the retarded speaker's tongue glued to the side of his mouth to get the accent right.

On the day of the referendum, I don't know whether to hide in a box and wait until someone breaks the news to me or listen intently to the radio knowing I will be disappointed.

"Oh, by the way, it's war." I did not mean to be insulting and derogatory but I ask you to take it in a self-examinatory way. Of course we were aware of the sensitive nature of the situation, the 'Whole-of-Ireland-as-One' Thing. The English having being there for centuries, Catholics, Protestants, it was extremely difficult. We all know that.

"For one moment, lift your vision from the dirty, shameful, and oh-so-important past, which should be about the size of a full stop on your desk, to the future." If only I could lecture that demented hateful uncivilised moron.

I remember an expression from my childhood,

"It is better to be dead than red." It was of course a reference to the then ongoing confrontation with communism.

I once worked with a Sikh. My thoughts at the time were,

"That creeping dirty influence, soon the whole of England will be wearing turbans, the sooner that it is realised as a threat the better." However I am glad to report that I believe that I woke up.

"They have a lot to offer to us. Are we really proud of our society's relationship with alcohol? Do we as a society know what reverence, respect, and worship is any more? Do we as a society treat our criminals properly? Do we really understand how they treat their wives and women? Is not the Catholic God the same one that the Protestants worship? Does it really, and this is the crux of it, really matter which side of the line one is on? Instead of haggling and wrangling over issues that were so irrelevant to those who were able to see beyond, why not start on something big. If we were going to have a common state, whether it was Europe or the 'Union of Peoples that Have Decided to Live Together in Peace' we are going to need a common language. I looked deep into his face, imploring him. Man to man, he would have to see reason, or was I just one of the infidels on the other side that he wanted to simply irradicate?

"Whatever happened to Esperanto? Yes exactly, get off your fat comfortable arse and do it for me for every child in the 'Union', they should learn it as their second language. In the second generation they would be learning their 'mother' tongue as their second language. Stern stuff huh? Nonsense. Instead of rushing to find reasons why it was not possible, which at the end of the day might make your seat less comfortable, get on with it! Please Mr Sensible-Bloke-Politician…" I could see that I had lost the debate

"…What's the use, let's face it, it is easier just to carry on with the war..."

I leant back in my chair and sighed heavily, knowing that at the end of the day my contribution towards anything would be zero. Perhaps I could make the shop a success? Perhaps I could get a degree and become a world authority on genealogy; perhaps I could win the lottery, buy a large house and fly like a bird…

CHAPTER SIXTEEN

... reason defeated by bigotry ...

Sunday Club, Senior Group; St Michael's Hurley 3rd May 1998. One of the biggest crises in my life had always been to try and work out the meaning of it all. Initially at school, most of Christian teaching I simply accepted without question. Then as an adult, the teaching of Evolution, the Big Bang, most wars fought in the name of religion, all caused confusion and doubt in my already disturbed mind...

After the previous week's fiasco, I think that the reason why they called me 'Joss the Flop' was because it was such an unmitigated disaster added to the number of disasters on the previous Sunday. I was getting quite steeled to it. Would all the adult helpers turn up, would all the children turn up, would anybody turn up, would, would, would anything go right?

Jonathan turned out to be a genius with clay, Leslie had to be pulled away with a crowbar and Katrina was covered from head-to-toe and those were just the adults. The model churches turned out brilliantly. We had used Bob Jenkins' proposed plan as a guide. The next week we only had to do the finishing touches, which was going to be even more fun.

Now the point of this chapter was not to illustrate how much fun Sunday school was. Indeed it was to try to draw the analogy between different peoples working happily towards a common goal, and the 'heckling' that can be heard regarding the Millennium proposals. First, understand that I was the very first person, quaking at the knees, to oppose the plans. However, I did not sit at the back of the General Meeting and,

"Ah Yes... but if... well not really, no, etc., etc." There are proper channels to conduct any organisation's proceedings. If one opposed the first plans and still opposed the amended plans this did not mean that proper channels were entirely closed. One could of course write letters to the appropriate body. Can they not see the beauty and simplicity of the revised plans? Obviously not. For those that didn't hear Father Short from Upper Maidenbottom talk at the AGM, he had said that they had sent their first architect to Coventry and commissioned an inspired genius. For those that felt that we should sack Bob Jenkins because he was not up to it would be the same people that would say nothing when given the opportunity when the new plans were drawn up, but would snipe away from the back because they felt that a bit of disunity was in the best interests of the Church. Grow up fellow Christians; if they couldn't take a bit of a telling off then let them kick me out; I will still be a Christian. The building that we worshipped in is precisely that, a building. Belinda and I have worshipped in outdoor services, in tents, in huts, in very old buildings and in brand new buildings. The body of the Church is not the building, but us, so let's put this petty bickering behind us. I could hear them say,

"The arrogance, Mr Smith Wesson, how can you have the audacity to lecture us on church unity at St Michael's, on Christian principles? You have not been a member of our Church for long, you are less than half the age of most of us, how dare you come on all pious on Christian principles?"

"Well folks the answer is...when you lot were hounding Bob at the AGM I was quaking with anger, and I was trying to compose myself to say something. I wanted to say, 'Friends, Romans, Countrymen, Friends – I know all of you by name, Romans, we are all citizens together – Christians and Countrymen – Hurleyites, lend me your ear! Can you not see that that plan was the right plan, the inspired plan, and God's plan? So let's get behind it. Let's break some ground rules and raise the money tonight. Seriously folks, if we were all totally behind these plans, we could make a serious indent in the total amount required before Christmas.' But I did not say anything because I was too frightened... simply because I am right! Please do not react by saying or thinking, 'We'll see about that!'"

If I were to have said that, their response would be to simply not come into my humble shop. I did not wish to antagonise anybody, so I simply asked them to pray, as I did after studying the first plans. God would guide them. Jesus was a revolutionary in that he said what the authorities did not want to hear. They had the opportunity to crucify me;

however, I believed that when they realised, after prayer, that these plans were meant for us, were the right way forward, then they would forgive my impertinence. It may have been that I was further in the red than most of them had been in the black, which gave me a clearer insight. I believed that I, as a Christian, in every situation I would try to do the will of God. If I ever were in that queue I would have to say, 'shoot me'. However, I was also a husband, father, brother, son and friend. They all depended on me, would they forgive me if I made a tactical decision to pray another day and spit that day? Look at the single issue of being a vegetarian. I strongly believe that future generations will look back on us in disgust, as we have the knowledge, the opportunity but not the will to stop this unnecessary cruelty. I do not drink or smoke. These activities are not the Will of our God, as I understand Him. I do not eat chocolate. I believe that I do not need it and that it was one of the primary causes for the destruction of the rainforests. Crops such as cocoa, coffee and sugar are grown when the forests are cleared for a few years before the land is able to sustain them and the farmers simply chop down another part of the virgin forest. You could argue that the list of products or companies that are ecologically or humanly unfriendly is endless and of course it is. I strongly prefer to buy Fair Trade coffee that we buy from Oxfam, which Belinda drinks. Belinda and I have been supporting a child in Kenya for longer than we have had children of our own. To the Church we give what we can afford, something that the more pious members do not seem to want to understand. There is a story of the rich men in the temple mocking the poor beggar for only giving a few coins; what if the beggar was a professional beggar and was in fact a millionaire and the rich man was in great debt? I did not know the answers to these questions, other than to spark a seed of doubt in my belief that the Church and its congregation were the followers of the same Christ I know.

CHAPTER SEVENTEEN

... no surprise retrospectively...

To gain an insight into the place of desperation I had arrived at by the end of this book, I have retrospectively inserted this short chapter. The purpose is to prepare the reader for the sharp change in my state of mind. 'Mental Health' as a subject is hard to define. We live in a ridiculous age in which every behavioural trait has a cause and therefore a treatment. The vast majority of our ancestors were happy to just be alive. Still, in this age, I found myself in the care of quite the most remarkable doctor who has made it his business to ensure that I was not only going to recover, but stay recovered. What his reason for this is, I do not know. Perhaps it is because I am responsible for the welfare of my family etc.

If one has had an episode of 'Mental ill Health', does one get labelled as 'Mentally Unsound' forever? In my case there is (apparent) recovery and I am delighted to say that there is a 'happy ending' as such. Although how 'happy' I am, I am not sure. I hear of fellow 'Manic Depressives' that miss the extreme highs of the roller coaster that was our everyday life. I also can certainly look back wistfully at the extreme beautiful highs. To defeat the dreaded lows I have accepted that I must continue the daily medication, thereby also eliminating the magnificent off-the-wall highs. Yes, a pretty boring life. So I am resigned to taking the 'Happy Tablets' for the rest of my innings. It must be much the same for heroin addicts. On the few occasions that I have decided that enough is enough, and to do 'Cold Turkey', my body has refused to function anywhere near properly. I am not able to hold a conversation or even speak coherently; I almost immediately go back into a vortex of black sombre thoughts of self-destruction and of varying methods of doing the deed. Physically, my face goes numb; there is an electrical arcing feeling inside my head that hurts my brain. I honestly believe that I am hearing voices. I am tortured at night by unending horrific nightmares that prevent me getting rest from sleep, waking with black bags under my eyes. I genuinely believe people hate me and I become a social recluse within a few days.

So to keep from my episodes of divergence from the straight and narrow, I am attempting to stick to the 'sweeties'. The sad truth is that, in many respects, I know that I am no longer the exuberant, eccentric, flamboyant, extremely energetic individual I once was (when I was not depressed) and have become slow in thought and speech. The closest I can now get to a 'high' is an excessive amount of alcohol. The irony is that, after relatively little, my speech slurs and I start to talk gibberish. But hell, I am 'happy' in my own world!

To work in the twilight shift.

I'm driving. It's dark, very dark. The hedges beside the road become insane monsters from the planet 'Deepest Nightmare', enormous serpent-type devils that screech hollow death into the core of my being. Otherwise tame trees transform into ghoul-like beasts that lurch and stretch towards me, their tentacles in the howling winter wind intent on devouring my very soul.

To work. Another mind-numbingly, non-challenging, non-academic job whose most difficult aspects I had defeated in the first hour of the first day.

The road is dead straight. So would be the demented hedges if not for the wild wind. That night there was no other traffic so my mind was tortured further by the demons both inside and outside my head. I know this road. I have travelled along it hundreds of times. In daylight the trees, hedges and bushes are, at worst, hardly noticeable and, at best, part of the glorious landscape that is Mother England. That night though, they conspired together, determined to become part of my awful terminal nightmare.

The road has a maximum speed of 50 miles per hour. I was doing 80, my headlights slicing their way through the black starless night. In the far distance another vehicle appeared, perhaps at least two miles away. Perhaps it was a bloke on his way home, just finishing work. Perhaps he was just off to the pub. Did he even notice the furious trees lashing wildly in the wind? No, it was an HGV as I began to see the outline of the red lights high above the oncoming headlights.

God – perhaps it was something really heavy, going very fast. My clenched hands began to sweat, and twitch on the steering wheel. My eyelids joined in, blurring my wet vision.

"Jeez, this is it!" I thought. Got to make it look like some dreadful accident. Plough straight into the front of him and I would disintegrate, disappear, cease to exist.

He dipped his headlights. If it were day I would probably have been able to see him clearly. He would probably have had a baseball cap on backwards, wearing a string vest, tattoos on his muscular working shoulders, probably humming badly to his favourite radio station, cigarette in his lips.

Now only 30 or 40 metres apart and I felt sick. "Why, oh why am I such a failure!" I screamed. This would end it all and all the people that have the misfortune of being entangled in my life could make a fresh start. I began to cry, sobbing loudly. Oh, God, what about him, the other driver? What if he was also killed? No. There has just got to be another way. Just do what the rest of the suicide loser squad do. Slit my wrists; jump in front of a train or off a tall building. I could knock back my own small pharmacy of pills in one hit and that should do it.

So in the end I flew straight past the truck.

The next night, that feeling of sickness and self-repulsion grew yet stronger.

Again the next night and the next ... blacker and blacker...

What is it with us suicide morons! OK. If I were a starving orphan in Africa with no prospects of another meal ... ever ... or in my final year at university expecting to come out with top honours – fail – get dumped by my long-standing girlfriend – parents get killed in a horrific motor accident and I get diagnosed with terminal cancer. OK, now. If ever one should get sympathy for even contemplating the deed these might be considered.

I, on the other hand, have three gorgeous daughters and an equally gorgeous wife who has stuck by me through all this crap. I have all my faculties, have a diploma in farm management, and have run my own business for six years.

Surely any normal person's response should be, ought to be,

"SNAP OUT OF IT MAN!!"

I can't explain the difference between the two extremes. The point of this book, I would like to believe, is to illustrate that it is possible to get to the horrendous point of 'the bridge' (which is where I believe I was going just before I was interned), by apparently relatively minor incidents. Somewhere it started when I became obsessed about never winning anything. The lack of success I had had compared to my contemporaries, peers and friends both at school and at college, all of whom, with the exception of two, I have completely lost contact with. Probably because my deep inner feeling is that they would be looking down on me with contempt for the meagre amount I had achieved in my pathetic, insignificant, meaningless life.

The critical reason (if ever there is such a thing) was that I was so far in debt that I did not honestly believe that there was a way out. As insane, believable, plausible excuses go, this would probably be the best, as a condition of buying the business was to take out a life insurance policy. The event of my 'timely demise' would eradicate all debts...

CHAPTER EIGHTEEN

... held together by sticky tape ...

Almost out of the blue, a National Convenience Chain with outlets throughout England, Wales and Scotland approached us. They had just had a massive reinvestment and were looking to acquire additional outlets. We were in an ideal location so when their letter arrived we allowed them to court us. They continually forgot that it was them that wished to buy our business and not us wishing to sell and so as a result the process dragged on for around eighteen months. They would insist that certain conditions were met and then we would simply tell them that the business was not for sale. Eventually they agreed and the sale went through, much to our relief. It had become more than a burden.

Our bank allowed us to go up to £30,000.00 overdrawn, but it often veered as high as £40,000.00 and that was in the summer, which was supposed to be when we made money! However, it depended on the timing of the deposits, which could be as much as £8,000.00 over a weekend, to the size of our orders. It was always a catch-22 situation in that reducing the order had an impact on sales. My frustration, anguish and ultimately my depression were because of my own apparent inability to control this downward spiral. If only I could find and successfully prosecute the staff members and members of the public who were flagrantly stealing from me. Perhaps the apparent success of the business led them to believe that I would be able to support their grazing. If only the issue of price differential with the major supermarkets was not such an issue. Many customers would delight in telling me that certain of my products were considerably more expensive than they were, say, in Tesco's or Sainsbury's. People were so fickle and appeared to hold no loyalty to me at all. Some weeks they would come in and greet me cheerfully, and buy what we might describe as a month's end shop! Other times the same people would come in, scowl, and demand some unusual product and deride me for not having it. Many customers abused our account system and on the final day we closed we had to write off a few hundred pounds. There were people who inexplicably never darkened our door, either because they felt that the service was not satisfactory or because they had decided upon a personal vendetta. One particular individual I caught in the shop one day just after we had had a refit. He presumably thought that the business had changed hands. I greeted him cheerfully as he rushed past me to get out. I determined at that moment to get my revenge on the bastard. I plotted to pour petrol into his letterbox one night and burn him and his house to the ground. If he wanted to hate me, well, I could out hate him in return.

Come the big day of the sale, I truly believed that my problems were behind me. We had not sold the business for a fortune but, certainly short term, I did not need a job. We went on holiday to visit my parents in Cape Town and came back totally refreshed. I almost fell into the trap of believing that getting a normal job would be a formality, and so it immediately depressed me further when after the fifth or sixth interview I was found to be apparently unemployable.

My younger brother Jonathan was by now an Area Manager for an American coffee company and he suggested that my managerial skills would be transferable to run one of their outlets. I applied to them and was delighted when they accepted me. The unit was inside a major supermarket only twenty minutes drive away from home. Everything was going wonderfully to start with. It was an enormous challenge to recruit and train suitable staff. I was also asked my opinion on the layout and style of the premises because of my own experience in doing the same for my own business. It was very exciting to see it develop. I was very fortunate to find a wonderful bunch of people to work with and we all got on extremely well. The wheels started to fall off when I realised that I had no input on the gross profit on the outlet, although I succeeded in reducing the running costs well below the average for the company. My job began to revolve around wiping tables and smiling sweetly at complaining customers who would not understand why there was such an incredible difference between what the growers in the Third World received for the coffee and what they paid for a cup. I attempted to cheer myself in engaging in the companies many in-house competitions, coming second in the highest single sale competition, for example. The store was one of the smallest and it was something of a surprise to have an outlet in regional England doing well at this sort of thing. The stores in central London usually won. We had an incredible record of the lowest man-hours used to run an outlet. I managed this simply by scheduling myself as a barista, an employee that operated the coffee-making machine. I would do the banking at the quietest moments, leaving only one member of staff on duty. Fortunately, the bank was also inside the supermarket. I began to get increasingly despondent with the menial nature of some of my responsibilities and yearned to stretch what I still considered to be my true potential. Perhaps if I had had patience, I might have also been able to take the route Jonathan took with promotion inside the company. After all, one individual that had been recently promoted was little more than an idiot.

I would return back to Hurley in the evening and would invariably bump into old customers of ours who would plead with me,

"For God's sake Joss, take the shop back; it has fallen to rack and ruin. The whole village is in despair!" I had just had another depressing interview in which I was again rejected due to unsuitability and felt that if they were to offer me the same package then, it would be worth it for me to return to manage what had been my own business. There certainly appeared to be good reasons for it. I would not be ultimately responsible for its success. I would have the backing of an enormous head office and I would get extensive training on how to do the job. I would not have to drive and I knew most, if not all, the customers.

So after less that a year with the coffee company I found myself commuting an incredible distance down to Southampton to do my training. I was put up in a small hotel for one or two nights a week. The manager and his staff were all pleasant enough. In fact, in many ways I quite envied them. It was very much a family affair with both sons and daughters-in-law working for the shop. They kept saying,

"Well, of course, you will have to somehow do all these things on your own," as if I was some kind of octopus. These responsibilities included a plethora of small but time-consuming jobs, such as counting all the newspapers in the morning, getting the entire newspaper rounds ready before six o'clock before the delivery boys came in. Perhaps I was too far gone to quit; I certainly could not go back to the coffee company, and so I doggedly carried on the training for months, becoming more and more tired and despondent. Come the big day of my passing out examination, I was nearly spared the following chapters, as it were, by coming close to failing. Still, I didn't and with some gusto I was thrown into my old haunt.

The Relief Manager was an old hand who knew the Managing Director well and he was not going to be persuaded to open the business from six to ten. He simply shut at six. On day one the Regional Manager came to see me. In my office (Jonathan and I had built it), he stated that the purchase of the store had been a disaster for them and that the reason that they had taken me on was because if I could do it for myself, then I could do it for them. There was to be no excuses, the store was to be open from six until ten. Now, had I had my team of young men who held the evening shift together it might have been possible. It might have been possible if there was anyone that could do it. As it was, there was no one yet they still demanded that I should still somehow do it. By this time of course, the little money that we had from the sale of the business had disappeared and it was crucial that I had a job and the family had an income. The whole issue of failure and depression no longer weighed like some far distant cloud to consider. It was a sudden rush of certainty that I had to liberate my family and myself. I wrote a foolish note to Belinda saying,

"I am sorry I am such a failure."

Somehow she found the note as I was on my way to nowhere and dragged me up to the surgery. Fortunately my own doctor was on duty and he saw me immediately. It did not take much convincing that I should be admitted to a secure psychiatric hospital.

"You need a lot of rest and recuperation. Also you may need to think about the kind of people that you want to work for," he added pragmatically.

He telephoned the hospital and drove us there immediately.

CHAPTER NINETEEN

... collapse ...

Jeez William, Will, Bill, Billy, Buddy, only because you always scraped the labels off your bottles of Bud – well, also because you were the nearest thing to a Buddy I had. You asked me to write down the experience. It seems as though it was twenty years ago – really only a few weeks. There was no real start and certainly no real end point, as yet anyway.

This is the meat of the whole story, so apologies for the strange becoming bizarre, the real becoming unreal and the norm becoming frighteningly surreal. It is where I actually found myself inside a mental hospital. (No, Bazar did not become bazaar, which then became bizarre). Michael James Hunt, Richard Nathaniel Kingdom Head, Pedro Darling, Loony Leslie, Lesley Bien, a hideous German woman, Erma Pratt, and other loony characters including Doolally Sally and me in the Local Loony Bin.

Belinda was weeping buckets on my shoulder. A kindly dear offered to make us tea. I call her a 'kindly dear' because it is too early in the tale to refer to them all and me as 'loonies'. We were ushered into a tiny office where she continued to blub away. I suppose I was in some far away state believing myself beyond hope. Belinda and an ageing doctor – grey, balding, frowning, stereotypical half glasses, stethoscope, pens and thermometers, go head to head.

"What has caused this to happen?" he asked sympathetically.

"He is under a tremendous amount of stress at work and it has just got on top of him," Belinda tried to explain through her tears. I don't recall him doing some Loony Test such as looking inside my ear and seeing if he could see any vipers or vapours, but I do recall him asking a lot of questions.

"He has been getting progressively worse for the last few years," Belinda wailed. Apparently I had even given up on the idea of claiming that somehow I was in fact coping.

"Yes, but what specifically do you think is making him mentally ill?" His furrowed brow lowered menacingly at her as if it were an entrance examination. Belinda's determined concern to see me get the best and most appropriate treatment left the consultant in no doubt that I was either under incredible stress, or mad enough to be admitted.

I suppose, looking back, there must be loads of people looking for a free holiday and if they could only persuade the overworked, underpaid, idiot doctors, they would be in to the Holiday Camp of a lifetime. Although, I don't think that he needed much persuading that I was doolally (orghay, orghay). I was given a small suitcase of medicine, most of which was too frightening to remember, and was led away to the boys' dorm.

"Aargh!" I moaned and cried into my pillow before the various chemicals quickly carried my mind away.

The first three days were tremendous, as I did nothing else but sleep. I later came to realise the true meaning of sleeping as there was a chap called Roland who was a professional sleeper. If it were ever an Olympic event he would undoubtedly have been a champion.

Before I went in, I think I had thought I was essentially just an off-the-wall extrovert eccentric, not an actual full-blown loon. The whole episode inside the psychiatric hospital was actually very frightening and I was reminded daily that there were no clear boundaries. I frequently referred to the place as the 'Bin', almost to show that I was not afraid to. However, I hope that you, dear Reader, will not be offended if I refer to it as the 'Bin' again in the future. I was surrounded by fears.

Fear that I was not really bonkers and that I would wake up sane again…

Fear that I really was bonkers and that it was just the beginning…

Fear that Michael James Hunt would actually get into my bed. I managed to fend him off for the duration of my stay. My ridiculous line of defence was to get paper clips and clip my curtain closed. The only way I got in and out of my den was to do an army commando crawl under the curtain. I hoped that if he were intent on making a nightly sortie it would jangle the things I had hung on the clips.

Fear that my life was irretrievably damaged.

Fear that I could no longer look my peers in the face without them knowing, "You've been sectioned in a Loony Bin!"

Fear that the pills they were giving me were in fact just placebos as the desire to save my family, the weight of my torment, still drove me to consider option B. Possibly why I felt drawn to the seat by the river.

Fear that all the well-intentioned medication I was receiving was changing my whole character and personality into a lesser, altogether different, unknown person.

Beauty woke me that night. I knew it was her, she had the standard nurse uniform, complete with pens, thermometer, watch clipped to her top pocket and her same sweet-corn perfume. In the half-light, I recognised her beautiful pouted kissing lips that were once mine. She touched my forehead as she had done many years before.

"I have brought you treatment." She smiled quietly that same radiant, beautiful angelic smile.

"Beauty, Beauty," I whispered, "Only you can save me."

She slipped naked into the bed with me and without waking the other loons we quietly made wet beautiful invisible love. The same ripe, timeless, peach hips were mine again, the same golden brown breasts with button hard nipples. I could feel her and I could taste her. She haunted me and tormented me; her magnificent imaginary body rode and exhilarated me from the past. She held me in her grasp as we rolled and fought again. Had I really defiled her? She was so willing... perhaps she was my real love... perhaps, perhaps...

Beauty

Put your hand here, touch my stomach
Yes, your stomach, you remember now
Touch my breasts, these two breasts
Feel them, caress them, they are yours
These are my buttocks, touch them also
Put your hand on my bare knees, please
Run your hands through my willing hair
Give me what you owe me, pleasure
Now my body is yours, then and tonight
Gently rub my calves, my inner thighs,
Touch my womanhood, make me shudder
Eat me, devour me, but don't forget me.
Leave me wet with exuberance of love
Remember me as I was, willing to please.

Belinda's soft, small, warm, caring hand came through the chemical cosh saving me from drowning in my own rotten, putrid thoughts. She did not ask for explanations, or even a timetable; she was always totally confident that somehow I would put the whole episode behind me. She was aware of the demons that possessed me, but she believed that she had to be there for me when they finally left me. Beauty, Simone, Sally, Kerri and the many that I had never actually met, all tore shreds into my mind. They did seem to have an agreement in that they did not share the same nightmare. Often they would appear suddenly in an otherwise normal situation and then we would be doing something erotic together, usually making strange love and usually outside in warm clean grass. Always Belinda would somehow exorcise the ghost, almost like a semi-transparent medieval maiden in white shining robes. At the moment of climax I would open my eyes in the dream and the woman underneath me would change from fading Beauty to beautiful Belinda, from golden brown to florescent white, from lucid past to wretched present, from wild imagination to physical reality.

The first place of interest in the asylum was the kitchen. To many of the loons, it remained the only place of any interest, all that potential to do damage, broken plates, electricity, boiling water and sharp knives. There were many deep cruel moments when I thought that some of my fellow inmates were there for the kitchen/gravy ride. Sad old outlook on life, but imagine it, four meals a day and as much tea and coffee you can put down. Zottie, an Albanian and a veritable working machine was in charge of the kitchen. If I ever go into business again, I will have to find him and make him a partner. One particular old crone was quite possessive about the kitchen space.

"What are you doing in here?" she dribbled dementedly. With her dressing gown filthy and her matted hair, she looked as if she was about to audition for a part as a hag in *Macbeth*.

After the kitchen, the lounge was almost as interesting. When I first arrived I had no idea as to the many applications of a settee. There were two computers. I use the term 'computers' in a very generous loose fashion. There were screens and boxes that looked as if they might once have been the brains. They might of course have been part of some clever exhibit. Anyhow, they were rubbish, to be beyond polite. Still it took me a couple of intrigued hours of fiddling to discover the fact. Then there was a cupboard full of puzzles. I hoped that I never became that sad that I ended up doing puzzles. Before one asks, yes, I did... To stop us inmates becoming too attached to our puzzle creations, the Bin policy was to deliberately remove one piece. The previously mentioned, sought-after settee, a couple of chairs, those soft floppy things that hippies, loonies and dogs sit in and of course the telly. Yes, all the windows were bolted. Or rather they were prevented from opening more than a few inches. Although, let's face it, in the event one of us jumping out, we were unlikely to kill ourselves. Perhaps break a few bones, unless one managed to land directly on one's head. One could of course escape.... The girls' dorm door was straight out of the lounge. Ours was just off the main corridor. I never had the urge to go into the girls' but I got the impression that the midnight journey between the two was not such an uncommon thing as I stumbled upon the condom machine. They would not have put it there for show, would they? The thought of loons happily breeding and producing a generation of super loons would have the voters a bit jittery, especially as it would be at the taxpayers' expense.

The lounge was also the dining room and as such had five or six tables and chairs. Daytime telly was, no doubt, invented for the likes of us that end up inside. The pecking order as to who sat where was not as you might imagine, first-come-first-served; well, it sort of was if you did not mind being surrounded by doolally, smelly dribbling old maids. Beyond the comfort of these two rooms lay the huge hall that was the rest of the ward with many various adjoining rooms.

The medicine room was one in particular that life revolved around, particularly when one became more familiar with one's surroundings. I will spare the sordid details, except to say that come bedtime it was a bit of a haggle as to whether one had enough medicine. I always got the impression that the measure of how ill one was was how many pills one was issued with. I had a significant psychological advantage in that I felt that my many vitamin pills and asthma pumps counted, as I was also a raving veggie by then.

It was really a strange and surreal environment. The main hall had a pool table and a table tennis table. In one corner there was, in the past-past tense, as it had been put out of its misery, a music machine. Doolally Sally attacked it one evening when it was playing the wrong music.

"Take that, scum!" she screamed as she hurled it against the wall. The little chain that was designed to prevent it from being stolen was not sufficient to save it. "Who the hell is Beethoven, anyway?" she added when she had finally calmed down.

During that first few weeks I was not allowed out unaccompanied. Actually, during the first few days, I was not allowed out at all. I remember the brightness of the sunlight hurting my eyes. The otherwise gorgeous English sunshine was too hot for me and I couldn't go out of the shade. Initially it was great to be able to sit on the benches just outside the ward entrance and just breathe. I can't remember who introduced me to the bench by the river but it certainly was a special place I enjoyed. Once I somehow escaped without the warders noticing. There were always doctors, nurses, numerous trainee nurses and other auxiliary staff coming and going so although the door was supposedly kept locked at all times there were invariably lapses in security. I probably muttered to one of the junior trainees that I was going out just as she ended her shift without her passing on the vital bit of information. They never did find which nurse I supposedly told. Actually I felt sure that I really had told one of them; but hey, who was I to argue, I was a nutter.

Stefan, one of the fitter warders, came sprinting down as if he was about to overtake Linford Christie, saw me, sweat pouring off him, and without a word he bolted back to HQ to report on my safe whereabouts. That would have been a good moment to jump into the river and drown; it would have taken them hours to find my body. Still, I could swim, so it was not really an option. The serious option, Option B, was Suicide Alley. It was that B road notorious for having large heavy trucks speeding along it. I just had to swerve in front of one of them coming towards me...

...there would not be a lot left...

Doolally Sally was good for a laugh in a manic kind of a way. She had obviously been in a couple of times before and knew when was the best time to throw a fit and when best not to. On a couple of occasions she would be rampant, usually with the warders. I think on the one occasion it was because some money had supposedly been stolen from her cupboard and if they did not search all the cupboards, she was going to call the police. She knew her rights, although I could not see the Old Bill hurrying around to the Bin for that sort of thing. Anyway on a quieter moment, she, Roland and I were playing pool.

"Actually Roland, playing pool with you is a bit like playing with a shark. You are too good for us. So to make it a bit more interesting..." She challenged him with a wink, "Let's play strip-pool!" Sally and Roland were probably not much older than twenty and in normal life might have been quite suited to each other. He had his football supporter's haircut and she had her gypsy skirt and frills. She was quite a sight, whirling around on top of the pool table barefoot, teasing us with glimpses of her pretty red knickers. I don't think she actually got to take any of her kit off as Stefan forced a change in the rules, back to the way they were, and Roland immediately lost interest. Sally disappeared soon after that. She was diagnosed as having some condition that meant that she would not be able to work for the rest of her life. But I also think that it meant that technically she was not loony, which must have been a relief.

Despite the fear, there were moments of happiness. The definition of which I think I had laboured hard over long before and since. It may well be a short-term spasm of shared laughter of over repeated jokes or the realisation that despite the illnesses, and private agonies, we were all able to recognise the parts not torn in each other. All loonies are part genius and hopefully one will recognise that many out there on the outside are part loony. It is a fine line. It was also difficult to recant and repackage the words that made those hysterical jokes here with the screen staring blankly back at me. I will kick off though with an incident that sort of got the boys dorm laughing at me and hopefully, but perhaps I am just a dreamer, with me. The first week or so, sleeping was not an issue as my body craved it so badly and anyway, they certainly were not shy in handing out the sleeping tablets, I could have slept next to an operational road drill. But when I started to slowly come round, as it were, I realised that I might as well be sleeping in the jungles of Borneo, that the 'All English Indoor Snoring Competition' was being fought here in the Gurney Ward Men's Dormitory with a vengeance. I say being fought; actually, the competition was really only for second place. Pedro was light years ahead of the rest of the field. In fact, to describe the noise he made as a humble 'snore' would be insulting. He was undoubtedly a roarer!! A serious lion in full charge, I'm-coming-to-eat-you type of roar! Another bloke had his bed opposite Pedro's, I can't remember his name but we sort of exchanged pleasantries,

"What you in for?"

"Slashed my arteries," that kind of stuff, would probably come second. He was also a true artist in his own way; he had two snores! An in-snore and an out-snore, both subtly designed to prevent anyone within one hundred yards of even thinking of going to sleep. So, what did I do about it? Remember I was fairly **(Ed. Does one read, 'very'?)** tired and could have done with at least a bit of sleep that night. Well, I thought I would tackle Pedro first as he was the nearest and the loudest. If I could shut him up, the other blokes' tidal roaring might just seem like part of my disturbed dreams. Now how was I to know that the night the police arrested him, they kicked his foot to get him into the police car and broke his toe? Being a big man who knew his rights and of course felt that they shouldn't have done so, he proceeded to take legal action against them. It would happen to be the same foot whose toe I chose to tweak. Roland had great memories of the event, saying something like,

"You're in full flow!" Full flow, full flow was the only bit he remembered. Pedro of course did not remember anything of that except he woke up with his toe in blinding agony!

"Who did that, you bloody bastards? I'll kill you!" he screamed with venom. Fortunately the pain prevented him from doing a full investigation at the time. Perhaps he feared that one of the serious loons kept a hatchet under his pillow and would swing at him if he were to wake them up to ask,

"Did you wake me up?" he demanded as I sneaked past.

"Not me." I hunched my shoulders. After that I gave up on toe tweaking and crept into the lounge, hoping to sleep on the settee. Prettyish, youngish, heavily pregnant Jennie – seriously and totally doolally - was already there. I made the fatal mistake of waking her up and asking her to go back to her bed. In my mind I didn't imagine women snoring with quite such ferocity.

"F*%k $$f!" she cursed venomously and loudly as she rolled on to her other side. Plan C. I found a spare pillow and put it over my head and that way managed something near to sleep. Like many stories, it improved each time it was told, almost to the point that I did not recognise it when Pedro and I went back for a reunion to try to spring Richard

Nathaniel Kingdom Head aka Dick-Ed. Roland was in hysterics long before Pedro got to the punch line,

"Full Flow, Full Flow!" Everyone was in stitches...

It must have been after at least three days that I did not go straight back to bed after being forcibly woken for food or medicine. Even then I did not leap straight into the first Eleven Snorers. Beyond sleep I had little interest in my immediate surroundings. On a scale of one to ten, my bed at home being a ten, this was a nought.

"Come on Joss, you must get up; it is the fifth time we have called you for dinner. You know you must eat." The pretty African nurses would poke their heads into my territory and attempt to persuade me to come out of my drug-induced slumber. It must have been in the manual not to shake the customers, well in my case, it never got that bad; they just had to shout louder each time. Although, it may well be that I missed a few meals as on one occasion I awoke famished. I certainly had lost all track of time and if I was told that I had in fact woken up a week later, I would not have been surprised.

I had had a terrible experience when Belinda had come to visit and had brought Felicity. Cool-Dude-Flick luckily was wearing her shades. It was the middle of summer and she was about to go to the swimming pool with a friend. I completely did not notice the streams of tears coming down the precious child's face. This was partly because she was intent on looking away, and because of her dark glasses and mainly because of my selfish determination to tell Belinda the full extent of the horrors of the place. I did notice however, when they suddenly erupted into loud sobs. I think that was one of the major factors that made me realise that I simply had to get out of there.

"Sophie cries herself to sleep every night because you are not there." Belinda brought home the realities to me. "She wants to know when you are going to come home to read her a bedtime story," she continued. I knew I had to get out as soon as possible, whatever it took.

Belinda would arrive almost to the minute. My meagre failure of a life, I am still not sure that I have resolved that particular issue, revolved around her arrival.

Almost from the very beginning I felt that the other inmates were envious of the attention I was apparently getting. There were some poor folk in there for whom one visit a month was about their ration. She would lead me to our bench and happily chat sanely about all things happening at home.

"My mum is coming out in a few weeks so when you come out she will be able to help with the children over the summer holidays."

"That will be nice. She has always wanted to come over. A pity it is in these circumstances. She could always go and visit her brother in Manchester if things don't go well with us," I replied.

"Oh, she will love to be here and she will love to be helpful, even if it is only doing the housework." Belinda was the most resilient character; she was determined to stick with me through thick and thin. Perhaps she took our wedding vows at face value. Whether I would have had the strength of character to do the same for her I did not know. But then it was totally inconceivable that she would ever be in such a situation; somehow, she was always in control. Her mother, Pauline, was a nurse and would be a great help around the flat, with three children and a loony husband and Belinda working full time. She was determined to help me regain my sanity. She ordered the Open University prospectus for me. At the time it did not make sense to me, as I could not see how we, as a family, could afford for me to study, so to be honest when it arrived, I immediately threw it away without looking at it. Later, I managed to realign my brain and realise the importance of doing some studying. I wanted to study Medieval History and at some later point go into further depth on this genealogy thing. Anyway, I think that I really would spend the rest of my life regretting that I did not take the opportunity to do so. Sadly I had already missed the opportunity to enrol for that year. However, again, I was determined to turn that around and study something else in the meantime. Like for instance, exactly which 'word' is the right 'word' to study, 'life', 'sanity', 'purpose' or 'Microsoft Word'? I would also like to do a typing course. One should see me here with my two fingers. This has all come about because I have made a fundamental decision regarding my employers. I know in my heart of hearts that if I were to attempt to do the job of Store

Manager in what was my own business, I would very quickly go back downhill. I had written to them saying that I need longer to recover and will only work twenty hours per week.

"So one's not been in a loony bin? Well one might have visited someone, but has one been inside his or her mind? It is scary really!" I was trying to persuade Jessica, but in my haze, I could see I was not making progress. I was no authority based on the fact that I managed to escape after a mere eight weeks or so, which would indicate that I was not a full-blown loony. The terms of my home leave were that I was to report back every week for an assessment. That went on for a further three months and I have now progressed down to one a year. The seriously ill patients would typically go in for a few months recuperation, be let loose, either neglect to take their medication or society would become too much of a burden to them and they would end up inside again, in a never-ending cycle. I am certainly of the opinion that loonies are only so in parts of their minds. The other parts are probably further developed than supposed non-loonies. Certainly I was able to relate to many of the wonderful people that were in there to recuperate and/or to recover from similar illnesses. In fact there were many times, as an inmate, when one felt totally abandoned by one's so-called friends and the people that one found oneself chained to were increasingly misunderstood and I could understand, sympathise and empathise with them. One sympathises with someone with a visible ailment one may have had, certainly one could understand. Without having been there, please don't patronise us by saying that one empathises. At the end of the day, I think, actually in the cold light of day, I was certain, I would rather be actually dead than have to spend the rest of my life being mentally dead. But then, comes the awful day, one is beyond the ability to have the option and would simply be parked in the system's chemical cosh.

Richard Nathaniel Kingdom Head, Pedro and I were The Escape Committee. Our plans varied, depending on whether Richard Nathaniel Kingdom Head had had his bowel movement, from a tunnel underneath the settee, to a superb plan that involved a submarine that would meet us at midnight on the Thames just beyond my bench. All new arrivals were vetted as to their suitability to be on the committee. Most failed the very strict physical and mental **(Ed. You will not let it alone will you)** requirements. Actually, I think that they thought that we were mad and, as one will have spotted of course, we were! Pedro, the clever schemer, had his own escape plan, which to be fair he did bring before the committee but it was thrown out because it was far too serious. He gave it a run in his second week and was promptly thrown out, on the grounds that he was a menace and would bring the institute's good name into disrepute. He embarrassed the senior Hospital Management by illustrating that their fire standards were woefully below standard. It certainly would be a predicament if one were to go in as a nutter and come out with First Degree burns because one could not be evacuated fast enough, or not at all. Richard Nathaniel Kingdom Head's real plan, if he had one, I think involved chatting up the head shrink whose name was Katie KizWillie and getting her to throw him out on the grounds that she hated the weekly assessments more than he did. Mine was a subtle combination of the two.

One of the more frightening, and also strangely very reassuring experiences I had was once I had successfully escaped or rather been discharged. The condition was that I had to go back for an appraisal or check-up every week. Going back for one of these interrogations, I went into the ward for the first time with my clean shirt and clean shave. The remaining inmates looked a million miles away from my world. As it happened Belinda was not able to take time off to come with me.

"Great," I reasoned to myself, "it means I must be making progress if I can no longer relate to them any more." The check-up was a hoot. I made the mistake of thinking that I would be signed off, as it were. I needed a change in medication was the decision after what seemed like an hour or so of deliberation – they more or less doubled the happy pills I was already on.

The loonies then proverbially had me for breakfast. Richard, Erma Pratt and the two Lesleys and even Stefan joined in for toast and coffee. We talked about the tunnel; I was going to start burrowing from the other side of the river, the Open University and the World in general. It was like being back with old friends.

Pedro, the winning snorer, telephoned. He said he didn't snore any more, thanks to me – and we agreed to meet at the Bin to cheer up Richard Nathaniel Kingdom Head, our fellow committee member. As it happened it was of course impossible for us to just visit one person and it turned out to be a very pleasant evening. In an ordinary evening there would usually be some sort of incident involving much shouting and violent abuse of fellow inmates. On a few occasions, the lucky winners would be carted away to the secure ward to be sedated. So it was nice to be able to see the healed side of those people, and in truth I am perhaps able to relate to them better than the nutters on the outside.

If I were to try and summarise my illness and my stay it would be to try and make real the incredible moments of anguish, hopelessness, fear and self-hate. Also the equally incredible moments of laughter, of hope, of camaraderie and the feeling that as one in five get some sort of mental health problem, we were not an abandoned species; that we do have a contribution to make to the big world out there.

However, having being released back into society, I don't feel part of it. I had just failed to renew my subscription to the social club after having been a member for many years. I was only able to go in on the very few occasions when I had a 'friend' to meet there. These had become fewer and further apart. Belinda insists that it is my own imagination and is probably down to my lack of any money, rather than being social ostracisation. My job in the evenings is never going to make the family into millionaires but it is sufficiently challenging to keep me plugging away at it. I was nominated to be 'Employee of the Quarter' after only my first quarter. I love listening to Radio Four on the way there and back, and particularly I love missing the seriously deranged television that the rest of the family insists on watching – mainly the soaps and pop shows. I have been able to make progress with my various essays, for instance on the causes of the English Civil War with all the uninterrupted time I have in the mornings.

The meaning of life beyond cubed cyber space

Learning... earning...completely nearly nothing
Mankind's ancient ancestors learned to jaw-jaw
Today man is not still further away from war-war
Following Millennium – He goes on with existing
Understanding, knowledge and communicating
Ten million years on, he has to find the flaw-flaw
His terrible atrocities are stuck in our craw-craw
That age of clever science will end our suffering
Your dirty obsession with all your personal gain
Your property, salaried, money, holiday, pension
Actors, authors, sports personalities – morons on
More money than the whole of Sudan and Spain
Your national despairing grieving communal pain
Your wicked indulgent world heading for The Sun

CHAPTER TWENTY

... recovery ...

A perception of success is perhaps a large house, car, kids at university, holidays in exotic places, etc. Well, I have none of these, but all is relative. My three daughters are all extremely bright and well placed to succeed in society. My beloved wife Belinda enjoys her job, which she is extremely proficient at. My job is going well and my Open University course is going exceedingly well and I believe that in five years I should have a degree. This year Belinda and I will have been married twenty-one years – doesn't time fly when one is having fun? As Sophie needs less attention, and is able to go to after school club and friends, I should be able to take on a more serious job.

However, that is really just a poor excuse to explain my lack of integration back into society. The truth, by almost any standards, is that I have yet to 'make it'. Life can be very cruel and the forces of nature do seem to be conspiring against me. We did have for over seven years two guinea pigs that were adored family pets until they died last year. Felicity was heart broken and kept begging that we get something new.

"I can't talk to humans the same way I can talk to animals, Dad!" she implored. After seeing some delightful mice in a hardware store, I brought them home to surprise her. She was of course, delighted but the consequence is that my asthma has become permanent and almost debilitating. I have taken steroids, antibiotics and am now on three different inhalers, all without effect.

About three years ago, when I was working in the village, I thought it would be great if I could become a retained fireman and duly applied. I sailed through the fitness, vertigo and IQ tests and was then sent to a doctor for a general medical as part of the application. I thought that my asthma might be an issue so I was pleasantly surprised to be informed that I could still join. However, there was a problem with my urine. To cut a long story short, after numerous and many embarrassing tests, one of which involved having an ancient chappie doctor peering down the end of my chopper with a tube accompanied by two particularly fit nurses - it might not have been quite so embarrassing had they been ugly old hags - it came to light that I only had one kidney, which was riddled with stones. Although I have not gone through the agony of passing a stone, I have now been twice for surgery to have them removed and the tests continue as to what is causing them. Three short years ago, I still looked vaguely like what I looked like at college. I could still run with the rest of the boys and sprint over the bridge to the gym where we met. Now with this kidney and asthma problem, doing any exercise has gone out the window, so I am now also technically obese. A very fat, asthmatic loon diagnosed with Bipolar Affective Disorder or Manic Depression with one faulty kidney, what hope do I have?

"...argh, all in a day's march, ha, ha!" says the man in the street.

Well, from a very different perspective, I feel it necessary to end on a positive note. Perhaps all my life I was obsessed with failure, defeat, coming second and at best not achieving my objectives. I muddled on through from one apparent disappointment to another. All my previous relationships, without exception, had failed. One particularly good friend from college, Matthew and I swore that we would remain friends to the end. But for whatever reason, I did not pursue contact with him, perhaps using the excuse that I had been in South Africa as the reason, or perhaps I persuaded myself that my flat was probably the size of his dog's kennel and he would no longer be on the same playing field as I.

Since making the decision to attempt to write this book, I timidly and almost reluctantly showed it to a true friend – **(who is now also Ed. Ed, if you dump me, I will of course forgive you. You are quite the most remarkable person, apart from Belinda, that I have ever met. Incidentally, before I am accused of lying, Belinda is not just a wife. She is my companion, soul mate, alter ego, conscience, editor, supporter and friend. She is also my best critic, my courage, my reason, and my purpose in life. As a woman, and a beautiful, desirable one at that, with my track record with girls, I desperately,**

desperately want to keep her as a friend – just a friend – a friend that can call on me when she needs me.) After handing it to her I immediately regretted it. We worked in the same office and, up until then, she had no reason to believe that I was anything other than normal. In the parts in which I expose the deranged side of myself...I was truly afraid that she would hand it back to me in disgust. A few days of anguish and torment went by. Her attitude towards me did not appear to change. Everything in the office was as happy and as busy as it usually was. Then one day, after everyone had left, it appeared out of her bag. She clutched it to her chest. This was it, she was going to tell me that she had got as far as page ten and that I should not give up my day job. She had read every page, carefully marking in the margin my many grammatical errors. Her shiny, enthusiastic, exuberant eyes said it all. She was delighted to have been given it to read and considered it a privilege. Her constructive, objective, totally dispassionate critique of my attempt overwhelmed me. The parts that a less kind person might describe as 'crap' she simply said needed more attention. However, she said that there were parts that were excellent. Some of the poems she was particularly impressed with. The biggest fault of the book as it was, was the ending. I was **NOT** a failure. The fact that I was capable of working in the stressful environment of the call centre industry was testimony to my 'normality.'

Initially I was not able to agree. The job was not really a real job, being a measured 43 yards from our front door. I was in the enviable position of being able to take Sophie hand-in-hand to school everyday and she was delighted with the number of friends she went to after school. Also I felt I had become a master of disguise in that I could hide behind my other self. When I first went into the hospital and a good few months before, I was convinced that all the many tablets I was dining on were merely placebos. Later I came to realise that they did indeed have an impact on the working of my brain (whether I will have to be on them for the remainder of my innings I have yet to see). Slowly, I became too aware that the person I was pretending to be was in fact really me.

"Joss, the fact that you are able to confront your madness and defeat it is a triumph. Very few people that suffer from mental illness are able to put it behind them as you have. We all have some 'madness' inside us to some degree and your ability to tell the story of your journey from apparent normality, through severe debilitating depression to recovery is wonderful. You must end the book on this note."

It is for this reason that the additional chapter on the Comrades is included. However the following two poems, on close examination, probably reveal more about my self-destructive mind than I intended.

Woman

Sensible, logical, creative, conscientious, absorbing,
Intelligent, industrious, exciting, direct, sad and caring;
Consuming, friendly, happy, honest, trusting, perennial,
Single-minded, persevering, honourable, capable
Thorough, courageous, selfless, strong and loyal
All of these... yet... you to me are also female.
Woman, exceptionally beautiful, penetrating eyes
Magnificent rounded breasts – beauty personified.
Curved graceful strong adult buttocks and stomach
Do I confess to loving you for your attractive personality
Or do I admit that I am also in love with your body?
Have you even sat on a washing machine on spin?
Have you ever had multiple orgasms? Oh Woman,
Let's persist in gazing meaninglessly at each other.
And never ask the question... for friendship's sake,
Become androgynous, sexless, fraught in splendour.

Do I acknowledge lying, deceiving you yet again?
I never really loved you, never was interested.
I just want you, need you, to caress and smother
Have you and hold you tightly, kiss you all over
Passionately make love till we both lie exhausted
Our bodies quivering with love's tingling after burn
Already regretting and savouring our obsession
God no! What is infatuation, without passion,
Without soul, without truth, without sense?
Perhaps as an emasculated celibate eunuch,
As an empty hollow shell without expression.
Love is not a piece of equipment, a tick-box
Love is not conditional ...or understanding
It just so happens, woman, that I love you.

Glorious Africa! Our shared vision of all that is beautiful
Great, mythical, divine, shrouded, heavenly mountains
Reaching into our inner beings, beyond drizzle, traffic
Here and now, calling us home. Cleansed sparkling
Euphoric, reborn, virgin-earth springs. Sky so true blue.
Blue! Blue that is eternal, infinite, pure, so mesmerising
Lungs drink in sacred potion, invigorating and rebuilding
Multi-cultured ethnic beautiful noble peoples that differ
In tones and clashes of browns, yellows and whites.
None complete without the others, perfectly balanced.
Our shared sight, our common image of this planet.
We are not lovers, carnally committing secret crimes
Some damned terrible violation of God's vengeful laws.
We stand innocent before **YOU** to be judged as friends.

We are fundamentally, diametrically different,
In composition, thought, outlook, and gender
We are friends, she with the wiles of womanhood
Graces, posture, culture and all female advantage.
It is not possible for any man to disregard her allure.
However, she is not some girl-dream from my history
That I have not been able to properly exorcise.
She is not a beautiful dream, conjured into reality.
She is conversation, therapy, healing, she is trust,
She is honesty, objectivity, someone there, here.
She is not an alien, a competitor, or monster.
Between anger and frustration is hidden truth
She would rather walk away from me forever
If she felt she was remotely coming between us.

She is a just friend, a colleague, a charming character.
Our marriage is not based on fear of ugly competition
Or misconstrued unintentional hurtful passing comments.
It is of total, absolute and uncompromising love and trust.
I like her as a lost spirit, as a fellow traveller, as a friend.
YOU are my being, my reason, my existence, my soul
My sanity, my happiness, my alter-ego and my future.
Everything I do, I do for you; **YOU** are my beloved wife.
I adore beyond words, beyond time and understanding.
YOU I adore beyond and above contractual acquaintance.
Today, I worship you more than ever before, my darling.
Forgive any hurt that I have caused; I love you too much
Our bond is not a physical arrangement between players.

Your dream

My gaba, my boet, my bra, my eie broer!
Words, gibberish, propaganda, sound,
Talking around circles, talking into voids,
Meaning nothing, meaning everything.
You talk to my soul, to my inner being,
You talk and talk harmony and discord.
You heal and wound with your words.
You lift and destroy my intimate thinking.
Like two random asteroids lost in space
You're chained, shackled, truly bonded
To your ignorance, to your blindness
To your ridiculous unsustainable lifestyle
Me to mine, our minds accidentally met
Miraculously crashed and forged together.
Be there for me when I cry with aching hurt
When I die; brother, scatter me near you.

Your hand in mind, so hard, so gentle,
My garden, God's birds, flowers, trees,
We two sit together endlessly entwined,
Music of your voice, touch and your mind,
Under the shade of my crab-apple tree,
Together on my little bench of heaven.
Mottled sunlight playing on your brain,
Flowing and downloading into mine.
Now your hand pulling slowly away
For milliseconds I hold your fingertips
You look into my eyes, the way you do
Getting up, momentary paradise over
For those rare precious dying seconds
You were my brother and my only friend
We spoke about beauty, about real life,
About pain, about those remaining aches.

Wrestling and tossing endlessly
The pain in my head intensifying
You are with me here and now.
You soothe and comfort me
Your body is my true medicine
In my torment I try to reject you
Yet I am frail, you are too strong
We love and bind into a contract.
An imaginary illegal dream marriage.
Our minds reluctantly fused into one.
Only you are my saviour, my temptation
You are my understanding, my laughter
My coach, and my closest ally, my consort
My hungry soul needs you to restore me
Give me succour, give me your strength
Give me light relief, give me your all.

I lie here in this stinking forgotten pit
Unrepentant, poisoned, punished
My deed so dreadfully foul, yet for love
Remembering exquisite fading pictures
Your eyes, your sweet, sweet touch
Recede into dirty vacuums of my mind
Your translucent hands becomes skeletal
Your sunken eyes dead and accusing
My sick mind floats into willed subconscious
You stare with hatred passion – why oh why?
I take you, your frail decomposed body
Crushed against my burning chest
In the dreadful silence you scream
A nauseating, repellent invisible sound
I envelope you, you are mine again
I did it for you, you must understand.

We lie naked together, us two again
You're alive now, these breasts awake
You smile that smile, conquering all
Our eyes half meet again in truth
Your handsome face inches from mine
You are all who you were before.
Your strong arms around my waist
My wet longing hands hold you tightly
Then you hold my elbows, pulling me closer
I stand upright, my shoulders into yours
Your rugged cheek turned slightly against mine
Take me away from here. Let us fly together.
Our single body a plane of imagination
We fly south, over European decadence
Over well strewn fields and pastures
Over the Mediterranean to total poverty
We fly over man's sad inhumanity

South, south to South Africa, our home.
We fly into Cape Town near Boulders Beach
My secret place. Jackass penguins roar
A *Piet-my-vrou* bird sings "piet my vrou"
Gloriously familiar washing of the waves
Hubbub of Munt Afrikaans intertwined
Magical twang of English spoken by my people.
Rhythmic clicking of the African Cicada
Your beautiful body, your mind, your soul
Totally at ease, at peace, eternal joy
You snuggle into me as we lie on the sand
My feet behind you, the cockpit of our plane
Sandy wind, crispy enchanted sun setting
Behind bent nature-torn gnarled bushes
You lead me through alleys of pure heaven
Into darkness we fly on, our bodies now one.

Upwards, outwards, darkness deeper
Blacker, more frightening, terrifying,
In space somewhere, we cling together
What have we done, us two criminals?
Children of passion, playing with love.
This bi-plane no longer capable to withstand
Fear, violence and evil threatens to crush us.
Yet, we are still together, one mind.
Seeing, but not seeing, as now,
I look into your eyes, let us land
Your strong hands take the controls
Holding my elbows again, leaning forward
Your strength defeats the evil, my fears
Quietly through a maze of blackness
We land in front of my familiar sink
Still clutching each other tightly

You whisper coarsely, "I love you"
And kiss me with your eyes and soul
For seconds we embrace thus
A car crunches up the drive
I whisper softly, "I love you."
Oh precious Creature from Heaven
What have we done to each other?
Oh pea, magic love device, secret switch
So vital to man's understanding of love,
His ability to make proper relationships,
Critical for all women to be complete.
Men make a vague, wrong vile attempt,
Fondle, a grope, – it's there somewhere
My breasts, you know where they are
You suck, caress, lick and massage
Yet the little key is left off, unattended.

It's here, it's here! Please find it, gently now,
Rub tenderly, softly, lovingly, make me squirm,
Make me moan, make me cry, make me scream!
Must I really show you? You were born into this world
It's your responsibility to know unlike illiterate millions,
You've escaped an education. Accept here and now,
My orgasm is not from you. My orgasm is not virginal,
The secret is in the key, re-entry care of my button.
Blurred and searing white-hot brain burning
Starting here at Da Vinci's sacred lower torso
Trembling, vibrating nerve endings tingling
My whole body engulfed by your electricity
Surging power of a million triumphant victories
Tides of glorious ecstasy and near agony
Wash away all mortal consciousness
To total exhilaration beyond living hell.

Our Elicit Love

My love for you
Is like being in heaven
Is like talking to God
You are my eternal angel
My guardian, my salvation.

My love for you
Breaks all the rules
We fly through breaking glass
Through molten lava
Through watching eyes
Through social snares

Yet our love still grows
Like an ancient oak tree
Its cooling shade covers
And defeats competitors
Spreading its roots still
Further and further with time
Spreading comforting shade

To caress and hold us.
Now your love, you
My darling, my wife
Is like a delicate possession
Held gently in my sweating palm
Age, wear and earthly cruelty
Have caused tiny fractures
Fissures where the paint peels

I turn it over
I turn from her
The beauty and the charm
That once were hers
Now faded and lost

I turn to you;
New, shining, illustrious,
Magnetic, hypnotic, enchanting
Totally, totally beautiful

I am in awe of you
Why is such an angel
In love with mere mortal me?

I have no right, no right at all.
Yet you do, you strangely love me
You look for reasons not to
But find none – why?!!
I am so imperfect,
So flawed and so damaged.

Yet as I am, I see you
See your love,
Its simplicity, its purity
Its honesty, its strength,
Its pride and passion

I humbly stand before you
Your love,
As your love toy,
Your love beast
Your love forever

I am yours, take me
Hold me, scold me,
Treasure me, argue with me,
Get angry with me, spank me
Spank me hard –in love

I will love you likewise
I will treat you like
My personal angel
Like a precious thought
Known only to us.

I will love you
As if you were
Born to be mine.
With all my heart
With all my soul
With all my being.

My Love for you

I love you like a clear blue bright sky
Like an unending awe inspiring sunset
Like walking in warm summer rain
Fingers entwined as we transfer thoughts

I love you like a Caribbean hurricane
Violent, desperate without any logic
Violent to anything that stands between us
Desperate to be with you always

I love not because of your beauty
Although you are and I do
I love you not because of your intellect
Although you are and I do

It never occurred to me
In my married misery
That I would ever find you.
I love you because I do
You, my Saviour, You, my Angel
You are Goddess, my everything.

I love you with a passion
I have never felt before
I love you now, tonight tomorrow
And always
Thank you beautiful maid
For coming into my life
And loving me in return.

I want

To entwine my eyelashes in yours
To feel your fingers in my hair
To feel your breath on my face
To taste your tongue with mine
To go to bed with you
To make love with you
To wake up to you
Your arms around me
To share your dreams
To talk with you
To talk and talk
To stare into your eyes
To laugh with you
To share beauty with you
To cry with you
As we struggle
Against the world
I want you
So much it hurts
I want you
To want me.

Your love

Your love is like a
Warm strong sea wind
I am a decorated Japanese kite
Bobbing, weaving, alive in the sky
You lift and hold me with you.
Your love is like a
Perfect ocean wave
I am a surfer skating magically
Defying gravity flying high
It is you that puts me here
Your love is like a woollen blanket
Surrounding me in love
In bliss to wash the day away
You with me here now

Your love is like a war shield
Amidst all the rage and the hate
You protect and save me
Bringing me always back to you.

My Promise to you

I promise to always try to live up
To your expectations of me
To put your needs, hopes, desires
Dreams and aspirations before mine

To love you like a wife, a lover
But above all, like a devoted friend
To be there for you when you experience pain
To share your happiness and to make you laugh
To share your pride in our children's pride

To share the responsibility of teaching them
Guiding them to appreciate beauty in the world
To tell you at least twice a day
"I love you"
With all my heart, all my being, all my soul
I love you now and will love you to the end

I promise never to hide things from you
To lie to you, to never raise my voice to you
To never end an argument without resolution
To always try and surprise you with love
With gifts, with beauty,
Doing unexpected things for you.

I promise to hold you to my heart
Like a most treasured possession
I promise to always treat you with respect
Courtesy, dignity and honour
All born out of love.

Swzi woo!!

You are to me amazing!
Your smile makes me happy!
Your voice makes me laugh
I love you woman, I really do!
Swzi, Swzi, Swzi woo!!
Do I love you like a hungry lion?
Do I stalk you to make you mine?
Do you see my swirling thoughts?
You and I dancing naked together!
Do you Swzi, Swzi woo?
I am so hungry for you
I feel like a caged animal
Straining unreleased desiring
To ravish and plunder you
Could I Swzi, Swzi woo?
Every single thought I think
Every single word I speak
Swzi woo, in clouded mists of
Reality, you are here with me
Swzi, Swzi woo, thank you.

...Your Kiss ...

...your kiss...
...like ripe golden peach...
...such bliss...
...like sweet summer...
...sunshine strawberry...
...stop me hold me my darling...
...I'm falling into your abyss...

...Your kiss...
...like strong red wine...
...my heartbeat takes a miss...
...intoxicating, overpowering, heaven...
...hold me, squeeze me, make my twist...

...Your kiss...
...Like a priceless diamond...
...blows my mind into senselessness...
...Into unknown erotic pleasure...
...your body I must possess...

...your kiss...
...like an untamed hurricane...
...starts to tear apart...
...our DNA, yours and mine...
...each molecule, each cell...
...combine to hold us together...

...your kiss...
...a tenth of a second...
...nay – two whole seconds...
...we are bound together...
...like two slaves to our sin...

…your kiss…
…you are his…
…I am hers…
…yet I am yours…
…to have and to hold…
…we play this endless game…
…for love for fun for pleasure…
…for friendship, for understanding…
…but most of all…
…for simple pure love…
…in your eyes I see it shining…
…without words you say it loudly…
…you peer into mine, deep into my soul…
…you see my innermost thoughts…
…my desires, my hopes, my dreams…
…my burning, seething enduring…
…love for you…

…yet…

…yet, we are apart…
…to be such by society…
…by our families…
…by our better judgement…

…we love each other from afar…
…let our love grow and grow…
…like the same ancient oak tree…
…let us wait our moment…
…when we can wake in each other arms…

Scrambled Smashed God and Blessed Belinda

You're a cosmology of energy
My sun and my moon
You make my world revolve
My world revolves around you.
You are food for my mind
The purpose for life
You are the thing that I love
Beyond all measure
Beyond time, beyond compare.
I still love you today
I loved you yesterday as a child
Like an irresponsible adolescent
Now I am grown
So has my love.
I realise now
That I love you enough
To let you go
Yet my love is still growing
I love you so much
My child's heart in this
Old man's body aches
At the loss of you.
I will wait now, today
In pain, in memory
My memory will grow
As will my pain
I have the patience
To wait forever.
I have hurt you so
Such pain is excruciating.
Fly amongst the clouds
Fly with the beautiful people.
Find a hero.
Be happy.
Make me happy,
By being happy…
You grow stronger
Day by day by day
I grow weaker

More dependent on you
More pathetic
My character draining away
Second by second.
You are more confident
More beautiful, more radiant
You grow with happiness
Your gorgeous teenage hips
Your gorgeous hair-do
Your warm inviting lips
You have become yourself.
Without you, I am nothing
Drained of soul,
Meaning and purpose.
I am left like a fish
Out of water.
Darling, I'm begging
You for mercy.
I've hurt you so badly.
You have emerged the victor
I, the looser.
Please take me back.
I will dedicate my life to you
I will live to make you happy
I will do whatever you want.
I know it sounds selfish
But I am dying without you.
You say you still love me?
It's been long years of Hell
I swear that I am now
And always will be
True only to you.
Surely you see that
You hold me in your hand.
Sitting here, trains flashing by
God I'm in agony.
Reasons to be alive.
Sophie and you
You and Sophie.
Reasons not to be.
Jesus an end to this pain
My useless life with its

Purpose shattered.
You say that you'll
Never never
Come back to me.
Oh God, my heart
My brain, my soul
My entire being
Burns in agony.
Train easier than pills?
Pills are easy…
Trains…oh God…
My brain is on fire
I have cramp in my neck
My face is hot and numb
I see in triplicate
My throat is sore
God, what a hypochondriac
I so enjoy suffering
My body malfunctioning
I'm too old
Too fat, too insincere
Too self-centred
Too tired
Too…
…suicidal.
I know it is cheap
I know you hate me for it
But I am dying rapidly
My reason for living
Has gone.
When will you know?
You have found yourself
Your revenge be complete
When will you be happy?
Beloved woman
Dare I say "mine?"
I love you so
I am consumed by you
Thinking of you
Every second of every hour
Of every day.
Please be mine again

I will honour you
Treasure you, look after you
Love you like a friend
Like a wife
Like a saviour
Please be mine.
You tell me to get on with life
To find myself
To go out with my friends
Don't you see?
I have no friends but you
Without you, I am no one
I don't want to be anyone.
Let me be with you
Let us be together
Darling I love you so
I want you so much
Please want me again
Before there is nothing
Left to have.
I know that you'll never
Read this, or any of my poems.
They are just the mad
Deluded scribblings of a
Demented ex-lover.
The fires within my head
Are more than physical
They are the drought
Caused without succour
From you.
Water me,
Bring me back to life.
I can be the man I was.
Exuberant, boisterous, witty,
Clever, charming, even funny.
OK, slightly extrovert,
Eccentric, even manic
But they were the reasons why
You loved me before.
I can be whoever
You tell me to be
I'll drop this family history crap

If it winds you up
I'll start jogging again
I'll even start writing again.
God the pain
Pour water on my brain
It hurts so.
My thoughts are all of you.
Please be mine.
Please say you will
We were so happy
You and I.
I really, really
Believe it will work
If you let it.
One day I will rise up
Like an Egyptian Phoenix
Claim my fame amongst
The literary folk on Earth.
Be remembered amongst the
Shakespeares and Blakes.
But not without you.
Without you, I am nothing.
Nothing to start,
Nothing to build on.
Empty.
So you see,
If I could turn the clock back
To that terrible time
And see into the future
I wish that we,
That woman and I,
Had never met,
Never crossed the threshold.
God, I was so wrong.
So very, completely wrong.
You are my life.
You are my beloved wife.
You are my reason for living.
You are the one and only
I love you so much it hurts
God punish me for hurting you.
You have every reason

To want to hurt me back.
You have every right
"To move on"
To not want me in your life.
I am just begging you
Like the pathetic child
I have become.
I have no self-respect.
I can't just wait for you
Don't you see?
I am diminishing before you
My ability to think, to reason
To live, are crumbling.
No, crumbled.
If ever I was anything
Married for 23 years
Father of three beloved children
Comrades Silver medal hero
Ran our business together
Advanced genealogist
Count for nothing.
Don't you understand?
Without you, they count for nothing.
Oh beloved Belinda
Your heart has turned to stone
You are happy to leave me.
I beg you again, please, please
Please don't go.
We were so great together
You and I.
We were so happy
Forgive me, and take me back
I swear I will never, ever
Take you for granted again.
Woman, beloved woman
Take me, hold me
Love me, feel me
Scold me, spank me
Thrill me, inspire me
Just be mine again.
For God's sake
For our children's sake

For your sake
For mine.
Please
Please, please, please
I am begging you.
Let me know happiness
Let me know taste
Let me breathe
Let me see clearly
Let me hear properly
Let me hold you.
To hold you would be Heaven
Oh sweet divine Goddess
I am just your plaything
I beg you not to tire of me
I am your toy.
Please don't consign me to the bin
As I did you.
I am the same toy that I was
Please play with me again.
I promise I will come alive again
Hold you enthralled with my vigour.
I can be your soldier
Earn you respect again.
I will be your slave
Your beloved husband
Your friend
Your ally
To be there when you need me
To protect you
To make you laugh
To help you.
Electric spasms shoot
Through my brain
Thinking these happy
Yet unthinkable thoughts.
God, oh great God
You can be so cruel.
Everyone around me
So apparently blissfully happy
Yet here I am rotting
Dying in despair.

Just one last kiss.
In my dirty subconscious
My thoughts conspire to believe
That your remaining semblance
Of cordiality or civility
Is because of your intention
To deliver the death knell.
To tell me that you no longer
Wish to cohabit with me
Living in the same building
Being just too much.
You will never read this
It dawns on me I am becoming
Increasingly Godly. God.
God knows. Oh God. Oh yes.
Yes – God is listening
To my pathetic pleas.
Oh God, please open her ears
Open her heart
Ask her to take me back.
Otherwise I will be knocking
On Your door.
Rejects like me who commit
The ultimate crime get sent
To the fires of damnation.
My loser mind thinks of it
It becomes the only way
This time, no mistakes
No return, no come-back
All my pills, a bottle of whiskey
Some pain killers to start
Sit naked in a warm bath
With a new Stanley knife.
Or hop in front of the next train
Oh so easy, my hand jitters
My heart trembles
Why am I such a loser?
One kiss would make today
A look of possible tenderness.
At the moment of impact
She lowers her head and
I kiss her on the forehead.

Enough to keep me going
I suppose, just one kiss, it was.
Loneliness is so dreadful
Everything is black.
Everything tastes of metal.
Everything is blurred.
Everything is muffled
Everything is an effort.
Oh God, even my retarded job
Devoid of complication
In my state of weakness
Of dizziness and doubt
I suspect my days are short.
The question is whether
I will be ignominiously fired
Or will I ceremonially resign?
Slight irony in the question
The day of my work review
Is the day of my
Mental health review
My lifeline to the insane world.
My psychiatrist, my doctor
My shrink, my friend,
I am petrified of her.
She is going to section me.
Imagine the hell.
Dribbling shot-away weirdos
Threatening to kill me because
I looked at them strangely,
Or because I did not.
Hysterical half-wit
With a carving knife,
Crazed inmate
Smashing furniture
With the remnants of
Her tattered brain
Me, with my delusions of love
My delusions of madness.
Maybe that is why
I am so afraid of her.
She will see beneath my
Veneer, my façade, my pretext.

Who in their right mind
Would pretend to be mad
Other than a madman?
She is bound to see
I am as likely to commit suicide
As anyone
So
"Go on, give it your best shot"
She says.
So, do I go and do it
And finally kill myself?
Final shut-down
No longer queries
No longer pain
No longer thought
Just permanent shakes
Permanent death
Thoughts of comfort
Are no longer.

2nd May 2008 - another day

Time ticking away
I'm 48, 49 in a few months
Will be 50 next year.
My wretched miserable useless life
I have achieved nothing.
Is it purely circumstantial?
Is it down to poor health?
Inadequate intellect?
Insufficient resilience?
Inappropriate education?
Fate?
Andy Warhol famously said,
"Everyone will be famous
For fifteen minutes."
I wonder if I have had mine?
So you don't see my strange animals
Yet I recognise your intensity
Your unique desire to be right
All signs of insanity to me.
The world is as likely to implode
Tomorrow as any other day
Also I'm a little bemused now
A gathering of a dozen cracked pots
Who claim to see crystal balls in their hands
Will do anything to change anything

CHAPTER TWENTY-ONE

... struggling for words ...

I was inspired to complete this book upon seeing a poster in the London Underground attempting to explode the myths of mental health (one of the many that 99.9% of the population don't notice). I was vaguely tempted to write in the convenient space on the poster,

"Thank you – this poster has significantly helped me. I am determined to come out a stronger, more purposeful and therefore a better person compared to the wreck I was. For those of you that still see me as a leper... please stop. I really, really am back in control."

It's funny, but the thought crossed my mind that had I done so, more people might have taken notice of the poster.

I have recently been sectioned twice, arrested and handcuffed six times, spent three nights in police cells and attempted suicide twice. I was twice hospitalised – the non-mental kind, and ambulance "blue-lighted" through central Reading. I was apparently unconscious for 3 days.

I apologise again if you, the reader are unfamiliar/ unhappy/ dissatisfied with my attempts at poetry. There were moments of extreme sadness and confusion where my simple mind could only think in terms of one-line connecting phrases. I suppose I should add quickly though that some of my critics/ reviewers have said that my poetry surpasses my prose.

Of course one reason for putting pen to paper again, is continue with the train of thought on the poster in the Underground and thereby enlighten you, the general public, as to an experience of mental health. Yes, you may be next. My serious, genuine hope is that more people would accept that just as there is physical ill-health and recovery, there is mental ill-health and recovery. I have been out of the hospital for three years now, although there have been a few moments where I have felt myself spinning out of control. Fortunately for me, I have close family and friends who have steadied me.

However, I have to confess again, from the onset, as to my real reason for writing this and therefore why it will never be published. It is by way of a pathetic apology to Belinda for my despicable behaviour. I understand entirely why she left me; I had become a hateful arsehole. I just so wish I could undo the pain I caused her. I know in my soul that it is never going to happen, but I would give anything, agree to anything to have her back. She, quite rightly, has put me behind her to find happiness with someone else. I genuinely hope and pray that she/they are happy together. I on the other hand, still wear our wedding ring that has been on my finger these past 24 years. Her birthday is engraved on the back of my Rolex and on my right wrist is a bracelet with "I Love Belinda Forever." I suppose that at some point in the future, I have got to stop punishing myself and do likewise, and put her behind me. Does it take a year? Ten years?

I don't know where to start really. Many contemporary authors like to start in the present and then go back to the beginning, occasionally flicking through time.

After going through the dirty details of my confinement, I am not sure that there is a "happy ending/conclusion." Yes, I have escaped and yes, I am back at work but each passing day compounds my sadness. Perhaps if I just set out on this voyage, the ending will just happen… (She will come back to me…)

This book will probably only get as far as a single *Lulu* edition, left for you, my grandchildren to find. It gave me some solace to confide my thoughts and poems to paper, which, ironically sadly, frustratingly, Belinda has sworn never to read anyway.

My friends and family repeatedly tried to convince me that my liaison (pause for thought...I need to think of a name for this awkward, delicate and ultimately destructive character...) with Ellen was simply the last straw. I heard them, but somehow preferred to suffer with my own guilt. I was entirely to blame. It was only when confronted by Belinda's angry and frustrated mother that it suddenly dawned on me that they were right. I set about writing her a truly terrible, vitriolic letter stating all the many breakdowns in the relationship that were Belinda's fault and taunting her to get Belinda to deny them. Hindsight is great and had I given it further thought, I should not have written such a hateful letter. Now, not only will I never be reconciled with Belinda, but her mother as well.

Ellen. The truth is that despite the above, I still feel responsible. Ellen could have been any number of women. She just happened to be there. Oh hell, well, here we go...

I was rather flattered by her having read my first draft overnight and said that it was fantastic. When she saw me, early the next morning, she ran to embrace me and kissed me on both cheeks. It had been published by a charity specialising in mental health publications, whose proof reading, she said, was little more than a general scan through. She immediately asked if she could copy-edit so to create a "marketable product," this being her profession. I of course, agreed. She set about the task with enthusiasm. At the time I had been laid off work after painful treatment to remove a number of stones from my remaining kidney. Yes, her husband went off to work and yes, we found each other alone... alone editing some of mine and Belinda's intimate lovemaking scenes. She had clearly led a rather cloistered sex-life, and perhaps mine was slightly more adventurous, but certainly I now believe that she fell in love with the persona I had created. Retrospectively I almost wish we had had sex... had we done so, perhaps she might have felt emotionally bonded to me. I think we both qualified our relationship as "intellectual", so it was no heartbreak for her to call it off. I say for "her" to call it off... here I sit in *Costa* at Stansted waiting for Malc's plane... and in the dim echoes of my memory, I now remember that it was me that ended it...

So, I instantly hear you ask, nay demand, "Why the sudden case of insanity?" Rather than a seemingly meaningless sentence/ paragraph, I think I will leave it to you, the reader, to fathom an answer. Perhaps you will join with Belinda in finding me totally guilty (perhaps that's it…the awful burden of guilt was too much for my conscious mind to handle…yes, ridiculous…).

I am going to stop now, partly because Malc's plane should be here any minute, and partly because I have inadvertently done what I intended not to, namely break the logical chronology of events. So again my apologies, I will try and work from the summer of 2007.

CHAPTER TWENTY-TWO

... another day in the life of a telemarketer ...

Ricky Gervais is the geezer who wrote and starred in that hysterical comedy sitcom, *The Office* – my apologies, Ricky, for any similarities.

Bal wears a smart suit, brand new silk tie and shirt every day. He believes that he is the MD and so do any naive New Starters. However, as with the joke about the balloon, he lets himself down occasionally coming to work in his pyjamas. A frequent routine of his is this: He slowly raises his left arm to a vertical position in front of him, and while continuing to babble into his mouthpiece, mechanically brings up the other arm up underneath forming the 'T' signal. 'T' is for tea, totty and toilet. He has long mastered the art of expending maximum time away from his desk. Time is money... We both rise ceremonially and meet in the aisle heading for the coffee machine. We are past the point of worrying whether anyone (especially management) has noticed that we take an additional twelve breaks a day. All around there is a sea of smartly dressed, (sorry, relatively smartly. No one does it like Bal, including the actual directors) executive telesales marketers. Most of them live in the belief that that is what it stands for. We who are in the know know that TM stands for Telesales Monkey. As we stroll nonchalantly through '*The Office*,' we bring ourselves up to date on any new talent that has recently started. There are usually half a dozen or so every week. All sense of continuing to pretend to be adults is long forgotten when one finds oneself letching at women that are probably younger than one's own daughters.

Taxiing gently into the zone, a whole complicated procedure begins. Bal has exactly two sachets of white sugar, two sachets of coffee creamer and of course the coffee. I stick to my tea and milk. I hate tea, but I will come to that later. While one of us is mother and plays with the machine, the other is at liberty to turn away from the machine (still engaging in heartfelt man-to-man discussions – such as where we should go to for lunch) and gawp. Some of these gals are pros, knowing that they are entering the cave of a testosterone-charged laboratory, their little skimpy skirts more suitable for the beach. They don't have to eye around them; they are safe in the knowledge that every (normal) male is visually eating them.

We amble slowly back to the cutting floor. It is sometimes possible to suck in the gentle whiff of the potential victim's perfume without looking too obvious. However, introductions will have to be made later at the regulation breaks. Before the final descent, a minor conversation into the ear of lovely Sarah, usually trying to persuade her to buy my book in instalments. She is one of those girls that means "yes" when they say "no." Her current excuse is that she is reading Harry Potter's latest... For some funny reason she has a provocative picture of a French can-can girl in full swing in front of her, on her desk partition. Sarah hasn't a boyfriend which is a crime and a waste seeing as she is stark-staringly beautiful.

Where was I? Oh Yes – our standard day consists of having to make a minimum of eighty calls to certain lucky winners (unfortunate bastards that have forgotten to leave their telephones on answer-phone) and, theoretically at least, one 'Op' a day (an 'Op' is defined as where sufficient information is gathered from the victim to ensure that when an account manager visits them, the sale is more or less a formality). Yes, to any other normal humanoid, potentially mind-blowingly boring. But Bal and I are master-mechanics. Bal has perfected the art of nodding off with his eyes open and I peer over Martin's shoulder at his on-going interesting Internet porn – he is a genius that boy, Martin. Bal only does this job because his main job is generally at weekends. He is a professional photographer so one can imagine the amount of 'sickies' he has to pull. What Martin's story is, I am not sure. I think he is into weed. He speaks Afrikaans every now and then to confuse me but on the other hand, can't speak Zulu. It's a pity there are no Zulu people I could ring up to confuse him. Martin is meticulous about his dress code. Every day he takes a shirt from the bottom of the laundry basket (under the sexually-abused-rotting-skid-marked pants), carefully rolls it into a bundle which he then stands on to get the creases just right. He is also just as particular about personal hygiene and does not come to work without having first rolled in a fresh heap of steaming dog-shit.

Now the mighty Louis, he ends up talking to his victims (actually they are more like personal friends to him) about where they are going to go for their holidays, their children, their wives and the women they wish were their wives! Yes, he should take up counselling. He does not approve of the coffee machine muck. Downstairs, on the ground floor, there is an in-house restaurant and coffee bar. Normally he and I would meet there at 8.50 in the morning and order hot water. No, not that sad. At his desk, next to mine, there is a miniature *Twinings* exotic teashop with an enormous selection, depending on his mood, but I think his favourite is Wild Chinese Nettle. Louis is the spitting image of that bad-lad on TV, Russell Brand, but far more interesting. He is essentially a retiring sort of gent but once I had got to know him, he turned out to be quite scary. He is also a registered loon (oops should I mention that?) but far better at hiding it. When he was young he was also going to be interned into the Fairmile but his parents said that they would take responsibility for him. He had been going through awful episodes of agoraphobia. He had found himself in the middle of Southampton, where he was at university, huddled up in the foetal position screaming hysterically. He also suffers from the most horrendous asthma, which he bears with the most incredible tolerance and courage. However the most amazing thing about Louis is his sense of humour. There is not a day that goes by in which he does not lean over and share some of his gems. "Phew, someone just dropped one!" he would exclaim. I would state that it was not me but probably Martin who just stank. "Yes, that's true, as you would roll up a sheet of paper, cut some strategic holes in the tube and play a tune with your arse!" He has had some of the most amazing adventures. Once he ended up in police cells for the night. When he was fifteen, he was in the army cadets at school and they had a healthy disrespect for the navy types. He and his posse kitted themselves out with all their commando gear, helmets, camouflage war-paint on their faces, realistic guns, grenades, the works. It was at the height of the IRA bombing. The poofy navy types saw these assault warriors stalking them through the woods and promptly called in the real army, police, bomb squad, ambulance, air & sea rescue, and anybody and everybody that might come to their immediate aid. It was not a fair tussle as Louis' men's guns could not actually fire bullets so they lost the battle and were ceremonially beaten up, cuffed and thrown into cells...

Louis has now gone over to the dark side and has become Kate's bitch. Yes, awful. I have seen Kate's naked bum – but I will also have to come to that later. He was promoted as he is something of an Op machine and is now a project leader. Kate is his boss (actually he is still a diamond). He has always maintained that his other half, Helen, is fat and ugly but it came as no surprise that she is the complete opposite, gorgeous and more gorgeous. Oh, one other thing before I move on... Louis is not a man to be held by the constraints of company policy. He would often amble out on the presumption of going to the loo and come back ages later. He confessed that when he was bored, he would go for a nap in the disabled toilet.

Now, who else can I grass on? You know that episode from *Father Ted* when Ted has to judge a girls' beauty contest and the final challenge is which of the remaining contestants has the sexiest laugh? Well, Vicky's laugh is so immoral, so deliciously wicked, and so wrong that she is the outright winner. She often wears kit so tight that there is very little left to the imagination. She has the body and mind of an experienced pole dancer. She could probably do a mean lap dance too (or are they one and the same thing?). What there is to giggle, laugh, titter and flirt about on the phone all day is beyond most of us but it seems to work for her. Well, presumably it does, otherwise she would have been tin-tacked ages ago. She is also a pro-temporary member of the lunchtime boozing gang. I imagine that when she is not drinking with us she is catching up on her daily allowance of sex (I wonder if she laughs like that when she is on the job...?). The main reason for the existence of the boozing gang is that the prices in the restaurant downstairs are so exorbitantly expensive that we have decided to boycott it. *The Carvery* however, is able to offer 'all-you-can-eat for £3.50' which of course is a far better deal. While we are there it would be a shame not to take advantage of the ridiculous price of their ales too. The most the mighty 'B' & I once managed was four pints of Guinness and two doubles of Jack Daniels (did I mention that it is essentially an incredibly boring job, and that one has the IQ of a gerbil?). Usually, in our drunken haze, we would fly through the afternoon and bag some top pheasants. The two temptresses that work at the bar call me 'Mr. Pimms.' Once "*Barbie*" was clearing away glasses nearby and heard a bit of our conversation which included me mentioning my frustration at my sexual inadequacies and that my wife has long since defeated me in the game. (I think it was that day that I chased Barbie around the bar and into the kitchen.) It is of course a topic of much mirth to them whenever we go in. Now Bal was the captain that particular day as he was driving. He usually drove because my car looks worse than a Johannesburg taxi that has never been washed. The tree under which I park must be home to a multitude of some flying creatures that are a cross between albatross and polar bear that suffer from extreme diarrhoea. Bal's BMW is like flying with BA first class, not that I ever flown first class but it must be luxurious. He had this crazy idea that he was going to take five of us to this amazing pizza place over by Cemetery Junction halfway across town. This of course would have meant that we would have spent the majority of our lunch break cramped in his car getting there and back, so it was not much of a surprise that when he mentioned the planned voyage, the crew mutinied and voted for the *Carvery*. He then said that he just had to fill up with petrol and then stop off to get some money. Hey! Us pirates had not signed up for this either, so when he disappeared into *Morrisons*, I requisitioned his ship and sailed up the delta to the pub, and ordered the beers, then had a sudden conscience attack and went steaming back to find him. To say that he was unimpressed would be an understatement! After handing the vessel over to the rightful owner, I climbed into the back as he did a vicious skidding turn and flew back up the road doing about 70 mph past the pub. Fortunately for me the lights were red so I was able to swim ashore. Vicky and her shipmates were there so I changed allegiances and joined her ruffian crew. Up close the laugh is even more erotic! Her first mate is baldy Hor-zay (Bal is also a baldy) who is weird. He does not have to put on any make-up to look like a pirate, comes from Spain and yes, talks funny. Has a genuine what looks like a sabre or cutlass scar on his bald head. The other member of the crew is Sandra (she insisted that I change her name – but everyone in the entire English-Speaking world knows who I am referring to). She is also weird. She used to be on my hate short-list. Long story, but I accidentally assaulted her (no, she did not end up pregnant and no I didn't go to jail). Going from not saying a single word to each other for months and months, we ended up as the best of mates, even to the ridiculous extreme that at our staff party I accidentally kissed her (no, not tongues). Sandra is particularly weird because she is a project leader but socialises with us riff-raff. She went to see *Metalica* over the weekend, you see...weird!

Who else deserves a mention? Ah, my fellow authors. Sly Simon is well into his second book. His first is about... (hum, will he thank me if I tell you? – if I don't you won't know what you are missing). It is called *"Red Light."* It starts as a very entertaining espionage about a criminal who gets enmeshed in the world of South American drug smuggling. However, the book leaps into a different genre when the hero decides to wipe out cocaine. It is extremely well researched and highly plausible and I would thoroughly recommend reading it. In my humble view its importance is that it is far more than an ordinary book, rather a manual on how to eradicate narcotics or illegal drugs. Simon has a beautiful girl friend/fiancée. The two of them peddle to work together until they part company and she goes to wherever she works. It is very romantic to see them part...

Mad Sam's book is quite remarkable. Sam is the in-house psycho. He is about nine feet tall so calling him names is definitely not advisable. His book is certainly no light read. It is called *Amazingstoke*. It takes the reader directly into the mind of a homicidal killer similar to the man that walked into a police station in Newcastle and announced that he had executed four members of his family; or the bloke in the States who randomly murdered thirty or so fellow students. It takes the concept of manic depression, failure to conform to society's recognised norm, anger management, vastly excessive alcohol and drugs to the extreme. The extreme not being a place of isolation inhabited by the anti-hero, but by hundreds, possibly thousands of otherwise ordinary citizens in this country. It is a tragic tale of someone determined to be remembered, irrespective of the consequences. It is far more than a book about downwardly spiralling immorality, decadence, crime and drugs. Like Simon's book, Sam's book leads the way in its field. It illustrates how the mind of a psycho killer works and, as such, it should be mandatory reading to anyone studying the subject.

Jeez– that was heavy.

Who else won't appreciate being lied about? There's mad march hare Steff in the canteen-restaurant. She is always good for a snog. She absolutely adores and worships Gerry. Gerry? Gerry disappeared about eighteen months ago. He is now the lead singer of the rock band *SixNationState.* Aside from Louis, Gerry is one of the coolest dudes I know. I was as shy as a mouse when I first started (as you might imagine as I was doing my best to pretend that I had not just been signed out of the loony-bin so did not to say a word to anyone). Gerry sat next to me and would have none of it and forced me into his gang. It consisted of him and a New Zealand guy call Nick. He was also cool for cats. Didn't get to know him very well though, as he left quite soon (he must have been cool as he was the only person who dared to come to work in shorts, sandals and Hawaiian shirts). And a wild-child chick called Ruth. She once succeeded in spending thirty hours in one week on MySpace before she was fired! I think Gerry was quite impressed with my suggestion for an alternative name for his band, *SixNationState* being a bit strange in that there are only five of them in it. Now everybody knows that kids these days are becoming increasingly affluent and they are the ones who will be buying his records. Most of the little blighters have seen, remember and can relate to the films about *Shrek.* You know the bit where Pinocchio says, *"I'm a real boy!"* Well the cool name for a top group is "*The Real Boys"* screamed in a high-pitched Pinocchio squeaky voice. Gerry is a cross between an Abominable Snowman and a Yeti although quite tame (only because I have yet to see him eat anyone). He looks vaguely like a younger, bigger version of Ronnie Barker. I can't remember whether he adopted me as his father, or I adopted him as my son; either way, he always called me Dad, and I called him Son. He invited Belinda and me to one of his concerts. It was great in that our actual kids were well into the whole rock concert thing, but as yet had not 'done' one, so we beat them to the draw. It was a small gig down the back end of Reading organised to try and persuade the powers-that-be that Reading is in fact a city and does have its own music culture. I will never forget him dedicating a song to me, "I hate the summer, but I love the rain." For us it was absolutely mind-blowing and I have since adopted the rest of the band. Richard is cool and looks like the guy in *My Family* that replaced Nick. He has this insane, inane grin on his face while he plays his guitar and every now and then goes mad with a whistle. John insists on playing barefoot which can be a bit of an ordeal in amongst broken glass. He still owes me a version of Jimi Hendrix's *Hey Joe* (You know why Dude). Alexey has grown a beard, plays the drums and looks as if he could represent England in the Olympics in something. Neil is a blond veggie and plays bass... actually, they are all dead cool on stage – very, very active. (...he don't give a damn coz them kid is a Gangster,,,! ...Up, down...!)

Are you ready for the bit about Kate's bum? Nah... it is the only reason you're still reading!

Oh, yes back to Steff. She is amazing in that she makes it her business to know everyone's names from their day one. She talks incessantly and tries to be cheerful but sometimes the world conspires against her and she breaks down sobbing. She is leaving at the end of this month to go and live in Devon where I sincerely hope she will be happy. She was delighted with my rhyme (which I think I remembered from primary school) and took pleasure in saying it to all her customers. There must be at least 400 of us in this building.

One fine day, in the middle of the night/ Two dead men got up to fight/ Back to back they faced each other/ Drew their swords and shot each other.

Lillian is drop-dead gorgeous, come to think of it so is her mate Agi. They could both win beauty contests if they put their minds to it. Agi is beautiful in a picture kind-of-way but Lillian, however, is the living representation of Beauty. Beauty the maid. Beauty the beautiful girl of my past, although I doubt I would recognise her now. Since seeing her last, and I don't believe that I will ever see her again, I have put on four stone in weight. Lillian seems happy to play the part of a girl that I vaguely knew long before she was born. She always smells divine but not in the same magical African way Beauty did. She dresses immaculately, seemingly with an unending wardrobe. Lillian liked my joke, 'What smells of poo and sounds like a bell? – Dung!' She laughed! Secretly I live in hope that she will force me into the disabled loo and ...

Malc! What he is doing here God only knows. He has an IQ of ... well off the Richter scale. He has read every book ever written at least twice, and is great mates with the entire shadow cabinet. He is only eighteen so one has to forgive him in his outrageous belief that the Conservative Party stands a snowball's hope in hell chance of winning the next election. Apparently if you cut him in half, he is Conservative to the core. I think he is voting for Arnie to be the next Prime Minister.

Ciaron, the little shrimp, is afraid of becoming a national statistic of paedophilia. He looks as if he is about twelve with a stick-on beardy thing. On Red Nose Day it was close, although I managed to hold myself back. He is also seriously annoying in that he gets about twelve Ops a day (how, nobody knows).

Nav – another twat. He is part of the in-crowd and can be seen every break on the decking outside enjoying the delights of yet another Marlboro or whatever he can scrounge. Actually top bloke, and somehow on my short list of best mates.

OK. I'll mention you, my daytime wife! Sara sits opposite me and occasionally we find each other staring into each other's eyes... Actually the daytime wife gag started at the office pool contest. Sara had had far too much to drink (as she always does) and presumably in her drunken haze had either mistaken me for someone else, or someone had told her that I had a fourteen-inch chopper and was good with it. Either way, before I knew it, I had this slavering-slobbering animal-woman-she-beast attempting to eat my tonsils and impregnate herself on me; she certainly stole a fair share of DNA strands off me. It was scary! The staring into each other eyes... there is nowhere else to look in the office! But before you report me to the Thought Police, I even find myself looking for inspiration from the mighty Bal!

Hang on – there's Victoria, completely different person to naked Vicky. She has a laugh of her own which is very sweet. Her sneeze is adorable but what is really cool is when she lets rip at whoever winds her up! I used to sit opposite her so we were quite friendly and I had been promising and promising to take her out to lunch. Eventually she tied me down and we had a very enjoyable meal together at Pizza Hut, despite the fact that Bal and his gang had stalked us! Afterwards there was an ice-cream van outside and I bought two spiral ice creams (apparently calling them Whippys is rude). I think she was quite surprised as to how much of a gent I was. I think that I like her too much to treat her otherwise. She is lovely. It is part of the office routine that I get a kiss off her every Friday.

Now the purpose of course of this slightly zany chapter is to try and convince you, the reader, that I have returned to something close to normal. Louis is able to take one look at me in the morning and state correctly whether or not I have forgotten my happy tablets.

This is my final proof of normality. On Red Nose Day the office had various schemes to raise money. One was that if us T-Monkeys donated a pound, we could come in dressed in civvies. Well, for £1.00 I was going to give them their money's worth! That green thing sticking out of my collar is the Oxfam price tag for the bow-tie. I have saved the whole outfit for next year.

Kate's bare bum? Thought I nearly forgot, huh? I think that if I were to tell the truth I would end up being sacked/ sued or both...

And me and tea? Now that is so seriously boring that even if I were to make up something, you would never read another book I wrote!

I let rip with another stormer (fart) and move to the window to let it escape before it kills me. I pick at the open wound across my wrist as beloved friend Sally/ Lizzie/ Jenny phones. Why she does not give up on me, Heaven only knows. I promise I will write her a poem, so here goes...

Sally/ Annie/ Jenny (you know who you are)

My beloved South African friend
A is for Aardvark
A long-nosed cutey
Road destroying maniac
B is for biltong & borevors
Staple diet of our mutual
Stamvaders
Raw dead meat
C rarely used
In Afrikaans
It's a K
D is for Doord or dogter
Dead or daughter
I have three exquisite of the latter
Which is why I am not the former
E is for...Armageddon...
F is for sex
G is for spot
H is for stop this.
Oh Sally, forgive me
My brain is comatosed
But you know how I feel.
I am now and always will be
Deeply in love with you
Now and always
My special female friend

I spend most of the morning practising the ancient art of passing through time - asleep. In the afternoon I finished my "Joss loves Belinda" plate, mug and eggcup. Nurse Abbey gives me a grilling (sounds as if there ought to be an alternative word there...) *"Give up on her, she is never coming back to you..."*

"It would be useful to for you to digest things from your relationship." she said

"It is self-destructive to compare yourself to the person who has taken your place with Belinda."

"Ensure that you get help when you need it."

"Live your life as well as you can and do not let feelings for Belinda consume you."

"Focus on yourself, push away from her."

"You need to be stoic, strong in mind and enduring and have the capacity to carry on regardless."

"She would want to see me strong as she is more likely to be attracted to this."

"You need to be able to grieve for the loss of the relationship."

"If it was not with Felix, it would probably have been with someone else."

CHAPTER TWENTY-THREE

... Waiting ...

02/05/2008. I have carefully packed away all my possessions into my Starbucks bag. At the top, sticking out, is the soft monkey I bought yesterday. It is symbolic of the fourth child Belinda and I never had. She was ten days late with her period in January. She said categorically that had she been pregnant she would have had an abortion. I would have been devastated. It could have been the child that kept us together... If it were a boy, I would have called him Joss Smith Wesson Junior and possibly just "Junior" for short. My monkey is called Joss Smith Wesson Junior.

I phoned Belinda six times in the last hour.

1) To tell her that I had bought her a present. Her immediate reaction was that she did not want it. I wondered if this meant that she would not be buying me anything for my birthday or Christmas.
2) To ask her to bring me some mints as the metallic taste in my mouth was worse.
3) To ask her to bring in a Pritt stick so I could continue to stick stuff into my diary.
4) To ask her to bring me some nice bananas as I was determined to use them as my secret weapon in losing weight.
5) To ask if there had been any response from the estate agent.
6) I asked if she could make my bed. She agreed. I said that I was going to be at either of my two brothers when I came out so why did she not return to our marriage bed? The thought of my exquisite wife back in our bed brought tears to my eyes. God, let me live to the day when we are back together. I will worship and treasure her. My pathetic brain seems to mush from rationality recalling our happy times together.

Belinda phoned to ask what her mother in South Africa's telephone number was. I was delighted to be able to help her but was annoyed with myself for forgetting to say that I often thought of her and to send my love to her. I wondered if I would ever see her again. I desperately hoped so as I genuinely loved her. Not as much as I loved her daughter, obviously. I am sitting at a standard A frame picnic table in the garden under a cherry tree. It is quite beautiful but at the same time quite sad because the whole event of spring seems to have passed me by. This might seem a strange contradiction, as there are a number of flower presses at the back of my diary. They are my childish way of trying to say "Joss loves Belinda," all of which have failed miserably; all I have succeeded in doing is making a mess of my diary.

Her visit turned out to be a disaster. On the phone just before, I had broken down in tears so she said that she was not going to come. Sophie also burst into tears saying that she did not want to see her parents fighting and so did not want to come. I promised that I would not fight with Belinda, so she said she would come. We went to a coffee bar in Headington. Belinda walked three or four strides ahead of me. It was probably this that caused me to break down again, despite my promise. However, Belinda did remember Sophie's Lacrosse tournament in Winchester on 17/05/2008 and promised that the three of us would go down together. It would have been absolute Heaven had this come about.

As I childishly waved as the car disappeared down the drive, I again dissolved into tears. If only I could "move on," if only I could stop loving her. But it is impossible. Each atom of my being craves for her. As always, she surprised me with how magnificent she looked, her skin glowing with health, her hips looking every inch a teenager's. Her *Jennifer Aniston* hair-do, yet somehow more beautiful. Her eyes the same beautiful azure deep blue.

A quote courtesy of a fellow inmate Tim Pander-Johns
"Love is level
Love is kind
Love is patient
Love gives and never counts the cost
Love drives out fear"

To-morrow, and to-morrow, and to-morrow
Creeps in this petty pace from day to day
To the last syllable of recorded time;
And all our yesterdays have lighted fools
The way to dusty death. Out, out, brief candle!
Life is but a walking shadow, a poor player
That struts and frets his hour upon the stage,
And then is heard no more.
William Shakespeare
(Although in my own view it was written by Sir Henry Neville, my uncle.)

CHAPTER TWENTY-FOUR

... Some theories according to Stephen Housemeister ...
(another clever loon)

Time doesn't matter
Only people are subject to time.
Nobody dies. Our ancestors are all around us.
An idea for a novel would be to combine the culture of the Bible and the Koran.
The end of time happens when the event horizon narrows. In the last 10^{-43} seconds the whole universe collapses back into the horizon and a new universe begins. E.
Another good title would be "Seconds Out Of A Dinner Conversation With A Creationist."
$10^{-43} = E$ is the equation that explains the physical universe and includes a key to the spiritual universe.
The essence of the universe comes down to being a scrap metal merchant.
Present=eternity=standing still.
Matter cannot travel in two different directions at the same time (antimatter? Quarks etc.)
Darwin was only able to look at evolution from the inside. Stephen says that he is able to look at it from the outside.
He is certainly one of the strangest patients that I have come across. I reserve the right to use the word "pleasure" to have met him as he believes that in previous lives he has been Adolph Hitler, Jesus, Joseph Goebbels and is currently some German musician. He occasionally plays his guitar and he has hardly passed "beginner" stage. While watching *Silence Of The Lambs* he totally spooked me out by passing me the following notes:-
"Paddy, kick the habit or the system kicks you!"
"How do THEY get the information out of her? THROUGH THE TOILET.
TOILET: garbage in – garbage out compost.
Substances = Plastic > Plastic <u>cannot</u> be composted = bad karma

Walking through Oxford was painful. I walked with my deliberate purposeful stride, albeit undoubtedly more slowly than in my youth. Many young lovers, their fingers entwined, walked slow, casual, almost directionless steps as they hung on each other's words and then occasionally faced each and locked lips, their eyelashes completing the embrace. Then eventually, idly they break apart and continue ambling nowhere, but in love. My heart hurts so to see them. It only seemed such short weeks before that Belinda and I used to walk together just the same. I have to be the biggest fool in Christendom, on earth, nay, the entire Universe. Why oh why did I mess around with Ellen? I don't hate her, but I wish I had never met her.

Sunday 4th May 2008

I thought that I must have been getting better as when I was told that Belinda was going to be spending the night with Felix I did not immediately break down into tears. However, this did not turn out to be the case; when I spoke to her later in the afternoon she was happy, saying that the two of them were now lovers. I ended up begging her to take me back between my sobs. I phoned back later to ask if she had the tax letter that had been sent to me by my employers. She exploded into anger saying that I always portray her in the worse possible light to my brothers (Daryl believing that she had not done my tax return. I was unaware that we did not need to do them). She put the phone down on me saying that she did not want to speak to me again.

CHAPTER TWENTY-FIVE

... Another pathetic letter ...

Belinda I beg you, I implore you, I beseech you to reconsider. Please, please, please forgive me for the terrible mistake I made with Ellen. We have had 22 ½ years of happiness between us, we can have another 23 years. Oh Belinda, please let it happen, I will honour and treasure you.

Stuck in here with nothing but loneliness as my companion is it not forgiveable that all I think of is you, my darling? Your beautiful face, your beautiful mouth surrounded by laughter lines, those beautiful blue eyes with their larger than usual pupils.

I adore your stomach, the way it descends into your legs and how you carefully keep your secret zone trimmed. It is just so beautiful. The thought that I will not lay down next to you is agony. My only reason for living is the belief that we will be together again.

CHAPTER TWENTY-SIX

... emails ...

JOSS: (I sent Belinda a picture of a kiss)
BELINDA: *Why?*
JOSS: Coz I love you!
BELINDA: *Joss, We are separating, please do not make this difficult. Belinda*
JOSS: Sorry... but did you like the one before though?
BELINDA: *I have signed the agreement with James but not the details for the property. Paul Owen will put them through the door tonight for us to check, sign and return. Thanks, Belinda*
JOSS: I think that you will find that to sell the flat requires both of our signatures on the agreement with the estate agent.
BELINDA: *I did ask the Paul Owen that same question and he was happy with just my signature. Are you now saying you don't want to sell?*
JOSS: No, I'm not saying that. But I would rather you stopped treating me like an old coat that you can now just throw away. I want to talk to you before signing.
BELINDA: *I can't believe you can say that about the old coat. You were quite happy to do that to me last year in such a brutal way. I am trying to get my life back and be me. I'm sorry if you can't accept it.*
JOSS: I am sorry. (I cannot put it more succinctly than that as you will no longer read my notes to you - except I have virtually written another book begging for your forgiveness - yes I did discard you but as we agreed, at the time of relationship was at an all time low - I had begged you on two previous occasions to come with me to marriage counseling.) Darling can't you see, you have already flowered into the new you. You look magnificent; you are confident in yourself and have a new found ability in your job.
However, none of the above is what I want to TALK (as opposed to email) to you about. I honestly do love you and...
BELINDA: *Joss, Please accept that our marriage is over. We both need to move*
on with our lives and be good friends for the sake of the children. We always will be good friends and I certainly don't

want to throw that away. Please don't make this difficult for both of us to move on.

JOSS: Darling, I am not going to be drawn into a conversation by email (about what I want to talk about), however I will address some of the points you have raised.

a) Our marriage is not over. You say/said/keep saying that you want a separation to find yourself and to have some space (as you say that you have forgiven me for my affair). Are you now going beyond this into divorce? You have always said that you do NOT want a divorce which led me to believe that at some point in the future we could come back together. (My understanding of this is probably when you decide that I have become sufficiently repentant and worthy of you again, which is something that I am prepared to spend the rest of my life trying to do.)

b) No, I do not want to make it difficult but equally, you seem determined to take advantage of my illness (my inability to think rationally at the moment).

c) I cannot image us being "best friends" and you being married to someone else. Be honest, you would not want a mentally ill person anywhere near your new family.

BELINDA: *Last week I made it quite clear and even phoned Fiona and told her that it was over. You were in your room and heard the whole conversation. I can't take any more of the emotional blackmail; it is unfair to everyone. I have told you that I do not love you as a husband any more. I think that it would be better for us to part company, separation initially just to see what happens but if you would prefer to go through with the divorce then I won't stand in your way.*

Please don't make threats to me about you being mentally ill. It is not my fault, I have not done anything wrong, you were the one that started this. I don't see why I have to spend the rest of my life being scared of you because of all your threats of being mentally ill. Your threats have made me realize that you do not own me and we should not be together any more. Your threats are also frightening to the children so please can I ask you to be more understanding for their sakes. If you want them to grow up normally then you should just stand back and let me go!

JOSS: Dearest beloved Belinda, can I just say something in my defense? You say that you spoke to Fiona and I was in the next room and heard the whole thing. Well, I honestly did not and she did not refer to it when I was there on Friday evening. Love you.

BELINDA: *Please stop doing this to me. I have a job to do and I am not going to change my mind. It is over and we are splitting up. I just can't cope with this any more.*

JOSS: If you think that I have run out of options you are very much mistaken.

BELINDA: *Why do you always have to be nasty? I am phoning your family when I get home because your behaviour towards me is unacceptable!*

JOSS: Dearest darling Belinda, OK so I rose to your bait. I am truly sorry. You say that I am turning nasty. As it happens I have forwarded our entire emails home so I can illustrate how you choose to ignore my questions etc. Read them... you are the one that has decided to turn nasty. I say I still love you and I desperately want to keep you. You think it clever to stick to your "I've made my decision" thing (which the more we go into it seems to be purely out of revenge). I have said that I will do whatever you want. I will delete all female contacts off my phone, I will only ever go out with you. Why oh why do you hate me so suddenly and dramatically? (Please don't lie!!) PS It does seem strange that you have not asked what it is that I want(ed) to speak about.

CHAPTER TWENTY-SEVEN

... Text messages ...

22/04/2008 08:17 I told you to get out of the flat.
22/04/2008 08:25 *Joss please may I ask u 2 b civil 2wards me for the sake of the children. U r frightening all of us. Please remember ur 3 beautiful daughters love u and need u. fm Belinda.*
22/04/2008 08:31 F..k off. You missed your chance to part as friends now I am going to hurt you as much as you are hurting me.
22/04/2008 08:42 *Don't u realise the stress strain and damage u r doing to our children? They r important to me and I do not like u frightening them. They r innocent in all this so please do what they want and not what u want.*
22/04/2008 08:53 F..k off. Losing the children would not make my pain any worse
22/04/2008 10:06 Bitch. Tell my brothers that I have been sectioned thanx to you and I will not speak to them as they betrayed me to u.
22/04/2008 10:15 *Joss ur bros have not betrayed u. They love u dearly and want to help u. Please don't push them away. They are there to support u. Please try to get well 4 ur children, they love u and need u. Don't discard that love, they will always love u. fr ur best friend Belinda*
22/04/2008 10:21 F..k off I will get my revenge
22/04/2008 14:42 *Joss, Felicity and Sophie r coming 2 c u today, is there anything else u wld like them 2 bring? Please can I ask u 2 stop taking ur anger out on our children by trying to be as nasty as you can to me. It is upsetting them. As a parent u shld b thinking of them and not uself. Please can we b civil 4 the sake of our children. They need us both. Fm Belinda.*
22/04/2008 14:51 F..k off you evil bitch. U have turned them against me anyhow. Tell *Felicity* if she doesn't want to come then not to bother.
22/08/2008 15:08 *Joss u know that isn't true. I am not like that. We have many good memories 2gether. Our 3 beautiful daughters 4 starters. They love u dearly and want their warm loving dad back. Please don't let them down. Please could u find out y Sophie can't visit 2nite, she really wants 2 c u. fm Belinda*

22/04/2008 15:15 Bitch. U know y Sophie can't come. I am writing an ultimatum to F & T that it's either me or you.
22/04/2008 15:21 *Joss that is not fair to T & F. Why r u punishing everyone for your mistake?*
22/04/2008 16:28 And the three princesses and their evil stepmother lived happily ever after.
22/04/2008 16:46 *Joss please can u b civil 2 ur own children they love u very much. Putting them on the spot is a clear indication that u need them. Please rethink and don't break their hearts. They love both of us. U r blaming everyone 4 ur mistake. U also hate everyone who disagrees with u. Please reconsider as I can't have sex with u 1 last time! Fr Belinda*
22/04/2008 16:47 Pity.
23/04/2008 09:35 I can't get the image of you sitting naked on me with me inside you and sucking and kissing your perfect breasts. Please forgive me. What moments do you remember?
22/04/2008 20:03 How does it feel?!
23/04/2008 11:37 No I recognise I committed a terrible sin. I am not blaming anyone else. I am just begging you to forgive me, please.
23/04/2008 14:42 Darling Belinda please forgive me for these few days. I am so so sorry. After Ellen I understand u not being able to trust me. After your Felix, I still want you back. U r my soul mate. Let me be yours. U know it makes sense! Please trust me. I beg you. I love you. Joss.
23/04/2008 16:00 Darling, if I had not met Ellen and u Felix would u still want to divorce me? Belinda darling, I know u r angry and u have every right to be, but I believe that deep down u still love me. Darling, I swear I love u, as Sophie says, a billion times over. Say u will?
23/04/2008 17:26 Darling Belinda. I hope I have not made u ill coz I have been so horrid. It has some as a bit of a shock. P/s forgive me. I do love u!
[On the 24th, your birthday, we were going to make love, and had taken all our clothes off, when we heard Tilly and Sebastian coming through the front door.]
25/04/2008 09:21 *I have left the key in a brown envelope in the little blue house out the back.*
25/04/2008 09:21 Thanks.
25/04/2008 10:22 *R u on ur way home?*
25/04/2008 10:43 Has Dr. Elwell phoned u?

25/04/2008 12:12 I'm at Oxford station should be home by 1.
25/04/2008 13:00 *Hi Joss have u arrived home?*
25/04/2008 13:30 Did you remember Sue's birthday?
25/04/2008 13:34 *Thankx 4 letting me know. I forgot Sue's b'day.*
25/04/2008 13:35 OK. Do you want me to get a card?
25/04/2008 13:39 *I have a card. Thanx. Plse don't text me back or call unless absolutely urgent as I am getting strange looks.*
25/04/2008 21:35 P/s remind me to phone Melissa.
25/04/2008 21:46 Goodnight.
26/04/2008 22:15 R u OK?
[The 26th was the day that Belinda went out with this guy Felix to Beale Park in Pangbourne. I could just imagine them holding hands and kissing.]
26/04/2008 22:30 Dearest Belinda. I am hoping u r still awake. I am thinking happy thoughts about your lovely day. Darling I am trying to be strong. This is not emotional blackmail but I so desperately want you to be happy. Otherwise the little time we r talking I want to be there for you and Sophie but I seem to be falling apart as much as I don't want to. I think that I need to go back into hospital. Please help me. Joss.
28/04/2008 12:02 Thanks Belinda u r an angel. I promise I will get better. Thank u again for your support. U r amazing. How is Felicity? Joss
29/04/2008 00:04 Hi Belinda. I'm going forward, there are 2 things that I have learnt today. 1.U r wrong to confuse my passion for my genealogy for destructive obsession. 2. We were fighting long before we met the Davidsons and were probably going to get divorced anyway. What I have learnt is that u are much more concerned about yourself.
29/04/2008 09:21 Belinda. I have just re-read my text to u last night and it did not make sense. Since being separated we r getting on better than before. U seem more aware and concerned about my illness and I have fallen totally and completely in love with u.
29/04/2008 17:54 Can I ring u later?
29/04/2008 20:25 Would u rather I didn't contact u?
29/04/2008 20:50 Please answer...

29/04/2008 20:57 *Sorry I have just got out of the bath. Y don't u just phone the house in the evenings 4 a chat and leave txts 4 emergencies fm Belinda.*
29/04/2008 20:59 Thank you Belinda. U r a friend indeed.
01/05/2008 13:58 Please forward this to your Felix. Sung to Dolly Parton's Jolene. Felix, Felix, Felix mate. Please don't take my wife just because u can. Joss Smith Wesson
03/05/2008 11:02 Hi Belinda. When u speak to your mum and dad, please give them my love and say that they are always in my thoughts.
04/05/2008 23:25 Dearest Belinda, funnily enough I am not hurting at the prospect of you two consummating your relationship as much as I thought I might. Yes, I am coming to terms with it. I will always love u my angel. I will always be waiting. Love Joss.
05/05/2008 20:19 Hi Belinda my friend. I was hoping that u might talk to Nat about her exams. I understand that she was out last night. PS How do u do number in text?
05/05/2008 11:38 Hi Belinda. I hope u had a really fabulous weekend. Please give me a ring. I want to talk to u about Felicity. Love u. Joss
05/05/2008 12:21 Hi Belinda. I'm so sorry. I don't mean to fight with u. I really want u to be happy. I am so glad that u have found Felix as I am sure that he will keep u happy. Thank u for all the happiness we shared. I will always love u and will always be waiting. Joss.
05/05/2008 13:03 *Joss, Sophie and I r at Swindon stn waiting for our train. Bcoz of how angry u were when I called I didn't think u would want 2 c Felicity. I now know that u want to c them. Thanks fm Belinda.*
06/05/2008 09:08 Hi Belinda. Hey! They want to let me out for a day. Has Dr Elwell phoned u? Could I spend Saturday night at home so u could go out? Dearest Belinda, I know we are thru but I desperately need your help. Could u, Sophie and I go for a walk together? Obviously I would not expect to hold hands and we could have Sophie between us? I am shaking like a leaf and crying as usual. Please grant me this? Otherwise I could stay with Daryl or Jonathan. I am sorry to have bothered you last weekend. Will u still come down to Winchester for Sophie's lacrosse tournament? Joss.

One-Millionth Poem to love-lost

How can my love for you grow deeper
When their roots penetrate my very soul?
Could my love for you be any stronger
When thoughts of you occupy my every
second?
When will my flying love be allowed to land
When you keep the airstrip closed?
My love, let this tired soaring eagle
Come back to your welcome nest.
Why has this bird been ejected from home
This loving partner, gentle lover, betrayer of
trust?
Oh creature so vile and loathsome
Dare you beseech such a fair maiden?
Yours is just dessert and reward
To be punished for all eternity.
Oh my darling, my beloved
Oh creature so divine
My love for you is like a rock
Smashed and battered by the
Worst of angry winter storms.
Your anger cutting and hurting me
Your fury making my love more steadfast
You are right to be furious my angel
When you needed me most, I betrayed you
I ask for your forgiveness
I am repentant. I am full of remorse
I wish to God I could make you love me
I am the world's greatest fool
You are my only love.
Oh broken heart be mended
Rip thoughts of her out of your soul
Move forward find another partner
Put your own needs first
Oh wise words advising councillor
This frail creature seems unable so to do
She is embedded into my psyche
Jump to my death, hang myself or head-on-
collision
Would be so easy and yes, I want to.

CHAPTER TWENTY-EIGHT

... The Lion of Israel ...

Boyd Boy David of Israel. When he arrived in the Vaughn Thomas Ward with his Bible he caused quite a stir as all the Satanists ran away from him. "Today," he says "at 13:10 is Armageddon." So I stood barefoot in the park at the allotted time, waiting. At the moment of impact I got someone to photograph me lying in the Sea of Cherry blossom.

Before I had met Boyd, he somehow knew of me. I wondered if it was because I looked like a ponce or because of my reputation although what I might have a reputation for I did not know – perhaps I looked like one of THEM.

Stephen – pronounced Stefan – and I have being having an amicable chat here in my room for the past two and half hours. Stef is the weirdo I mentioned earlier who believes that he is/was Hitler etc.

Tim's a raving nutter, another one of God's disciples. Tim believes that he is Michael, as in Archangel Michael who throws the Damned to Hell and is also the leader of Jesus Christ's army. He invited me to join his loony brigade. I said that I would if he were to pay off my mortgage. He promptly went off, got his chequebook and wrote me a cheque for £180,000.00 quid, smackers, lolly, currency, money, pounds. I am of course going to bank the cheque tomorrow and then (once it clears) start my new career as a raving disciple!

I went to Tim's famous friend Boyd who Tim recognises as Jesus Christ, the Tree of Life and whose father is God Almighty. Boyd says he was at Church on Sunday and he saw a man whose leg had been amputated and saw the leg re-grow. Boyd took me aside and said that he agreed that the cheque would bounce but not to worry because my mortgage would be paid. He also said in such a way that I believed that my book would be published.

09/05/2008 09:54. Just leaving Oxford Station, will be home in half an hour. Today could well be the first day of the rest of my life. God, the thought brings such unimaginable joy. I realise of course that it is highly unlikely that the cheque will be honoured but in the event that it does, it will be like winning the lottery. If I were to win (i.e. the cheque clears) I will give all the money to Belinda. She is right. She has had 23 years of misery being married to me. The money would certainly not make up for my terrible neglect in these last few years. But it would be my attempt to do so. I would not even tell her that the money is in the account; I would just leave it to her to find on her own. My stupid ridiculous insane mind is already doing overtime with the possibilities that it could lead to. I so want her back.

Incredible – already in Didcot - Chav City.

I am delighted to have found my wedding ring and have it back on my finger. Inside it reads, "Joss & Belinda 15/12/1984 Forever." I am also wearing my Quartz Oyster Rolex watch my father gave me for my 21st. It has my name and Belinda's date of birth engraved on the back. In my trouser right-hand pocket there is a picture wallet of her and our three beloved daughters. Oh God, the pain of it. I just can't bear to be apart from her.

I drop everything at home to and get back on the train into Reading to get a tattoo over my heart. "Joss loves Belinda" and "Belinda is the most beautiful woman in the world" on my forearm.

What would it be like to be free of debt? I am shaking uncontrollably at the thought that I hardly dare think it. Would Belinda ever reconsider me? I have lost loads of weight... I know money is not everything, but I love her so much. When she finds out, will she immediately transfer all the money over to her Felix? I am deliberately going to leave it so that she does not know the source of the funds. Knowing that she never opens the post, it could be months before she realised. Would I be blowing my cover to say to the staff in the bank to ring her when the cheque clears?

Ironically really, Brother Tim (Col. Archangel Michael, God's slayer), I had only spoken to him for the first time yesterday (previously it had just been the standard passing greeting of one loon to another).

I usually associate with Bryan frequently playing chess with him. I don't know for sure but I think that he has advanced Multiple Sclerosis. Sometimes it is virtually impossible to understand him. However he is very patient and knows that it is a bit of a lottery to be understood and doesn't mind being asked to repeat sentences. He is hopeless at chess though but just loves to play. (I had to go up to Oxford in March 2009 and was resoundingly beaten by him!) It is an excellent way of passing the time and virtually every game is accompanied by cups of tea.

"Thgnoong thugaarh," he says, translating roughly as, "No sugar."

Rob the Karate Kid punches a wall and breaks the bones in his hand. Poor Rob is in a similar situation to me, except he is not in love with his ex, he has a problem with getting used to the idea of having limited access to their daughter, Emily. His ex-girlfriend's name is Yvonne.

Just on the train into Reading, unable to bank the cheque at either HSBC or Lloyds and failed to change the status on Belinda's Lloyds account from "dormant" to "in use." I always used to have signing power on the account.
I made the fatal error of telling Daryl about the cheque. He of course advises that I should tear it up. My argument is that I will never know if it would have cleared or not.

It is amazing how time flies when one is writing on a train, just half a page between stations. I wish I could do that to real life. I wish I could see what the future holds. I wonder how many more times I am going to end up in mental hospitals? I obviously have a propensity or panache for them. I suspect that the next time will be the end of me.

I was only given one day's medication, but I was authorised to have two days' leave so I am supposed to go all the way back to Oxford to pick them up tomorrow. They can get lost.

Past Pangbourne, past Tilehurst, surprisingly "Tickets please". In all the time I have used this train service I have never had to show my ticket on board the train. Past *John George & Sons*, past Throckmorton where my beloved Belinda and her boyfriend, Felix work; the train slows down coming into Reading.

Oh God. I should never have presented the cheque. I am highly embarrassed to find that the amount in words did not equal the amount in numbers.

Belinda Smith Wesson 24th March

Thank you for your love, your care, your kindness,
Your hope, your strength and your belief in me.
Thank you for being there for me
Thank you for seeing me through
For putting up with me; for putting me straight.
Thank you for just being you.
When I am down
When things are black
When the world seems wrong,
There you are with your smile
Your beauty, you're mine, I'm rich.
I love you so. You are my reason
You're my being, you're my happiness.

CHAPTER TWENTY-NINE

... Another Strange Day ...

I woke almost in a trance at 4:30 to the most magical sounds on Earth – the spring morning chorus. I am ashamed to say that I do not know which bird makes which sound, except for the exhilarating sound of a Blackbird (in the same way I do not know which instruments make which sounds in an orchestra) but the combined and individual sound is truly uplifting. I stood in our humble kitchen with the window overlooking rooftops and cried and cried. I wished that I could get back into our bed and that Belinda would be there; knowing that she never would hurt so much. She had been out with her Felix the night before and had only returned at 01:00 am. I forced myself back to bed and eventually returned to a snoring dead-man's slumber (God, if only). I woke early at 07:30 and spent a few hours on my PC researching my ancestors before Sophie woke. I so much wanted to be well for her as well as wanting to go to church so she could be with her friends in the Sunday Club. When I looked into her room she was lying with no blanket or duvet in just her knickers. Belinda must have been equally hot as she had tossed the duvet off and I could see up her legs to her panties. I spontaneously burst into tears and beg her to take me back. She truly is a wonderful woman as she immediately gives me a hug.

I had already packed a few things into a bag and then spent a few more moments on the PC so that my streams of tears are not visible as the desk faces the window. Charles phones to see how I am. I say that I am about to go back into hospital. He suggests that he collects me at 11:00 and then takes me to the accommodation he has found for me. He arrives and I let him in. We chat and he makes some suggestions regarding house-selling tactics and then we leave to go to this place. He and his fiancé Jenny rent a cottage in a livery stable. There must have been upwards of forty horses stabled. The accommodation on offer is a jockey's room. It has a tiny kitchen and loo but the surroundings are incredible and would certainly be a shot in the arm for a sick Joss. I could just see myself helping to muck out horses before going to work, or even learning to ride. Come to think of it, I already smell of horse!

Charles went on and on about the runs we could do and that it would only take a few minutes to pedal to Hurley and Pangbourne and that it would be an ideal way to get fit. In the few moments that I stood beside him in this wonderful spot for very select people, I could actually see myself whole again. His glorious financee Jenny returned from her horse-riding tournament (dressage I think) and we had lunch together. Jules had had a painful divorce from Ben (a wanker in Goring) and it was her idea for me to use the room. It seemed almost too much like heaven to be real – there had to be a catch. The room is free for three months. The only "catch" as such would be if it were to rain while I was on the bike... but even that did not detract me as much as it might.

Charles set his Sat-Nav machine and we set off. A remarkable piece of equipment as most people already know, but in my usual behind the curve kind of way, I had never seen one up-front and active.

Back at the ward I introduced Charles to Abbey White the Duty Staff Nurse and he explained my circumstances, which were that I now had alternative accommodation but that I had had two bad breakdowns.

The cheque that Tim had given me for £180,000.00 turned out to be a bit of a dud. The fact that the cheque is void only comes to light while I was attempting to bank it at the HSBC in Reading. I had gone through the long laborious process of opening a new account which I suppose will be handy once we do sell the flat and I need my own account.

CHAPTER THIRTY

... Saturday, a day of misery ...

I had started to clear out old paperwork and came across the many love letters Belinda and I had written to each other. I had come back to England just after we had met to go to Mike Dixon's wedding up in Cumbria. We wrote to each other every day. It is a strange irony that the forceful and upfront character I was then was a turn-on to her whereas now it is just the opposite. I totally broke down reading them. I phoned the ward to say I wanted to come back. Neither Felicity nor Belinda would give me a lift so I was going to go by train. My real intention was to jump in front of the first Intercity. Belinda refused to let me go.

Today is Sunday – the supposed meeting took one minute as I read out my list and then asked to be taken back in tears. My desire to commit suicide is as strong as it was the first time. I just wish I had never met Ellen Davidson. I want Belinda back so badly.

I found the newspaper cutting announcing our engagement in The Telegraph of 14th April 1984, ten days before her birthday.

Charles phoned. He had found me some accommodation. Some jockey place near him. Apparently it is unoccupied for the next three months. He is going to arrive here at 11:00 to take me to see it, to go to the pub for lunch and then to take me back to the hospital. Belinda has been amazing. During one of my worse sobbing fits she gently hugged me. It was heaven to be in the arms of the woman I loved and hell to know that she no longer loved me in return.

Monday. Charles arrives promptly at 11:00 as promised for the meeting with Dr Ellwell for 11:30. Maria Wells was initially sitting in on the meeting. I had worked for Charles after selling the store for a few months. He was far more than an employer and a customer in my store. We became life-time friends. She was Belinda's advisor (the bitch who I believe advised Belinda to leave me). I said that there was a conflict of interest and asked her to leave which she did. I briefly explained that I had had the breakdowns and that Charles was offering me accommodation. I suggested that it might be best if I were to stay inside for two more days and be released on Wednesday. This was the plan that was ultimately agreed on so that I could meet Dr Ellwell in Henley on Thursday.

I have just spoken to Felicity who says that she will pick me up from the hospital on Wednesday to take me to Charles' flat. Charles had had another key cut. Belinda phoned to find out where I was. She was a little annoyed, as I had not mentioned that Fran's mum, Tina, had agreed to look after Sophie until 19:00. She had gone to collect her at 18:00 and was told to come back in an hour. She was a little surprised that I was still at the hospital.

After Charles had left after lunch, I walked down into Oxford. I had my Rolex put to the correct time and made it fit me. It gave me an enormous feeling of well-being as it completes the three things on my person that display my love for Belinda. It has my name and her birthday engraved on the back. In my right hand trouser pocket there is a picture of her and I together and another of our three beloved daughters. Of course I will be wearing our wedding ring until the end of my days. It has "Joss and Belinda 15/12/1984 Forever" engraved inside. I went to a tattoo parlour and was surprised and annoyed to find that the tattoo artist had just resigned. They suggested I try a shop in Banbury. I know where there is a place in Reading where I will get *Joss loves Belinda* in a heart shape tattooed over my heart.

I arrived back at the psychiatric ward/ lunatic asylum/ loony bin to be accosted by Boyd and Tim who tried to give me lessons on seeing with one's "Mind's Eye." I had to close my eyes and imagine something. I imagined Belinda and I sitting on the bench at the top of Lardon Chase overlooking Hurley & Maidenbottom. I then had to open my eyes and say what I could see. All I could see was grass in front me. I got up crying as I left them.

I lie in this hospital bed consumed by thoughts of my beloved wife, my beloved Belinda. Surely she cannot question my faith and trust in her now? I love her enough to let her go, to let her go to make love with another man, whilst my own heart is broken. I know that I will win her back. It is as certain as the sun will rise tomorrow, I just don't know when or how. Perhaps it will only be when I get to Heaven and then I suppose I will have to share her with her Felix. Oh God, even that I would not mind so long as I had her back.

I have already broken my rule, my promise I made to her, not to spend any money. I have ordered and paid for a bracelet with "Joss loves Belinda, forever" on it. Along with the others, I will wear it forever. Oh God, what do I have to do to make her fall in love with me again?

Anna and Rob

Rob and Anna
There's mad as a hatter Tim
He thinks that Boyd is Jesus
Boyd also thinks he is Jesus
There's screaming Rose
Man, she's good
Smashed the clinic-room door
In one of her friendly fits.

Now there are loads of loons
All of them so spaced out
On anger, fear, guilt or heartbreak.
Rob is your average loon
High on suicide
The Carfax tower beckoning
Smashed his fist into a wall
In pent-up rage and frustration

Now there is also Anna
She is pretty, she is quiet
She is also shy and very hurt.
Here in this awkward
Most unlikely of places
They fall in love.

Love is level
Love is kind
Love is generous
Love gives without counting the cost
Love makes no demands
Love is all there is
Love makes new that which was broken
Love grows greater with care

Rob in his pain has found Anna
Anna in hers has found Rob
Rob and Anna are in love, it's official
They're madly in love,
Today, tonight, tomorrow and forever.

Rob sent this as a text to Anna on 12/05/2008 at 21:45
She replied,
"Oh Wow! I'm crying now. That is lovely and sad and hopeful all at the same time. I will write it down tomorrow. Please thank Joss for me."
I made a ceramic bowl for Rob and Anna with the following spiralled words leading into the centre.
"Love is a fruit in season and within reach of every hand. Love is something that begins when nothing is looked for in return. Love is not gazing at each other but looking outward together in the same direction. Love is a game that two can play and both win. Love is all you need. Love is like quicksilver in the hand; leave the fingers open and it stays, clutch at it and it darts away. Love is that which can be divided endlessly and still not be diminished. Love is the force that drives you around the circle. Love is proud of itself. It leaks out of us even with the tightest of security. Love is a great beautifier. Love is insanity with a collaborator."

1 Corinthians 13

1 If I speak in the tongues of men and of angels but have no love, I am only a resounding gong or a clanging cymbal.

2 If I have the gift of prophecy and can fathom all mysteries and all knowledge, and if I have faith that can move mountains, but have not love, I am nothing.

3 If I give all that I possess to the poor and surrender my body to the flames, but have not love, I gain nothing.

4 Love is patient, love is kind. It does not envy, it does not boast, it is not proud.

5 It is not rude, it is not self-seeking, it is not easily angered, it keeps no record of wrongs.

6 Love does not delight in evil but rejoices with the truth.

7 It always protects, always trusts, always hopes, always preserves.

8 Love never fails. But where there are prophesies, they will cease; where they are tongues, they will be stilled; where there is knowledge, it will pass away.

9 For we know in part and we prophesy in part.

10 But when perfection comes, the imperfect disappears.
11 When I was a child, I talked like a child, I thought like a
child, I reasoned like a child. When I became a man, I put
childish ways behind me.
12 Now we see but a poor reflection as in a mirror; then I
shall know fully, even as I am fully grown.
13 And now these three remain, faith, hope and love. But the
greatest of these is love.

Dear God, you who knows and understands everything, even when I am ill, afraid, lonely, anxious, sad and depressed. Help me now to trust You because You love me and promise to be with me always. Amen

John 3:16 in Afrikaans
Want so life God die wệreld gehad, dat sy eniggebore seun gegee het, sodat elkeen wat in Hom glo, nie verlore mag gaan nie, maar ie ewige lewe kan kệ.

Mark 10

2 Some Pharisees came and tested Jesus by asking, “Is it
lawful for a man to divorce his wife?”
3 “What did Moses command you?” He replied.
4 They said, “Moses permitted a man to write a certificate of
divorce and send her away.”
5 “It was because your hearts were hard that Moses wrote
you this law,” Jesus replied.
6 “But at the beginning of creation God made them male and
female.”
7 “For this reason a man will leave his father and mother and
will be united to his wife
8 and the two will become one flesh, so they are no longer
two but one.
9 Therefore what God has joined together, let no man
separate.”
10 When they were in the house again, the disciples asked
Jesus about this.
11 He answered, “Anyone who divorces his wife and marries
another woman commits adultery against her.
12 And if she divorces her husband and marries another
man, she commits adultery.”

Ephesians 5

21 Submit to one another out of reverence for Christ.
22 Wives, submit to your husbands as to the Lord.
23 For the husband is the head of the wife as Christ is head
of the church, his body, of which he is the saviour.
24 Now as the church submits to Christ so also wives should
submit to their husbands everything.
25 Husbands, love your wives, just as Christ loved the
Church and gave himself up for her
26 to make her holy, cleansing her by the washing with
water through the word

27 and to present her to himself as a radiant church, without
stain or wrinkle or any other blemish, but holy and
blameless.
28 In the same way, husbands ought to love their wives as
their own bodies. He who loves his wife loves himself.
29 After all, no-one ever hated his own body, but feeds and
cares for it, just as Christ does for the church
30 for we are members of his body.
31 For this reason a man will leave his father and mother
and be united to his wife, and the two will become one flesh.
32 This is a profound mystery – but I am talking about Christ
and the church. However each one of us must love his wife
as he loves himself, and the wife must respect her husband.

CHAPTER THIRTY-ONE

... David Fox. C of E Accountant with Social Awareness ...

13/05/2008

The Holy Spirit is the bit that most people do not recognise and do not submit to. It is something that cannot be seen or be touched, tasted, or smelt, but it seeks one out. We have just gone through Pentecost which is the time the Holy Spirit alights on God's people, which is everyone. Since I have been in here there has been a cyclone in Burma and a major earthquake in South West China. We are witnesses to the story that was started with creation of Alpha and Omega. Alpha being the beginning and Omega the end. We are witnessing a new creation of God's Kingdom. Whilst everyone has not been living the lives God intended, no one has been forsaken or left out.

CHAPTER THIRTY-TWO

... Breakfast with Pete R ...

The full equality of women with men is one of the most important but least acknowledged prerequisites to world peace. The denial of full equality to half the world's population cannot be justified on any grounds, biological, moral, physiological or psychological. This denial creates in men harmful attitudes that are taken from the home to the workplace and ultimately to international relations. Until women are welcomed by men into every arena of human endeavour, the psychological climate will not be created in which world peace can emerge.

An extract from a document called "By the Universal House of Justice. The Promise of World Peace 1985."

To submit to true love one has to be strong and obey or risk the wrath of the new race of men who will consider social ostracism. To obey I feel constrained to trust in what I do not understand, to submit to authority which I know to be good although logic tells me it is tyranny, all in the name of love for the manifestation of the Spirit incarnated in the physical frame of a beautiful woman who by virtue of her spirit of service has won my heart and taken on the role of being my soul. As Baha'u'llah says in "The Seven Valleys":

"A man must abound in sanity to merit The Malfunctions of a Bipolar Mind love."

"When the fire of love is ablaze it burneth to ashes the harvest of reason."

- Baha'i from 5/1/1975, who finds himself apparently in love with one person to the exclusion of all others including God, fearing God's wrath but perceiving her beauty to be only a faint reflection of the beauty of Abdu'l-Baha who as a kind father seems an extremely harsh task master.

Abdu'l-Baha 1844 – 1921, eldest son of Baha'u'llah 1817 – 1892 and his successor as head of the Baha'i International Community.

12/05/2008 09:48. Recalled from memory by Pete Rose.

CHAPTER THIRTY-THREE

... Tuesday 13th May 2008 ...

My feet ache from walking all day. I found a tattoo parlour in the Cawley Road and made a provisional appointment for 08:45 the next day. The tattoo artist's name is Curley and he is covered from head to foot in tattoos. As I walk back into central Oxford I pop into Oxfam and enquire if they have a Gideon's Bible. They don't but have a really cool box which if it is still there tomorrow I will buy. I waited for Daryl at the Carfax tower at 02:30. He duly arrived and we went to Georgina's café in the covered market. We were the only customers. Late in the evenings I could imagine it heaving with university types. He loved his carved wooden elephant bowl I gave him. We wanted to wander around the Ashmolean museum but it was being refurbished and was in a strange state of un-readiness.

CHAPTER THIRTY-FOUR

... denial ...

What I had was not an affair. I had a non-sexual encounter, a liaison. We did not spend much time together. It was not planned or calculated. It was just a moment of madness which very few would have had the strength of character to resist. I got no pleasure out of the relationship. I have paid a huge price for no gain and become mentally ill. We are all sexual creatures. The drudgery of married life overtook feelings of living together and I momentarily stopped seeing Belinda as my life partner with feelings and needs. Life had changed me. It is better to have loved and lost than never to have loved at all. Live love and leave a legacy. We are all victims of victims. Our love-life experiences transcending our upbringing. So you see, it was not an affair...

A Poem for Serenity in Adversity

I sit here quietly, desperately thinking
thoughts
Activate my mind, pull it away,
Away from the abyss
Away from total sadness
Away from suicide.

Here I sit, pen in my numb hand
Writing without thoughts
Thoughts of home
Thoughts of lost happiness
Thoughts of Belinda.

Oh God, serenity eroding
Fast flying incoming tears
Belinda my darling
Oh to be with you
To hold your hand
To kiss you now.

Be kind to me please
This traitor, this betrayer of trust
This monster that dares to look at you.
Please, just a soft word
I don't need a kiss
Just don't be cross with me
It hurts so much.

CHAPTER THIRTY-FIVE

... Let's split together ...

An article from the Sunday Express Modern Life 18/05/2008

You always said your love would never die, and you would be friends forever, come what may. But now your relationship is over and you face the acid test – can you stay friends?

Words by Rosie Staal, Crowded House.

You were so proud and happy when you bought your first home together. Now you'd give anything to turn your back on that property – and your partner. But you can't: there's a mortgage to be paid and although the flat's been on the market for months, there isn't a buyer in sight.

So how are you coping? Apart from the fact that one of you is kipping on an air-bed in the living room, while the other finds themselves alone in the master bedroom, are you managing to stay friends with your former partner?

Probably not – and that is a shame, says divorce coach Jackie Walker (www.thedivorcecoach.co.uk). But she is confident that there are ways of making this awkward – and increasingly common – scenario work.

"You must set boundaries," advises Jackie. "Without any rules you're in danger of slipping back to where you were before you reached this truce. For example, if one of you starts a new relationship, can you bring this new person home? Don't wait until it happens – establish at the very beginning what each of you will tolerate."

Staying civil under the same roof

Set ground rules and stick to them. Be considerate – this is another human being under your roof, not a monster. Bite your tongue – absolutely no shouting and no door slamming. No intimacy. Beware the late-night drunken tumble "just for old time's sake."

Family matters

Dan rings Gail from work every day at 11am. They talk about their children, the family dog and Gail's widowed mother. To an outsider it sounds like a normal conversation between a couple – normal in all respects except one: Dan and Gail are not a couple any more. They divorced last August and live five miles apart, with their two daughters dividing their week between the two houses.

"It's odd that we get on so well now," says Dan. "I'd describe Gail as very much a friend. She's a nice person but we were not compatible enough to be married," he explains. "Getting divorced was the best decision for us, even though it was awful at the time. Now there is peace in two households, where there used to be endless rows and unhappiness in one." Gail, too, is pleased that she managed to remain on good terms with Dan.

"The children like to see that Mummy and Daddy are still able to have a laugh and a chat together and, to be honest, I like having Dan as a friend. Without the rows and tensions that there were in our marriage we see each other differently."

Being friends for the sake of the children

Rock-solid unity in all family matters is essential, as is total reliability and perfect time-keeping. Don't make any attempts to gain favour by spoiling the children. Set a good example in your behaviour – it will be a positive influence on your ex and your children.

We can work it out

Running their own business was something Steve and Kim had always wanted to do. Hard work helped them achieve their ambition, but two years later their marriage fell apart when Steve had an affair.

Even after their divorce, they had to continue to work together as company directors because so much was tied up in the firm's future. "At first, my feelings of bitterness and revulsion were so strong it was difficult to keep them hidden from the staff," recalls Kim. "But over the past four years, because I've continued to work alongside him, I've come to regard Steve differently. I don't think of him as a cheating husband. He's a colleague, and a good friend for whom I have respect. I like him now, whereas not long ago I loathed him."

Keeping the peace as colleagues

Reassess your levels of interaction carefully. Could a little delegation make life a bit more bearable for both of you?
Don't use pet names – no calling each other "darling" or using familiar language.
No lapses in behaviour – if you must work late, make sure your meeting stays strictly business.
Be utterly professional in your role.

Social taboos

An amateur operatic society – and a production of *Calamity Jane* in particular – brought Rod and Sally together and has played an important role in their lives for eighteen years. Now the pair are bringing the curtain down on their marriage but they both want to carry on being active members of the club.
"I'm certainly not willing to give it up," says Sally, and as Rod is rehearsing for *HMS Pinafore* in June, he obviously isn't either. "So even though we've fallen out over most other things, this is one area of our lives that we feel we can still share. It means we often see each other socially, with mutual friends, so it is important that we don't make them feel awkward," explains Sally. "We're being very sensible about it and actually, Rod is quite a laugh to be around now that the stress is off. I wouldn't say he is a friend exactly, at least not yet, but we're certainly not the out-and-out enemies we might have been."

Getting along without giving up on mutual friends and interests

Don't encourage your mutual friends to take sides.
Don't react spitefully if any of them side with your ex.
No bad-mouthing of your ex – words come back and bite you.
Be aware that some of your friends may find the situation strange.

It's all relative

When a relationship breaks down, it isn't just the couple who become the victims. The shock waves ripple out into extended family, affecting parents, siblings and children too. But by staying friends with your ex you can not only maintain considerable dignity – and earn the admiration of the family – but also remain on good terms with the whole tribe of in-laws who might otherwise become outlaws.

Grandparents and grandchildren stand to lose the most: a divorce can shatter their relationship too, cutting them off from each other and causing untold sadness and irrevocable loss.
Julie and Mark, who split up six years ago, get together for Christmas and the children's birthdays, and always make a point of involving the grandparents. "Julie and I have been civil to each other through it all," says Mark, "and that's what I'd recommend. It helps you to be seen by the whole family as the same person you always were, not some ogre."

Keeping the in-laws on side

Be polite and say nothing to family members you might later regret. Don't encourage your "side" to close ranks against the other. Be fair to your ex partner's parents, involving them in plans where possible.
Be the one who initiates family get-togethers – they'll be unsure how you feel, so take the lead.

A little respect

Friendship is a two-way thing, and ultimately, being friends with your ex means treating them the way you would expect to be treated yourself. "You don't even need to like your ex," maintains Jackie Walker. "But you must respect them as a human being and remember that the situation isn't just about you. Look beyond your needs and feelings and learn to consider the other person's point of view. That shows respect."
Rosie Staal is the author of How to Split Up and Stay in One Piece, published by White Ladder Press, price £7.99

Reading this article makes me break down into streams of tears and snot. I so wish I could be in control of myself instead of being this blubbering mess. I have broken every single one of these rules. It is no wonder that Belinda hates and despises me. I just wish I could fix it and for the two of us to be back together again. I know she never will agree to that which is why I must get my tattoo and die. Life without her is just too miserable.
I have persuaded all and sundry that I have been in control all weekend. Nothing could be further from the truth. I am just waiting for the first opportunity to get out of here and the only way to do that is to pretend to be normal. Rob caught me crying in the lounge reading the above article but luckily there were no staff about.
It is hardly any wonder that people in prison get suicidal. It is therefore also understandable why the State spends a fortune keeping in-mates occupied and therefore the reason why they are accused of being too soft on prisoners. If I were to be interned for any great length of time I would very quickly lose my grip on reality. I would initially attempt to occupy myself before finding some means of killing myself.

My first failed relationship was with my mother. When I was first sectioned in the Fairmile mental hospital near Wallingford and was diagnosed with Bipolar, my parents were actually in the country. (They lived, at the time, just outside Cape Town). They visited me once before hurrying back to South Africa. This was a terrible crisis in my life and I needed all the help and support I could get. Belinda was absolutely amazing, arriving like clockwork every day. My mother did not use my name to greet me, "Hello there," was all she could manage.

The grudge I held against her (I suspect it was mutual) was over her behaviour at Daryl's wedding. The poor (poor as in unfortunate and destitute) staff had come in at 06:00, probably having to travel for two hours to get there. At the end of the long day they were still washing dishes at 23:00. I had done my brotherly thing with the in-laws knowing full well that I would never meet them again. I was fully aware of the colour divide; white equalled honoured guest, black equalled humble staff (for staff, read serf or slave). So I took it upon myself to go and help out with the enormous pile of dirty cutlery and crockery. Mother came storming into the kitchen and demanded that I be with the guests and that being with the blacks was no place for me.

To cut a long story short, I said that I would be on my flight back to England the next day and that would be the last she ever heard from me. My beloved sister Melissa managed to calm things down but only on the surface.

CHAPTER THIRTY-SIX

... thoughts of suicide ...

By any standards, this room is well furnished. There is a bed, wardrobe, chair, bin and small side chest. The radiator and all pipes are all covered. The ceiling is about ten feet up with no possible hooks with which to hang oneself. I am quite certain that if I genuinely actually wanted to commit suicide, I could do so in this room. As I sit here and write, I note that the edge of the cupboard is quite sharp. It would be quite painful but hypothetically I could saw away until I hit an artery. I could lift the bed up on one edge with my legs and then let it fall on my head. I could do what Bryan tried and jam my thumb into the base of my neck. I could easily nick an eating knife out of the dining room, jam it into the cupboard and then fall onto it.

I am afraid that if I were to ever somehow win Belinda back, I am so badly damaged that I would not be able to return to who I was before. I would probably break down crying at the slightest provocation.

Oh beloved woman, hear my prayer, please, please come back to me. I wait and wait for you endlessly... I am so afraid that I will end up like your father who has spent the last forty years waiting for your mother. I bet he was a character in his youth. I would love to meet some of his school friends or army friends to add to his biography. Perhaps you could ask your brother Barry to add a bit? I feel so cut off from him. I bet he phoned this evening. Did he send his love to me?

Suicide or fall in love. I just met Rita, lovely green eyes, short blond hair and very pretty. She was born on 9th Feb 1958. I certainly felt that I would never fall for a fellow loon, but hey, it beats suicide. She has a neat almost military skirt which she bought from Oxfam. She has gorgeous laughter lines around her eyes.

Deuteronomy 28 53

53 Because of the suffering that your enemy will inflict on your during the siege, you will eat the fruit of the womb, the flesh of the sons and daughters the Lord has given you.

27 The Lord will send on you curses, confusion and rebuke everything you put your hand to, until you are destroyed and come to sudden ruin because of the evil you have done in forsaking him.

22 If a man is found sleeping with another man's wife, both the man who slept with her and the woman must die. You must purge the evil from Israel.

Romans 8 28-29

And we know that in all things God works for the good of those who love him, who have been called according to his purpose. For those God fore knew he also predestined to be conformed to the likeness of his son that he might be first born among many brothers.

2 Corinthians 4, 8 & 9

We are hard pressed on every side but not crushed, perplexed but not in despair; persecuted, but not abandoned; struck down but not destroyed.

CHAPTER THIRTY-SEVEN

... Joss loves Belinda ...

19/05/2008 21:45. I made this cushion – see!! It says, "Joss loves Belinda!" in huge letters. The cover is in a maroon pink and the writing in blood-red. Not having ever done sewing, it was something of an undertaking. It is finished and I am proud of it but I know in my broken heart that she will not accept it or even look at it.

Monday morning routine, i.e. loaf about until such time as one is seen by the consultant Dr Ellwell, the prat, the arsehole. He can't seem to decide whether to go for permanent detainee or unceremoniously kick me out to commit suicide at my leisure. My philosophy up until this assessment has been to tell the whole truth with a view towards helping him to get me better. I now know that being interned in here is not doing me any good at all. I urgently need to get back to work to earn a living and live in the flat.

Weird. Masses happened today. I feel naked without my diary. Immediately after the review I set off for the tattooist. Frustratingly he had a policy of appointments only on Monday and Tuesday so I went and bought the beautiful box. Hey! I might have to open my own box shop! I don't know where this strange desire to purchase different ornamental boxes comes from. I was out for less than two hours. I want to lull them into a false sense of security.

I spoke briefly to Belinda. As always, she could not resist the temptation to be horrid to me. I know that there will be some disappointed /sad people around when I to do the deed. If I were to try to list them they would include (in no particular order), Tilly, Felicity, Sophie, Daryl, Jonathan, Mum, Dad, Melissa, Charles, Anne (and a few other associated people). This is the master plan. I am going to do my best to be "normal" tomorrow and then first thing at 08:00 I am going to be sitting outside the tattooist parlour. Then after I am done I am going to make my way home. I will lock myself in and barricade the door. I will have bought a half bottle of cheap whiskey and then down all the medicines in the house including any bleach I can find. It would be just my f..king luck that I chunder the whole lot up and not die. I just want out. C'mon Joss, you self-centred arsehole, try and think of something beautiful to end the day on.

Perfect Woman

She was a phantom of delight
When first she gleam'd upon my sight;
A lovely apparition, sent
To be a moment's ornament;
Her eyes as stars of twilight fair;
Like twilight's, her dusky hair;
But all things else about her drawn
From May-time and the cheerful dawn;
A dancing shape, an image gay,
To haunt, to startle and waylay.

I saw her upon nearer view
A Spirit, yet a woman to!
Her house hold motions light and free,
And steps of virgin liberty;
A countenance in which did meet
Sweet records, promised sweet;
A creature not too bright or good
For human nature's daily food;
For transient sorrows, simple wiles,
Praise, blame, love, kisses, tears and smiles.

And now I see with eye serene
The very pulse of the machine;
A being breathing thoughtful breath,
A traveller between life and death;
The reason firm, the temperate will,
Endurance, foresight, strength and skill;
A perfect woman, nobly plann'd,
To warn, to comfort, and command;
And yet a Spirit still and bright
With something of angelic light

William Wordsworth 1770-1850

Two Loves

"What is thy name?" he said, "My name is Love."
Then straight the first did turn himself to me
And cried, "He lieth, for his name is Shame,
But I am Love, and I was wont to be
Alone in this fair garden, till he came
Unasked by night: I am true Love, I fill
The hearts of boys and girls with mutual flame."
Then sighing said the other, "Have thy will,
I am the Love that dare not speak its name."

Lord Alfred Douglas 1870-1945

I Love You

Spanish	- Te Amo
French	- Je T'aime
German	- Ich Liebe Dich
Japanese	- Ai Shite Imasu
Italian	- Ti Amo
Chinese	- Wo Ai Ni
Swedish	- Jag Alskar
Akrikaans	- Ek het jou liefe
Zulu	- Ngiyakuthanda!
Welsh	- 'Rwy'n dy garu di.
Urdu	- Mujhe tumse mohabbat hai
Irish	- taim i' ngra leat
Hebrew	- Ani ohev otach
Vietnamese	- Anh ye^u em

Someone I love very dearly said that the only true magic in the world is love.

Let me not in the marriage of true minds
Admit impediments, Love is not love
Which alters when it altercation finds,
Or bends with the remover to remove:
O, no! It is an ever-fixed mark
That looks on tempests and is never shaken;
It is the star to every wand'ring bark,
Whose worth's unknown, although his height be taken
Love's not Time's food, through rosy lips and cheeks
Within his bending sickle's compass come
Love alters not even at the edge of doom:-
If this be error and upon me proved
I never writ, no one man ever loved

William Shakespeare 1564 – 1616

How do I love thee, Let me count the ways.
I love thee to the depth and breadth and height
My soul can reach, when feeling out of sight
For the ends of Being and the ideal Grace.
I love thee to the level of every day's
Most quiet need, by sun and candlelight;
I love thee freely, as men strive for Right;
I love thee purely, as they turn from Praise.
I love thee with the passion put to use
In my old grief's, and my childhood faith.
I love thee with a love, I seemed to lose
With my lost Saints, I love thee with the breath
Smiles, tears of all my life! – and if God choose
I shall but love thee better after death.

Elizabeth Barrett Browning 1806 – 1861

CHAPTER THIRTY-EIGHT

... no it's not, it's Sunday ...

Thursday 17th. I was going to say that the importance of today is that I can show I am still vaguely in command... ha ha!!

Diary » distracted thoughts, less suicidal, still 100% certain that given the first opportunity I will get my tattoo. I am hoping that this will happen after my review next week. God, it seems an eternity in this awful place. The thing that makes it so bad is that nine years ago in the Fairmile hospital Belinda used to visit me every day. In here she has only come once and that was the day before she announced that she was going out with Felix. I love her so much. I know that this diary/ novel will never be published because it is so boring; every other line reads, "I wish to God I could turn back time and make her love me again." With Sophie playing lacrosse this afternoon, she has probably organised for Felicity to pick her up so she can spend two days with Felix. I do hope that she will be all right and that he does not also break her heart, but in the dark recesses of my evil heart, I hope that he does as it is the only way I could get her back. I wonder if she considered my ridiculous idea of sharing her. I don't even need to be a physical lover any more. I just need her as a friend. Why does she not want to come and visit me? Why is she always so horrid to me? I suppose she is trying to force me to stop loving her. But it is impossible – I love her too much. She has said that the reason why she stopped loving me was because she could no longer trust me. I am obviously guilty of this as I fell in love with Ellen. God, if only I had not. I think that I started taking her for granted when I stopped wearing my wedding ring for the ridiculous reason that it was supposedly too small for me. With soap I force it over my knuckle, determined that it is going to stay there until the day I die.

19/05/2008 21:45. I finished another "Joss loves Belinda" plate and another "Joss loves Belinda" mug. I wrote Sophie a card wishing her luck in her lacrosse tournament. I carefully made an envelope to keep all of Belinda and my love letters.

I decide to follow the order of suggested Bible readings which begin with Peter and John being arrested after Jesus' crucifixion, resurrection and ascension. They were brought before the Sanhedrin who were unable to find fault with them for curing the crippled man that sat by one of the city gates.

I then looked up the passage directing the reader when looking for help when afraid or fearful. It began...

"Of David. When he pretended to be insane before Abimelech, who drove him away and he left."

I wonder if I am just pretending to be insane, depressed, and heartbroken or whatever which is making me act crazy. If Belinda were to take me back I am sure that I would recover instantly. So I suppose that this is evidence that I am just putting it on...

Sorry...

Today is the first weekend day that I have not had a visitor. I suppose that it is something that I need to get used to. I remember at the Fairmile some of my fellow inmates did not get visitors for weeks on end. Hovering in the corridor is lovely Nurse Anna doing her fifteen-minute ward rounds. She looks scarily like Agi at Advanced Telesales and Marketing Solutions Ltd (where I work). Weird thing, I really, really miss being at work. I miss Martin, my adopted son, Louis, Becky, Hywell, Sara and John who amazingly bought my first draft. I miss simply being near them and their frequent sarcastic remarks about my telesales ability (or rather, lack of!)

There is the Cup Final on the telly, Portsmouth verses Cardiff. It is not really my scene. I cannot whip up enough enthusiasm to watch. One guy, Matthew, is fast asleep on the settee. I wonder what percentage of the crowd are football hooligans, waiting for the signal to go berserk? The rest of the world must view English football with contempt.

I can hear quiet sobbing down the corridor. I have no idea who it is but it is growing in intensity. I go and tell Linda who thanks me. I wonder what it is that Linda had said to whomever it was that made them stop crying.

I must have had an awful dream last night because I awoke with a start having bitten my tongue quite badly. Blood and the permanent taste of metal...

A quote from this book, two of the four Buddhist truths are:-

"If you are alive you suffer, and there's a reason for your suffering." Wow! Heavy stuff. Something almost as profound as pretending to be insane. What if I am not pretending and what if the reason for this suffering is to teach me the real meaning of love?

My first experience of love was with a girl whose name I am ashamed to say I have since forgotten. I have even forgotten the name of the cool pub she worked in. It was a classic colonial pub where the ultra-hard drinkers hung out. I remember a tale that once the whole of the loo floor was six inches deep in vomit. The South African and Zimbabwe (then Rhodesian) boys would play down-down drinking games which involved the consumption of 500% more alcohol than was normal. She worked behind the bar and was a tremendous dancer. It was the age of John Travolta as Tony from Saturday Night Fever. I can't dance now and I doubt that I could then. The difference is that I didn't care what people thought then. The disco was in the hall above the pub. After playing the equivalent to a game of rugby in the amount I had sweated in dancing we retired to her room. In my virginity I was surprised that come the hour my willy was not standing to attention. I began by kissing and licking her breasts, her stomach and then somewhere down between her legs. I had no idea what I was looking for but I nibbled and sucked everything and anything I could find. Retrospectively I have absolutely no idea whether she came or not but the exercise brought on the necessary erection. The cruel irony is that from that first internal squirt, she became pregnant.

Almost immediately she went out with the first team fly-half and not long after came to me to ask for a lift home where she was going to get an abortion. She, he and I will never know who the father was, or is that bollocks? Am I just reassuring myself because a woman is bound to know whom she is made pregnant by? I can't remember why my friends were so adamant that I dump her. She was pretty and horsey. I vaguely think, retrospectively, that she was quite rich as the house outside which I dropped her was more of a mansion. Of course her father might have just been the gardener there, and her mother the cook. I bumped into her on one other occasion. She was sitting rather sheepishly on a barstool in the aforementioned pub. I greeted her and she showed me the hospital tag still on her wrist.

So, on a rating of love.
Physically:- 8/10 (Dropped two points due to my own lack of geographic knowledge of the female anatomy, also I remember that she did not participate much, just lay there and thought of England.)
Emotionally:- (retrospectively) 0/10 (The fact that I cannot remember her name and never think of her.)

Girl number two (Jeez, I was a whore!) I also cannot remember her name. She was the underage girlfriend of the First team captain. One night the two of them were in the corridor outside our room in the hall of residence. He was beyond drunk. Mike, my room mate called her down to our room. Our room walls were completely covered in porn. It must have been a bit of a turn on to her because she started rubbing her crotch against Mike's chair arm. It only took Mike seconds to assess the situation and we manoeuvred both of our chests of drawers in front of the door and put our beds together. He gave her a good shagging with the only condom. Strangely she spent the night hugging and kissing me. I was too petrified to move. Bare in mind that I was about nineteen and she was about fourteen. Early in the morning she rolled on top of me and slipped herself onto me. I was too inexperienced or did not care about sexually transmitted diseases or pregnancy but I do remember that it was beautiful. Mike woke just at the exciting bit and rebuked me for doing it without a condom. I can't remember the boyfriend's name but he took her out to Zimbabwe and apparently started a family.
Physically:- 8/10
Emotionally:- 0/10 ditto previous girl.

Girl Three was Sally whom I waxed lyrical about before. I know I was, and still am, in love with her. The truth is that time does heal and in this case it has taken 25 years and a broken marriage for me to realise that she is at long last in my past. It was my well-meaning friends that demanded I dump her.
Emotional:- 10/10
Physical:- 10/10. I was still an idiot when it came to female anatomical geography, but what we lacked in accuracy, we made up for in frequency.

I ought to remember the name of the next girl I had sex with as the relationship was on and off for quite a while. I think that the reason for forgetting is because I have her pseudonym from my first book stuck in my mind. Sorry, Simone Thomas. Sexually, she also was not an animal; she was more a girlfriend of convenience. At any social (read rugby) event, one would have to be gay not to be accompanied by a suitable girl. Once we went parachuting and made love on the floor of the hanger afterwards. Another time we slept together in a single sleeping bag. Because of the extreme cold, sex was impossible.
Emotionally:- 1/10 (I know in my heart that neither of us were in love)
Physically:- 1/10 again because of my own inadequacies in the art of love-making.

Next, Belinda:-
Emotionally:- 10/10
Physically:- 10/10

In order to bring my women into perspective, it would be appropriate to mention some of my post college girls I had crushes on. I had already bought my tickets to South Africa when I met Angie. She was short, cute with an infectious laugh. She was extremely athletic, playing tennis, squash and skiing amongst others. I remember us crawling along the M4 at about 40 mph to go and see a Peter Gabriel concert (in which he sang "Free Nelson Mandela"). I have no idea why we never consummated our relationship. Had we, I would never have had such an affinity with South Africa and a love for Belinda.

I think I fell partially, (OK, almost totally) in love with Anne. Anne is oh, so beautiful, she is so wise and without doubt a very good friend. She refused to let me cross the boundary of gender which is why she has remained such a good friend. Why is it when I speak to some supposed friends, what they say sounds like nonsense? But Anne always has the right advice at the right moment, very much like my sister Melissa. Perhaps also being South African and having a strong desire to be there makes us kindred spirits.

We once almost accidentally kissed each other on the lips and at that moment my hormones went wild, but she sensibly restrained me (and possibly herself).

Before we were married I had a crush on Beauty, an exceptionally beautiful black woman. She is known as Mshlope, which in Zulu means white. I think that my infatuation with her was more of a fantasy and I doubt that it was ever reciprocated, as she certainly never showed it.

Ellen. If I were to view the relationship in reverse, I have not spoken to her since. She continued to contact me after the awful day four years ago, in early October 2007 when I told Belinda I wanted a divorce. Ironic really, one would have thought that instead of being in a loony bin broken hearted over her, I should be out there shagging her like there is no tomorrow. I believe the reason I am not is the sad realisation as to the terrible awful mistake I had made with Ellen.

Every morning I awoke and found myself still next to Belinda I would thank my creator. Every evening I would try to make special in one way or another. Belinda was clearly affected by my actions and immediately stopped eating. She went to see Dr Robertson who referred her to Maria Wells, a psychiatric nurse in Henley. Despite her protests otherwise, I believe that it was Maria that put the thought into Belinda's head that she needed to be independent of me. I wondered if I would ever find out. Every day we were together up until Christmas, I fell further and further and more deeply in love with her. I recognised the awful pain I had caused her and did everything in my power to put it right. She had said that she had forgiven me and that the incident was in the past. However it clearly was not and although she had said she had forgiven me, deep within her heart she had not and came to despise and even hate me. As her anger and frustration rose she emailed me with the famous "we have got to talk" message. My heart sank into my shoes. There was only one thing that she would want to talk about: she wanted to separate. God, I wanted to die. We agreed to go and see Apa together. Apa was Dr Ellwell's number two. Belinda said that she did not see the point in going again together as she did not want to continue the relationship. We had been to three sessions with Relate. Frustratingly I wanted to stop them because I felt that the councillor was clearly blaming me. Later we were to cite that the reason we stopped going was because she had no experience of dealing with my Bipolar and Belinda's eating disorders. Belinda's weight had dropped alarming. She was an attractive 18 and overnight became a stunning size 12 looking totally gorgeous. She had always been proud of her looks and never went out without all her make-up on and her hair done properly. In another life she could have been a model. It is clear where Felicity gets her glamour gene from.

It is probably too early to say where Sophie sits; my guess is that she will be more like Tilly who spends no more than ten minutes on her hair and face before going out. Tilly has long brown curly bouncy hair. Sophie's is slightly less bouncy.

Of my three daughters, Tilly is the oldest. To be honest, she is probably the one least scathed by this whole parents separating thing. She is at Leicester University doing Computer Science. She is in her second year and seems to be doing very well. She has a wonderful boyfriend called Sebastian who dotes on her. They have been "going steady" (if the phrase still exists) for about a year and half. They are planning on going to Disneyland in Florida in August. She is right in the middle of some key exams which is probably why I have not heard from her in a while. She is very shy but once started she has a contagious giggle. I can just imagine "giving her away." I am ashamed to say that I have forgotten Sebastian's parents' names. We met in strange circumstances. Roughly this time last year Tilly was diagnosed with Type 1 Diabetes. It was very traumatic for her as well as for Sebastian, both sets of parents rushing to Leicester hospital, meeting and making polite conversation in the hospital reception.

I understand that Sebastian will be earning a fortune when he starts work. He had either a second or third interview during the week. I was hoping that they might ring and tell me how it went.

I am certainly not the kind of father that could be accused of favouritism. I love my three daughters (and my wife) equally. However, the reality any parent has to face is the flying-the-coup syndrome. Tilly has flown the coup and is 100% emotionally independent of her parents. When she is not at University in Leicester, she is in Northampton where Sebastian lives.

Felicity has a fiery character and she seemed from the age of twelve to seventeen to be in one long permanent argument. Parents were good ammunition, although I would like to think that I was the weaker out of the two of us and would invariably give in to her. A classic example of this was the fiasco at her 16th birthday party. After we refused point blank to allow it in the flat, we organised to use the village hall. She was quite adamant that there were only going to be a few invited friends. It turned out to be total mayhem. Fortunately it was all over by 10:00 because the local PC intervened. He gave me a sever rollicking for being so irresponsible as to leave them unattended. Belinda and I spent until midnight cleaning up the place. The gents were awash with broken glass, blood and vomit. There were splatterings of vomit strategically deposited all around the hall. It was an unmitigated disaster. Early the next morning I dashed into town and bought a new mirror to replace the one in the gents. A few weeks later we were sent a huge bill for the damages which I refused to pay, partly because they were charging us for items which Belinda and I had seen to be there when we left at midnight and partly because we simply could not afford it and partly because of the countless hours my father had put into restoring the hall.
Felicity is very loyal to her friend David who has moved down to Devon. He is like a brother to her. She and her friend Sophie P go out at least once a week. She is a very social animal and is able to rate all the clubs in Reading. Her life is one huge juggling act. She is right in the middle of some key exams. Sadly the truth is that she will not do as well in them as she might simply because in her list of priorities college attendance was right down the bottom, below working, drinking and learning to drive (passing first time, phew, a load off the Dadster's mind as I was the Chief Teacher. Belinda ended up shouting at her and of course Flick would give it straight back!).

CHAPTER THIRTY-NINE

... Belinda's autobiography ...

"I moved to South Africa in 1969 with my mother and two brothers. I obtained a University pass from Maris Stella in Durban and later a Diploma in Computer Programming (Basic). I broke in thoroughbred horses and prepared them for the track before working for Marley in Pietermaritzburg. My interests include horse riding, sewing, knitting, typing, cooking, cake decorating (I made our wedding cake), and crosswords. I prepared the accounts for the business on my own. I am currently doing a Diploma Course in Bookkeeping through the Mid Kent College. I worked for Entranet in Hurley, then later at Throckmorton in Reading. I want *Love, Oh Love* by Lionel Richie to be played at my funeral. Everyone must have the words so they can sing along and I want my ashes scattered in a poppy field near Hurley. Feb 2000.

My ideal virtue... honesty
My ideal of beauty in nature... sunset
My ideal of beauty in art.... Monet -Poppy fields
My favourite study.... Law
My favourite flower... Rose & daffodil
My favourite colour... Blue but I like to wear red in the evening - has to be V or U necked (NOT polar)
My best asset... my boobs!
My favourite qualities in man... sense of humour
The most beautiful woman was… Princess Diana
The most beautiful woman is… Nicole Kidman
My greatness happiness... having children
My favourite entertainer... Lee Evans
My favourite residence... Hurley
My favourite authors... Robert Ludlam & John Le Carre
My favourite musical instrument.... Flute played by Rachael
My favourite hero in real life... Churchill
My favourite heroine in real life... Princess Diana

My favourite actors...	John Thaw, Matt Damon, Ewan McGregor & Kevin Costner
My favourite actresses...	Nicole Kidman, Claudia Schiffer & Kiera Knightley
My favourite James Bond...	Pierce Brosnan
My favourite film...	Mission Impossible (spy type films)
My favourite musicians…	George Michael, Travis, Keane & Sting.
My favourite animal...	Horse
My favourite bird...	Cockatiel
My ambition...	to pass the ACCA examinations to become a qualified Accountant
My favourite time of year...	March/ Spring
My favourite walk...	Along the towpath in Hurley
My present state of mind...	tired

01/01/2008 Self

My Suicide Note – Heartbroken

"What" I exclaimed, after running out to the car park with his trousers and fleecy top and finding him standing there in his white Boddington's T shirt with the slogan "By 'eck you look gorgeous tonight, Petal" and his grey *Buzz Lightyear* boxer shorts. As he stood there with his shiny new mobile phone glued to his ear and with a scary Cheshire cat grin on his face, he announced to me "Yes Darling, we are getting divorced because I love Sue." To say I was shocked and stunned was an understatement. My whole life was ruined, what was I going to do now, how was I going to survive on my own? It drew a cold shiver down my spine and I threw his clothes at him and stormed back into the flat. Why didn't I just throw his clothes in the bin, it was right there, and leave him to freeze on that October Sunday morning? Obviously the shock had set in. Every day I keep pinching myself, thinking that I am still stuck in this dreadful dream. Will it ever go away; will I ever be normal again? Secretly knowing that the answer to both questions will be no; my nightmare lives on.

I know that I am not perfect, no one is, we all have faults and I still don't understand why Joss hated me so much to put me through this. What was he thinking? I guess it was his revenge for me arguing and standing up to him. I have always trusted him with my heart and felt that he would never have an affair because we loved each other. How wrong I was. I have been slapped in the face with a double whammy. I feel as though I have had my heart ripped from my body and broken into tiny pieces and scattered across the floor for people to trample on until it becomes dust and eventually disintegrates before my eyes. I now realise that he didn't really care about me or the consequences of it all as in his cloud cuckoo-land mind he was going to live in perfect harmony, with the perfect woman, in the perfect home, with the perfect children and have the perfect life forever. Now back to reality as his friend Anne would say, a few kisses and cuddles here and there whilst she threw herself at him raving about his book and he hardly knew her at all.

At the end of the day I gave up everything for him and worked like a Trojan. It's ironic that I use the term

Trojan, as that was my nickname for her cycling machine "The Trojan Horse." I know that I don't own Joss. We all do what we think is best for ourselves. That is of course the selfish way of looking at it because life is not so simple. In a marriage there are partners and children to consider. If you don't respect them and realise that they too are individuals with their own feelings that need to be taken into account then you definitely will land up on your own. I know I don't have a right to stand in his way and as the saying goes, love is proved in the letting go. I am totally devastated, shocked and stunned that I don't quite know what to do. Please dear God tell me the right answer as I am totally gutted, my life ruined, I have nothing to live for any more and I am empty.

The children will be fine as they all go on to lead their own lives and what future do I have... as Blackadder would say "None whatsoever."

Felicity, this is your promise to me, when I die and it probably won't be long now (I wonder how long I can survive without eating), please ensure that on my tombstone are the following words: Here lies Belinda Smith Wesson nee Swart, Completely heartbroken. At my funeral, please pick the worst hymns possible and I would like someone to stand up and say that I died of a broken heart. Please can you ensure that Joss pays for my parents to fly over to attend the funeral. I want all my clothes/belongings burnt so that they don't bring bad luck to anyone else.

My engagement ring is to go to Tilly as she is the oldest and the earrings, one to be given to you and the other to Sophie (Joss must have them made into rings for you and Sophie). The ring that will be going to Tilly is worth far more than the earrings so I would like you to also have the V shaped ring. Sophie can have my wedding band. Please promise me that you, Tilly and Sophie will always love your father and you will look after him for me and support him when he needs you.

My advice to all three of you is to make the best of your lives. Make sure you are independent, that you have qualifications and earn the most you can. Look after yourself first, don't do what I did and give everything up for someone. One day they will let you down so look after yourselves and be a little selfish. If you ever need someone to speak to other than Dad, I would recommend Aunty Fiona. I will never forget any of you - love you all so much

Tilly,

You have done so well in getting to university. I know it has been a struggle but you must be proud of yourself as you have done it all yourself. When you have finished university you will be able to walk into a good job. Well done my love, I am so proud of you. Always be true to yourself. Sebastian is truly the best for you and it is so lovely to see you both so happy together. Love you both lots

Felicity,

You are going through a tough time at the moment. Always remember you are a highly intelligent young woman and you can do anything you put your mind and heart to. Please don't waste your time. Time is so precious and can flutter by so quickly. I am so proud of you and know that whatever you decide to do will be right for you. Remember that whatever you do choose to do is not set in stone for the rest of your life. You have to live a little to find out who you are and where you are going. At seventeen this is very hard to discover and you won't get it right. Just don't give up keep trying I will be willing you on. Love you lots

Sophie,

My baby, you have grown up into such a beautiful young girl. I know you keep on about being so tall. One day you will understand that it is an asset and not a liability. Keep strong, hold your head high and always do the best for yourself. I am so proud of you, look after yourself and always remember me. Love you lots

Please ask for the following to be put in the Hurley Gap.

Belinda Wesson Smith (24/03/62 to XX/XX/2007).

Belinda moved to Hurley in 1987 from South Africa. She gave up everything to be with her husband Joss and raise her children in a more stable country. Together Joss and Belinda had three beautiful daughters. In 1992 they purchased the local village store called Welcome Stores. After the sale of the shop four years later they continued to stay on in Goring. As they had both moved around so much in their youth they wanted to keep their family settled in one place. Then Joss became ill and unable to work, and Belinda was thrown into the workplace and became the breadwinner. Many people in the village found this very difficult to deal with as in their minds the man was always the breadwinner. However when faced with a crisis and not wanting to live off the state, it was a case of survival. For a few years she worked seven days a week to keep the family together and put food on the table. As Joss slowly recovered he eventually took on employment and is now happily working full time. Sadly the tale does not have a happy ending as Belinda died of a broken heart, betrayed by the one she loved the most.

Belinda is often very tired and often spends hours asleep on the settee and loves to sleep in late on weekends. She is one of those women that are naturally very good looking. She has beautiful blue eyes; I can see them clearly as I write this. She is serene and radiant. I know that she is understandably angry with me and I wish I could speak to her without her rage boiling over. I love her so much that I let her win the argument. I am slowly diminishing to nothing.
She loves watching programmes like Big Brother, the X Factor, Strictly Come Dancing, I'm a Celebrity Get Me Out of Here, The Apprentice, Britain's Got Talent Reality and interactive telly. Sometimes when she is in the mood, she enjoys cooking and throws herself into the kitchen with gusto. She enjoys playing Sophie Cluedo although it is not a game I was born to play. She is very good (I mean very, very good) at Sudoko and all number games and fairly good at crosswords. After living with her for 23 years I have come to realise that she is highly intelligent. My biggest regret ... (yeah, yeah...) She does, however, love to make sure that she looks absolutely stunning before going out. Last year she was studying so hard it was incredible. There were many times that she would get home at 21:00 and then study until midnight. She very much enjoys a good joke and she is particularly beautiful when she smiles or laughs. Sadly the truth was that I was less able to make her laugh closer to the end. Strangely even the hospital staff now thinks that I am going doolally over her.

Show the world and all its people
All the wonders love can bring
Give us strength and understanding
Give us all one song to sing
Let the music play
Play it loud and make it clear
It's time to stand up
To a new world that is now so near
From the bottom to the top
To the leaders of the land
We all have one heart
Everyone of us must lend a hand
And let there be joy in the world
And let there be no sorrow
(Let there be)
And let there be peace on earth
And let there be peace on earth
For all the world
We've got to see

That love, oh love
What a blessed thing (oh, yeah)
Say it loud
Make it clear today

All the walls are falling down
No more children off to war
If we search in our hearts
All the suffering will be no more
And let there be joy in the world
And let there be no sorrow
For all God's children
Let them see
That love, oh love
What a blessed thing (oh, yeah)
Say it loud
Make it clear today

And freedom, no more lies
We can save this world if we try
One world I know we can make it
Yes, it's only in your heart
Yes, it's only in your dreams
You can climb the highest mountains
You can make the whole world sing
Love, oh love
What a blessed thing (oh, yeah)
Say it loud
Make it clear today

[Lional Richie married Brenda Harvey, on 18 Oct 1975. Ironically during their marriage Lionel began a relationship with Diane Alexander in 1986.]

CHAPTER FORTY

... Felicity's autobiography ...

"My nickname is Flick, Feline-Felicity or Felicity with a very weak "T." I was born at 7.24pm on 12 Dec 1989 at Heatherwood hospital in Ascot. My godparents are Melissa West nee Smith Wesson, and Daryl Smith Wesson and I was baptised on 07th April 1991 at St. Thomas of Canterbury in Hurley by Rev. Philip Nixon.

I know the names of all my toy animals. I love animals and love my pets very much; they are Nibbles (the guinea pig) and Scampie, a beautiful Spollie (cross between a Collie and a Spaniel!) I love taking him for walks with Dad, especially to Maidenbottom Park and to the Hollies. Very sadly, we have had to part with him. However when we do get a house, we are going to find Scampie and get him back. My favourite programme on TV is the Simpsons. My second best holiday was when the whole family went down to Woolacombe for Easter 1998 but my best ever holiday was Christmas 1998 when the whole family visited all the family in Durban and Franschhoek, with Nana and Grandpa, Uncle Stephen, Auntie Melissa, Uncle Daryl and Auntie Fiona. My hobbies are swimming, and netball. I played in the school netball team. My favourite subject at school is Art. My favourite teacher, in Year 3, was Mrs Catherine Wood. Self Aug 2001

Scampie

It was a Sunday morning when my dad promised to get me a dog. I had always wanted a dog, for as long as I could remember. It was the kind of thing that every seven year old that doesn't already have one wants.

But of course, with every good thing, comes a bad thing. My dad made a deal with me: to get my dog I have to go to Church. Normally this would have been too much. Normally spending hours and hours having the Bible read to you and singing hymns would have been like your worst nightmare come true, but nothing could have ruined my excitement and I agreed.

So we're in church, singing hymn number 257. I'm singing my heart out, as loud and as tunefully as I possibly can, and surrounding people are either covering their ears or giving me and my dad very weird looks.

Finally, after what seems like forever has gone by, we're in the car with Mum and my sister Tilly driving somewhere. I don't know where of course, but we're going to get my dog, and that's the most important thing.

I couldn't believe it, after another eternity we were actually there! I was so excited! I looked out of the window at the kennels. I could see a German shepherd in the first kennel, and it was huge!

"Dad, Dad! Can I have that one Dad?" I pointed out the window at the German shepherd.

Dad laughed, "But it might step on you and squish you," Dad said.

We all got out the car and while Dad went to speak to the managers, I ran as fast as I could to see the German shepherd. As I got closer, it seemed to get bigger and bigger until I was right up next to the kennel staring up at it. Mum and Tilly were looking at some very uninteresting small dogs that were lying in their beds looking very boring.

"Mum please can I get this dog?" I begged.

"No. But how about one of these lovely dogs?" I scowled; She just wanted me to have a boring dog that didn't do anything.

"What about this one?" Dad had re-appeared and was standing by a large black and white dog that looked like it was in serious danger of knocking down the wire door that separated him from Dad.

So that was how I got Scampie. Of course I had tried my hardest to make Dad get the German shepherd as well, but I unfortunately didn't succeed.

Scampie was the best dog ever, he was totally crazy, but I wouldn't have wanted a normal dog. There are so many different stories to tell you about Scampie; like for instance the time he mistook my new-born sister Sophie's bald head for a tennis ball and nearly bit her. Or there was the time I was taking him for a walk when he decided to chase a speeding motorbike down the High Street, dragging me along behind! Or when we took him to obedience classes and he thought he'd terrorise the other dogs and their owners and urinated all over the floor.

One thing I remember very clearly about Scampie was that he never liked getting in the car. We had to force him into the boot. We weren't sure why; it might have been because he was terrified that we'd take him back.

We all loved Scampie, so I never understood why we had to give him away. The truth is that there are many reasons apart from his Attention Disorder; we lived in a flat and it was unfair on him, Dad got asthma, he was very expensive to keep, etc. etc.

It was very tearful the day we gave Scampie away; I remember sitting crying in the kitchen with him. He seemed to understand that there was something wrong and he curled up next to me.

I insisted on going with Dad to take him back to where we got him. As we got in the car, he put up more of a fight than usual to get in the boot. When we turned into the kennels, Scampie knew where we were and was barking constantly. In tears again, I gave him a big hug goodbye and as he was put into a free kennel, he struggled to get back to us. I remember watching him getting smaller and smaller as we drove away, knowing that I would never see him again.

04th December 2004

When we bought Scampie I was not working as I had just come out of hospital and I was able to take her for long walks twice a day so she was in beautiful condition. I would take her up to Lardon Chase where she would go mad chasing rabbits and butterflies.

Flick was about to finish at Henley College and was not sure what she wanted to do next. The last I heard is that she wanted to work on an ocean going liner for a year. It would be fun.

My daughters are very close and love each other very much. Tilly and Felicity would take it in turns to look after Sophie. Sophie is ten years younger than Sarah. Sophie would have been ten years older than the child conceived in December 2007. Very sadly for me, it was not to be. At 46 Belinda would not have been the oldest of mums but she would certainly have had to give up her sacred career. She claims that we had not been sleeping together for ages before she met and went out with Felix. Having kept a diary of the pertinent dates, it is clear that at some stage she was having an affair. Either way, I suppose, it is academic as we are separated and every moment without her is exceptionally painful. I wish to God I could get her back…

Sophie is a little bundle of fun. She loves being the youngest and the cutest. She is very good at the flute. Sadly on the day of her exam, she was only a few marks off a distinction, due to the tension between Belinda and me. Belinda, Tilly and Sophie have similar brown curly beautiful hair whereas Felicity's is naturally blond.

CHAPTER FORTY-ONE

... Sophie's autobiography ...

"My best friends include Charlotte, Sophie, Fran, Amy, Chloe, Beth, Holly and Molly. My first name was chosen by Felicity because her best friend was called Sophie, and my second name is my mother's second name. When I was born I weighed 8.2lbs and had light brown hair. I arrived at 8.22 in the evening. My family received over sixty cards when I was born! I appeared at a month old to look identical to my sisters Tilly and Felicity at the same age, and at the age of three I was the splitting image of Tilly when she was three. Some of my favourite phrases were, 'I did it!', 'Eyeah eyeah, eyeah' and 'want it', meaning 'I don't want it' (or so Mum and Dad say I supposedly said!) My favourite toy is Catty!

My ideal virtue...	patience
My ideal of beauty in nature...	view of a sunset from a penthouse
My ideal of beauty in art....	"Marilyn Monroe" (Andy Warhol)
My favourite study....	Science & Music
My favourite flower...	Lavender & bluebells
My favourite colour...	Red (because I am in Langtree), purple & blue
My favourite qualities in man...	kindness
My favourite qualities in woman...	prettiness
My greatness happiness...	being with family
My greatest misery...	having stitches
My favourite amusement...	Sports day & Thorpe Park
My favourite residence...	Swanage, Woolecombe
My favourite authors...	Michael Lawrence, Holly Webb, Daisy Meadows & Sue Bentley
My favourite poems...	The dog ate my bus pass & I did not eat the goldfish

My favourite composer & instrument…	Edvard Grieg, Flute
My favourite hero in real life...	my Daddy!
My favourite heroine in real life...	my Mummy!
My favourite actors and plays...	Zoe from Blue Peter in Peter Pan on Ice
My favourite animal...	Hamster, Cats, Guinea-pigs & rabbits
My favourite names...	Hannah, Lilly, Daniel & Amy
My favourite quotation...	"Silly-billy"
My present state of mind...	bored & tired

11/4/2007 Self

Our Teacher

Our teacher thinks she's very tough
So she makes me
run around the P.E hall which puts me in a huff
She writes something on the white board
I put my hand up to say
But she ignores me anyway
My teacher's very mean
She always shouts at me
Says I've never seen
Someone let me be
She gives us a dare to be quiet for the day
Does she really think that we'll obey?

Sophie is particularly good at the Maths Grid test. She has on a number of occasions come first in the weekly test they do. I have been rather naughty in accusing her of having Ben Leeman-Brown as a boyfriend. She is a master of almost all computer games. The only one I can beat her in is boxing as there is virtually no skill involved!

Of my three daughters Sophie has been most affected by the separation. She now frequently wets her bed and is often crying. I confess that I am closer to Sophie than to Tilly and Felicity simply because the six years of running our own business I worked very long hours and therefore did not see the older two as much as I would have liked. When I started working at Advanced Telesales and Marketing Solutions Ltd, I began a new and more orderly life in which I saw her both before and after school. We are great fans of the author Michael Lawrence having read all his seven Jiggy McCue books at least three times each. When Sophie is not playing the flute, she is playing her electric piano or some of the other instruments she has. I wish I had the money to buy her a piano. Perhaps I should start saving to buy her one. I wonder how much they cost.

Sophie was playing lacrosse in Winchester yesterday. Her team came second. About a month ago they played in a tournament in Reading which they won. She also loves football, gym and judo. She is the second tallest in her class.

All the adversity I've had in my life, all my troubles and obstacles, have strengthened me... You may not realize it when it happens, but a kick in the teeth may be the best thing in the world for you. **Walt Disney**

CHAPTER FORTY-TWO

... Sudden excitement ...

A young girl called Rebecca has just escaped. I feel as guilty as hell as it was I that grassed on her but she is unlikely to get better treatment elsewhere. I was unable to give directions to the chasing staff. Shame, the poor child. She will now have someone staying within six feet of her for 24 hours a day; that is of course if they catch her. The police are also looking for her.

The place suddenly seems to have descended into a proper nut-house. Pete is stomping around a-la-Forrest Gump saying in his pseudo-American accent, "Life is a box of chocolates." Mad Daniel with his permanent hoodie and dark glasses (yes, indoors!) repeats over and over, "I'll be back!" Mad Terry (if that's indeed her real name - the staff call her Tracy – and they should know) is hysterical and grips her sides as she cackles horribly.

Just spoke to Belinda and as usual she made me cry. She said that Sophie doesn't want to speak to me any more because I make her cry. Oh God, what a wreck I am. What a total bastard I am. If only I could escape... escape from here and escape from life. My reasons for living are supposed to be for Sophie and Belinda. Sophie won't speak to me and it is now six months since Belinda and I separated.

Did 25 press-ups from the second step by the phone. Can certainly feel the hum in my chest muscles. Back in my room I do some running on the spot. I'm beginning to feel as if I have to go to the base of the mountain. I have got to find the old Joss Smith Wesson.

In that awful instant I destroyed my own and Sophie's happiness. Ironically Belinda says that she has never been happier. She says that our marriage was 23 years of torment to her she would not come back to me for £1m or for a million years. It breaks my heart to hear this. However I am absolutely committed to getting the tattoo over my heart. I will never forget her. I will never move on. I will never sleep with another woman. I will live like Grandpa Joe and find myself a tiny room and live in isolation.

I make another pathetic attempt to talk to Sophie. She apparently just cries when Belinda asks her to speak to me.

Oh, God. I know that I have another review tomorrow. On this occasion I am going to do my damndest into hoodwinking them into believing I am not a liability. I desperately want to just walk down and get my tattoo. After that nothing else matters. Until then I am naked.

No Joss, you moron! Think rationally. Think you can and then you will win her back. You will get your book published. You will make a lot of money. You will be able to buy a nice house (with no mortgage), a nice car. You will be able to win back her respect and love. Not much of a tall order then…

So you can see why despair seeps through this flimsy armour of my chemical defence. I am so ill, so determined that the only way out is death. No other thought enters my brain. I try to imagine Belinda and me holding hands sitting on the bench at the top of Lardon Chase and laughing together.

CHAPTER FORTY-THREE

... Requiem for a Dream for a Couple of Queens ...

14th June 2008 19:21. I once dreamt circa 1989 to 1994 that I was walking along a grey path between two fields of green, manicured lawns. In the air around me was a thick pea soup fog, a mist so thick I could see in front of me perhaps only a couple of feet. I felt I was walking slowly, plodding with no purpose, no reason, no knowledge of anything, calm, aimless, emotionless, thoughtless, as if in a waking strange sleep. I looked up, to see vertically above me, through thicker mist, the battlements of a fortress. I reasoned that if they were vertically above me, the entrance to the castle must be very close. I was wearing a rug sack. As I gazed at these battlements of the fortress, I felt overwhelmed by feelings of majesty; awe, grandeur, beauty and the overpowering might of the fortress. Such was this feeling of being overwhelmed, that I was "slain in the Lord" and fell back, onto my rug sack, unconscious, dead to the world, insensible, having passed out, fainted away and the dream was at an end. If the castle was Windsor castle, the New Jerusalem, "the fortress of well-being and salvation" of Batiai marriage then maybe I feel like this dream has just come true, that I was approaching the fortress of St James when the Old Bill suggested that my health came first and I should get my feet looked at. Then another dream came true. I was being admitted by my "friends," Steve and Becky with only the pyjamas, slippers and dressing gown I was wearing. Already liquid, cooked into total mental numbness by psychotics as an inpatient to a psychiatric ward in "Chinnor" hospital. I felt utterly desolate, defeated and dispirited that my life was again in ruins with no future to live any more, all over again. Since this dream, I have consciously tried to avoid psychotics and hospitalisation and have concluded that Steve has effectively "destroyed my life" for the second time, and I have decided to have absolutely nothing more to do with him. Steve is Iago and I am Othello and Desdemona is in the guise of Sandra, and Sarah's potential relationship with little me, has been denied me twice from 1978 to 2004 and from 2006 to 2008. Thanks Steve, you're a pal!

So now the dream is over, I am lacking in all consciousness, spirit, faith, hope, love, emotion with only materialistic reality left and my "fantasy world" of faith in dreams again burnt to ashes. As Woody Allen said, "Life's a bitch and then you die," and Blofeld said to Sean Connery, "You only live twice Mr Bond," so I must not expect Sandra and Sarah to appear in the bleak future, and I am not available to anyone who feels minded to fill their shoes. My only emotion is a desire to expose, discredit and destroy Iago, once and for all. As said by Singh Nooniam Khan, "Vengeance is a dish best served cold." In "The Wrath of Khan Star Trek 2" Steve is also "my father," and I am Oedipus, who has been for the umpteenth time denied his "mum." My mum having been "reinvented" in the form of Alison Coon, Linda Parker, Nicola Goeting, Jenny Walker, Yesesptek Yoroughi, Sandra Hardy, Anahita Khosrain and Susan Martin. However, reason, logic, pragmatism, love and forgiveness will not win. My intense desire for justice demands retribution and punishment of the guilty and I will not rest until something is done. There will be no third way, third love, third chance of life until Sarah Martin is restored to me, or my life will continue to be full of an insistent desire for justice, full of hatred, recrimination and hostility for the rest of my life.

Pete Rose 14th May 2008

CHAPTER FORTY-FOUR

... One for Sorrow, Two for Joy. Magpies. Who says ...

Funny thing how things go around... After yesterday's review I am allowed out so I started things quite quietly by going to a Creative Art session and was delighted with the cover I made for my diary. I then started in the Relaxation session but gave up when I could not hear waves in my ears.

Jonathan arrived with Mum and Dad, also known as Nana and Grandpa. We went to a pub and I went through the motions as I knew that any hint of suicide would be reported back to HQ.

After supper I plodded off to Headington, my gaze no more than a few feet ahead of me. Walking along the pavement, my thoughts were along the following lines, "If I had had my tattoo by now I would have the nerve to jump out in front of a bus."

Plodded back down with the same thought intensifying. As I turned into the grounds I saw a magpie and thought, "One for sorrow." Depressed and sad, I was saving the best of the worst of my emotions for tomorrow. You could see the headline; "Manic Depressive suffers from Bipolar Affective Disorder – who was the idiot who let him out?"

But hey...in the space of an hour things look completely different. Felicity phones to say that there is a letter for me from Athena Press, a review of Aargh! (The previous title of the draft of this book). This completely catches me by surprise, after all the months, nay years that I believed that it was going nowhere.

CHAPTER FORTY-FIVE

... a scene overheard from the next room ...

30th April 2008, early evening

"Back off!"
"Get out of my room!"
"Get out!"
"Get out of my f..king room!"
"Don't f..king touch me!"

...Strange, screaming, gurgling sounds...

A different calm voice, "Stop struggling..."

"Get off me!"
"Get out!"
"Mummy..."
"Get off me!"
"Get the f..k off me!"
"Get the f..k off me!"
"Piss off!"
"F..king cunt..."
"Get off me..."
"F..k me..."
"Prick, get out, get off!!"

Calm voice... "Stop shouting."

"Don't even f..king start..."
"Get off, you can f..k off as well!"

...Loud sobbing...

...Wailing, struggling, thrashing...

"Ouch, ouch, Mummy, you are going to lose your f..king job, you prick..."
"It's called pain compliance. I'm going to smash your f..king head off!"
"My head hurts..."
"Get off me! If you break my wrists I am going to sue you...!"

Silence…

"Gee-art off!! Gee-art out!!"
"Mummy..."

…Wailing…

> *"Get off me!"*
> *"Get off me you psychopathic bastards! You're control freaks, now f..k off!"*

The performance had started at dinnertime. Jason took his meal to his room with his parents, I think. There was some bitter dialogue between them. Jason was determined that his family were wrong and that he could eat his meal wherever he wanted. There was an initial effing and blinding. I had been making notes on the causes and symptoms of bipolar and the side effects of the many medications I was taking. I did not have a leaflet on ***Rispiradal*** and went to the Clinic to ask for one and mentioned the altercation in the room next door. The nurse immediately popped down to see if everything was all right. Clearly everything was not all right as Jason also raged at her that he would eat his food in his room if he chose to. She realised that it was not a situation she could handle and went for reinforcements.

Poor Jason. Still, it made me realise how lucky I was; just a few more notches of loony and hey, one finds oneself pinned down by the equivalent of the whole English rugby scrum, each of the monsters weighing over twenty stone (and probably also do boxing and other martial arts). Jason was a Tintin look-a-like; his chances of smashing in the face of just one of them was about zero.

Later. A nurse's hurried footsteps to next door, checking on him. Jason didn't respond, as he was effectively dead. She immediately pressed the alarm and about four sets of additional footsteps came running fast down the corridor followed by the squeaking wheels of the monitoring equipment.

"... Pip, pip, pip ..."

...Long silence...

"... Bleep, bleep, bleep..."

"Can I have some oxygen..."

"Can I have the emergency drugs out..."

"Is the doctor coming..."

"I have no pulse..."

"Get the ambi bag out of here..."

More panting, loud panic-struck running...
Sounds of oxygen hissing...

"Still no pulse..."
"Put a probe on his finger to see if there is a pulse..."
"Have we had a 999..."
"Yes, they're on the way..."

"...pip, pip, pip, pip..."

"...pip, pip, pip..."

...Hissing...
...Whispering in lowered tones...

"... pip, pip,...pip..."

"Josephine, it's too late to have you walking out now..."

"... pip, pip, pip..."

21:19 No ambulance...

"pi...-...pip" – slower...

21:20 Ambulance arrives. Mental hospital staff become quite orderly…

"…That's Ian…"

Ian quickly briefs the ambulance staff as to what had happened. Things are generally much calmer.
Ian explains Jason's actions of the day before. (I had only become aware of his antics on arrival that night) "When and if Jason pulls out, I am going to ask him how he got to being in the hospital," I thought to myself.

21:23 All seemed under control next door. Jason is still unconscious. (I was assuming that he was unconscious and not dead because of the orderly activity). He certainly came close to being dead though.

21:25 *"… pip, pip, pip …"* The ambulance staff bring in a stretcher. I found myself regretting not introducing myself earlier that afternoon.

21:28 "Jason, you are going to feel a sharp scratch on the back of your hand, OK?"

"… pip, pip, pip…"

"OK mate?"

"… pip, pip, pip…"

21:29 *"How you doing?"*

Silence…

"Relax Jason. Well done. OK mate?"

21:30 *"… pip, pip, pip…"*

"Can you tell me what happened, Jason?"

"What has happened this evening?"

"Aargh!!"

"Jason, have you got any pain anywhere?"

"In your head..."

21:32 "Jason, we're going to take you to the general hospital in Oxford as we believe that you have had a seizure."

No sound or comment from Jason.

The sound of new people arriving, possibly parents or additional staff.
"Ooh, my back hurts..."

"Turn around Jason – well done."

21:35 The parents must be there as someone calls him "Darling."

21;36 The activity moves to the corridor, Jason strapped onto a stretcher. I again rue not introducing myself as he taken away. My guess is that he was no more than 19. When/ if he recovers, will they bring him back? Will he have learnt from the experience that it is simply not possible to kick against Big Brother? Or, is it possible that Big Brother might have actually learnt something and be more considerate when dealing with individuals like Jason?

22:40 Had my medication. ***Venlafaxin, Depacote, Risperadil, Zopiclone*** mixed with a snort of ***Seratide*** *and* ***Ventaline***.

Some of my fellow inmates' comments regarding Jason's dice with death:-

- Angry Andre had seen the ambulance and thought something was "up."
- Insane Ian thought it was a "life or death" situation.
- Rob the Karate Kid said we should celebrate by getting in some Chinese.
- Anna (Rob's Babe) was going to pretend to be a nurse to get a better view.

- Jumping Josephine reckoned that Jason looked as if he was only fifteen.
- Doolally Mary said that it had nothing to do with anyone, "surely."
- Mary (with a bad foot) said that she was particularly depressed all day.
- Overstressed Tom said that it was time to escort his wife Sue out.
- Silent Joe said nothing (as usual).
- Barking-mad Rose said something, but I forget what.
- Clever Tom said they must have given Jason an injection to calm him down which caused his heart to stop.
- Robert went on to explain, as an ex-psychiatric nurse himself, why it is necessary for five nurses (read rugby forwards) to restrain the patient.
- I was thinking of having my own rehearsal later.

01/05/ 2008, early the next morning.

Much to my amazement Jason is back in his room. I walk in and introduce myself.

"Hi, I'm Jay." No wonder he's mad – his family can't even call him by his preferred name. He cracks a joke when I mention that the heating is on full-blast.

"Your children don't want to see you dead as they love you. You need to move on from Belinda."

" Wise words Jay."

"Would you get back together with Belinda?"

"Categorically..."

"You should recognize that she is never coming back and you should move

on." He adds that I was not a loony, just hurt. It was at this point that Jay went off at a tangent as I was about to hypothesize on how to regain the love, respect and admiration of my dearly beloved wife.

Mid-afternoon and Jay is still fast asleep. The staff are becoming concerned. Lindsey comes to ask me if I am OK. Ha, just a ruse to peep into Jay's room.

Emits revolting vile green fart...

So, the remaining opportunity to achieve world acclaim would have to be through my writing. I certainly do not see myself as the next "JK," however I must set myself the objective of bringing the plight of the mentally ill and the system they are mangled through to the public conscience.

OK, so it has given me some consolation that some of my fellow inmates/ loons have thought I was a doctor. One even presented me with a full set of keys that might have come in handy had I not been so stupid as to hand them in to the proper authorities myself. Despite being more expressive, erudite, articulate, I am still suffering the same mental pain and anguish they are (with the possible exception of Doolally Mary, who is entirely shot away).

23:41. I want to make an observation as my hold on reality slips away as the medication sets in. I feel dizzy, woozy, and unsteady on my feet. The sensible thing would be to admit defeat and go to bed....

I have a ridiculous uncontrollable attack of sadness; start crying again and resolve to send Belinda an emergency text. I write,

"Dearest Belinda, please forward this to your Felix to be sung to the tune of Dolly Parton's *Jolene*.

"Felix, Felix, Felix,
Please don't take my wife,
Just because you can.
She is everything to me.
I love her so.
(This is an emergency text)"

I suspect she will go ape-shit. I am at my wits end; suicide is the only way if I can't be with the one I love. I wonder what her reply will be? I know ultimately I should never have sent it.

I am re-classified as "Level Three" Observation which means that I have to have a nurse within six feet of me at all times.

CHAPTER FORTY-SIX

... a letter from Belinda's Mum, Shirley ...

18th June 2008

Dear Joss,

I am so sorry to hear that you are not well and in hospital. My thoughts and prayers are with you and hope that you will have a speedy recovery. Be strong, you can overcome this set back. Be prepared to help yourself, get back on the road to recovery and be stronger than before. You can do it. Take deep breaths, relax and meditate. You have three beautiful daughters who love you dearly. Please do it for them, if not for yourself. You also have two brothers and a sister, mother and father who love you too, together with your in-laws and friends. Take a minute to relax and think of all the good that has taken place in your life. Try not to dwell on all the negative parts. Remember all the good times and be grateful for all the love and support shown to you and for you. You are a special, intelligent and kind individual and deserve to be happy. Pick up the pieces and rebuild. Everyone on this planet has troubles – some more than others. We all have to deal with them. Everyone makes mistakes, but we all have to take responsibility for our mistakes and deal with them in the best way possible that we can manage, or take the help that is offered. Turn towards your family, Joss. I am certain that your brothers and sister, mum and dad are all willing to assist you to pick yourself up. Dust yourself off and walk tall again. Many marriages have fallen apart, but that does not mean the end of the road for either party. They both move on amicably, especially where there are children involved. Please do not burden your beautiful girls with their parents' troubles, especially little Sophie. She is only ten years old. It could have a devastating effect on her life. She loves you and Belinda – her parents - dearly. She needs you both so much without fighting. Please take care of number one – you Joss. Get all the help on hand at the hospital, and come up stronger and better than before. Many people are praying for you in this stressful time Joss and many people send love and support to you. Thank you for all the love you have sent to me via Belinda; much appreciated. Good luck with your next book. I am crossing my fingers for it to be successful. See, you have so much to be grateful for. **Sterkte, ou maat**. You can do it. Go down to the river alongside the hospital and feed the ducks and take in all the beauty around you. Be strong and get better soon.

Lots of love Joss. Look after yourself

Love Mum

CHAPTER FORTY-SEVEN

... My reply ...

Shirley,

It is ironic that both Grandpa Joe and Uncle Barry are able to realise that it takes two to cause a separation and do not hold any malice towards me but you in your wisdom have decided that it is entirely my fault.

It was after our second phone call whilst I was in South Africa that I realised that I am innocent in this separation between Belinda & me. Your daughter is heartless and used the incident last year to separate from me and used it as an opportunity to make me feel guilty. I now know in my heart that it was your advice that made her go ahead and do so. (I clearly remember how you heartlessly similarly referred to your fifth husband Sam while you were here in England). I will always totally love Belinda, but I cannot accept or forgive you for your acrimonious and unnecessary attack on my character without knowing all the facts. I do however have you to thank for making me see the situation in its proper light.

So I challenge you to put the following accusations to Belinda. I suggest that you will not bother, knowing that she is guilty of them all.

Belinda: –

Do you deny that in your suicide note you stated that all you wanted was to have me back? Yet once you had had me back you immediately began plotting to get rid of me.

Do you deny the irony that you had lost you mother's telephone number and had to phone me for it in the hospital? Indicating that at the time, she was more important to me than to you.

Do you deny that on the occasions when you had to work very late in the evenings at the office last year (often up to 11.00 pm), I would come just to be with you? (Similarly over the weekends)

Do you deny that now that you have started this relationship with Felix you rarely work overtime and never weekends, which speaks volumes?

Do you deny that you admitted to me that you would often work late because you did not want to come home?

Do you deny that you admitted to me that you have "known" Felix for two years?

Do you deny that you "began" your relationship with Felix in March 2008, the same month that we were still making love?

Do you deny that after 26th December 2007 when you moved out of our bed, we made love at least a dozen times? You later claimed to have done this as "friends" yet you know that I am deeply devotedly in love with you. It also begs the question of the morals and scruples of anyone who makes love but is not in love, specifically if it is to their spouse.

Do you deny that we made love on 16th and 17th March and then on the 18th we went happily hand-in-hand into Reading shopping together? You might remember we went into your favourite coffee shop, the one in WH Smiths. We even romantically looked at duvet covers together!

Do you deny that when your brother Dirk and my brother Jonathan met us here in the flat in February you insisted that you were still in love with me? Do you deny that at the time, you only wanted "separation" to have time on your own to think things through? Do you deny that you had agreed with them that once we sold this place, we were going to rent a place together?

Do you deny that after I had attempted to commit suicide you promised to continue to live with me until we had worked things out? Instead what happened was that you met your Felix and saw a brilliant means of blaming the whole failure of our wonderful marriage on me, sending me into a fearful self-destructive cycle of guilt.

Do you deny that it was in your interest to have me as ill and as ranting as possible as it only made your new "knight-in-armour" look all the more attractive?

Do you deny that you lied about where you had been the night before I was admitted to the hospital? You later confessed that you had been seeing Felix.

Do you deny that you used the time that I was in that dreadful hospital to cement your relationship with Felix?

Do you deny that although I was in hospital for over four months, you only brought Sophie to see me once?

Do you deny that during the incident at your office which resulted in my arrest, you used your most dramatic schoolgirl cinema put-on scream? Appearing to supposedly fear me is again good for your case with the new lover. You need a reliable strong, young, handsome, rich lover, all of which I am not.

Do you deny that your reason to ultimately leave me because you were supposedly unable to trust me was a lie? I accept that I had committed a terrible awful sin, but afterwards you said that you had forgiven me and that you loved me; is this not what love is? Yes, I had broken our bond of trust. I was prepared to leave as you wanted me to. I begged you to forgive me which you wholeheartedly did. By forgiving me and saying and acting as if you loved me, you cannot deny that meant that you trusted me again? Just because it suited you, you later then decided to remove this trust and start your relationship with Felix.

Do you deny that prior to Valentine's Day 2007 you only wore gaudy, boring very unsexy underwear? Do you deny that it was me that bought you all that beautiful clothing which you are now happy to wear for your new lover?

Do you deny that I made for you a beautiful birthday present and that you had the audacity to tell Felix that I had forgotten and had not bought you anything? When I reminded you of what I had made for you and had spent over £200.00 on it, you then cruelly said that you did not want it.

Do you deny that once you had lost all that weight and were wearing a complete new wardrobe (and completely new sexy underwear) and were looking stunningly gorgeous, you simply believed that I was no longer good enough for you, being the overweight slob that I had become?

Do you deny that despite it taking me over twenty years to write, you have never bothered to read my book, despite it being a eulogy of my love of you?

Do you deny that prior to our even meeting the Davidsons (the woman I had the affair with – although I am sure you will agree that to have an affair necessitates having sex, which we did not, going out together, which we did not etc.), I had begged you to come with me to a marriage guidance counsellor on two occasions?

Do you deny that after you had supposedly forgiven me for my liaison with Ellen Davidson, we lived happily together for nearly three months? Why the sudden change of heart, other than your mother's interference?

Do you deny that when we became increasingly at odds with each other you made no effort to resolve our differences? You enjoyed TV programmes such as East Enders, X Factor, Big Brother, and Strictly Come Dancing etc. But during the few programmes I enjoy, you would usually continue a conversation with the children in the room so I would inevitably get up and leave.

Do you deny that during our many heated augments you were happy to turn your back on me and go to sleep without attempting to resolve the issue? On a few occasions you simply resorted to the "silent treatment." Do you deny that it was I who always tried to resolve these issues?

Do you deny that your claim that you frequently went to sleep in tears was an outright lie?

Do you deny that virtually every evening as we prepared for bed, we would chat for hours?

Do you deny that after we had had a fight, and made up, we always enjoyed making love more than ever?

Do you deny your desire to "get revenge" on me for something I supposedly did early in our marriage?

Do you deny that you seemed totally determined to ignore my cries to live within our means and spent money with no concern as to how our mounting debts will be repaid?

Do you deny that you stole £5,500.00 out of our "Joint Account" and put it beyond my reach despite promises to myself and my brothers that it would be returned?

Do you deny that you have stolen the access cards to the "Joint Account" so I cannot see its activity?

Do you deny that you knew that I had given Felicity £110.00 just before Sophie and I left for South Africa but you still gave her an additional £200.00? What would she have needed all that money for in a fortnight (as well as earning her own money)?

Do you deny that I gave you £150.00 of the £400.00 I had withdrawn, leaving me just £90.00 to spend on holiday? (Of which I gave £50.00 to Sophie which you owed to her anyway.)

Do you deny that you have hidden my HSBC chequebook, paying in book and credit cards?

Do you deny that the £11,000.00 Marks & Spencer loan is your responsibility?

Do you deny that the Lloyds Visa debt is also entirely yours?

Do you deny that the outstanding loan on the car is yours? (Unless we are going to share its use.)

Do you deny that when doing the weekly grocery shopping you grossly overspend, much of it ending in the bin?

Do you deny that staying in Woking has at least trebled your petrol consumption? You yourself admitted that Roger's car was terrible on fuel consumption. This was presumably coming out of the "joint account."

Do you deny that you are paying your brother Dirk rent, presumably also coming out of our "Joint Account"?

Do you deny that by last year you had become mean, vindictive, aggressive, spiteful and lacking in any sympathy towards Sophie? You became obsessed with your career to the degree that you almost totally neglected her. You have never read her a bedtime story and very rarely kissed her good night. You very rarely listen to her practise her flute, preferring to close doors so that you can watch TV uninterrupted. You frequently raised your voice to her when she was innocent of any wrongdoing, making her cry and worse of all you frequently smacked her (until I got so angry on that weekend we went to Dunster last year, when I forced you to stop). You promised that she could accompany Felicity on holiday to South Africa to visit our various families last year. It was while I was actually on the phone to my parents that you decided to change your mind and not let her go (even though they were paying for her to go). At the time I too taken aback and felt that I needed time to decide how I was going to react to this act of incredible cruelty. How it will affect her in later life I do not know. If you naively believe that she will forget, you are mistaken. By way of a supposed alternative, you promised that we would take her to Disneyland in Paris. Do you deny that you did everything in your power to delay and stall the application of her passport? We were then supposed to go to Ireland instead. That was then replaced by that three-day weekend in Devon.

Do you deny that in going to South Africa this year you again attempted to prevent Sophie from going? Firstly by securing her passport at the solicitors and secondly by attempting to manipulate the poor child the day before departure into believing that her father was some sort of monster that could not be trusted.

Do you deny that Sophie is just an inconvenience to you? You do not truly love her and I have tried my hardest to make up for your failure and I will contest taking custody of her. Without her, you will be able to get on with your beloved career and new lover. It was only when the separation issue became apparent to you that you started to look upon her as a commodity and feigned love for her.

Do you deny that you are more concerned with your relationship with your new lover than you are with your children? Incidentally, none of them are vaguely suffering without your presence in Goring. Sophie is delighted to walk to school and take a packed lunch every day, saving a fortune. Either Felicity or I pick her up and the three of us enjoy watching a video together in the evenings (without the previously inevitable heated arguing, you always insisting on watching "adult" TV).

Do you deny that when we first met you treated your father appallingly and this is how you came to treat me in the last two to three years?

Do you deny that you did everything possible to prevent friends from visiting us?

Do you deny that you never once accompanied Sophie and I to the Free Church, despite knowing its importance to her?

Do you deny that you did not follow my lead trying to encourage Felicity to improve her attendance at Henley College and to spend more time on her course work?

Do you deny that you said that we would part as friends? However you have been so vindictive and beastly to me since you started your relationship with Felix.

Do you deny that you have taken every opportunity to turn my family against me?

Do you deny that you lied that one of my family had suggested to you to take the NatWest money away from me. You have successfully portrayed me as the financially reckless irresponsible spender whereas in truth the reverse is the case.

Ultimately**, do you deny** that you used my very brief liaison with Ellen Davidson as an excuse to end our relationship? It was probably more to do with seeing an opportunity to escape the dreaded flat which we both hate. It could be that you saw someone that earns twice what I do and saw what he could do for you (already supposedly paying for this holiday of yours to Ireland). Perhaps you erroneously blamed me for our spiralling debts. I know that you despise me for trying to save money by shopping for my clothes at second-hand shops. Perhaps you believe that I am an inadequate lover? Perhaps you think that I spend too much time on my/our genealogy? Perhaps you despise the fact that I earn less than you? Perhaps you have never really loved me and just used me to get to England? Perhaps you could not tolerate living with someone permanently ill with Bipolar? Perhaps you never believed that I have it and think that I only do strange things to gain attention? Whatever the real reason, I very much doubt that you have the strength of character to admit why you dumped me, but thanks to your mother, I am now certain that it had nothing to do with Ellen Davidson. (Incidentally, any of these theories could be right, but surely what a loving couple should do would be to try and work out their problems together – not just walk away from them like you did.) Many, many couples survive such tragedies (I do not pretend that it was anything less) yet with forgiveness and love they become stronger together. You, however, with your mother's advice, saw an opportunity to go for some of your other dreams such as a big house, fast car etc.
Shirley, I can hardly say "fond regards" or "love" etc. because if I never see you again I will not be too upset.

Joss (your ex son-in-law)

CHAPTER FORTY-EIGHT

... In the Reading County Court ...

Case No. RG08P01773
Children Act 1989
Family Law Act 1996
Mr Joss Smith Wesson
Applicant

and

Mrs Belinda Smith Wesson
Respondent

Statement in support of an Interim Contact Order of Sophie Smith Wesson
(DOB 24/12/1997) by Joss Smith Wesson

I, the applicant, Joss Smith Wesson apply to the Court for an Interim Order to secure legal rights to see my daughter Sophie Smith Wesson during what will doubtlessly be a lengthy proceeding to determine whether I am a supposed danger to her.

Unfortunately I suffer from Bipolar (my breakdown last year was largely caused by my wife's adultery). As I stated in Court on 19th Feb 2009, I regularly take medication, I see my GP, Dr. David Walters in Hurley-on-Thames on a weekly basis, I see my consultant psychiatrist in psychotherapy, Dr. Jennie Le Roux in Hurley-on-Thames, on a monthly basis. I also have a weekly informal meeting with my employer. I am therefore monitored on a more or less continuous basis with a view to maintaining my recovery and stability.

Prior to my return to work, my employer insisted that an independent psychologist, Dr. Michael Humphries in Oxford, assess me. The summary of his report was that I was no longer mentally ill, that I am not a danger to anyone; not to my wife, (I only include the word "estranged" here as she will be rushing to find errors and omissions in my statement) to my daughters, (Tilly and Felicity, both over aged 16) or to myself.

I am able to give character references from a number of people from various walks of life who will testify that I am recovered and capable of caring for Sophie when she resides with me.

My wife is waving the "mentally ill" card to prevent my seeing Sophie. It should be mentioned that my wife also has a history of "mental illness", frequently going to Henley outpatients' clinic for psychiatric treatment.

If I am (and I adamantly state that I am not) of psychological danger to Sophie, why is it that she has been allowed so freely into my presence, most weekends, for the last five months?

Clearly I am recovered and that this is an attempt to use my past illness against me to stall the process further.

My wife will immediately cite that it was I that caused the marital breakdown with the liaison I had (I use the word "liaison" as opposed to "affair" because the relationship never became physical). I enclose a letter I wrote to her mother in response to her vitriolic attack on my character over the telephone. It illustrates that my "relationship" with this other woman was simply the last straw and that my wife was equally to blame for the marital breakdown. I have slept alone since she left; yet she was sleeping with her new partner within days of the last time we were in bed together.

Prior to my being sectioned last year (in the Warnford Hospital in Oxford), my wife had become mean, vindictive, aggressive, spiteful and lacking in any sympathy towards Sophie.

She had become obsessed with her career to the degree that she almost totally neglected Sophie. She never read Sophie a bedtime story and very rarely kissed her goodnight. She very rarely listened to Sophie practise her flute, preferring to close doors so that she could watch TV uninterrupted. She frequently raised her voice to Sophie when she was innocent of any wrongdoing, making her cry, and worst of all she frequently smacked Sophie.

She promised that Sophie could accompany Felicity (our middle daughter) on a holiday to South Africa to visit our various families in 2006. It was while I was actually on the phone to my parents organising the holiday that she decided to change her mind and not let her go (even though my parents were paying for Sophie to go). At the time I too taken aback and felt that I needed time to decide how I was going to react to this act of incredible cruelty.

By way of a supposed alternative, she promised that we would take Sophie to Disneyland in Paris. She then did everything in her power to delay and stall the application of Sophie's passport. We were then supposed to go to Ireland which was replaced by a three-day weekend in Devon instead. (We did subsequently go to Disneyland in February 2008)

In the presence of her solicitor in the waiting room of the Reading County Court on Thursday 19th February 2009, my wife promised me that Sophie could go to South Africa for my parents' 50th wedding anniversary party. The next day, I received a letter from my solicitor attempting to impose unnecessary preconditions on this. I include these letters for consideration by all parties. My view, and I believe the Court will agree, that this is an act of spite, hatred and revenge and has no bearing on the welfare of Sophie. Clearly had I not taken the opportunity to apply for this Interim Order, my wife would have succeeded in prevented Sophie from going to South Africa with me.

I have absolutely no reason to stay or live in South Africa. Sophie's home is here. All her friends are here. Both my older daughters are here. My home that I love – and which I own - is here in Hurley. I love my job in Reading. My wife knows all this, but chooses to act accordingly. I am now genuinely afraid and concerned that she will succeed in preventing Sophie from going on this holiday that was prearranged years ago.

Sophie has a right to see her paternal grandparents and visit a land which is a significant part of her heritage.

Had Belinda not decided to appeal on the grounds of "danger" – a choice which from her correspondence appears to have been made by ticking a box - Sophie could now be spending weekends happily with me now. I am led to believe that this action is done out of vindictiveness rather than concern for Sophie's welfare.

Why my wife is so determined to smear my character is not clear to me as she goes to visit her boyfriend in Swindon every weekend and it would have been convenient to her to have someone who loves Sophie care for her while she is away.

I believe that my wife would have preferred that I had not recovered and had stayed in the state of illness I was in last year. It would be satisfying for her to have me labelled as mentally unfit and a potential danger to my daughter. This, however, is not a satisfaction she will have. I am prepared to submit to any humiliating exercise in order to prove my fitness, recovery and stability. I am totally and unreservedly confident that any independent psychologist will concur with Dr Humphries that I am fully recovered; I can also summon pertinent character witnesses to testify to my fitness.

To me the care of Sophie is of primary concern. However, it is also important that the Court appreciates that it has been five months since Sophie was my responsibility and that it will be another three months of the CAFCASS process, during which time I believe that my wife will find another legal mechanism to stall proceedings still further to prevent me seeing Sophie. During this time she continue the process of alienating me from my daughter.

The questions I would like the CAFCASS Officer to indirectly put to Sophie include:
Before separation from your father last year,

- Who reads to you every night?
- Who listened to you practice your flute every night?

- Who brushed their teeth with you, encouraging you in the habit?
- Who took you to the loo in the middle of every night because of your bed-wetting problem?
- Who chatted to you from behind the curtain whilst you showered?
- Who walked you to school, holding hands the whole way?
- Who watched you and photographed all your sports days?
- Who photographed you at every stage of your life, lovingly storing the pictures?
- On the many trips back and forth from Bristol, who preferred to chat happily away about future kitten names and other stuff? (As opposed to have you sit in silence all the way in the back.)
- Who often took you and friends to Beadle Park?
- Who frequently took you to the cinema?
- Who carried you on their shoulders way past the age where you were still a small child?
- Who took you to various lacrosse tournaments?
- Who accompanied you to the Hurley Free Church?
- Who went on endless bike rides with you?
- Who went on long walks with you?
- Who has loved you with a passion since the day you were born?
- Who is in agony without you?
- Who encourages you not to phone your father?
- Have you frequently asked if you can stay with him?
- Why do you not phone him?
- Do you fear your father?
- Do you believe your father still loves your mother?
- Why did you hold your father's hand all the way back on the journey from Bristol on 15/2/2009?
- Did your mother prevent you going to South Africa in 2006? (Y/N?)
- Are you aware that your mother is attempting to prevent you from going to South Africa this April 2009?

(The CAFCASS officer should thereby be able to deduce my fitness as a parent as contrasted with my wife.)

This is my statement of events. My wife in her hatred of me now will take this opportunity to deny them and vilify me. I enclose her statement of our initial Court hearing in October 2008 to illustrate her inability to recall facts, or rather her ability to distort and manipulate them and my response. I also enclose Dr. Humphries' letter to my employers, drawing attention to her recommendations (on the assumption that all these are not already available to this hearing).

(I also enclose a letter I hand-delivered to my wife's address in Pangbourne in November last year. The net result was to spend 24 hours in Reading police cells. I had ensured that when I delivered it, she was not at home. As can be seen, the letter is neither threatening, harassing etc. It simply requested resolution of the many outstanding matters, of which custody of Sophie was one. She had the audacity to have hand-delivered a solicitor's letter to me on the evening of 18th February 2009, i.e. without any opportunity to go over it, requesting that we use the time before the Case to resolve these other matters! Of course I want to resolve these matters, but not in a public, overcrowded, noisy waiting room with very limited time. We had had a mutually agreed meeting arranged for 12/12/2008 at her solicitor's office, Richard Wilson in Hurley. She chose to not attend this and by delivery of this solicitor's letter last night can only have had the intention of attempting to unsettle me. I had requested that this meeting be rescheduled. Clearly 19/02/09, fifteen minutes before my application for Contact to see Sophie is hardly appropriate.)

I would also like to take this opportunity to enquire from the Court the meaning of the phrase,
"*And upon the Applicant indicating to the Court that she will present & petition for divorce as soon as reasonably practicable.*"
[Reading County Court RG08F0117 14th October 2008]

Clearly five months is beyond reason. I have no intention of petitioning the Court, as I still love my wife and do not want a divorce, but equally, I do need to get on with the rest of my life.

The purpose of this application is to maintain contact with my beloved daughter Sophie and therefore I would also like the Court to draw to the attention to my wife the sentence in the same hearing,
"And upon the Applicant agreeing to ***support and facilitate*** *contact between the Respondent and the child Sophie Smith Wesson by* ***daily telephone contact****."*

This is simply not happening. I am asking for her assistance in this matter. I have been obliging in handing over all that she has requested (TV, bread maker, heaters, clothes, books, and Smith Wesson family heirlooms) but this goodwill is not being reciprocated.

I believe that the contents of this statement are true.

Signed
Date
Joss Smith Wesson
14A High Street
Hurley-on-Thames
Maidenbottom
RG5 9AR

CHAPTER FORTY-NINE

... Notes further to Belinda's statement in response to mine ...

READING COUNTY COURT

CASE NO. RG08PO1773
CASE NO. RG08F01717

Belinda's statement starts well in saying that we both want what is best for Sophie. However, things go downhill from there. The rest of her statement is an attack on my character.

My application is to gain Contact and Residency of our beloved daughter, Sophie. Belinda now sees this as an opportunity to put me on trial. Our outstanding financial difficulties are irrelevant to this case and my illness is of secondary importance to my real ability to cope. I have no doubt that the Judge will be aware of high profile celebrities, such as Peter Gabriel, that suffer from the same condition and both parent normally and live normally (e.g. point 16.4, 21).

I note that she does not contest that she denied Sophie the pleasure of going to visit our families in South Africa in 2006. This was going to be paid for by my parents and I was on the phone arranging this with my parents when Belinda changed her mind. She does not mention the mental cruelty she inflicted on Sophie (now that we are separated, clearly she is being amiable and pleasant to Sophie in the hope that the child will forget how beastly she used to be to her).

I additionally note with interest her passing comment that she has cash flow problems and I therefore wonder how she intends to pay Richard Wilson for their services.

2) She states that it would be "fair" to await the outcome of the CAFCASS report, then contradicts herself in attempting

to find additional reasons as to my unsuitability to parent Sophie.

3) Ditto. Without psychiatric expertise she proceeds to besmirch my character. What she chooses to ignore is that my (retrospectively ridiculous) attempt to commit suicide was out of love for her and understandable distress at her leaving. My doctor and the psychiatric evaluation will testify to my now much improved emotional state.

4) It is only fair that as my mental health is in question, that Belinda's own mental health is examined. She mentions that the records are available, are they made available to this court?

5.1) I think Belinda is getting confused with her own statement of the 14th October 2008 as the date of our separation is not mentioned in my statement.

5.2) Yes, she imposed the separation date of 26th December 2007. However, we made love a further eight times after this date, the last being 18th March 2008. So by her own admission, she started her relationship with her new partner only seventeen days later.

5.3) She contends that I have refused Cognitive Behavioural Therapy. I regularly see Dr. Jennie Le Roux (consultant psychiatrist in Henley) who as yet has not recommended it. However, I will be seeing her as of next Monday (30th January 2009) and will suggest Cognitive Behavioural Therapy.

Most of the symptoms she refers to here are from 2007. (I respectfully request that Richard Wilson note that I cc Dr David Walters who can be contacted to verify this). I do still have a poor memory on occasion, but this is not a serious disabling factor and I am making considerable effort to improve my memory.

5.4) I have no doubt that she now reads to Sophie in my absence but she certainly never did before. Of course Sophie, as an adolescent girl, is very capable of reading to herself; but reading to a child is important. I find it hurtful that Belinda in her rage and anger against me has the audacity to still blame me for Sophie wetting her bed.

5.5) Specifically who in my family? I suspect nobody, as I have never suggested this awful crime. I suspect that Belinda is jealous of the month of bliss Sophie, Felicity and I enjoyed together last September.

6) I believe that the events of these fateful days are documented and are available to the Judge. I make no defence for my behaviour. I can only say that I did not wish to live without Belinda. Her cruel contention that I did it deliberately to psychologically wound Sophie is wrong. Again, I cannot explain my thinking at the time; I just wanted to die. As I mentioned before, my doctor will testify that my psychological state is greatly improved.

7) As before, these events are otherwise documented. I cannot really defend the letter I sent, but I hope that the court recognises the irrational things that passion and distress can cause one to do.

8) My comments as to the validity of the PCAMHS report are below.

9) Belinda says that I am trying to use emotional blackmail to get Sophie to ring me. I believe that the Judge will see that the reverse is the case. Why is it that Sophie is so relaxed in my company? Why is it that she so enjoys riding her bicycle with me? Why is it that she so enjoys playing chess and Monopoly with me? Why is it that she so enjoys going to the pub with Felicity and I?

10) Yes, I indeed do this. I plead guilty. It was Felicity that made me see the error of my decision, although this was after she said that she had chosen me.

11) Yes, this did happen. I think that Belinda seems to have forgotten that I am still, and always will be Sophie's parent and have a right to reprimand her for inappropriate behaviour.

12) I do not believe that this is Sophie's view. This is either what Belinda has instilled into her or simply Belinda's imagination. Sophie often said that she would like to come and stay with me.

13) I understood that Sophie's phone was an old phone (either way, it is academic). However, I bought her £10.00 credit in order to phone me.

14) Whatever the reasons, I was Sophie's active parent at that time. Belinda is attempting to take this away from me. I somehow doubt that the CAFCASS report will corroborate that Belinda ever read to Sophie. Belinda was always far too interested in Reality TV & Soaps.

15) It is interesting to note that point 15 is dealt with so late in her statement as this is the nub of the Court Hearing. I do not believe that Belinda honestly believes that I am a "danger" to Sophie. She is acting out of revenge and spite.

16.1) Yes, I have attempted to take my own life twice. However, let the psychiatric consultants be the judge of what "danger" I present to Sophie, Belinda and myself. This is clearly an attempt to override any report and cloud the Judge's judgement.

16.2) Sophie and her sister witnessed me going down the stairs towards Belinda to put my shoes on. Belinda then did her best "audition scream" she could come up with. She knew she was in no danger but chose to exploit the situation.

16.3) This is ridiculous. This is the statement of one determined to smear the character of one she used to love. There is no truth in it.

16.4) I have every confidence that the Judge will mock this inclusion and probably commend me on my initiative in getting additional income in difficult circumstances. My friend and lodger says that he would be prepared to undergo a psychiatric profile and an advanced Criminal Records

Bureau clearance. He is not a 'stranger'; I have known him for some considerable time.

16.5) I had said that Sophie and I were going to go to South Africa and it turned out that it was possible that we were able to go in August despite Belinda's best attempts to prevent Sophie from going (including actually pulling her aside at the last possible moment).

16.6) I again can't see the relevance of this. In my despair, I found myself in dialogue with this woman. Yes, I desperately wish that it had not happened. As my wonderful and beloved father said when I told him that I had wasted this money, "Son, I have made worse mistakes in my life." I can just imagine how Belinda has continued to delight in repeating this story ad infinitum to denigrate me to my children.

17) Yes, my sister wrote the letter and I forwarded it to Belinda, however I agreed and concurred wholeheartedly with its contents. At the time I was too emotionally exhausted to rewrite it.

18) The Court would have to get a statement from Felicity as to whether Belinda had offered to pay for Felicity to go to South Africa. However Felicity was fortunate to recently inherit a sum of money from my brother so she was in a position to finance herself as she had frequently said she would. After Belinda's mention of having "cash flow" problems, I doubt that Belinda ever made this offer. My whole family is desperately looking forward to this family holiday together (It would have been all the more wonderful if Belinda and Tilly had been able to come). It is incidentally entirely academic whether I am taking them to South Africa or whether my parents are paying for them. There is a terrible fear in my heart that in her hatred of me, Belinda will still attempt to find some reason to spoil it.

19) Richard Wilson should have been aware that a solicitor no longer represents me. However, on our return to Heathrow airport, I will happily give Sophie's passport to Felicity.

20) I may have at an early stage of parenthood smacked our older children, however, in the same considered way that I decided to be a vegetarian, give up alcohol and coffee for nine years (yes, irrelevant to the case) I decided that it was wrong to do so. However, it is a lie for Belinda to state that it was a joint decision. She continued to do so until October 2007 when I got particularly angry with her for smacking Sophie.

22) I was unaware of any plans that I should live elsewhere. Belinda is guilty of adultery and it should be (and was) her that had to leave the family home.

23) Yes, I did try to contact her. I delivered a letter stating the funds she owed me, not in itself a threatening item. I particularly enjoy Humphrey Gilbertson's creative writing, "...the applicant cycled from Hurley to Pangbourne at 11pm at night (when else is 11pm?) after an evening in the pub to deliver a letter..." It was after a long evening compiling the letter, obviously! Felicity has yet to "pass on" any thanks for the many items that I have given to Belinda, which I was not otherwise obliged to give her.

24) It was me that started and encouraged Sophie to play the flute. I am delighted that she is continuing to do so well. I am also so pleased for her that she is enjoying her lacrosse.

25) I am absolutely delighted that Sophie has been selected to go to the David Beckham Academy. However the relevance of this point is somewhat lost on me. If the point of it is that Sophie will be collected by Felicity and I, as opposed to by me on my own, then I would like to point out to the Court that on many occasions when Felicity and Sophie come to lunch on Sundays, Felicity spends time alone on my PC (on Facebook) and Sophie and I go off together on long bicycle rides together.

26) It is a strange lie to make as surely the court can check on this. It was I who applied for Sophie to go to Langtree School last September.

28) I respect that Belinda loves our children, but in her hatred for me, she is trying to prevent me from having a natural relationship with them.

The PCAMHS Summary Review

I have never shown any aggression to my daughters and the only time I was aggressive to my beloved wife, Belinda, was when she openly phoned her lover in my presence. Most husbands would probably get equally angry. I had never "moved in" with my brother Jonathan. I stayed with them for about five days.

I have never received any material from the organisation.

In the Action plan:-

Belinda was to arrange a meeting with my psychiatric nurse and Sophie. This, to my knowledge, and I see her monthly, has never happened.

I interpret the next statement as, "Belinda will continue to indoctrinate her hatred of me into Sophie".

CHAPTER FIFTY

... Patient's Information Leaflet No. 7 ...

Patient's Information Leaflet 7
Mental Health Act 1983 Section 3
Admission to Hospital for Treatment

Patient's Name...
Joss Smith Wesson
You have been admitted to... Section 3
Your Doctor is... Dr. Ellwell
Date of Admission... 28th April
2008

Why am I in hospital?
It has been decided to admit you to this hospital or mental nursing home so that you can be given the treatment and care you need. You can be kept in this way because of section 3 of the Mental Health Act 1983. This means that the doctors who said you should be admitted to the hospital think that you have a mental disorder for which you need to be in hospital for medical treatment.

How long will I be here?
You can be kept here for up to six months so that you can be given the medical treatment you need. You must not leave during this time unless a doctor tells you that you may. If you try to leave, the staff can stop you, and if you leave, you can be brought back.

What happens next?
The doctor will tell you when she or he thinks you are well enough to leave hospital. If the doctor feels you need to stay in hospital for longer than six months, she or he will talk to you about it towards the end of the six months.

Can I appeal?
You can ask the Hospital Managers to let you leave hospital. If you want to do this, write to them at:-
Mental health Act Office
Littlemore Mental Health Centre
Sandford Road
Littlemore
Oxford
OX4 4XN

Your nearest relative can also write to the Hospital Managers and ask them to let you leave. The Managers can take 72 hours (three days) to look at the request, so that they can get a report from your doctor. Your doctor may say in his report that you should not be discharged and if she or he does you will have to stay in hospital.

My Guardians

With every passing moment
They are sat there
Looking for symptoms
Symptoms of suicide
If only they could read my thoughts
It's just as well they cannot.
Suicide, suicide
Internal death
Death to self.

I phoned Belinda and amazingly she was pleased to hear from me, although she had not changed her stance vis-à-vis getting separated, presumably as I did not ask the question. She asks whether I was going to be coming out soon and if so would I be going down to Bristol. I of course say that I do not know and would let her know as soon as I did.

I also speak to Sophie who is not keen to go and stay in Bristol but says that she would rather go to Longleat with me. I am not sure how I am going to field not going to Bristol and keeping Sophie happy which would be my main priority. We could go after Longleat. I think that the reason why she does not want to go is because she is so embarrassed about her bed-wetting. I know from my own experiences that it can be numbingly embarrassing.

I desperately want to see Belinda even if it is only fleetingly. I know I have lost the battle to keep her as a partner but just want to keep her as a friend. The problem is that I am petrified that I will burst into tears at some insignificant thing that would cause her to despise me even more. I wish I could do something that would make her proud of her "association" with me.

What with this current episode in the bin, it is highly unlikely that it will be something that will happen in the foreseeable future at work. I believe that the reality however, is that I am capable of being a project leader and had I not started the slide into this state back in October/ November 2007, I would probably have been promoted by now. Is it possible that it might come out of my genealogy? Potentially yes, realistically no...

Quick joke...
Son to Dad, *"Dad, what is the difference between potentially and realistically?"*
Dad, *"If I were ask your mum whether she would sleep with George Clooney for £1m, would she say yes?"*
Son, *"Yes."*
Dad, *"If I were to ask your sister to sleep with George Clooney for £1m, would she say yes?"*
Son, *"Yes."*
Dad, *"If I were to ask you if you would sleep with George Clooney for £1m, would you?"*
Son, *"Yes."*
Dad, *"Well, potentially we are sitting on £3m, realistically we have two whores and a homo!"*

Cotswold Cottage

Imagine you and I in a Cotswold Cottage
A little cottage far from anywhere
A perfect place with no traffic
No bills, no debt, no hassle.
We could walk and talk for hours
Friends could pop in and stay
It would be our refuge
From this hectic life.
But in reality it will never happen
The Cotswold house is merely
A sign outside my room
Another lunatic ward
Opposite my sealed window
A million miles from you.

Oxfordshire and Buckinghamshire Mental Health NHS Foundation Trust

Mental Health Act Office
Littlemore Mental Health Centre
Sandford Road
Littlemore
Oxford
OX4 4XN
Tel: 0845 219 1270
Fax: 0845 219 1275
11 June 2008

Mr Joss Smith Wesson
Wintle Ward
Warneford Hospital
Headington
Oxon
OX3 7JX

Dear Mr Smith Wesson
The Mental Health Act Managers' Committee are meeting to review your detention under Section 3 of the Mental Health Act (1983).
The meeting has been arranged for Wednesday 25 June at 10:30am and will be held in the MHA Tribunal Room day Hospital Corridor Warneford Hospital
Copies of the Psychiatric Report and Social Circumstance Report will be sent to you via the Nurse-in-charge. I am enclosing a patient information leaflet.
On the day of the meeting, the ward staff will inform you when the managers are ready to see you.
Yours sincerely,

Carol Bannister
Mental Health Act Administrator
Enc. Patient Information Leaflet
Cc: Shift Co-ordinator, Wintel Ward Warneford Hospital, Headington

CHAPTER FIFTY-ONE

... Mind for better mental health ...

Mind for better mental health

How to cope with relationship problems

"I felt angry and bitter that my husband was running out on me. Friends were a great support, while work gave me my day structure and took my mind off my problems. But it was sheer determination that got me through. I had to prove to myself, and to my ex-husband, that I could cope and provide stability for my children. My job in a hospital has given me back my self-esteem. I have status that I didn't have before and I have gained the respect of many people."

What can cause relationship problems?

Relationship problems may be triggered by an unexpected event, like the loss of a job, illness, or the death of a child. But any major life changes, even some we may have chosen ourselves, such as moving house, having a baby or inviting an elderly parent to live with us, can place huge pressures on a relationship. In some ways, these everyday events are easier to overlook, because we think that everyone experiences them. So we try to cope, ignoring the signs of stress.

Many people are living in highly stressful relationships, with partners who are abusive or alcoholic, who have long-term illness, are unemployed, or who are having affairs. You may be doing your best to cope, to carry on as normal, and may even be admired for doing so.

Whatever the problem, the first step towards dealing with it is acknowledging it. Here are some of the most common sources of stress, and suggested ways of coping with them, which may save your relationship.

Babies and young children

New babies bring pleasure and joy. But they also bring broken nights and change the balance of your relationship. Sometimes a mother is so involved with her baby that her partner feels excluded and jealous. Many women go off sex for a period after giving birth. Second babies may bring jealousy from the first-born, and generally more demands. A partner who is feeling neglected may then withdraw and stop communicating, or spend more time at work.

It's essential that you have time alone together, away from the children. You might book a babysitter and go out for the evening, or leave the children with friends for part of the weekend. The main carer is also likely to to be pretty desperate for time away from children – alone or with friends – on a regular basis. Try to work things out between so that you are both getting you needs met. This can relieve a lot of the pressure on your relationship.

Step-children

It's quite common to feel jealous of, and competitive with, your partner's child or children; perhaps almost feeling like another child yourself. These are uncomfortable feelings. Remember that your partner has chosen to live with you and that you have an adult-to-adult relationship that is quite different from the parent-child relationship. Try to establish your own relationship with the child, for example by finding an enjoyable activity that you can do without your partner.

Some stepchildren may feel deliberately hostile to a step-parent. They may feel that aggression is their only source of power in this situation, and will express it openly or by silence or withdrawal. You will need to talk to your partner to get support, but be careful to talk about your feelings and not to criticise the children.

Starting an affair

Many of us fall in love and start a relationship hoping that it's going to meet all our needs and that we will live happily ever after. When we run into problems, whether at home or at work, it's easy to blame the relationship and think that we are with the wrong person. At this point, it may be tempting to give up on the relationship or start an affair with somebody else.

Having an affair does not necessarily mean the end of the relationship. The impulse to have an affair is often a symptom of underlying problems between the two of you.

The third party might be the right person, but it's just as likely that you will take the same problems with you into the new relationship.

To tackle this dilemma, it's crucial that you start listening to each other's disappointments and needs, and for this you may find that you need professional help, from a relationship counsellor, for instance.

Sex

Although sexual difficulties are often a symptom of other problems, in some relationships they are the basis of the difficulty. People often feel shy or ashamed of acknowledging them, but problems are solvable with expert help.

Unemployment and redundancy

Redundancy is usually sudden and shocking. Whatever the reason, it's likely to dent someone's self-esteem and so make them feel bad-tempered and moody, as well as anxious. At the same time, your partner may start to feel resentful if they are now the sole breadwinner. This may be aggravated if, quite understandably, the jobless person is keeping busy by seeing friends or taking up pastimes. In this situation, it's a good idea to talk about rebalancing things, so that the working partner gets more support and doesn't have to do all the domestic chores.

If neither of you works, you're both likely to get anxious and, unless you express these feelings, tense, angry or simply withdrawn. Long-term unemployment, whether it's you, your partner or a grown-up child, is draining for the whole family. The unemployed person will often feel inadequate and powerless and this may mean they withdraw sexually. They may also feel sad, depressed, or humiliated.

Money problems

Shortage of money can produce a lot of anxiety and fear, and can easily become the main focus of a relationship. Share your feelings as much as you can, rather than withdrawing in panic or blaming you partner for earning enough. You could contact the National Debtline or go together to your local Citizens Advice Bureau (CAB). All CAB staff are trained to offer help with debt and redundancy problems. They can help you check whether you are getting all the benefits you are entitled to, and discuss whether other options are available.

Many money problems are actually power struggles being played out through money. If this is what is happening to you, a counsellor is probably your best source of help.

Long-standing illness

This puts an enormous strain on any partnership. Apart from the extra work involved, the well partner will often have unwelcome feelings like resentment, hatred or jealousy. It's essential that you have a place to air feelings, so that they don't get in the way of your caring or damage your own health and well-being.

Bottling them up will only increase the pressure on the relationship. It can also take the pressure off if the ill partner has a place to talk. There are organisations that support people with specific diseases and those caring for them. Your hospital or social worker should have details of groups dealing with your partner's illness.

Alcoholism

You may have knowingly teamed up with a drinker, or your partner may begin drinking later in your relationship. One of the hardest things about living with an alcoholic is their mood swings. They may be quite abusive, even violent, when drunk, but charming when sober; affectionate and attentive when they're drinking, but very withdrawn again when they stop. And the expense of drinking may cause money problems. Your partner's alcoholism need not lead to the end of your relationship, if you are both willing to get help.

Physical violence and emotional abuse

This is probably one of the most difficult situations to deal with, but there is increasing support available to both partners, which could save the relationship. The physical violence doesn't have to be frequent to make you a victim.

More common, and perhaps even more frightening and undermining, is the emotional abuse. Slamming doors and threats like, "Don't you ever do that again" evoke a constant fear of violence. You may begin to adapt your behaviour so that you don't provoke your partner. You may feel confused because your partner becomes loving after an attack, telling you that it wasn't that bad, that you should forget about it, perhaps even forget that it happened, so that you begin to doubt your own experience.

Your partner may be in the habit of humiliating you in front of your friends, or making constant critical remarks about what you do and how you look. This kind of verbal abuse may happen again and again, and can be devastating over time.

Emotional abuse may also take the form of silent withdrawal. In this situation most people feel ugly, worthless, ashamed and unloved. You may start to move away from your friends and become withdrawn at work. As your self-esteem plummets, you may feel increasingly dependent for friendship and love on the very person who is abusing you.

Partners may resort to violence in response to their feelings of inadequacy, insecurity, loneliness and depression. The patterns involved in a violent and abusive relationship usually run very deep and you will need professional help if you are to save your relationship. Acknowledging what is going on is an important first step. You might want to start by talking to friend.

Counselling and psychotherapy

At this point in your relationship, talking to an independent third party, on a strictly confidential basis, can be enormously helpful. You may have a friend who has been to see a counsellor or a therapist and can give you a personal recommendation, or your GP may be able to refer you to someone.

What do I do when I know it's over?

Even if you have decided your relationship is over, it can be very difficult to leave, especially if it's an abusive one. However bad it is, it's familiar and we are all scared of the unknown.

You might be afraid of being lonely, and feel that you will never have another relationship. If you have been married a long time, you may feel ashamed and not want friends and neighbours to know.

If you have been financially supported by your partner, or shared bills, you will probably have anxieties about money. There may also be a period of doubting, when you think this relationship may be as good as any other, and that "everyone has problems."

Getting help

Once you have made the decision, you will find your separation goes more smoothly if you have help. Most conflicts at the end of a relationship centre on housing, and possessions, money, and children. A lot of power struggles get played out in these areas, and discussions tend to get very emotional. Consider seeing a counsellor to get some support during this stressful period. Another option is to go to a local legal advice centre, which should have a free surgery at least once a week. They can refer you to a solicitor specialising in conciliation. If you have any difficulty getting access to either of these, a CAB should be able to help you. They can also advise you about your legal rights, and various options available for dealing with financial or housing problems.

If you are leaving a violent relationship and living with the threat of being hit, you are deemed to be 'homeless.'

However, you will not necessarily be regarded as being a priority need for housing, unless you are pregnant or have children.

It is worth contacting your local housing department to discuss the situation.

How will separating affect the children?

One danger after separation is that parents use children as pawns, playing out their own unresolved feelings of anger and hurt. This might be by withholding maintenance. Or you may want to exclude your ex-partner, who doesn't have custody, from parents' evenings, or prevent them from coming to your home. These power struggles are damaging for you and your partner. A counsellor or conciliation lawyer could help you with this.

Behaviour patterns to avoid

Children and parents tend to react to separation in certain patterns. Being aware of these can help you to deal with them. One pattern is that the child and the parent they live with will become much too dependent on each other (especially if it's just the two of them). Sometimes, if there are a number of children, the parent opts out and the children evolve a system amongst themselves, so that an older child may take on the role of parent. Another trap is for the parent to overcompensate, out of guilt, and feel compelled to do everything for the children to make up for what has happened. She or he may be too lax or too anxious about setting limits because of this. There is also a danger that the other parent may stop seeing their children because of the pain it involves.

Children in trouble

Too frequently, a child starts extreme acting-out, either with abusive behaviour towards the parent or by bullying behaviour or withdrawal at school. A danger here is that the behaviour may be excused and tolerated because the child has had such a rough time. There are now many voluntary organisations offering counselling to children, and it may also be available through their school or GP.

How do I move on?

The first step is to acknowledge how you are feeling. If you have been left, you will probably be feeling abandoned and negative about yourself. You may fear that you'll never have another relationship and that no-one will ever love you again. These feelings give way to anger, which is natural and the healthy response to being left out. Expressing it is one of the one of the best ways of raising your self-esteem and not sinking into depression. Even if you feel relieved or have chosen to end the relationship, you are still likely to go through a grieving process.

If you have been in an abusive relationship, you will need to work on freeing yourself from repeating the pattern. You may find counselling or psychotherapy a useful tool.

Rediscovering your identity

If you have just ended a long-term relationship you may feel quite lost, asking yourself, "Who am I now I'm not in a relationship?" If you are a woman leaving a marriage, you may find yourself dropped by one-time friends who see you as a threat. Talking to people in your situation can be helpful. This is also a good time to look back at what was positive or nurturing and what was negative and undermining in your relationship. This can give you more sense of self and help you move on. You might also review your life generally. Which friendships or activities are still satisfying? How do you feel about your work?

Two common responses to ending a long-term relationship are to rush straight into another, or to close off the possibility of intimacy. Whether or not you follow these impulses, this is a time to focus on yourself.

Useful organisations

Mind

Mind is the leading mental health organisation in England and Wales, providing a unique range of services through its local associations, to enable people with experience of mental distress to have a better quality of life. For more information about any mental health issues, including details of your nearest local Mind association, contact the Mind website:
www.mind.org.uk
or Mind*info*Line on 0845 766 0163.

Al-Anon family Groups

61 Great Dover Street, London SE1 4YF
tel. 020 7403 0888, web: www.al-anonuk.org.uk
Supports partners and family members of problem drinkers.

British Association for Counselling and Psychotherapy (BACP)

BACP House, 35 – 37 Albert Street, Rugby CV21 2SG
Tel: 0870 443 5252 web: www.bacp.co.uk

British Association for Sexual and Relationship Therapy

PO Box 13686, London SW20 9ZH
Tel/fax. 020 8543 2707, web: www.basrt.org.uk

Childline

Helpline: 0800 11 11 (24 hours0
Web: www.childline.org.uk

Marriage Care

1 Blythe Mews, Blythe Road, London W14 0NW
tel. 020 7371 1341, web: www.marriagecare.org.uk

National Debtline

Tel. 0808 808 4000, web: www.nationaldebtline.co.uk

National Family Mediation

7 The Close, Exeter EX1 1EZ

tel. 01392 271 610, web: www.nfm.u-net.com

Parentline Plus

Highgate Studios, 53-57 Highgate Road, London NW5 1TL
Helpline: 080 800 2222, web: www.parentlineplus.org.uk

Relate

Herbet Gray College, Little Church Street, Rugby CV21 3AP
Tel. 0845 456 1310, web: www.relate.org.uk

Women's Aid

PO Box 391, Bristol BS99 7WS
Helpline: 0808 2000 247, web: www.womensaid.org.uk

CHAPTER FIFTY-TWO

... Warneford Crisis Day Service ...

Coping with psychosis

<u>What is psychosis</u>

The facts

- Psychosis is a mental health term. It describes experiences, such as hearing or seeing things or holding unusual beliefs which other people don't see or share.
- Everyone's experiences are unique. The majority hear voices, but others experience non-verbal thoughts, images, visions, tastes, smells and sensations which have no apparent cause.
- Your thoughts may jump around very quickly, so you may find it difficult to voice them in a way others can understand.
- Many people can find these experiences highly distressing, disruptive and interfering with everyday life.
- Depending on other factors, diagnosis can be severe depression, schizophrenia, bi-polar disorder (manic depression), paranoia, psychotic illness, schizoaffective disorder.
- If you experience psychosis, you may think it hard to talk about your experiences and understanding of the world, because you feel no words can describe how you think and feel.

References

www.mind.org.uk , www.rethink.org , www.sane.org.uk

CHAPTER FIFTY-THREE

... Antipsychotics ...

ANTIPSYCHOTICS

(An –tea –sigh – cot – icks)

Why have I been prescribed an antipsychotic?

Antipsychotics are medicines used to help treat schizophrenia and similar conditions, such as psychosis.

When they have schizophrenia, many people hear voices talking to them or about them. They may also become suspicious or paranoid. Some people also have problems with their thinking and feel that other people can read their thoughts. These are called "positive symptoms." Antipsychotics can help relieve these symptoms. Many people with schizophrenia also experience "negative symptoms." They feel tired and lacking in energy and may become inactive and withdrawn. Antipsychotics may help relieve these symptoms as well. Antipsychotics are also useful to help manage agitation, anxiety, mania or hypomania, nausea, sleep problems and many other conditions.

What exactly are antipsychotics?

Schizophrenia and similar disorders are sometimes referred to as pychoses, hence the name given to this group of medicines, which is the "antipychotics." They are sometimes also called neuroleptics or (incorrectly) major tranquillisers. Some examples of antipsychotics include **chlorpromazine** ('*Largactil*'), **haloperidol** ('*Neulactil*'), **pimozide** ('*Orap*'), **promazine**, **thioridazine** ('*Clopixol*'), and **haloperidol** ('*Haldol Decanoate*').

Are the antipsychotics safe to take?

It is usually safe to have antipsychotics regularly prescribed by your doctor, but they don't suit everyone. Let you doctor know if any of the following apply to you, as extra care may be needed:

If you suffer from epilepsy, diabetes, depression, myasthenia gravis, phaeochromocytoma, Parkinson's disease or glaucoma, or suffer from heart, liver, breathing, kidney, or prostrate trouble.

If you are taking any other medication. This includes medication from your pharmacist, such as antihistamines.

If you are pregnant, breast feeding, or wish to become pregnant.

How should I take my antipsychotic?

Look at the label on your medicine; it should have all the necessary instructions on it. Follow this advice carefully. If you have any questions, speak to your doctor or pharmacist. Most medicines are now supplied with an information leaflet.

What should I do if I miss a dose?

Never change your dose without checking with your doctor. If you forget a dose, take it as soon as you remember, as long as it is within a few hours of the usual time.

When I feel better, can I stop taking them?

No. If you stop taking antipsychotics, your original symptoms may return, but this may not be for three to six months after you stop the drug. You and your doctor should decide together when you can come off it. Most people need to be on an antipsychotic for quite some time, sometimes years. This is not thought to be harmful. Antipsychotics are not addictive.

What will happen to me when I start taking my antipsychotics?

Antipsychotics do not work straight away. For example, it may take several days or even weeks for some of the symptoms to reduce. To begin with, most people find that this medication will help them feel more relaxed and calm. Later, after one or two weeks, other symptoms should begin to improve.

Unfortunately, you might get side effects before you start to feel better. Most side effects should go away after a few weeks. Some antipsychotics suit some people better than others.

Seven Ever-Changing Women

Nata, you Russian whore.
Can mention you by name, you bitch.
Stole my heart, my hopes, my money and my dreams.
Off the list coz you never existed.

Woman Two. No, Ellen is not a contender.

Sally, Lizzie, Jenny – pick one.
Yes, I'm totally in love with you.
Exquisite, tangible sweet creature.
Your glorious intellect defines you.
Woman Four. Belinda. Stop there.
Woman Five. My Shrink...also stop dead...
Woman Six. Stealing my air, gulp by gulp
Down there in beloved South Africa.
Alive with an exuberance that I love.

Woman Seven...

Woman Seven I will worship and make every accommodation for, make whatever sacrifice necessary to retain her. I will kiss her feet daily. I will treat her like a Goddess. I will make her happy for every second of every remaining day. I will write her poems, sonnets, and stories. I will spend the rest of my life reinventing and evolving my love for her. If after this she follows Belinda and decides that I am not enough, I will still love her.

All these six women are surreal and beyond my reach. Somewhere between reality and myth, between honesty and mind games, between the present and the future lies Lizzy, aka Elizabeth Lucy. Either one of us was mad, and it was definitely not Lizzy. Bursting from the blocks, determined to prove to one and all I was not gay, that I was over Bloody B and that I was ready to take on society again, I set forth for Oxford, the known centre of fornication. I fumbled about in alleyways until eventually finding the right, appropriately seedy address. Yes you have to be desperate and yes, the sad looking guys there certainly looked as if they could do with remedial treatment. Twenty babes all dying to meet me, well Mr Right anyway, so that would count me out. The idea was that for four minutes one would babble away to each consecutive babe/victim in turn. She/ you would ask carefully veiled questions to reveal what kind of delinquent you/ she really was. Four minutes is nothing! (Four minutes to save the world...) There is me trying/ lying to be as funny as possible and at the same trying to squeeze the whole (missing strategic bits) of my life story into two minutes (being a gentlemen, one had to give the opponent/ victim the same opportunity). I remember one that must have been mentally retarded (or French as I did not understand a word she said), one that had knockers the size of melons (and no bra!), and buttocks the size of pigmy hippos, (yes, each buttock equal to one hippo!), one so ultra-fit, she ate marathons for breakfast and one was so brainy I was afraid to say anything in case she realised what a thicko I was/ am.

Actually, I made all that up. The truth is that I didn't actually remember any of them.

The first actual memory of any of the supposed candidates from the bizarre chat-up that jammed itself into my hard-drive, was after chatting with the only candidate I picked and incredibly also picked me. We started "chatting" on the internet and then by phone and then we agreed to meet again in person, for longer than four minutes. It was outside Debenhams in Oxford. I was totally bowled off my feet when she danced happily across the street, casually sidestepped menacing traffic, and without a moment's hesitation, kissed me, smiling broadly, on the cheek. I had fallen totally in love with Lizzy.

Lizzy my love, you are and were then, absolutely gorgeous. Your happy cheeky smile and funny teeth. On the day of her birthday in early September as our first date, we met at the most beautiful spot on Earth for a picnic. I brought my picnic blanket made up of dozens of South African Tea Towels, sandwiches I had spent ages making and some juice. Lizzy brought the Champagne and elegant glasses.

The weather was perfect. It was on the top of Maidenbottom Hill overlooking the whole valley in a quiet secluded spot which no one knew about. We twined our arms together, clinked glasses and kissed. It was a totally blissful romantic day, we both in love.

Lizzy has an amazing sense of humour. She can weave long complex jokes which have me falling about. We both love the Simpsons and laugh at the fact that most of the humour goes over our heads.

We shared a year of bliss in an idyllic, secluded romantic garden cottage. Our little cosy love nest tucked away in the backlogs of darkest Oxfordshire was so perfect. Cleaning the cottage together, gardening, cycling, running, endlessly chatting, cooking, travelling to both our families and cuddling endlessly. It was Heaven. It was just large enough to have all our combined stuff and a spare room for Sophie to come and visit. We were always so busy. And of course drinking or having meals in the many wonderful characterful pubs nearby (that I have already slandered!). We found a local farm-gate shop that sold cider and often stocked up on the good stuff. We often had barbecues, inviting our many family and friends around. The garden was attached to an enormous enclosed park so it was possible to allow small children to wonder off without fear of being eaten/ stolen/ getting lost etc. Yes, getting eaten is more of a parental fear I might have brought from Africa, because as everyone knows, there are marauding lions and tigers roaming the streets in search of waifs and strays. Still, the English are afraid of everything, the said wondering child might get eaten by ants, worms etc. I remember eating worms (funny thing – remembering – I don't actually know whether I remember, or whether my folks told me the story so often that they made me think I remember, I wonder if they brainwashed me into believing that all I ate as a child was worms?) and other garden creatures, "make a man of you," and "get them before they get you." etc. So said three years old could get to nearly fifty to sixty yards away before the said parent would do the Linford Christie and rescue the said toddler from...nothing... but a good rescue in front of the family shows you care. I never got round to enquire whether Lizzy's early diet included a healthy portion of earthworms. Did you know that if you (accidentally) cut an earthworm in two, it becomes two earthworms? (That's what my mother always told me, so it must be true.) Did you know that earthworms travel underground by means of waves of muscular contractions which alternately shorten and lengthen the body? Did you know that Darwin estimated that arable land contains up to 53,000 worms per acre? Did you know that you could potentially write a whole book copy-and-pasting out of Wikipedia? And no, before you even think of asking, I haven't. (The introduction and the ending are original! lol) Lol- Did I just say lol? There must be an educated generation out there (over the age of about seventeen) that hasn't a clue what a lol is. I haven't either, but I am led to believe that it is like an exclamation mark, but louder!

Poor Lizzy works horrendous hours, either starting at seven in the morning or at one in the afternoon. If she was starting early, I would always get up with her and make her a cup of tea. (I always tried to entice her to have some breakfast before she did battle with the day but she was not much of a morning type of person.) In the evenings when she came home late I would always cook a meal for her so it would be ready for when she got home and would also have a bottle of wine open. We would sit and chat for ages before going to bed. I am not sure whether it was because I was petrified of her finding out that I was the worst (well perhaps second worse!) snorer in England, but I would wait for her to go to sleep first. I felt it was part of my role to ensure that she was properly tucked in and that her shoulders were not out in the cold. I will never forget that after the many times we made love, she would fall asleep naked on my bare shoulder. I would lay motionless trying not to wake her and enjoying every second of this closeness and the intimate sound of her breathing. (Of course there were times when she was not exhausted and we would be at it like rabbits all night, but you don't want to know about that...)

As one gets further into a relationship it becomes easier to look for, and find reasons why, one loves ones partner. I love Lizzy for many reasons but undoubtedly the easiest and most honest reason why I am absolutely and will always be totally besotted with her is because she truly loves me, warts and all. When she is happy she has the most exquisite little smile that I adore. Shame, having me as part of her baggage, she does not have much to be happy about, but still she is. It sometimes comes when least expected, and when it does it conquers me completely. If you were to meet her, you would understand, she truly is an Angel, living here on Earth.

Our cottage was conveniently located half way between Oxford where Lizzy worked and Reading, where I worked. She drove and would get herself to Oxford. However my journey was a little more of a challenge. Firstly a bus to Maidenbottom, a train to Reading and then another bus too through Grenade Ltd in Green Park in Lower Reading, my place of work. Being an idiot, when I first saw the cottage and fell in love with it, I initially thought I could afford it. Of course I had not taken Council Tax and the additional cost of transport into account so I was on a hiding to nothing. The bus drivers all knew me as a fare dodger and would often let me on for nothing, as for getting past the gates at the station, I could write a book on that alone! Well, a small pamphlet anyway. It was a 15 mile journey and I began to do it more and more frequently on my bike, not because I enjoyed it but to simply save on the fares. Actually it was the most wonderful ride imaginable. Because I was frequently the first person alone on the forest footpath in the mornings, I saw many deer, badgers and other wild animals. I became much closer to nature than I had ever been before. I fell in love with the sound of the blackbird's call, each call seemingly different. There was also a farm I had to do battle with. On a dry day it was not too bad as the cows kept their powder dry. However on rainy or otherwise wet days, it was like Paint-Ball for real. There was a fifty metre patch in which it was impossible to avoid going through the slurry. No matter how slowly I went or tried going through the verges I would be covered from head to foot in cow dung; a great way to turn up for work (there was a shower...). Retrospectively, I should have got off and carried the bike through the liquid cow dung, but hey, perhaps I was secretly taking myself back to my farming roots. Perhaps, if the cows were not watching, I could have wallowed in the stuff. There was one interesting part on the footpath along the Thames in which the path does a vertical dive into nowhere. Being helmetless I would always take the precaution of carrying the bike down the Hill of Death (The brakes on the bike did not work either!) On a few occasions those bike nutter types, (you know, with spray on lycra body suites and with helmets that looked as if they were on back to front) would come along and just fly gracefully off the precipice. Of course the JSW reaction was, "if they can do it, so can I. " Fortunately on the one occasion I gave it a go (no I was not trying to commit hari-kiri, I actually thought I could do it) I was wearing a full rucksack. Now I mentioned that the brakes did not work, well, that was just the back brakes. Come the moment that I was airborne and a little excess on the speed side, the natural reaction was to clutch at the brakes. Coming back into contact with Terra firma and the front wheel was locked. I automatically did a couple of cartwheels down the remainder of the hill. The back wheel was buckled beyond repair and I had a nasty gash on my leg and the contents of the rucksack were severely compressed, probably saving my noggin. The worst causality of the PFPBA (as opposed to RTA – Public Footpath Bike Accident) was that my mobile phone refused to work again. Having been a Luddite for the first 99.99% of my life I had adamantly refused to embrace this new technology, sticking to the philosophy that if my ancestors managed without it, so could I. Then, damn, you find yourself married to the concept. "Yes dear, I am stuck at the bottom of Suicide Hill (yes I know I promised I would never attempt it), I have been captured by a particularly virulent bush of brambles and to top it all, I can't disengage myself from the bike, which seems to have wound itself around me, can you come and save me?" would have been a handy conversation to have had at precisely that moment. You know that TV programme when you see a poor upside down tortoise struggling against the odds to right itself? Usually they just die… I think that I decided that if I were to hypothetically just wait for the next rambler to amble past (equivalent to the zoo keeper in the tortoise analogy), I could have died of old age, so I set aside my fear of the brambles' dreaded poisonous venom and launched myself into its lair…

Lizzy my love

Lizzy you are my beacon
My lighthouse in a turbulent storm
You are my happiness, by being happy
You are my adult reasoned love
I love you because you love me
You are so easy to love.
Your beauty, your generosity
Your caring, your bubbly personality
I love your hair, the way it casually brushes on your face
Tickled by the flirtatious breeze.
I love your hair, the way it spreads itself on the pillow
When we are passionately entwined
Further adorning your already glorious body.
I just adore your smile at that very moment
At the simultaneous end of passion.
I love your clean pure thoughts
If ever a human deserved the accolade
Of being an Angel on Earth,
You, my Beloved are truly that Angel.
Thank you, thank you, thank you
For being part of my life and
For making me so intimately
Infinitely beautifully happy.
My love, it goes without saying
I adore your hands, your girlish curves
That face that shines beauty
My love, I love you so.
For all your womanly charms
But above all, I love you
For your unending, unquestioning
Friendship and support.
Your guidance, your advice
Your virtue, your selflessness
Your willingness to help me.
My love, for these, and a million more
I love you now, more than my mind
Can truly explain. I love you more than
I thought capable. I love you more than
I have anyone in the past.

Ode to a passing beauty that became mine

Lizzy, Lizzy, Lizzy, Dizzy, **LIZZY**!
Your beautiful intellect makes you shine!
You speak with such crisp, clear purpose;
To hear your voice is to hear a blackbird at night;
Being near your radiance makes me happy;
You are such a regal beautiful woman;
Your hands, your eyes, your mouth;
You are more beautiful than the sun setting.

Lizzy, Lizzy, Lizzy, Sizzling **LIZZY**!
What a beautiful sound! What a beautiful name,
For such a beautiful sweet maiden such as you!
Such laughing music to my humble unloved ears,
You bring the joy of summer into a cloudy day.
You blow away the idle, sad thoughts in my mind.
Your frown is beautiful when I say something wrong,
Disappearing in an instant as you smile that magic
smile.

Lizzy, Lizzy, Lizzy,Busy **LIZZY**!
Mortal souls twist to dust thinking of you,
Your eternal grace shining into our poor existence.
As passing ships we fleetingly glimpse each other
On the train, we tentatively exchange comments.
You on your way to exciting college, me to boring work.
You to me, a Goddess, Isis, Mary, Sophia and Gaia.
A special blessed angel from Heaven high above.

Lizzy, Lizzy, Lizzy, Saucy, **LIZZY**!
You gracious Queen, the world is yours to take.
I have so little to offer you, but all my time
Yes, not just some adolescent teenage crush;
No, not some little love between children.
I would be your biggest fan, your forever hero.
Let me fly you to faraway beaches,
To paradise, places together, to Heaven.

Lizzy, Lizzy, Lizzy, Sexy, **LIZZY**!
Let us gently reach out, touch fingertips,
Feel your hand in mine; lose your gaze in mine.
Gauge my pulse, feel my honesty, my sincerity.
Let me be your Prince, make your dreams come alive.
Let us slowly start this eternal journey, hand in hand,
Exploring each other's minds. Beautiful creature,
Let me buy you a drink and a chat, or maybe even
dinner
To know each other better, and laugh at little things.

When you are old and grey and full of Sleep,
And nodding by the fire, take down this book,
And slowly read, and dream of the soft look
Your eyes had once, and of their shadows deep;
How many loved your moments of glad grace
And loved your beauty with love false or true
But one man loved the pilgrim soul in you
And loved the sorrows of your changing face;
And bending down beside the glowing bars
Murmur, a little sadly, how love fled
And passed upon the mountain overhead
And hid amid a crowd of stars

W.B. Yeats
1865-1939

Romeo and Juliet

But soft, what light through yonder window breaks?
It is the east, and Juliet is the sun.
Arise, fair sun, and kill the envious moon
Who is already sick and pale with grief
That thou, her maid, art far more fair than she.
Be not her maid, since she is envious
Her vestal livery is but sick and green,
And none but fools do wear' it; cast it off.
[Enter Juliet aloft]
It is my lady, O, it is my love,
O that she knew she were!
She speaks, yet she says nothing. What of it?
Her eye discourses; I will answer it.
I am too bold. 'Tis not to me she speaks
Two of the fairest stars in all the heaven
Having some business, do entreat her eyes
To twinkle in their spheres till they return.
What if her eyes were there, they in her head?
The brightness of her cheek would shame those stars
As daylight doth a lamp; her eye in heaven
Would through the airy region stream so bright
That birds would sing and think it were not night.
See how she leans her cheek upon that hand.
O, that I were a glove upon that hand,
That I might touch that cheek!
Juliet Ay me.
Romeo [aside] She speaks.

Oh Speak again, bright angel; for thou art
As glorious to this night, being o'er my head
As a winged messenger of heaven
Unto the white upturned wond'ring eyes
Of mortals that fall back to gaze on him
When he bestrides the lazy-passing clouds
And sails upon the bosom of the air
Juliet [not knowing Romeo hears her]
O Romeo, Romeo wherefore art thou Romeo?
Deny thy father and refuse thy name,
Or if thou wilt not, but be sworn my love
And I'll no longer be a Capulet.
Romeo [aside]

Shall I hear more, or shall I speak at this?
Juliet
'Tis but thy name that is my enemy
Thou art thyself, though not a Montague.
What's a Montague? It is nor hand, nor foot,
Nor arm nor face nor any other part
Belonging to a man. O, be some other name
What's in a name? That which we shall call a rose
By any other word would smell as sweet
So Romeo would were he not Romeo called
Retain that clear perfection which he owes
Without that title, Romeo, doff thy name
And for thy name – which is no part of thee –
Take all myself

William Shakespeare **1564 – 1616**

CHAPTER FIFTY-FOUR

... Sleep and depression ...

Sleep and depression

Written by Dr. R H McAcllister-Williams, Carolyn Hughes and the Newcastle Disorders Group

Sleep problems are common. They can be caused by:

Stress

Physical illnesses that cause pain or frequent urination

having noisy neighbours

a partner who snores

having young children

an uncomfortable bed

working shifts

jet lag

Some medicines, heavy or spicy food and drinks (e.g. alcohol and those containing caffeine, such as coffee and tea) can also make it harder to sleep or disrupt the normal pattern of sleep. In addition to all of these causes of sleep disturbance, depressive illnesses also commonly cause sleep problems.

Disturbed sleep can cause a great deal of distress for people, whether it is caused by depression or not.

<u>What sort of sleep problems can affect people with depression?</u>

People with depression can have many types of sleep problems. Generally, these involve getting less sleep than usual and include:

Difficulty getting off to sleep – often because of lying in bed with thoughts going round your head.

Frequently waking up during the night.

Waking early in the morning and not being able to go back to sleep.

Even if people with depression do get a reasonable number of hours sleep, they often wake in the morning feeling 'un-refreshed' and feel tired through the day.

Occasionally, people with depression sleep too much, finding it hard to get out of bed and spending much of the day there. Again, this does not tend to lead to these people feeling less tired.

How common are sleep problems in depression?

Probably more than 80 per cent of people suffering depression have problems with their sleep, usually not getting enough.

Is it a problem of not getting enough sleep?

We are all aware that if we don't get a good night's sleep, we are less effective the next day. Important body processes occur during sleep that help to 'recharge our batteries.' If we get less sleep than we need, we are more at risk of having accidents in the home, at work or when driving.

In people with depression, not being able to sleep (especially when this involves spending hours awake lying in bed) can cause other problems as well. During this time, people tend to dwell on their problems.

If you are depressed, everything seems black and dismal. Such bleak thoughts going round and round your head can cause your mood to get even lower. A lower mood makes the thoughts even bleaker and a vicious circle can occur. Severe sleep problems in depressed people are associated with increased risk of suicide. On the other side of the coin, an improvement in sleep often indicates an improvement in mood.

How much sleep is enough?

Everybody's sleep needs are different. The range of time people sleep is as wide as three to ten hours. As a general rule of thumb, five to six hours sleep is probably a minimum below which your performance at work, when driving, etc. will be affected. Most people need between seven and eight hours sleep a night to feel refreshed.

Normal Sleep

Sleep can be assessed by measuring the electrical activity that occurs in the brain. By doing this, sleep can be divided into a number of different stages: we tend to go through stages 1 to 4 when we fall asleep and the reverse when we wake up. However, through the night we also make transitions between the different stages.

Stages 1 and 2 are regarded as light sleep. Stages 3 and 4 are deep sleep. During deep sleep various restorative

processes go on throughout the body. If we do not get enough deep sleep we feel tired and 'washed out.'
A fifth stage of sleep is called rapid eye movement sleep (REM) because although the eyes remain shut, they move around a lot during this stage. REM sleep is the time that we dream when we are asleep. Dreaming has important psychological effects, helping us to put 'things in order.' The content of dreams often includes things that have recently happened to us or that we have recently been thinking about. Dreams may be a way of making sense of all of this. The various stages of sleep can be plotted on a graph called a hypnogram. We normally undergo several cycles during the night, moving through the various stages of sleep. We have most of our deep sleep in the first half of the night and the REM sleep (when we dream) occurs later on. This explains why if you doze back to sleep in the morning, you will often wake and be aware of dreaming. It is not uncommon to wake during the night. Normally, these wakenings are so brief that we are unaware of them.

The pattern of sleep in depression

The sleep pattern of someone with depression is very different:

It takes much longer to get off to sleep.
The total sleep time is reduced.
There is little or no deep sleep.
REM sleep occurs early in the night.
There is more frequent wakenings during the night, which may last
long enough for the person to be aware of them.
The person wakes up early in the morning.

What can I do about my sleep problem?

It can be extremely distressing not being able to sleep. Fortunately, there are a number of things that you can do to try and improve your sleep. These suggestions are not miracle cures and they require some effort. This is good advice for anybody who has a sleep problem.

Get into a routine with your sleep times. Get up at the same time each morning, even if you have not had a good night's sleep. Don't sleep during the day, and don't go to bed early and get more sleep – you are likely just to lie in bed thinking over problems. Go to bed in the evening when you are tired.

Take some physical exercise during the day. This helps to make your body more tired in the evening and makes it easier to go to sleep. Exercise is good for you physically, and there is also research that suggests that exercise can itself be an antidepressant.

Avoid exercise two hours before bedtime. This is because exercise 'activates' the body, which can make it difficult to get off to sleep.

Avoid watching disturbing or violent films prior to bedtime.

Avoid drinking caffeine (tea, coffee, cola) in the evening after 6pm.

Caffeine is a stimulant and can prevent sleep.

Drink herbal teas or milky drinks such as Horlicks in the evening.

Herbal teas don't contain caffeine and milky drinks have been shown to

be as good as sleeping tablets for many people. However, be aware

that chocolate or cocoa milk drinks often contain caffeine.

Avoid heavy meals two hours before bedtime. It is extremely difficult

to get off to sleep with a full stomach.

Avoid alcohol in the evening. While alcohol is a sedative, it is not a good

idea to try to use it to sort out a sleep problem. This is because alcohol

does not lead to restful sleep. In addition, alcohol causes you to pass

increasing amounts of urine, which further disrupt sleep.

Unfortunately, a significant number of people with depression develop

an alcohol problem from using alcohol to help them sleep.

You should associate your room with sleep: avoid having a TV or radio

in your bedroom.

Your bedroom should be warm and familiar with a comfortable bed and quilt, etc. Ideally, the bed should be decorated in a relaxing way. This all helps in associating the room in your mind with restful sleep.

Use aromatic oils in the bath or on your pillow, such as lavender, which can help relaxation.

Use relaxation techniques, which you can learn from books or audiotapes. Reading in bed helps some people, but it can prevent others from getting off to sleep. If you do read in bed, only read light-hearted books or magazines.

If you are kept awake, or wake up worrying during the night, try the following:

At least two hours before bedtime, write down the problems that keep you awake. Also write down the next step you need to take towards resolving each problem.

If you find yourself thinking over the problems in bed, tell yourself you have the matter in hand and that going over it now will not help.

If a new worry occurs during the night, write it down or commit it to memory and deal with it the next day.

If you still do not manage to get to sleep, or you wake during the night and can't get back to sleep, get up. Do not lie in bed tossing and turning. Go and do something else like listening to relaxing music, having a warm bath or making yourself a milky drink. Go back to bed when you feel tired again.

CHAPTER FIFTY-FIVE

... Alcohol and depression ...

Alcohol and depression
[They both feed off each other: Malcolm Hartshorne 01/05/2009 22:48]
written by Dr Achal Mishra, Dr Hamish McAllister-Williams and the Newcastle Affective Disorders Group

How common is depression in people with alcohol problems?
Up to 40 per cent of people who drink heavily have symptoms that resemble a depressive illness.
However, when these same people are not drinking heavily, only 5 per cent of men and 10 per cent of woman have symptoms meeting the diagnostic criteria for depression – not that different from the rates of depression in the general population.
About 5 to 10 per cent of people with a depressive illness also have symptoms of an alcohol problem.

Why might alcohol problems and depression occur together?

Alcohol can briefly produce a pleasant and relaxed state of mind. However, alcohol problems and depression commonly occur together. There are several reasons for this:
Both alcohol problems and depression are extremely common. They may occur together completely independently.
People with depression sometimes use alcohol as a form of self-medication, for example either in an attempt to cheer themselves up, or sometimes to help them sleep. Although in small quantities alcohol can briefly lift mood, if used to try to cope with depressive illness, problems arise. Tolerance to the effects of alcohol can lead to individuals needing it in larger quantities to have the same effect.
Alcohol in large quantities, whether taken to treat a depression or not, produces a depressant effect on people's mood.

Why is an alcohol problem together with depression a particular worry?

Alcohol compromises judgement and makes people impulsive and likely to take risks. Alcohol also causes a loss of inhibition and increases aggressive behaviour and violent acts. Because increased alcohol consumption often occurs together with a depressed mood, this is a particular concern. Depression can lead to thoughts of suicide. The lack of self-control, compromised judgement and impulsiveness from the alcohol can increase the chances of a person attempting suicide. Generally, a higher incidence of suicide, both completed and attempted, is associated with alcohol.

The common problems of depression and alcohol are frequently complicated by social problems. Alcohol can often lead to problems at work in the form of absenteeism, sickness and under performance. The loss of a job has profound negative impact of a person's financial status and family life. Marital problems often arise because of an alcohol problem, although it may be difficult to say which started first.

Alcohol can cause a large number of physical problems. Few, if any of the organs in the body are spared. Liver problems commonly arise from heavy alcohol intake and take the form of jaundice (a yellow discolouration of the skin) resulting from hepatitis, cirrhosis of the liver or liver failure. Unchecked these will lead to death. Other common problems include:
Stomach ulcers.

Anaemia.
An irregular heartbeat.
Impotence.

Both alcohol intoxication and withdrawal have a damaging effect on the brain, and can cause:
Loss of sensation in the arms or legs.
Loss of muscle power.
Profound memory disturbances.

A shrunken brain.

Although alcohol can cause you to fall asleep, the quality of the sleep that follows tends to be poor. This is why people with depression should not use alcohol to try to improve their sleep, since it will actually have the opposite effect. Excessive alcohol intake can lead to legal problems. These may result from driving offences, drunk and disorderly behaviour, or violent crime due to the impulsiveness and lack of self-control caused by alcohol. Involvement with the legal establishment does not tend to help a depressed mood.

Alcohol problems account for:
33 per cent of domestic accidents.
40 per cent of fatal domestic fires.
15 to 30 per cent of workplace accidents.

Depression is also associated with increased rate of accidents and so the combination can be worrying.

Some antidepressants are sedative. If they are taken with alcohol, a person can be seriously sedated and at risk of their breathing stopping. In addition, many antidepressants are broken down in the liver. Because alcohol can damage the liver, the levels of these antidepressants in the body will be higher in people who are also drinking heavily. This can lead to an increase in side effects from antidepressants.

What causes the link between alcohol and depression?

There are a number of ways in which alcohol and depression may be linked.

Links with brain function

Over the last decade new research has shed light on the way alcohol affects the brain, and in the ways in which the brain is affected in depression. It is now known that some of the systems that are involved in producing the symptoms of low mood, anxiety, poor sleep and reduced appetite in depression are also affected by alcohol. This is one explanation of why alcohol can cause depression.

Psychological links

There are…

Bollocks!! What with Court case hearings, I have lost the rest of that handout. Sorry. Probably said the same as all the others, get your life back in line you sad loser and stop boozing and drugging. (On the other hand it might have said that there is something to be said for a little recreational smack and who ever hasn't boasted about the time when they were way, and I mean WAY over the limit?) I suppose if you really want to know, look it up on the Internet. I heard a report that by 2010, yes, next year, ha! the Internet is going to be suffering from major overload problems. As the fat ugly bag in Blackadder ("three things must ye know about the wise woman, first she is wise…) said, "Either kill yourself (that is why she was called wise – wise words you see), kill Bob, or kill the whole world!" This is annoying as I have been somewhat thrown off my thread. I was going to loop you wretched Reader (on the vague understanding that you are one of them – the ones on the outside!) into this world of expectation of lunacy, alcoholism, and drug addiction (of which I know nothing) with a view to the relevance to my own experience. There are loads of druggy books out there and it somewhat surprises me that one can write a crappy book about something innocuous like, I don't know, premarital sex and the masses flock to buy it. Write a masterpiece about how drugs are so readily available to all teenagers and the impact it has on their lives, and no one is interested. Well, this is not about drugs, it is about depression, suicide, vaguely, and about alcohol. I suppose I could include drugs insofar as I have become quite attached to the prescription cabinet of drugs I take on a daily basis. (I think my favourite is the sleeping tablet, two of those and the world's worries disappear ha! Still, in sad reality I know in my fucked-up mind that I would not cope without the uppers and the downers and the mood stabilizers in between. Just to make the pill-meal complete, I also take a blood-thinning tablet because I am a hypochondriac and for pudding I throw in a concentrated cranberry juice tablet, because I've only got one kidney which is frequently beset with stones…blah, blah…)

Just when you thought it was safe to carry on reading I found the leaflet on the Internet courtesy of Lloyds pharmacy:-
http://health.lloydspharmacy.com/health/alcoholanddepression.php
There are many potential psychological and social reasons for links between alcohol and depression.
Stressful life events can precipitate both alcohol problems and depression.
People with alcohol problems report more incidences of neglect and poor parenting as children than those without. These factors may also increase the risk of developing depression.

Genetic links

It is possible to inherit an increased likelihood of both alcohol problems and depression.
Alcohol problems are more frequent in the children of those who have severe alcohol problems. It is difficult to know what exactly is inherited. It could be a tolerance (or lack of it) to the effects of alcohol, or differences in the way alcohol affects various systems in the brain.
The genetic basis of depression is also well established. It is well known that having a first-degree relative (i.e. a parent or sibling) with depression increases your chances of having depression in later life.
Studies of depressed patients show that their relatives not only have an increased risk of depression, but also a number of other conditions including alcohol problems.

How much alcohol do you need to drink to affect the brain?

Many of the effects of alcohol on the systems of the brain depend on the 'dose' of alcohol taken.
At low doses (say one to two units of alcohol), alcohol has a relaxing and euphoric effect that makes a person feel confident, more social and jovial.
However, even small amounts of alcohol (one to five units) produce poor coordination, slowed reaction times and increased risk taking.

The legal driving limit in the UK is 80mg of alcohol per 100ml of blood. It is impossible to say exactly what this is in units. This is because the concentration of alcohol in the blood will depend on the size of the person, how quickly they drink and many other factors. On average, the legal limit will be reached after drinking around three to five units. But the legal driving limit is not a 'safe amount' of alcohol. Somebody with an alcohol level of between 50 and 80mg (ie below the legal limit) has a risk of a non-fatal accident twice that of a sober driver and is six times more likely to have a fatal accident.
With levels of alcohol above twice the legal driving limit, memory is affected and seriously poor coordination starts occurring.
At three to four times the legal driving limit, the breathing centre in the brain can be affected leading to death.
These effects may occur at very different blood alcohol concentrations in different people because drinking alcohol produces tolerance to its effects. This means that people who regularly drink large quantities develop effects at higher blood alcohol concentrations.

What is a safe amount to drink?

Current recommendations are that risks of problems (both physical and psychological) are greatly increased in men consuming more that 28 units of alcohol per week, and women more than 21 units. A unit of alcohol is:
half a pint of beer.
half a pint of a lager or cider (strong lagers and ciders can be up to two units per half pint).
a single pub measure of a spirit (a 'home' measure can easily be three to four units)
a small glass of wine.
These recommendations are not a 'safe' limit - it is simply a level above which the risks get significantly greater.
28 units (or 21 units for women) consumed all at once is certainly not safe and can cause serious problems.
You should aim for at least one or two days each week when you do not drink any alcohol.

When should I be worried if I have an alcohol problem?

There are a number of pointers that should lead you to consider if you have an alcohol problem. These include:
using alcohol to try to escape from your worries and troubles.
using alcohol to help you sleep.
if you drink every day.
if you are drinking more than the recommended units a week.
if having a drink starts being one of the most important things in your life.
if you are regularly drinking alone.
if people are advising you to cut down the amount you drink.
if you get annoyed by people criticising your drinking.
if you feel guilty about drinking.
if you need a drink in the morning to be able to face the world.
if you feel shaky in the morning after drinking heavily.
if you have periods when you were drinking that you cannot recall.
if you have ever had problems at work because of drink.
if you have ever been arrested or charged with any drink-related offence.

How are alcohol problems and depression treated?

Many of the symptoms reported by people drinking heavily resemble those of depression such as:
fatigue
disturbed sleep
early morning waking
poor energy levels
poor appetite.
These are simply due to heavy alcohol intake. This makes it difficult to be clear if a person is suffering from an alcohol problem plus depression or simply an alcohol problem.

The situation is further complicated because heavy

alcohol intake can lead to depression. As a result, it is normal practice to deal with the alcohol problem first and see if the depression gets better. If it does not, then specific treatment for the depression would be started.

Treatment with a selective serotonin reuptake inhibitor (SSRI) antidepressant can improve both depression and an alcohol problem. This may point towards a common cause for both disorders. There are a number of things that can be done to help people with alcohol problems.
1. Detoxification to help a person come off alcohol safely.

This involves the person stopping all alcohol intake, usually covered by the administration of medication such as diazepam or chlordiazepoxide to prevent a withdrawal syndrome.

Withdrawal symptoms include:
tremor
anxiety
restlessness
sweating
nausea
seizures
delirium tremens (DTs).
DTs usually occur three days or so after stopping alcohol and can last for up to seven days. The symptoms of DTs include those described above plus disorientation (being unaware of where you are, what time, day or year it is, and who other people are), hallucinations (seeing or hearing things that are not there) and delusions (having false beliefs about things, especially being frightened of certain situations and people).
2.Counselling

Support and counselling is used to help the person achieve abstinence or 'controlled drinking' within safe limits. More formal psychological therapies can be helpful, such as cognitive behavioural therapy.
3.Medication

Occasionally, medication can be helpful. This includes

disulfiram (Antabuse) and acamprosate (Campral). Disulfiram can aid abstinence because it causes a person to have an unpleasant and potentially dangerous reaction if they drink while taking it. Acamprosate may help to decrease the craving for alcohol. Both of these medicines will only be helpful if the person taking them is motivated to give up alcohol. They are certainly not magic wands.

What should I do if I think that I have developed an alcohol problem?

If you think you have a problem with alcohol, you may well have managed the first and hardest step in sorting it out - acknowledging the problem to yourself. What you need to do now is to speak to somebody about your concerns. Support and help for alcohol problems can come from a number of sources. These include:
your GP.
a counsellor in your GP practice.
a local alcohol counselling service (these are often advertised in GP surgeries and can be found in the 'Counselling and Advice' section of the Yellow Pages, and under 'Alcohol' in the business section of The Telephone Directory).
Alcoholics Anonymous (can be found in the business section of The Telephone Directory).
a drug and alcohol clinic run by the local mental health services. You may be able to self-refer, or you may need your GP to refer you - ask at your doctor's surgery.

CHAPTER FIFTY-SIX

... Schizophrenia ...

The Independent Thursday 2 July 2009 Front Page. Unlocked: the secrets of schizophrenia

Scientific breakthrough offers hope of new treatments of mental condition
By Steve Connor Science Editor

Scientists have discovered a remarkable similarity between the genetic faults behind schizophrenia and manic depression in a breakthrough that is expected to open the way to new treatments for two of the most common mental illnesses, affecting millions of people.
Previously doctors had assumed that the two conditions were quite separate. But new research shows for the first time that both have a common genetic basis that leads people to develop one or other of the two illnesses.
Three different international studies investigated the genetic basis of schizophrenia by pooling their analysis of about 15,000 patients and nearly 50,000 healthy subjects to find that thousands of tiny genetic mutations – known as single nucleotide polymorphisms (SNPs) - are operating in raising the risk of developing the illness.
Each mutation on its own increased the risk of developing schizophrenia by about 0.2 per cent but collectively they were found to account for at least a third of the total risk of developing schizophrenia. The condition is known to have a strong inherited component, accounting for about 80 per cent of the total risk, but is also influenced by upbringing and environment.
However, one of the most surprising findings to emerge from the three studies was the same array of genetic variations in SNPs was also linked to bipolar disorder, a discovery that is at odds with the orthodoxy in psychiatry stating that the two conditions are clinically distinct, the scientists said.
The findings are milestone in the understanding of both schizophrenia and manic depression – also known as bipolar disorder – which could eventually lead to new ways of either preventing or treating conditions that cause untold

human misery and cost the NHS hundreds of millions of pounds each year.

"If some of the same genetic risks underlie schizophrenia and bipolar disorder, perhaps these disorders originate from common vulnerability in the brain development," said Thomas Insel, director of the US National Institute for Mental Health in Bethesda, Maryland, which part-funded the studies. "Of course the big question then is how some people develop schizophrenia and others develop bipolar disorder."

Although the schizophrenia studies have so far only identified a handful of the many thousand genetic variations implicated in the mental illness, scientists believe it represents a breakthrough that will accelerate the understanding of the condition and the development of new drugs and treatments. "This is a pretty major breakthrough for us because before today you could count on the thumb of one hand the number of common [genetic] variants that have been reliably identified for schizophrenia," said Michael O'Donovan, professor of psychiatric genetics at the Medical Research Council's neurogenetics centre in Cardiff.

"However, what we have found so far explains only a tiny fraction of the risk of schizophrenia. Some of us were surprised to find that not only did these genes contribute to schizophrenia but that they also contribute to bipolar. So that really suggests that the two disorders are not really as distinct as we thought in psychiatry."

The three studies, published in the journal *Nature,* have been possible because of technical advances in the analysis of the genomes of patients, enabling scientists to rifle through vast amounts of DNA in order to make comparisons between patients and healthy "controls."

Eric Lander, the founding director of the consortium of eleven research centres in the United States, Europe and Australia behind the studies, and a member of Barak Obama's Council of Advisors on Science and Technology, said that the pace of research into schizophrenia was accelerating fast. "Over the past year, using techniques designed to study common DNA changes, psychiatric disease geneticists have detected more statistically compelling findings than in the previous one hundred years," he said.

Some of the genetic variations associated with schizophrenia appear to occur within a region of the genome known to be involved in controlling the immune system. This might help to explain why babies born in the winter and spring when influenza is rife, or to women who have slight flu during pregnancy, are at slightly higher risk of developing schizophrenia in later life, the scientists said.

"Discoveries such as these are crucial for teasing out the biology of the disease and making it possible for us to begin to develop drugs targeting the underlying causes and not just the symptoms of the disease," said Kari Stefansson, the head of Decode Genetics, the Icelandic company involved in one of the three studies. "One of the reasons this study was successful is the unprecedented size. Pooling our resources has yielded spectacular results, which is what the participants from the three continents hoped for."

The study also found links to schizophrenia with DNA variations in certain genes involved in the growth of nerve cells in the brain and the production of a protein messenger molecule that helps the transmission of signals from one brain cell to another.

Schizophrenia affects one in 100 people at some time of their lives. It is a chronic, long-term illness resulting in persistent delusions and hallucinations and is estimated to cost the taxpayer about £2bn a year in care and treatment. The costs to society at large – from the families of affected patients to the money spent by the criminal justice system – are thought to be least twice as high.

Professor David St Clair, chair of mental health at the University of Aberdeen, said the global drugs bill alone for schizophrenia is £12.5bn, not to mention other huge costs such as hospital stays, lost employment and diminished quality of life. "Our findings can be translated into new drug treatments. Much more work is also required for us to piece together the overall genetic architecture of schizophrenia."

Schizophrenia

Schizophrenia is a severe, chronic brain disorder that usually strikes in late adolescence or early adulthood and is marked by hallucinations and delusions. Sufferers may hear voices or believe that other people are controlling them or reading their minds. Such experiences can be terrifying and can cause fearfulness, withdrawal or extreme agitation. People with schizophrenia have reduced brain receptors for the dopamine messenger. They may not make sense when they talk, or they appear to be perfectly fine and normal until they are asked what they are thinking. Treatments can be effective, but most people have some residual symptoms that can stay with them for life.

Bipolar disorder

Bipolar disorder, or manic depression, is marked by unusual shifts in mood, energy, activity levels and the ability to carry out day-to-day tasks. Like schizophrenia, bipolar often manifests itself in late adolescence or early adulthood, although it may not be diagnosed for many years. The ups and downs are different from the normal ones that everyone experiences and they can result in damaged relationships, poor performance in school and jobs and even suicide. Sometimes a person with severe episodes of mania or depression has symptoms such as hallucinations or delusions such as believing that he or she is famous or has lots of money.

I hoped my son would recover soon. He did not.
Patrick Cockburn
Comment

At the time my son was diagnosed as having schizophrenia early in 2002, I knew little about the illness. Almost the only thing I did know was that it did not mean having a split personality.

Sitting in my hotel room in Brighton, where Henry was in a clinic, I spent hours at my laptop finding out as much as possible as I could about the illness. I was dismayed to discover that an eminent American doctor had said that what cancer was to physical medicine, schizophrenia was to mental illness.

I had already seen its shattering impact. Henry was a talented, prize winning artist before he became ill and the illness struck with terrifying rapidity over the course of a few weeks, though Henry later explained to me how it had gestated over a much longer period. The first sign that something was wrong came, in retrospect, when I noticed during a visit to Venice in the summer of 2001 that Henry, who had always drawn quickly and fluently, was having difficulty in sketching the human figure.

In January 2002 Henry started going barefoot and adopted a vegan diet, which might have been student eccentricity. But he also began to fear mobile phones, clocks and even Brighton's green-and-white taxis. He climbed up a high wall at Brighton station and passers-by called the police, who asked him if he had seen visions. Henry said he had not, although he later told me that he had seen a golden Buddha, though only for a instant, as he sat on Brighton beach. Later he watched a tree move its branches and speak to him.

Finally, on 9th February, Henry had set off for his home in Canterbury, walking barefoot along the foreshore until he got to Newhaven, where he swam in the near freezing water of the estuary. Picked up by fisherman who feared he was suffering from hypothermia, he was taken to Brighton hospital. I was in Afghanistan at the time and rushed back to see him.

I was told early on by doctors that one-third of people diagnosed as having schizophrenia have only one attack and recover; one-third have recurrent attacks but eventually show signs of recovery; and one-third never get better. In fact it is more complicated than that, but at first I hoped that Henry would be one of the lucky third who would recover fully.

This did not happen. Often Henry seemed to disappear into his own world of dreams and nightmares. Over the last year or eighteen months he seems to be more in control, referring to what he calls his "polka-dot day" when voices and visions return. He finds these painful and calls them "the torments," though he shows great courage in sustaining these agonies.

When Henry and I wrote about what happened to him last September, I was struck by how many people wrote intelligent and touching letters about this cruellest of illnesses. It struck me also that its treatment, and the treatment of other mental illnesses, were about at the stage that the treatment of physical illnesses had reached a century ago.

The causes of schizophrenia are suspected, but not known for certain. There are medications which control but do not cure it. Studies seem to bring understanding of the illness closer, only for others to disprove or qualify their results. Progress has been very slow.

Patrick and Henry Cockburn are writing a book about Henry's experiences, to be published in 2010.

CHAPTER FIFTY-SEVEN

… my will …

Scatter my ashes amongst the flowers in Belinda's garden.

Glossary of Names

The extended Smith Wesson Family

The Editor - me
Joss Smith Wesson - me, started writing this aged 19
'Nkosane' or 'Nkosi' - me, Zulu for Prince
'The Village Pirate' - me
'Joss the Flop' - me
'Mr. Pimms' - me
Belinda Smith Wesson nee Swart - my beloved girlfriend/ fiancée/ wife and now ex-wife, looks like *Jennifer Aniston*
Pauline Swart - Belinda's Mum
Sophie Smith Wesson - my youngest daughter
Tilly Smith Wesson - my oldest daughter aka Terrible-Tilly
Sebastian - Tilly's boyfriend
Felicity Smith Wesson - my middle daughter aka Feline-Felicity or Flick
Jonathan Smith Wesson - my younger wilder maverick brother
Susan Smith Wesson - Jonathan's wife
Daryl Smith Wesson - my second brother
Fiona Smith Wesson - Daryl's wife
Tim - Fiona's brother
Melissa West nee Smith Wesson - my sister
Stephen West - her husband
Nancy West - their daughter
Uncle Joss - my father's bother, who died before I was born
Mr Smith Wesson - my dad
Mrs Smith Wesson nee Wilkinson - my dad's mum
Mrs Smith Wesson nee Von Weillegh - my mum

The Kennedy Family

Mrs Sarah Kennedy nee Von Weillegh - my mum's sister
Mr Arthur Kennedy - my Godfather – owner of Make-me-Rich Farm
Mrs Jean Kennedy - Arthur's mum
Martin Kennedy - the eldest son
James Kennedy - the second son
Lyle Kennedy - the youngest son

The Baldwin family

Aunt Isabella Baldwin - my gran's sister
Steven Baldwin - owner of the farm The Heart of Africa
Dorothy Baldwin - Steve's wife
Bianca Baldwin - Steve's brother's daughter
Jordan Baldwin - Steve's brother's daughter
Beth Tomlinson nee Baldwin - Steve's sister
Sybil Baldwin - Steve's ex-wife

Old School Friends

Den Churchill - famously stole Jackie off Dave
Dave Green - At one time Den, Dave & I were inseparable
Jackie - girlfriend of both Den & Dave
Sam - Went to work in Paris
Kate Buckingham-Stratford - most gorgeous girl in the 6th form

Old College friends

Mike Dixon - Mike and I swore we would never lose touch…
Sandra - Mike's girlfriend
"Scuttle" Worthington - scuttle - A euphemism for rear entry sex

Den Churchill's Australian mates

Kerri MacFlattery	- I had something of a crush on her
Cathy MacFlattery	- Kerri's mum (ditto)
Mickey and Chalky	- Our hosts in Townville
Bernard and Katie Strange	- Our hosts in Sydney

Some Neighbouring farmers around Make-me-Rich farm - all mostly all involved in Polo

The Polo Club	- the centre of the White Community
Old MacDonald's farm	
Ian England's farm	
Murray Johnson's farm	
Mr Peppard's farm	
Alistair Smith's farm	
Armstrong's farm	
"String" Rodgers' farm	

Chris Smith's family, my friend at Make-me-Rich farm

Chris Smith - my wild South African friend

Caroline Smith	- Chris's mum
Alistair Smith	- Chris's dad
Louise	- Chris's girlfriend
Babs and Sandra	- Louise's much younger stepsisters
Andrew	- Louise's baby stepbrother
Murray Johnson	- Louise's stepfather

Other Europeans

Ludwig van der Hum	- Wildlife Vet on the farm the Heart of Africa
Marina Belring	- Wildlife Vet on the farm the Heart of Africa
Lorraine Jones	- Girlfriend of Ludwig v/d Hum
Malcolm Edwards	- Mechanic & Farm Manager on Make-me-Rich
Madeleine	- Malcolm's girlfriend
Sandra Street	- Ex girlfriend of my uncle
"Dutch" Benson	- Friend of Jonathan SW.
"Doc" Benson	- "Dutch's" father
Patty Benson	- "Dutch's" mother
Wayne Kerr	- Arrogant rich friend of Arthur Kennedy
Christopher "String" Rodgers	- Business partner of Arthur Kennedy
Mabel "Constable Els" Rodgers	- wife of "String"

Gays

Gerald FitzPatrick	- wife of Patrick FitzGerald
Patrick FitzGerald	- husband of Gerald FitzPatrick
Ben Down	- The Gaffer
Eileen Dover	- Wildlife Vet on the farm the Heart of Africa
Vilai Deesmai	- Will I ... (Yesh) Dessmai? (Asian and gay)
Pedro Darling	- Loony & gay (poor bastard!)

South African Police

Koojie Van As	- the Station commander
Jurgenina Hoelle	- his wife, Mr & Mrs Koojie Van As-Hoelle
Arma Duisdoo	- the Constable

English Police

William Metcalf	- Police Constable
Fiona	- his Beat partner

Afrikaners	(as well as the obvious Black/ White Apartheid divide, there was also a clear division between English speaking South Africans and their Afrikaans counterparts)
Karl Gut	- Stark Naked, literally
Naase Bittim	- Nice But Dim
Fik Bittim	- Thick But Dim
Sid Bittim	- Sad But Dim
Ivan Itchyanis	- My Bottom Needs a Scratch
Jan Grotéhuis	- A Hottentot (very small indigenous person)
Pin-yah v/d Westhuisen	- Had a flatulence problem
Nurse Virginia de Kok	- Nurse Specialising in genital dysfunction
Mudi Aazohl	- Bad tempered bastard
Blacks	
Tulip	- Sadly lost opportunity, a Classy Black African
Lipstick Red	- Sadly lost opportunity of a threesome
Beauty	- totally gorgeous in an adult way
Bedouin cattle herders	
Godson Banana	- Only just started the process…
Goodmansson	- moving on…
Arheddis Varkenjaab	- I don't like this job
Aywellbe Fayed	- I might be sacked
iNja	- Dog
Arhevbin Fayed	- I have been sacked
Bybeiev Rhibodie	- Chio
Gaucha Bitaguly	- Got him by the privates
yisiThutha	- Fool
Steelaygot Maowenbach	- Settled old scores
Tuka Piziniztee	- Revenge is sweet
Aynayda Pizaqvick	- Where are the loos out here in the Veld?
Malexa Kriest	- I'm bursting!
Awul Dasfilsshabeda	- Oh, over there, you should have said
Nowaynada Zheet	- Behind that bush
Makollig Jezvahted	- Was it you that made that noise
Levdaroum DeBahzted	- There's nowhere to hide out here
Zulu Farm staff at Make-me-Rich	
Ephraim	- Farm supervisor
Eleena	- wife of Ephraim and House Cook
Spongille	- daughter of Ephraim & Eleena
Tollie	- elder worker on the farm
Mangati	- wife of Tollie, Tribal Matriarch
Niki	- Tractor Driver
Mbonambi	- Wife of Niki -- had four small children
Tembi	- Either Wife Number Two of Niki or his niece
Esheena	- Second to Mangati in the Kraal Command
Dolphus	- Esheena's husband/ partner
Rita	- mother with no apparent partner
Tembiseni	- Rita's oldest son, about 14 – looked 10
Sipho	- Rita's 2nd son, about 10
Maxchu or "Horse"	- Rita's 3rd son, about 7 or 8
Samuel	- Rita's 4th son, about 3 or 4
Bongiwe	- Rita's youngest daughter, about 18 months/ 2 years.
Jablisse	- totally gorgeous in an illicit porn-star way
Bogkile	- old crone A
Jaina	- old crone B
Eunice	- old crone C
iButho	- father of most of the kids in the Valley – 2iC
Maruanda	- knew how to get seriously drunk

Gun	- apprentice to iButho
Sipho Ndlovu	- General Worker A
Jacob Ndlovu	- General Worker B
Elijah	- General Worker C
Silissor	- General Worker D
Mikeon	- General Worker E
<u>Asians</u>	
Yesh Deesmai	- Yes, there's my… unspeakable thing between my legs
Vee P. Elle	- Visible Panty Line – "Can you see though this dress?" A
Sheemha Krak	- Tarty Type – "Can you see though this Dress?" B
Gabbergass	- Was NOT a "Yes/ No" man
<u>Farms</u>	
Heart of Africa	- Orange River Tributaries, Orange Free State
Make-me-Rich	- Midmar Dam, Howick near Pietermaritzburg, Natal
Summertime Stud	- also Midmar Dam, where Belinda & I met
Sheep Heaven	- also Midmar Dam, where I grew up and left when I was eight
<u>My girlfriends and their retainers</u>	
Simone Thomas	- ex girlfriend
Altern Thomas	- her brother
Sally	- ex pregnant girlfriend, I still love her deeply
Peter	- her son (not mine)
Angie	- non-contact ex
Vicky Saunders	- Sally's best friend
Lizzy	- my best friend
<u>Staff in Smith Wesson's Convenience Store</u>	
Fran	- reliable teenager, probably now a millionaire
Jenny	- reliable teenager, probably now a millionaire
Ollie	- reliable teenager, probably now a millionaire
Jim-Bob	- our evening supervisor, his floor mopping skills towered over all others
Gemma	- his girlfriend, got roped into mopping the floor when Jim was cashing up
Jeffrey	- smartest member of staff
Legendary Linda	- our incredible legendary supervisor
Simon	- Linda's husband
Penny	- their baby
Hamish	- Linda's dad
<u>Some Suppliers</u>	
Ron	- the Cheese-man
John	- the Frozens' deliveryman
Mr McVitie	- the Biscuit deliveryman (lacked a sense of humour)
Mr Londis	- Built like an outdoor loo
<u>Youth Committee Members</u>	
Sharon	- had a heart of gold and was the soul of the village
Tracy	- liked to think she had a heart of gold.
Father Tim	- nearly a hundred. Absolutely no control over th[e] kids

Janette	- token 16 year old, giggled a lot
Sue	- token 16 year old, giggled a lot
Me	- argued a lot
<u>Sunday Club People</u>	
Jon Smith Wesson	- my brother, the expert in clay
'Joss the Flop'	- me, the expert in getting covered in mud
Katrina	- an enthusiastic adolescent member of my staff
Bob Jenkins	- the architect of the new Church, a fellow parent
Eight Sunday Clubbers	- normally getting kids to Sunday School was a challenge, but not when I was in charge
<u>Some Locals</u>	
Janet, James and Julian	- all worked at me on occasion
Rod and Chas	- repeatedly defeated me at squash, everyone did
Dom, Village Diamond	- frequently helped me evict underage drinkers
Sad Boy A	- underage drinker
Sad Boy B	- underage drinker
Quasimodo	- the North Maidenbottom Bell Ringer
Mr Davies	- local poet, gave me loads of books
Clive Wheelwright	- very old, wrote Church music
William	- inspired me to write this tale, I used to have him in stitches when he came to visit
His fiancée Jessica	- they had the most wonderful wedding
Ricky (friend of Jim-Bob)	- probably also now a millionaire now.
Nicola Blackwell	- loony… should have been locked up…
Eldred Hettersley	- extremely naughty…
<u>Local Pubs</u>	
The Old Cock Inn	- past the store on the right
The Farmer's Adopted Son	- just outside the village on the road to Maidenbottom
The Badger	- by the river
The Otter and Weasel	- down-market, one is most likely to get into a fight.
<u>Fellow air passengers</u>	
Jeremy Reeves	- about six, very well bred
Norman Stone	- very well educated, didn't like my definition of Apartheid.
<u>Fellow inmates</u>	
Michael James Hunt	- Mike Hunt
Richard Nathaniel Kingdom Head	- Dick Head
Loony Leslie	- loony
Lesley Bien	- loony
Erma Pratt	- a hideous German woman
Doolally Sally	- doolally (Grade One)
Doolally Rolland	- doolally (Grade One)
Doolally Pedro	- doolally (Grade Two)
Doolally Jennie	- doolally (Grade Two)
Stephen Housemeister	- pronounced Stefan, thinks he's Hitler
Tim	- a raving nutter; Col. Archangel Michael, God's slayer
Bryan	- had MS
Boy'd Boy David of Israel	- The Lion of Israel
Rob	- the Karate Kid
Anna	- Rob's Babe
Poor Jason	- a Tintin look-alike; aka Jay (to himself)
Andre	- Angry Andre

Josephine	- Jumping Josephine
Mary	- Totally Doolally Mary
Ian	- Insane Ian
Mary	- Mary with a bad foot but possibly not doolally
Tom	- Overstressed Tom
Joe	- always silent Joe
Rose	- Barking-mad Rose
Tom	- clever, but loony Tom
Rebecca	- succeeded in escaping – total respect
Doctors	
Katie KizWillie	- hated Head-Shrink - doolally
Stefan	- hated Hospital nurse, wannabe doolally
Nurse Abbey White	- Duty Staff Nurse
David Fox	- a Church of England Accountant
Rosie Staal	- From Crowded House
Dr Ellwell,	- Pratt, arsehole
Apa	- under qualified black quack
Carol Bannister	- Mental Health Act Administrator
Dr. David Walters	- my GP in Hurley-on-Thames
Dr. Jennie Le Roux	- consultant psychiatrist in psychotherapy
Dr. Michael Humphries	- in Oxford
Brian Harrington	- the CAFCASS Officer (totally incompetent)
Dr. R H McAcllister-Williams	- the Newcastle Disorders Group
Carolyn Hughes	- the Newcastle Disorders Group
Dr Achal Mishra	- the Newcastle Disorders Group
Malcolm Hartshorne	- the Newcastle Affective Disorders Group
Steve Connor	- Science Editor
Ellen Davidson	-the woman I had an affair with…
Felix	-Belinda's lover (probably looks like Satan)
Work Mates	
Bal	- bald, but cool
Martin	- my son/ his dad
Louis	- cooler than Russell Brand (whoever he is)
Kate's bum	- belonged to Kate…
"*Barbie*"	- waitress at the pub near work – well stacked
Hor-zay	- another baldy
Sandra	- Oh God, I'm in love with this woman…
Sly Simon	- Like me, aspiring author…
Mad Sam	- Like me, aspiring author… (except mad)
Steff	- gorgeous lady that worked in the canteen
Gerry	- Lead Singer of *SixNationState* – buy their albu **NOW!**
Nick	- rampant Aussy
Ruth	- work colleague famous for her commitment (lack of)
Malc	- Nerdy brainy prat
Ciaron	- seventeen next birthday
Nav	- doesn't play tennis, or is gay
Sara	- my daytime wife…
Victoria	- my dream daytime wife…
Lillian	- is drop-dead gorgeous
Vicky	- have difficulty in visualising her with clothes o

<u>*SixNationState*</u>	
Gerry	- huge, hairy, and should be up there with U2.
Richard	- is cool and looks like the guy in *My Family*
John	- insists on playing barefoot
Alexie	- has grown a beard
Neil	- is a blond veggie
<u>Random Guest appearances</u>	
John Wayne	- because he was fast
Clint Eastwood	- because he was fast
Barry Sheen	- because he was fast
Sterling Moss	- because he was fast
Jeff Archer	- arguably the best living author lol
Ronald Reagan	- arguably the best US President (satire...)
Nelson Mandela	- This book would not be complete without him
Prince Charles	- on a par with President Daniel Arap Moi
Princess Diana	- because I was/am desperately in love with her
President Daniel Arap Moi	- on a par with Prince Charles – yes, prat
Mahatma Gandhi	- a mover and a shaker
Peter Gabriel	- made great music
Neil Diamond	- made great music
UB40	- made great music
Jimi Hendrix	- made great music
Lionel Richie	- made great music
Dolly Parton	- made great music
Peter Gabriel	- made great music
Louis Botha	- because he tried
Bruce Fordyce	- because he was fast
Simon Mkize	- because he was fast (my all-time hero- sorry Bruce)
Billy Beaumont	- mates with my mate Mike Dixon, and good at rugby
John McEnroe	- because he was fast
Palmela Handerson	- because she was NOT a babe
Led Zeppelin	- made great music
James Herriot	- because this book is a prequel of his
Linford Christie	- because he was fast
Magnum	- token fictitious character
<u>General Places in South Africa</u>	
Kruger National Game Park	- Large Game Reserve
Lake Bloemfontein	- Near Bloemfontein, Capital of the Orange Free State
Red Bull café	- a café in Johannesburg
Fawn-Liza	- African township in KwaZulu
Monopump	- a Shop that sells irrigation parts
The Comrades Marathon Kingdom	- the old road between Pietermaritzburg and Durban
12 Woolacomb Drive,	- the Kennedy's town house in Durban
Imperial Hotel Pietermaritzburg	- semi mythical
Escourt	- superb Marathon
Grump	- a Landrover
Panga	- a long handled two edged blade
Kraal	- group of African homes usually very simplistic with no amenities
Aardvark	- EarthPig, Anteater, makes terrible holes in farm Roads
Pom	- derogatory term for Englishman in Australia and Africa
"Cor-Plug"	- Army cadet

Matato	- derogatory term for a taxi in Africa
Combi	- term for a Volkswagen kombi
"The Hotel"	- my vehicle
Bakkie	- South African term for a Utility vehicle
Ute	- Australian term for a Utility vehicle
Stoep	- Veranda or porch, Outdoor living area, Whites only.
Bangbang	- non domestic killer Rottweiler
Jessie	- the Labrador
Tomlinson Herd	- herd of cattle on the farm The Heart of Africa belonging to Beth Tomlinson

www.ingramcontent.com/pod-product-compliance
Lightning Source LLC
Chambersburg PA
CBHW020330270326
41926CB00007B/114
* 9 7 8 1 8 4 9 9 1 9 3 4 0 *